New Principles Of Gardening

To.6

√Q D

An Avenue in Perspective; terminating with the ruins of an ancient Building, after the Roman manner.

T. Bowles Sculp.

NEW
PRINCIPLES
OF
GARDENING:

Or, The Laying out and Planting

PARTERRES, GROVES, WILDERNESSES, LABYRINTHS, AVENUES, PARKS, &c.

After a more GRAND and RURAL MANNER, than
has been done before;

With Experimental Directions

For raising the several Kinds of FRUIT-TREES, FOREST-
TREES, EVER-GREENS and FLOWERING-SHRUBS
with which Gardens are adorn'd.

To which is added,

The various NAMES, DESCRIPTIONS, TEMPERATURES,
MEDICINAL VIRTUES, USES and CULTIVATIONS of
several ROOTS, PULSE, HERBS, &c. of the Kitchen and
Physick Gardens, that are absolutely necessary for the Service of
Families in general.

Illustrated with great Variety of GRAND DESIGNS, curiously
Engraven on twenty eight Folio Plates, by the best Hands.

By *BATTY LANGLEY* of *Twickenham*.

LONDON:
Printed for A. BETTESWORTH and J. BATLEY in *Pater-Noster
Row*; J. PEMBERTON in *Fleestreet*; T. BOWLES in St. *Paul's
Church-Yard*; J. CLARKE, under the *Royal Exchange*;
and J. BOWLES at *Mercer's Hall* in *Cheapside*.
M DCC.XXVIII.

ADVERTISEMENT,

To the Nobility and Gentry of *Great Britain*.

WHEREAS the Pleasure of Gardens, and Success of Plantations wholly depend on their manner of Laying out, and Judgment in the Choice and Planting such Kinds of Trees as are most natural to their Soils; This is to give Notice, that the Author's Advice may be readily commanded at all Times to any part of Great Britain, *or* Ireland.

By whom

Buildings in general are Surveyed, Valued, and Measured, as also Timber growing or felled.

Grottos, Baths, Cascades, Fountains, *&c. made, and* Engines *for raising Waters to any height required, for the service of Towns, private Families, Canals, Fish-Ponds,* &c.

Cities, Lordships, Estates, Farms, &c. *Survey'd, Measur'd, and Mapp'd, and* Sun Dials *of all Kinds made for any Latitude.*

Gardens *in general, Made, Planted and Furnish'd with Fruit and Forest-Trees, Ever-Greens, Flowering-Shrubs,* &c. *of the best Kinds, and Growths proper for all Kinds of Soils and Aspects, at very reasonable Rates.*

TO THE

KING.

SIR,

INquiries into vegetable Nature, being the Delight of Your *Majesty*, and Your *Royal Consort*, I humbly presume to lay at Your *Majesty*'s Feet, these Plans of *Parterres*, *Groves*, *Wildernesses*, *Labyrinths*, *Avenues*, *Parks*, &c. which are entirely new, but embellish'd with many of the most noble Antiquities now extant in other Countries.

I hum

DEDICATION.

I humbly offer the following Work to Your *Majesty's* Patronage and Protection, whose *Royal Regard* for the useful Arts of Planting and Gardening will sufficiently recommend their Improvement to the Nobility and Gentry of *Great Britain*.

May Your *Majesty*, and Your *Royal Confort*, long live to be a Blessing to these Nations, and at length transmit them, with Your *Imperial Crown*, to Your *Most Illustrious* and *Royal Issue*, is the fervent Prayer of,

Your Majesty's Most Loyal,

Most Obedient,

And faithful Subject,

Batty Langley.

THE
INTRODUCTION.

T O confider how many Authors (as *Evelyn, Meager, Woolridge, Cook, Lawrence, Bradley, London, Wife, Carpenter* and others, who) have wrote on Gardening, and the vaft Numbers of fine Plants that are, and have been for fixty years paft, raifed in our Nurferies about *London*, would make a Foreigner (that had not feen the Gardens of *England*) believe, that they excell'd all others in the World; more efpecially as we abound with the beft of *Grafs* and *Gravel* of any People whatfoever: But to our great Misfortune, *our Gardens are much the worft of any in the World*, fome few excepted, that have been laid out by *Gentlemen*, who have a grand and elegant Tafte in Defigning, known to very few Gardeners.

Among all the celebrated Books that have been wrote on the laying out Gardens, *The Theory and Practice of Gardening*, tranflated from the *French* by Mr. *John James* of *Greenwich*, and thofe wrote by Mr. *Stephen Switzer*, are the very beft. But even thofe are far fhort of *that great Beauty which Gardens ought to confift of:* For fince the Pleafure of a Garden depends on the variety of its Parts, 'tis therefore that we fhould well confider of their Difpofitions, fo as to have a continued Series of *Harmonious Objects*, that will prefent new and delightful Scenes to our View at every Step we take, which re-

gular

gular Gardens arc incapable of doing. Nor is there any Thing more *shocking* than a *stiff regular Garden*; where after we have feen one quarter thereof, the very fame is repeated in all the remaining Parts, fo that we are tired, inftead of being further entertain'd with fomething new as expected.

Thefe regular Gardens were firft taken from the *Dutch*, and introduced into *England* in the Time of the late Mr. *London* and Mr. *Wife*, who being then fuppos'd to be the beft Gardeners in *England* (the Art being in its Infancy, to what it is now) were imployed by the *Nobility and Gentry of England* to lay out and plant their Gardens in that *regular, stiff, and stuft up Manner* in which many yet appear.

And as *Gentlemen*, in thofe Days, were but flightly acquainted with the Pleafure of Gardening, they were the eafier impofed upon: Their Gardens were *crowded* with Ever-Greens and other Plants, fo that they had more of the Afpect of a *Nurfery*, than a *Garden of Pleafare*: But whether this over and above thick Planting proceeded from the Fafhion of thofe Times, the Ignorance of the Defigners, or the Advantages that might accrue from the greater Sales of their Plants, I am not able to determine.

And befides, their ftiff regular Plans were always ftuff'd up with *trifling flower Knots*, *Parterres of Cut work*, *Embroidery*, *Wildernesses of Ever-Greens*, and fometimes of *Forest Trees*, (tho' very rarely, for their Nurferies then abounded moft with *Yews, Hollies*, and other *Ever-Greens*) whofe Walks ever had a *niggard Breadth*: So that after a few Years the Growth of the Plants were fuch that they were hardly paffable.

Their *Wildernesses* and *Groves* (when they planted any) were always placed at the moft remote Parts of the Garden: So that before we can enter them, in the *Heat of Summer*, when they are moft ufeful, we are obliged to pafs thro' the *fcorching Heat of the Sun*.

Indeed, 'tis oftentimes neceffary to place *Groves* and open *Wildernesses* in fuch remote Parts of Gardens, from whence *pleafant Profpects are taken*; but then we fhould always take care to plant *proportionable Avenues* leading from the Houfe to them, under whofe *Shade* we might with Pleafure pafs and repafs at any time of the Day.

There

The *INTRODUCTION.*

There is nothing more agreeable in a Garden than good *Shade*, and without it *a Garden is nothing.*

That fine Terrace Walk at His MAJESTY's *Royal Palace* of *Hampton Court*, leading from the Parterre to the Bowling-Green next the *Thames*, being naked of Shade, is thereby useless, when the Sunshines; as is also that of His ROYAL MAJESTYS at *Richmond* next the River. There are divers other fine Walks in *England* that want this natural Embellishment of Trees that cause FINE SHADE, such as PLATANUS, *English* ELM, HORSE-CHESSNUT, LIME, *&c.* In whose stead, to my great Surprize, are planted *regular Yews* and *Holly* only as in Parterres, *&c.*

The very great Exactness that was observed in the laying out these regular Gardens, were often the *Loss* of many *fine Views*, as well as *sturdy* OAKS, whose *Herculean Aspects*, one would have thought, should have forbid those *base* and *ignorant Practices*. What a Shame it is, to destroy a *noble* OAK of two or three Hundred Years Growth, that always produces a *pleasant Shade*, and graceful Aspect for the sake of making a *trifling Grass-Plot* or *Flower Knot* regular.

Their *Parterres* of *Embroidery*, that consisted of *Grass*, *Sand, Shells, Brickdust*, &c. *crowded with Ever-Greens*, were the first Cause of these stiff Regularities; which indeed, when used, should be uniform; because the Eye being struck with all their Parts at the same Time, each opposite part should be equal: But afterwards, when we depart from this first regular Scene, then all the remaining Parts should consist of *regular Irregularities*: And the plainer *Parterres* are, the more *Grandeur*, for when they are stuff'd up with so many *small Ornaments*, they *break the Rays of Sight*, and the whole appears a Confusion.

Those great *Beauties of Nature*, HILLS and VALLEYS, were always levelled at very great Expences to complete their Regularity, or otherwise I may justly say, *the total ruin of the Gardens*. And their *Basins, Canals*, and other *Pieces of Water*, had always a very *mean Latitude* to their Length, as well as *improper Figures*, broke into many Angles which destroy the Beauty of fine Water.

Their GROVES (whenever they planted any) were always regular, *like unto Orchards*, which is entirely wrong; for when we come to *copy*, or *imitate Nature*, we should trace her

Steps

Steps with the greateſt Accuracy that can be. And therefore when we plant *Groves of Foreſt or other Trees*, we have nothing more to regard, than that the outſide Lines be agreeable to the Figure of the Grove, and that no three Trees together range in a ſtrait Line; excepting now and then by Chance, to cauſe Variety.

And ſince *Parterres* are moſt beautiful when *entirely plain,* I therefore recommend the removal of all Kinds of Ever-Greens from thence, and to have no more *Gravel Walks* about them than are neceſſary for Uſe. Whoever has ſeen thoſe *grand* and *beautiful* Plots or Parterres *of Graſs* in the Gardens belonging to Ham house in *Surrey*, oppoſite to the *Honourable* James Johnston at *Twickenham*, will agree with me herein; and were thoſe eight Plots, or Parterres, laid into *two* only, they would be the *moſt grand* of any in *England;* more eſpecially if that Grove of *Foreſt Trees*, joyning to them on the *Eaſt*, were taken in and made a part of that Garden.

The *Parterre Garden* at his Majesty's *Royal Palace* of *Hampton Court*, towards the *Park*, would have a very *grand Aſpect*, were thoſe *trifling Plants of Yew, Holly, &c.* and their Borders taken away, and *made plain with Graſs.* So alſo would the other *Parterre*, looking to the River *Thames.*

Beſides all the aforeſaid *erroneous Practices* in the laying out Gardens, I could mention divers others, almoſt without end; but as what has been hitherto ſaid is fully ſufficient to demonſtrate how little the laying out of Gardens has been underſtood, I ſhall therefore conclude on this Point with one other *very great* Error that's often committed, and even at this time, which may not be unneceſſary for my Readers to take Notice of, *viz.* When the Situation of Gardens ſuch, that the making of *Slopes* and *Terraces* are neceſſary, or cannot be avoided, they not only leave them *naked of Shade* as aforeſaid, but *break their Slopes* into ſo many Angles, that their *native Beauty* is thereby deſtroy'd. Thus if by waſte Earth a *Mount* be raiſed *ten* or *twelve Feet high*, you ſhall have its Slope, that ſhould be entire from top to bottom, broken into three, if not four ſmall *trifling ones*, and thoſe mixt with Archs of Circles, *&c.* that ſtill adds to their ill Effects: So that inſtead of having one *grand Slope* only with an eaſy Aſcent, you have three or four ſmall ones, that are *poor and trifling.*

And

And the only reaſon why they are made in this Stair or Step-like manner, is firſt to ſhew their Dexterity of Hand, without conſidering the ill Effect; and laſtly to imitate thoſe *grand Amphitheatrical Buildings*, uſed by the *Ancients*, of which they had no more Judgment, than of the excellent Proportions of Architecture that was uſed therein, when thoſe noble Structures were firſt erected.

In this low mean Manner I find ſome *Slopes* made at the Head of his MAJESTY'S *Canal* and *Mount* next the *Thames* at *Richmond*, which *Canal* is much *too narrow* for its Length : I alſo find the Plantation of *Foreſt Trees* on each Side thereof, not only *broken in the middle* without a Reaſon for ſo doing, but *ſtiff* and *regular* in their Situations, without any Regard to that beautiful Order, which *Nature* obſerves in all ſuch rural Operations.

I obſerve the like *Error* in the *Slopes* of the Garden of the *Honourable Mrs.* HOWARD at *Twickenham*, being view'd at the River *Thames*, and the ſame at *General Biſſet's* Amphitheatre (as called by its Architect) in his Garden at the ſame Town, as well as in that of the *Honourable John Gumley's* at *Iſleworth*, and many other Gardens too tedious to mention.

When very large Hills of great perpendicular Heights are to be cut into *Slopes* and *Terraces*, then we may juſtly endeavour to imitate thoſe grand Structures, (whereon their Gladiators exercis'd) by cutting them Concave, Convex, &c. as thoſe looking towards *Fair-Mile Heath*, in the Gardens of his *Grace* the DUKE of NEWCASTLE *at his Grand Seat of Claremont* ; but in ſmall Elevations they are poor and trifling, and therefore not to be uſed.

Having duly conſider'd theſe erroneous Practices, and what a great pity it is that *Gentlemen* ſhould be thus led on for want of being furniſhed with Deſigns that are *truly Grand and Noble*, after *Nature's own Manner* ; I thought that if I communicated ſome few in that Way, I might do no inconſiderable Service to my *Country*, nor Prejudice to any of my *Brother Gardeners*.

This Method of *laying out Gardens*, after the manner exhibited in the following Plates, being *entirely New*, as well as the moſt *grand* and *rural*; I have thought it neceſſary, not only to lay down all the moſt uſeful *Elements of Geometry*,

neceſſary

neceffary to be well underftood by every *good Gardener* that's imployed in *making and laying out Gardens*; but the manner of raifing and planting all forts of *Fruit* and *Foreft Trees*, *Ever-Greens*, and *flowering Shrubs* alfo; together with the right Ordering, and Cultivation of all fuch Vegetables are raifed in the *Kitchen Garden*. All which are handled at large in the firft, fecond, third, fourth, fifth, and feventh Parts.

The fixth Part contains *general Directions* for the laying out, and planting of Gardens in the manner aforefaid, exemplified by twenty eight Folio Plates.

Plate I. contains all the Geometrical Diagrams of the Problems contain'd in the firft Part, with an *octangular Lawn*, of which hereafter.

Plate II. is the *Plan* of a *Fruit Garden*, containing three quarters of an Acre, planted with the beft *Wall, Efpalier, Dwarf*, and *Standard* Fruits now extant in *England*.

Plate III. is the Defign of a *rural Garden*, after the new manner, where the front of the Houfe opens upon a fine *large plain Parterre*, environed with an eafy agreeable *Slope* and proportionable Verges of Grafs; adorn'd with *Apollo, Minerva* and *Pallas*, the *feven liberal Arts, Mercury* and *Pytho*.

The Goddeffes *Minerva* and *Pallas*, to be placed at A and B, *Apollo* at C, the *feven Sciences* at D, E, F, G, H, I, K, and *Mercury* and *Pytho* at L and M. In the Center of this *Parterre* is an *octagon Bafin of Water* which may be adorn'd with *Neptune*. This open *Parterre* is planted on the Sides P. Q. with double Lines of *Pines* and *Scotch Firs*. The *Terrace* S. S. with *Platanus*. The little Groves R. R. with *Lime Trees*. The open Grove O with *Horfe-Chefnuts*, and N with *Englifh Elm*. The middle or center excepted, which are Standards of *Scotch* Firs. T, T. with *Cedars of Lebanon, Cyprus*, and *Lignum Vitæ*. The Avenue V. V. with *Platanus:* The Groves Y, with Standards of *Holly, Yew, Bay Tree, Laurel, Ever-Green, Oak, Box* and *Phillyrea*. All which Trees throughout thefe feveral Plantations are planted at their Bottoms, with *Honey Suckles, Sweet Briers, white Jeffamine*, and the feveral *Sorts of Rofes*: And about the Stem or Body of every Tree are cut Circles about fourteen or fixteen Inches in Breadth fown with *Dwarf Stock, Candy Turf, Pinks, Sweet Williams, Catch-fly, &c.* which make no little Addition to the Beauty of our Plantations.

The

The *INTRODUCTION.*

The Groves N O are adorn'd with *Sylvanus* God, and *Ferona* Goddefs of the Woods. The Walks about the two Canals, and the Centers Z Z with *Apollo* and the *nine Mufes*; the Cabinets X, X, with *Ceres* and *Flora,* and V, with *Harpocrates* God, and *Agerona* Goddefs of Silence. And the other Statues in private Cabinets, with *Nymphæ* Fairies of the Woods, *Actæon, Diana, Eccho, &c.* and the large circular plain W. is open without a Statue: But if any Gentleman fhould be inclinable to place one in that Center, it fhould be *Hercules flaying Hydra.*

The *Serpentine,* and ftrait lined Walks within the Plantations of Wood or *Wildernefs Work,* are planted with Standards of *Oak, Beach, Elm, Lime, Maple, Sycamore, Hornbeam, Birch, Platanus, Wicky* or *Quick-beam, Alder, Poplar, Withy,* and the *weeping* or *mourning Willow* that was brought from *Babylon,* and now in great Plenty and Perfection in *England.* Particularly, in the Gardens of the late *Thomas Vernon* Efq; at his Seat of *Twickenham Park* in *Middlefex.* The Diftances that thofe feveral Sorts of Foreft Trees are planted at, and the Soil they delight in, are fully handled in the following Work.

The Hedges that are planted between the aforefaid Trees which form the Sides of the Walks are of *Englifh, Dutch* and *French Elms, Lime, Hornbeam, Maple, Privet, Yew, Holly, Arbutus, Phillyrea, Norway Fir, Ilex, Bay, Laurel, Laurus-Tinus, Piracantha, Juniper,* and the *Englifh Furze;* and indeed, a beautiful Plantation fhould not only be adorned with entire Walks and Hedges of Trees of all Sorts, as well Fruit as others; but intermix'd together in many parts, as if Nature had placed them there with her own Hand. The *agreeable Mixture of Fruits in a Wildernefs,* caufes great Variety and Pleafure, as well as Profit: In the *Spring,* when their beautiful Bloffoms appear, they then exceed all other Plants, and particularly the *Mirabalon Plumb* and *Almond,* of which I advife *Gentlemen* to plant entire Walks; for they not only make the moft beautiful Appearances in the *Spring,* which hold for fome Time, but afterwards are very pleafant, both in their Leaf and Fruits: As likewife are all our other Fruits, fuch as *Plumbs, Pears, Apples, Cherries,* the *Bruxel Apricot, white and blue Figs, Grapes, Mulberries, Quinces, Medlars, Services, Walnuts, Chefnuts;*

b   *Philberds,*

Philberds, *Berberrys,* *Goofeberries* and *Currants:* And altho'
they may not be in fuch great Perfection, as thofe that are planted
at greater Diftances in the free open Air, as in *Kitchen* and
Fruit Gardens, yet in *kind Summers* they will not be much
behind them; fo that from Plantations of this Kind, *Gentlemen* will not only be entertained with the Pleafures that a-
rife from them, throughout the feveral Stages of their Growth,
but receive fuch *Plenty of Fruits,* as to make *large Quantities*
of *Wine, Cyder, &c.* for the Service of their Families.

The Borders of each Walk are planted with *Violets, Primrofes, Snow-drops, &c.* as directed in the 22 and 23 Sections.
Part V.

The Quarters are filled up with Standards of the aforefaid
Kinds, planted at proper Diftances, and under them by Plants
of *Laurel,* which *thrive beft in the Shade,* and Flowers of a
ftrong Growth, as directed in Sect. 23. Part V.

FLOWERING SHRUBS are very beautiful when planted in the
Wildernefs as directed in Sect. 21. Part V. which are not to be
omitted, if we intend to have our Garden complete.

Our feveral Plantations being thus performed, we are, at
coming into the Garden, entertain'd with a *Plain* (but *Grand*)
Parterre of Grafs and Water, enriched with *Statues* agreeable to
their Situations, from which, on the right and left, we look
into two *pleafant Groves of Foreft Trees,* which complete the
firft Scene, at our coming into the Garden; then through the
Walks P R, or *Groves* N O, we pafs in the Shade to V, the
Entrance into the *Grand Avenue* V, V, where on a fudden
we are entertain'd with *two pleafant Canals* enrich'd with *Statues,* and *Groves of Ever-Greens,* and coming from thence to
the open plain W, we behold a pleafant crofs Walk, planted
with Standard Trees of all the *Varieties of Ever-Greens,* which
terminate in Cabinets, adorn'd with *Ceres* and *Flora.*

If we enter the Wildernefses at b b, *&c.* we are led through
their *pleafant Meanders,* with the agreeable Entertainments of
Flower Gardens, Fruit Gardens, Orangerys, Groves, of *Foreft
Trees,* and *Ever-Greens, Open-plains, Kitchen Gardens Phyfick
Gardens, Paddocks of Sheep, Deer, Cows,* &c. *Hop Grounds, Nur-
feries of Fruit* and *Foreft Trees, Ever-Greens,* &c. *Vineyards, In-
clofures of Corn, Grafs, Clover,* &c. *Cones of Fruit Trees, Foreft
Trees,*

Trees, Ever-Greens, Flowering Shrubs, Basins, Fountains, Canals, Cascades, Grottos, Warrens of *Hares* and *Rabbets, Aviaries, Manazeries, Bowling-Greens;* and thofe rural Objects, *Hay-Stacks* and *Wood Piles,* as in a Farmer's Yard in the Country. Which feveral Parts are difpofed of in fuch a Manner, and Diftance, as not to fee, or know of the next approaching, when we have feen the firft; fo that we are continually entertain'd with *new unexpected Objects at every Step we take;* for the Entrances into thofe Parts being made intricate, we can *never know when we have feen the whole.* Which (if I miftake not) is the true End and Defign of *laying out Gardens of Pleafure.*

By this Method of laying out Gardens, thofe that are but fmall, will be made to appear *as very large ones,* and thofe that are fpacious and large, *Grand* and *Noble.*

If we imagine that the Avenue B, Plate III. takes its Beginning from an *open Plain* or *Lawn* lying before a Houfe, as the *Avenue* V, doth of Plate II. from the plain Parterre there defcribed, we have another Defign that is *Grand and Noble,* which is fuppofed to be planted in the Manner aforefaid, the Walks about the Canal excepted, which fhould be of *ftately Pines,* and the Thickets B and D, which finifh the two crofs Views, fhould end in a *Mixture of Ever-Greens* back'd with *lofty Pines* behind them.

The *Groves* E, and F, F, that terminate the Water, have a much finer Afpect being planted in that *rural Manner,* than when ranged in Lines like a *Cherry* or *Apple Orchard;* as before noted in the Beginning of this Introduction.

Plate V. is a third Defign of an *Avenue* with its *Wilderneffes* on each Side, wherein is contain'd great Variety of Walking. The *Avenue* B, D, having its *Canal* terminated at both Ends with *Groves of Foreft Trees,* is fomething out of the *common Road* : But when the Bodies of fuch Trees are kept prun'd up about twenty Feet high, the Water makes a fine Appearance, being view'd through them ; as alfo have diftant Hills, *&c.*

The Walk E F, is fuppofed to be a *Terrace* from whence we have a fine View over the Country, which is planted with *Platanus,* or *Englifh Elms,* that always afford a pleafant Shade. In this Manner there are many *noble Walks* in *England* want

to be planted, to render them pleafant at all Times.

Plate VI. is a fourth Defign, containing *ftrait, angular, circular,* and *rural Walks* after a different Manner from the preceding.

Plate VII. confifts of four feveral Defigns for *Wildernefſes* and *Labyrinths* wherein A A, *&c.* are *Arbors,* or Places of Repofe.

Plate VIII. is an Improvement of that *grand Labyrinth at Verfailles,* wherein all the ftrait Walks are as they now ftand, and the curved or ferpentine Walks B B, excepted with their *Groves, Cabinets* and *Statues,* are Additions that may be made to that beautiful Place. *This I thought fit to communicate, as being the fineft Defign of any I ever faw.*

Plate IX. is an Improvement of a *beautiful Garden at Twickenham,* fituated on the *River Thames,* which paffes by the Line E F, and has a free communication with the Canals X and Z. That of X, continues the View of the Walk I H, away to X, and from thence over the *River Thames,* and there terminates in a pleafant Wood. At R, there is a *Ha, Ha,* of Water, which is a Fence to the Garden from the Road, and admits of a *free View,* which Iron Gates or Grills cannot do. I mention this to fhew, that *Hah Ha's* fhould be made in every part of a Garden from whence good Views may be had.

The Earth that came out of the *Ponds* B, B, raifed the *Mount* A, from whence is *a very fine View to the Thames,* as well as to *Richmond Hill, Peterfham, &c.* and underneath it is a very good Ice Houfe.

The Reafon why I mention this, is to fhew, that when the *Levels of Gardens are very flat,* and *good Views are loft* for want of proper Elevations, that then we muft dig *Fifh Ponds, Canals, &c.* if the Springs are not too deep; and with their Earth raife *pleafant Mounts, Terrace Walks, &c.* from whence we may enjoy the *pleafant Views* of the diftant Countries.

If the Walks leading up fuch *Mounts* as A were *contracted at their Top* K, to *one third* of their Breadth at Bottom I, that Contraction would caufe the Walk to appear of a much greater Length than it really is, being viewed at H. But then the afcending Walk muft be the whole Breadth at I.

There being a fine View from the Houfe to the River, the

Quarters

Quarters Q Q, muſt be planted with Fruit Trees of a low Growth; ſuch as Apples upon *Paradiſe Stocks, &c.* that will afford great Variety of Pleaſure as well as Profit, and not interrupt the View. The other Parts here offered being *Wilderneſſes, Labyrinth, Groves, &c.* as exhibited, need no further Explanation.

Plate X and XI, are Deſigns for Gardens that lye irregularly to the grand Houſe. In Plate X, the Houſe opens to the *North* upon the *Park* A, to the *Eaſt* upon the *Court* B, to the *South* upon the *Parterre of Graſs and Water* C; and Laſtly to the *Weſt* upon the *circular Baſon* D, from which leads a *pleaſant Avenue* Z X. The *Mount* F, is raiſed with the Earth that came out of the *Canal* E E, and its Slope H is planted with *Hedges* of *different Ever-Greens,* that riſing behind one another of different Colours, have a very good Effect, being view'd from M. I, I, are contracted Walks leading up the Mount. The remaining Parts being obvious need no farther Explanation.

Plate XI. hath its Houſe opening to the *North* upon a *plain Parterre of Graſs,* and to the *South,* upon a *Parterre of Graſs and Water :* From the Terrace E leads an Avenue I F, wherein at D is a *pleaſant Cabinet,* from whence we have five different Views, of which the Middle one through a *rural Grove* of Foreſt Trees, over a *Canal of Water,* terminated with the ſemicircular Grove of *Ever-Greens,* is very pleaſant.

The Walk P Q is ſuppoſed to be a *pleaſant Terrace,* planted with Foreſt Trees for Shade, in equal right Lines; but the Walk R S, is planted rural after *Nature's own Manner.* The reſt being very eaſy to underſtand, need no farther Explanation.

It is to be obſerved in theſe two Plans, that there's no regard had to the *Regularity* of the *Bounds of thoſe Gardens,* which hitherto were ſuppoſed impoſſible of making good Gardens, when in fact they make the moſt beautiful.

Plate XII. is the Deſign of a ſmall Garden ſituated in a *Park,* where the Houſe to the *North* opens upon *a noble circular Baſin of Water* B, in the *Park,* and to the *South,* on a *grand Parterre of Graſs,* from which over the *Canal* you have a boundleſs View into the Country.

The ſeveral *Avenues* and *Groves* contain'd in this Deſign, illuſtrate luftrate the great Beauty thereof, without any Regard had to the *Wilderneffes, Labyrinths, &c.* which are very fine in their Kind alfo. The other Parts being plainly exhibited, need no further Explanation.

We having thus paffed through all the moft pleafant Parts of a *delightful rural Garden,* we muft now fuppofe, that we are entering from X Y, of Plate III, at Z of Plate XIII, where we furprizingly behold a *pleafant femi-circular Lawn,* from which the *grand Avenue* V, V, of Plate III. is continued to H, *&c.* throughout the whole Eftate.

And we are here again in every of its Parts entertain'd with *different Views, open Plains, Groves, Thickets , open* and *private Fifb Ponds,* and in brief every Thing that's pleafant.

From Plantations of this Kind, time would produce vaft Quantities of Timber to the great Service of our Country and Improvement of Eftates.

Plate XIV. is another Specimen of a *Park,* after a different, but *grand and noble Manner,* where its Ifland is laid out in *rural Walks* and *Cabinets,* and the other Parts embellifh'd after *Nature's own Rules,* which is difcoverable at firft View.

Plate XV. is the Defign of a *Garden* and *Wildernefs in an Ifland,* lying before the View of *a Houfe, Terrace, &c.* B is *a Temple of View* erected on a *double Mount,* called (tho' improperly by *Gardeners,* an *Amphitheatre*) where 'tis to be obferved, that altho' the Slopes thereof are broke by the Angles, yet 'tis in fuch an agreeable *grand Manner ,* that they have a *noble Afpect.*

The other Parts being eafily underftood at View, need no further Explanation.

Plate XVI. contains great Variety of *Lawns,* or *Openings,* before a *grand Front of a Building,* into a *Park, Foreft, Common, &c.* with an elegant *Cabinet* in the middle of a *Thicket,* on the top of a Hill, in whofe Center at A, is fuppofed to be erected a fpacious Building *after the Form of a Temple,* from whence fine Views may be feen about the *Horizon.*

Plate XVII. contains the Defign of a *Fountain* and *Cafcade* after the *grand Manner at Verfailles.* From whence we pafs thro' thofe pleafant fhady Walks B B, to other Parts of our Gardens.

_When

When Figures of *Shell work* are erected in the midst of *Fountains*, we receive a double Pleasure of a *Fountain* and *Cascade* also, by the Waters agreeably murmuring down the rocky Shells.

Plate XVIII, contains divers curious *Frontispieces of Trellis Work* for the Entrances into *Temples of View*, *Arbors, shady Walks, Alcoves,* &c.

Plates XIX, XX, and XXI, are Views of *the Ruins of Buildings*, after the *old Roman manner*, to terminate such Walks that end in *disagreeable Objects*; which *Ruins* may either be *painted upon Canvas*, or actually built in that Manner with *Brick*, and *cover'd with Plaistering* in Imitation of Stone.

And since we are to build no more thereof than as much of the Shell, as is next to our View, I therefore recommend their Building before their Painting, not only as the *most durable*, but *least expensive* (if the Painting is performed by a skilful Hand) and much more to the real Purport intended.

To demonstrate what Effects they have when placed to terminate *Avenues, Walks, &c.* I have put one of them at the end of an *Avenue* in Plate XXII, which being viewed with one Eye through our Hand, or a piece of Paper roll'd up, so as to look through the same, you will behold its agreeable Effect with abundance of Pleasure. In the same Manner, the shady Walks of the preceding *Plates* are to be seen, and not according to the common way of viewing Objects with both Eyes at once.

The six last Plates at the end hereof, are Designs for *Kitchen Gardens*, of which the first is divided into equal Quarters, wherein is express'd the Quantity of each Vegetable that is necessary for the Service of a *Nobleman's Family*, as is also Plate II, and III. The *Italick Figures* denote the breadth of each Walk, as 6 signifies six Feet, 15 fifteen Feet, &c.

Plate VI. is the Design of the *Kitchen and Physick Garden*, with its Quarters environ'd with *Espaliers of Fruit.* The Design of this Garden is for the Use of Families, which require many Herbs for Distilling, as well as for the Use of the Kitchen, wherein the necessary Quantities are nearly adapted to the Use of most Families.

Plate

Plate V. is the Defign of a *Kitchen Garden* containing *one Acre, half,* and *twenty Poles,* and Plate III, another of *three Rood* and *twelve Pole* only, fit for leffer Families than the preceding. But as the Defign of thefe Plans are *more to inftruct in the Forms of Kitchen Gardens,* than their Quantities of Ground, or Herbs of each Kind as they may beft approve on ; therefore every one is at his Pleafure to fow and plant of each Sort of *Herbage, Roots, Pulfe, &c.* fuch Quantities as are neceffary for their Ufe.

For the *Temperatures,* and *Medicinal Virtues* of the *Kitchen* and *Phyfick Herbs* contain'd in the laft Part, I am obliged to that laborious *Herbarift Gerrard;* which being well underftood will prove of very great Service to us, in compofing our Sallads at all Times of the Year, fuitable to every ftrong or weak, hot or cold Stomachs, that are found in the different Conftitutions of People.

THE
CONTENTS.

PART. I.
Of Geometry.

SECT. I.
Of Lines.   Page 1

The CONTENTS.

SECT. II.
Of superficial Figures.

PART II.
Of Fruit-Trees.

The CONTENTS.

PART III.

Of Forest Trees, their Culture, &c.

PART IV.

Of Ever-Greens.

The CONTENTS

PART V.

Of Flowering Shrubs.

PART VI.

Of the Situation and Disposition of Gardens in General.

PART.

The CONTENTS.

PART VII.

Of the Kitchen Garden.

CHAP. I.

Of the right Ordering, and Cultivation of the several Sallet Herbs which are in Season, during the Months of JANUARY, FEBRUARY, and MARCH.

CHAP.

The CONTENTS.

CHAP. II.

Of the several Sallet Herbs, Roots, &c. for the Months of
APRIL, MAY and JUNE. page 103

CHAP. III.

CHAP. IV.

Of the several Sallet Herbs, Roots, &c. for the Months of
OCTOBER, NOVEMBER and DECEMBER. 141

I

CHAP.

The CONTENTS.

CHAP. V.

Of the Names, Defcriptions, Temperatures, Virtues and Cultivations of fuch Diftilling and other phyfical Herbs, that are abfolutely neceffary for the Service of all Gentlemen (and other) Families in general.

A Catalogue of Herbs to be dry'd, for Use in Winter.

(1.) For Distilling.

Angelica, Balm, Cammomile Flowers, Carduus Elicampane, Lavender, Liquorish, Summer Marjoram, Marigolds, Mint, Poppy, Tea Sage, Tansie and Wormwood.

(2.) For the Kitchen.

Summer Marjoram, Marigolds, and Mint.

A Table of aromatick Herbs.

Angelica, Anniseed, Balm, Cammomile, Chervil, Clovegilliflower, Dill, Hyssop, Lavender, Marjoram, Marigolds, Mint, Parsley, Southernwood, Tansie and Thyme.

Sweet Herbs for Kitchen Use.

Hyssop, Marjoram, Marigolds, Mint, Parsley, Penny-Royal, Savory, and Thyme.

Soup Herbs for Kitchen Use.

Asparagus, Beet, Borage, Cabbage, Carrot, Endive, Lettuce, Leeks, Winter Savory, Marjoram, Onions, Pease, Sellery, Spinage, Sorrel, and Turnip.

Herbs for Edgings in a Kitchen Garden.

Hyssop, Lavender, Spike and Cotton, Rhue, Sage and Thyme.

ERRATA.

PAGE 3. Problem. 5. Line 2. read *Interval.* p. 12. Paragraph 3. l. 1. r. *describe.* p. 34. parag. 3. r. *that naturally.* p. 38. l. 9. r. *that are good bearers,* and l. 10. r. *that are truly vigorous.* p. 39. l. 2. r. *therefore that you may not.* p. 48. r. *Benevolence.* r. *Do* in p. 73. 74. p. 54. r. *russelet, and note that Guisomadam is a summer fruit.* p. 55. *Blackpear of Worcester and Parkinson's Warden are the same fruit.* p. 56. r. *Kirton Pippin.* p. 57. *the early Flanders and Flemish Cherries are the same fruit.* p. 59. rule 5. r. *all that grow.* p. 60. rule 8. r. *that are in perfect health.* rule 13. l. 5. r. *to form the concave.* p. 64. r. June. p. 65. r. *Russelet.* p. 73. r. *the best season to prune the Fig, is the beginning or middle of June, and that the direction* p. 73. *is after the old method.* p. 77. r. *primordian.* p. 78. r. *Parterres.* l. 4. parag. 9. *for wonderfully* r. *much.* parag. 6. l. 4. r. *kernels that are saved.* p. 79. Sect. 12. l. 12. r. *those that are,* p. 80. parag. 5. l. 3. r. *and in April whom they begin.* p. 84. r. *Inkeward.* p. 85. l. 11. r. *cold winds,* and l. 2. Sect. 14. r. *that were.* p. 89. l. 6. r. *not admitting.* p. 90. parag. 4. l. 4. r. *garden:* p. 91. l. 5. r. *the soil they delight in.* p. 101. Corol. 19. l. 1. r. *terrace.* p. 102. parag. 3. l. 5. r. *than stewards, butlers, &c.* p. 105. l. 12. r. *primordian.* parag. 4. l. 14. r. *Russelet.* p. 106. l. 14. r. *la Royal.* p. 22. r. *Orleance.* l. 30. r. *Royal d'hyver.* p. 110. l. 1. r. *that are excellent good.* p. 115. l. 9. r. *that are.* parag. 5. l. 2. r. *best when planted.* p. 118. Sect. 2. l. 2. r. *such as is deep.* p. 124. r. *conduit joists, &c.* p. 131. parag. 2. l. 2. r. *If fell'd and sold.* p. 132. parag. 3. l. 9. r. *grow hollow.* p. 153. l. 6. r. *will discontinue.* p. 164. Sect. 14. l. 11. r. *water'd in very dry seasons.* p. 168. r. *Maracoc.* p. 169. l. 16. r. *greatly.* p. 174. r. *Lilac.* p. 182. l. 18. r. *their colours.* p. 183. r. *that is of the same colour.* p. 194. l. 10. r. *he never saw.* l. 12. r. *is not the purpose.* l. 16. r. *that is regular.* parag. 6. l. 2. r. *have been.* p. 195. direction 2. r. *with breadths proportionable,* and l. 3. r. *to their lengths of view.* p. 196. direct. 15. l. 5. r. *as the farther end.* p. 198. direct. 19. l. 3. r. *on Paradise stocks.* l. 6. r. *open plain environ'd.* p. 200. direct. 22. r. *Trelliss work.* direct. 30. r. *Plate.* 16, p. 203. r. *Jupiter, God of Thunder.* p. 204. r. *Hercules, God of Labour.* Part. VII. p. 8. l. 6. r. *where.* parag. 6. r. *Alleys.* p. 141. l. 18. r. *Clary.*

I PART

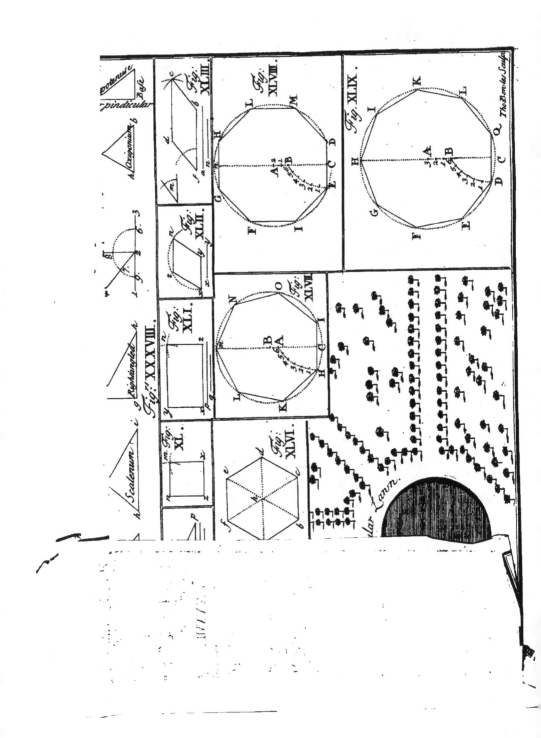

NEW
PRINCIPLES
OF
GARDENING.

PART I.
Of GEOMETRY.

SECT. I.
Of Lines.

N Confideration of the great Ufe as Geometry is
of to Gardeners, in furnifhing them with excellent Rules for their fure and fpeedy Execution of
Surveys, Meafures, Levels, Drawings, Working,
&c. therefore I have firft laid down all the moft
uſeful Principles thereof, and in a very concife
and familiar Manner.

B

PRO.

PROBLEM I.

Fig. I.

FROM *a given Point* (m,) *to draw a Right Line* (e z) *parallel to the Right Line* c b.

DEFINITION I. A Point in Practice is understood to be the leaft fuperficial Appearance, as can be made by the Point of a Needle, Pin, Pen, &c.

DEFINITION II. A Right Line is the neareft Diftance between its two bounding Points, as *c b.*

DEFINITION III. Parallel Right Lines are thofe which do not incline towards one another; and therefore if infinitely continued, would never meet, as *e a* and *c b.*

PRACTICE. Take the neareft Diftance from the Point *m*, to the Line *c b*, as *m o*, and on any Part of the Line *c b*, as at *f*, defcribe an Arch as *b b*; then by laying a Ruler from *m* to the Edge or Convexity of the Arch *b b*, you may draw the Parallel required. For by the firft, *a d* is equal to *a e*, *d g* equal to *g e*, and *a g* is common to both; therefore *a e* is parallel to *b e*. *Q. E. D.*

PROBLEM II.

Fig. I.

FROM *a Point given* (a,) *to draw a Line* (a e) *equal to the given Line* d g.

PRACTICE. From *a* draw *a e* parallel to *d g*, and join the Points, *a d* from the Point *g* draw *g e* parallel to *a d*, and the Line *a e* will be equal to *d g.* Becaufe in the Parallelogram *d e*, the oppofite Sides *a e* is equal to *d g.* *Q. E. F.*

PROBLEM III.

Fig. III.

A *Right Line being given* (a b) *to cut off a Part* (a f,) *equal to the Right Line* d c.

PRAC-

PRACTICE. From *a* draw *an* at pleasure, and longer than
dc. On *a*, with the Interval *dc*, describe the Arch *ef*; then
shall the Line *fa*, be equal to *cd*; because *fa* is equal to (*ae*
and) *cd*. *Q. E. D*

PROBLEM IV.

T O make an *Angle* (a b c) *equal to an Angle given*, Fig. IV.
(d e f.)

DEFINITION I. An Angle (called in *Latin Angulus*) is the
Corner (*d*,) that is made by the Meeting of Lines, as *fd*, and *de*,
&c. which Angle is greater or less, according as the Lines lean
nearer, or stand further off from one another: So the Lines *i d*
and *e d* make an Angle lesser than the Lines *e d* and *f d*, and
the Lines *h d* and *e d* greater than *e d* and *f d*, which is called
their Inclination. Therefore, when several Lines have the same
Inclination, they make equal Angles.

DEFINITION II. Angles are either right-lined, as *i*; spherical
or curved, as *k*, or mix'd, as *l*. When an Angle is mentioned
by three Letters, the second or middlemost Letter always denotes the Angle or Angular Point: So *a* denotes the Angle
b a c, or *c a b*, &c.

PRACTICE. Make *ac* equal to *df*. With any Interval, as
df on *d* describe *fe*, and on *a*, with the same Opening the
Arch *c b*, make *c b* equal to *fe*, and draw *a b*: So shall the
Angle *a b c* be equal to the given Angle *d e f*, because the Triangle *a b c* is equal-sided to the Triangle *d e f*. *Q. E. F.*

PROBLEM V.

T O divide an *Angle given* (a) *into two equal Parts.* Fig. V.

PRACTICE. On *a*, with any Iterval, describe the Arch *b c*,
and with the same Opening on *b* the Arch *f f*, and on *c* the
Arch *e e*, crossing in *d*: Join *d b* and *d c*, and draw *d a*, which shall
divide the Angle *a* in two equal Parts. For the Triangles *a b d*

and *a c d* are equal-fided, being Radius's of equal Circles, and *a d* common. Therefore the Angle *c d a* is equal to the Angle *b d a*. *Q. E. F.*

PROBLEM VI.

Fig. VI.

FROM *a given Point* (a or h) *to let fall or raife a Per-pendicular* (a h.)

DEFINITION I. *Perpendiculum*, or Perpendicular, (from the *Latin, perpendo,* to hang down,) is a Right Line falling upon a Right Line with equal Inclinations, (as *b a* on *b c*,) where the Angles on each Side (*b a b* and *b a c*) are equal to each other; and therefore are called Right Angles.

PRACTICE. With any Interval make *a c* equal to *a b*, and with the Diftance *b c* on *b* defcribe the Arch *e e*, and on *c* the Arch *f f*, croffing at *b*, join *b a*, and 'twill be the Perpendicular required; for *b b* is equal to *b c*, and *a b* to *a c*, and *b a* common. Therefore the Angles at *a* are equal and right-angled, and *a b* perpendicular. Secondly, on *b*, with any Interval, defcribe the Arch *b c*, join *b c* and *b b*; divide the Angle *c b b*, (by the preceding Problem,) and the Line *b a* is the Perpendicular required: For the Angles at *a* may be proved to be Right Angles, as before. Therefore, *&c. Q. E. F.*

Fig. VIII.

To let fall a Perpendicular from a Point, as at *i*, over or near the End of a Line, draw a Right Line (*i n o*) from the given Point (*i*) to any Part of the given Line, as to *o*, which divide into two equal Parts at *n*, and on *n* defcribe the Semi-circle *i l o*, draw *i l* the Perpendicular required. *Q. E. F.*

To raife Perpendiculars at the End of a Right Line, take the following Ways, *viz.*

Firft, From *a* raife the Perpendicular *a g*.

PRACTICE. With any Interval on *a* defcribe an Arch, as (*y c d*,) make *y c* and *c d* each equal to *a y d*; and with the fame Opening on *c* defcribe the Arch *d d*, and on *d* the Arch *c c*, croffing the other in *f*, draw *g a* through *f*, the Perpendicular required.

Secondly, From *b* raife the Perpendicular *b p*.

PRACTICE.

PRACTICE. With any Interval on *h* defcribe the Arch *i l z,*
make *i l* equal to *h i,* and with the fame Opening on *l* defcribe
the Arch *i m n o,* make *i o* equal to thrice *h i,* draw *o h,* and
'twill be the Perpendicular required.

Thirdly, From *q* raife the Perpendicular *q v.*　　　　Fig. VIII.

PRACTICE. With any Interval of your Compaffes place
down at a Venture one Foot thereof as at *s,* and with the other
defcribe the Arches *x x* and *w w*; lay a Ruler from *r* to *s,*
and 'twill cut the Arch *w w* in *t*; join *t q,* and 'tis the Perpendicular required.

Fourthly, From *a,* Fig. VIII. raife the Perpendicular *a c.*

PRACTICE. Draw a Right Line, as *d e,* and open your Fig. IX.
Compaffes to any fmall Diftance, as from 1 to 2, and thereon
prick off ten of thofe Divifions: Take eight of the faid Divifions, and place it from *a* to *b,* with the Interval of 6 on *a*;
defcribe the Arch *ff,* and with the Interval of 10 on *b,* the
Arch *g g,* croffing the former in *c*; join *c a,* and 'tis the Perpendicular required.

When Perpendiculars are to be raifed from an Angular
Point, (as *n m* from *n,*) open your Compaffes to any Interval,
as *n h,* and on the Angle *n* defcribe an Arch, as *g h*; then opening your Compaffes to any greater Diftance, as *g o,* on *g* defcribe the Arch *r r,* and on *h* the Arch *o o,* croffing the former
in *m*; draw *n m,* and 'tis the Perpendicular required.

PROBLEM VII.

T O *divide a Right Line into two equal Parts, by a Right* Fig. VII.
Line, as a b *by* n m.

PRACTICE. On *a,* with any Interval greater than *a i,* defcribe an Arch, as *d d,* and with the fame Opening on *b,* the
Arch *c c,* croffing the firft in *n m*; from which Points draw
the Line *n m,* and 'twill divide *a b* in the Middle; for *n b* is
equal

equal to the Radius of *n a* and *n i* common, and the Angles at *i* right-angled; therefore the Side *a i* is equal to *i b*. *Q. E. F.*

PROBLEM VIII.

TO *divide any Line (as* a b) *in a given Proportion, as* c a, c e.

Fig. X.   PRACTICE. *a b, a c,* being drawn at any Angle, draw the Right Line *b c,* and draw *e d* parallel to it; therefore, as *b a* is to *d a,* so is *c a* to *e a. Q. E. F.*

PROBLEM IX.

Fig. X.   TO *find a fourth Proportional* (b d) *to three given,* viz. a e: e c :: a d : d b.

PRACTICE. Join *e d,* and draw *c b* parallel, and continue *a d* to *b,* and *d b* is the fourth Proportional required; for as *a e* is to *e c,* so is *a d* to *d b. Q. E. F.*

PROBLEM X.

TO *find a third Proportional* (n m) *to two given,* (z y, y x.)

Fig. XI.   PRACTICE. Make *z n* equal to *z y* at any Angle, and join *y n.* Continue *z n* infinitely, and from *x* draw the Parrallel *x m; m n* is the third Proportional: For, as *z y* is to *y x,* so is *z n* to *n m. Q. E. F.*

PROBLEM XI.

BEtween *two given Lines* (i k, n o) *to find a mean Proportion* (c h.)

DEFINITION. A mean proportional Line, is such a Line, whose Length being multiplied into it self, its Product is equal to both the Products of the other two Lines between which it is a mean Proportional.

PRAC-

PRACTICE. Make *d b* equal to *i k* and *n o*, make *d c* equal to Fig. XII.
n o; and from *c*, raife the Perpendicular *c h*. Bifect *d b* in
a, and on *a*, with the Interval *a d*, or *a b*, defcribe the Semicircle *d h b*, cutting the Perpendicular in *h*; *h c* will be the mean
Proportion. For, (*h b*, *h d*, being joined) the Angle *b h d* is
right-angled. Therefore *h c* is the mean Proportion between
c b and *c d*. Q. E. F.

PROBLEM XII.

TO divide a Right Line (b f) *in extream and mean Pro-*
portion.

DEFINITION. A Right Line is faid to be divided in extream
and mean Proportion, when the Whole is to the greateft Segment,
as the greateft Segment is to the Leffer.

PRACTICE. Make *w v* equal to *b f*, and bifect *w v* by
x h, in *r*; through *h* and *x* draw *s t* and *z y* parallel to *w v*; and
through *w* and *v* the Lines *t y*, and *s z* parallel to *h x*;
on *t*, with the Interval *t y*, defcribe the Arch *y n o s*, cutting
h x in *n*, and *w v* in *o*. Draw *o h*, and on *h* with the Interval *h o*, cut *h x* in *a*, fo fhall *h a* be the greater Segment, and
a x the leffer; and confequently *h x* is thereby divided in extream and mean Proportion. Let *x o* be drawn, and with that
Interval on *x*, defcribe the Arch *o c*, and on *b* the Arch *o a*, and
draw the Right Lines *o a* and *o c*; then will the Angle *h c o* be
equal to the Angles *c x o*, and *x o c*; becaufe thefe two Angles
are within, the other without the Triangle *c x o*. Likewife
the fame Angle *h c o* is equal to the Angles *o a c* and *a o c*
and *o c a* equal to *x o c*; alfo the Angles *o x c* and *c o a* are
equal to each other. Therefore the Triangles *x o c*, and *a o c*,
have two Angles equal to two Angles of the Triangle *c o a*,
and therefore equal-angled. For as *o x* or *o h* is to *o c*, fo is
o c, or *o a*, to *a c*. Therefore *o c* or *o a* is a mean Propor- Fig. XIII.
tional between *h o* and *c a*. On the Right Lines *o x*, *o h*, make
h d and *x e*, equal to *h c*, and join *d e* and *d c*; then will *d o*
and *o e* be equal, and *d e* parallel to *h x*, and confequently the
alternate Angles *d e a*, *x a e*, and *e d a*, *h c d*, are all equal to
each

each other, and the Rhombus *x e d a* equal to the Rhombus *b d e c.* Therefore the Lines *x e, e c, d a, d b, b c,* and *o a,* are equal to one another. And as 'tis plain, that *o a* is a mean Proportional between *b a* and *c a,* fo likewife is *x a* (equal to *o a*) a mean Proportional between *b a* and *c a*; for 'twill be, as *b a* to *a x,* fo *a x* to *c a*; and being compounded, as *b a* more *a x,* (that is, *b x,*) to *x a* more *a c,* (that is, *x c* or *b a,*) fo likewife is *b a* to *b c*; therefore *b x* is divided in *c* and *a*; fo that the whole Line *b x,* a Part *b a,* and the remaining Part *b c,* likewife *x b,* a Part *x c,* and the remaining Part *x a,* are continual Proportionals. Therefore *b a* (that is, *b o*) is the greater Segment of the Right Line *b x,* divided in ex-tream and mean Proportion. *Q. E. D.*

N. B. Thofe Segments may alfo be found as follows: Continue *x b* to *k,* making *b k* equal to *b r*; on *k,* with the Interval *k v,* defcribe the Arch *v a o,* which will cut *b x* in *a*; fo will *b a* be the greater Segment. *Q. E. F.*

PROBLEM XIII.

Fig. XIV. **T**O *find the Center of an Arch (or Circle) given* (g h i) *or to defcribe a Circle, whofe Circumference fhall pafs through three Points given.*

PRACTICE. Join any two, as *b g* and *b i,* bifect each by Perpendiculars, croffing in *n,* which is the Center; for each Perpendicular is a Diameter, and confequently the Center muft be where they interfect.

PROBLEM XIV.

Fig. XV. **T**O *draw a Tangent* (n h) *from a Point given* (h)

DEFINITION. A Tangent (comes from the *Latin* Word *Tango,* to touch) is a perpendicular Right Line without a Circle falling upon the End of the Diameter, as *n b.*

PRACTICE. Draw a Right Line from *b* to the Center *k,* bifect *b k* in *i,* and thereon defcribe the Semicircle *k n b,* cutting

ting the Circle in *n*; join *n k*, *n b*, so shall *n b* be the Tangent required. For the Angle *k n b* is right-angled. *Q. E. F.*

PROBLEM XV.

TO *cut off a Segment* (o s) *from a Circle given, that may* Fig. XVI. *receive an Angle equal to an Angle given, viz.* s n o *equal to the given Angle* t.

DEFINITION. A *Segment* (*Latin*, from *seco*, to cut) of a *Circle*, is a Figure contain'd between a Right Line and any Part of the *Circumference* of a *Circle*, as o *x* s, or s *w* o.

PRACTICE. By the preceding draw the *Tangent* r *m*, touching in o, making the Angle r o s equal to *t*; therefore the Angle s n o (in the opposite Segment) is equal to *t*, so that s *w* n o, is the *Segment* required.

PROBLEM XVI.

TO *divide a Right Line* (z a) *into any Number of equal* Fig. XVII. *Parts*, (*suppose six.*)

PRACTICE. Draw a Line at Pleasure, as r *s*, and thereon prick off six equal Divisions of any Size, as those at 1, 2, 3, 4, 5, 6. On *s*, with the Interval r *s*, describe the Arch *x x*, and on r the Arch o o. From *b*, the Point of Intersection, through r, 1, 2, 3, 4, 5, *s*, draw Right Lines infinitely; make *b b* and *b i* equal to z a, and join *b i*; then will *b i* be *divided* into *six equal Parts* by the Lines *b n*, *b n*, &c. *Q. E. F.*

PROBLEM XVII.

TO *divide a Right Line* (z n) *in such Proportion, as an-* Fig.XVIII. *other is before divided*, (*as* a b.)

PRACTICE. Draw a Line at Pleasure, as r *s*, on which prick off the several Distances or Divisions of *a b*, as *a* 1, 1, 2, 2, 3, 3, 4, 4 *b*; at the Points *n n*, &c. make s *t* and r *t* equal (by the preceeding,) and from, *t* through the Points *n n*, &c.

C

draw

draw Right Lines infinitely, make *t q* and *t w* equal to *z n*, and draw *q w*; then will *q w* (which is equal to *z n*) be divided in such *Proportion* as *a b*. *Q. E. F.*

PROBLEM XVIII.

TO *describe* Spiral *or* Serpentine *Lines, either single, double, treble, or quadruple.*

Single Spiral Line.
Fig. XIX.
PRACTICE. (1.) Draw the Line 1, 2, at Pleasure, and bisect it in *y*, on which, with half the assigned Distance of the Line, (suppose *a x*,) describe the *Circle v w*, and bisect *v y* and *y w* in *z* and *x*, which are the *two Centers* on which the Line is described, as follows: On *x* describe *v t*, on *z*, *t s*, on *x*, *s q*, and on *z*, *q r*, &c. and so in like manner, you may turn the said *Line* about, as often as required.

Double Spiral Line.
Fig. XX.
(2.) Draw the Line 3, 4, at Pleasure, and bisect it in *y*, and, as in the preceding, describe the *Circle r w*, and its *Centers x*, *z*, which being done, on the *Center x* describe *w q*, and on *z* describe *r v*; also on *x*, *u p*, and on *z*, *q t*, and *p s*, and, so in like manner, on *x*, the Arches *t v* and *s u*, &c.

Treble Spiral Line.
Fig. XXI.
(3.) Make the *Equilateral Triangle a b m*, with its Sides, equal to the given Line *x a*, and by PROB. V. divide all the *Angles*, and draw the Lines, *a* 11, *f w*, *b* 7, *i* 8, *m* 9, and *o* 10. On *m* with the *Radius m b*, describe the Arch *b c*, on *a* the Arch *m e*, and on *b* the Arch *a d*; then on *o*, with the Interval *o c*, describe the Arch *c g*, on *f* the Arch *e l*, and on *i* the Arch *d n*. Again on *a*, with the Interval *a g*, describe the Arch *g h*, on *b* the Arch *l* 1, and on *m* the Arch *n v*; then beginning again at *o*, with the Interval *o v*, describe the Arch *v x*, on *a* the Arch *x y*, and on *f* the Arch *y z*, &c. and the like of others, to any Number of Revolutions required.

Quadruple Spiral Line.
Fig. XXII.
(4.) Draw a Right Line at Pleasure, as *g s*, and bisect it by the Line *i o*, and draw *d c* and *a b*, as also *b c* and *a d*, parallel to the Lines *i o*, and *s g*, at the given Distance of the Lines 5, 6, intersecting each other in *a b c d*, the *Centers*; on which the Lines are describ'd, as follows, viz. on *d* describe the Arch *b i*, on *a* the Arch *z y*, on *b*, *n m*, and on *c*, *o p*; then beginning again at *d*, describe *y k*, at *a*, *n l*, at *b*, *p q*, and at *c*, *p f*; and so in like manner may be continued about to any Number of Revolutions required.   PROB-

PROBLEM XIX.

*T*O *describe a serpentine Line about an Ellipsis.* Fig.XXIII

PRACTICE. By PROB. IX. SECT. II. describe the *Ellipsis* *a b c d*, according to its *Diameters given*, and extend out the Lines *e g*, *e h*, and *f g*, *f h*, infinitely : Divide *f h* into four equal Parts, and make *f i*, *h k*, *g l*, and *e m*, each equal to one Fourth of *f h*, which Points *i*, *k*, *l*, *m*, are the four *Centers* on which the Line is described as following, *viz.* On *l* describe the Arch *n p*, on *i* the Arch *p o*, on *k* the Arch *o v*, on *m* the Arch *v w*, on *l* the Arch *w x*, and on *i* the Arch *x g*, and so (as before in the *circular Spirals*) this may be continued about as often as required.

PROBLEM XX.

*T*O *describe with Compasses*, &c. *any rural or irregular* Fig.XXIV, *Curved Line, as* z w m.

PRACTICE. *First*, with a *Pencil* trace out the Line, and at every *Turning*, as *w*, *i*, *h*, make a Point. *Secondly*, in every such *Division* assume another *Point*, as *r*, and by PROB. XIII. hereof describe the Arch *z r w*, and then proceed in like manner to find the *Centers* of the Arches *w i*, *i h*, &c. till the whole Line is described as required.

SECT. II.

Of Superficial Figures.

SUPERFICIAL FIGURES, necessary to be understood by *Gardeners, &c.* are the *Circle, Ellipsis, Triangle, Square, Parellogram, Pentagon, Hexagon, Septagon, Octagon, Nonagon, Decagon,* &c. whose *Definitions* and *Constructions* are as follows.　　　　C 2　　　　**P R O-**

PROBLEM I.

Fig.XXV. TO *describe a Circle of any possible Magnitude required.*

DEFINITION. (1.) A CIRCLE is a *plain Figure,* bounded with one *Line,* called the *Circumference*; in the *Midst* whereof is a *Point,* from whence all Lines drawn to the *Circumference* are *equal,* which Point is called the *Center thereof,* as *a.* (2.) The *Diameter* of a *Circle* is a *Right Line* (*b c*) passing through the *Center a,* terminating at each *End* with the *Circumference,* and dividing the *Circle* into two equal Parts. (3.) The *Radius* of a Circle is the Semidiameter, as *b a,* or *a c.* (4.) A *Semicircle* is the Figure (*b n c*) contain'd between the *Diameter* and half the *Circumference.* (5.) A *Segment* of a Circle. *Vide* PROB. XV. SECT. I.

PRACTICE. A CIRCLE is usually described by the Revolution of a *Right Line,* having one of its Ends fix'd on the *Center,* while the other revolves round the same; as if *d b* was fix'd at *b,* (as the *Joint* of a *Sector, Two-foot Rule, &c.*) and to be moved from *d* to *l,* to *n,* to *v,* and to *d;* its former *Position,* the End of the Line *d* would *describe* the *Circumference,* and the *Line* the *Circle* itself. When a *Circle* is described by *Compasses,* the Distance between the two *Points* or *Legs* thereof, is to be considered as the *Radius* or Right Line aforesaid. It often happens, that *Circles* are required to be described where 'tis not possible for the *Radius to move round its Center,* as before; and therefore at such Times observe the following Rule:

Fig.XXVI. *How to aescribe a* CIRCLE *without the Center being known;* Let *d b g* be the given Diameter, which bisect in *b,* and thereon raise the Perpendicular *b l,* which make equal to *b d.* Continue *b d* towards *f,* and make *f d* equal to two Sevenths of *d b;* on *b,* with the Interval *b f,* describe the Arch *f m* at Pleasure, make *b v* equal to *b l,* or *b d;* on *d,* with any Interval greater than half *d l,* describe the Arches *k k,* *s s,* on *l,* the Arches *i i,* and draw *b b,* cutting the Arch *f m* in *a;* then with the Interval *d c,* or *l a,* on *l* describe the Arch *o o,* on *n* the Arches *p p,* *r r,* and on *v* the Arches *q q,* *t t,* interfecting
each

each other in the Points *a, y, w, x*; join the Right Lines *a l, l y, y g, g w, w v, v x, x d, d a,* each of which divide into any Number of equal Parts, as 1, 2, 3, 4, 5, &c. Draw Right Lines from the Divisions of *b d,* to those of *b l,* from *l y* to those of *y g,* from *g x* to those of *x v,* and from *v w* to those of *w d,* and their Interfections will describe the *Circle* required. *Q. E. F.*

PROBLEM II.

TO *divide the Circumference of a Circle into any Number of equal Parts, not exceeding ten.*

Fig. XXVII.

PRACTICE. By the preceding describe the *Circle a f e g;* draw the *Diameter a e c,* and 'twill divide the *Circle* into two equal Parts; make *a b* and *a d* equal to *a e,* and draw *b d,* which will divide the Circle into *three equal Parts*; draw *f g* at Right Angles to *a c,* and join *f a,* which is the *fourth Division*; on *a,* with the Interval *a f,* cut *a c* in *i,* and join *f i,* which shall divide the Circle into *five equal Parts*; the Radius *e a, e c, &c.* is the *sixth Division, b b,* or *b d,* is the *seventh*; draw *e k* through *o,* and the Line *a k* will be the *eighth*; one Third of the Arch *b a d,* viz. *d l,* is the *ninth,* and *e i* the *tenth* Division. *Q. E. F.*

PROBLEM III.

TO *divide the Circumference of any Circle into 360 equal Parts, or Degrees.*

DEFINITION. A *Degree* is the three hundred and fixtieth Part of the *Circumference* of any *Circle,* (*be it great or small*;) each of those *Degrees* are divided into *fixty equal Parts,* called *Minutes*; and each of those into *fixty Parts* more, called *Seconds*; and fo to *Thirds, Fourths, &c.* But fuch Subdivifions has no Place herein, any further than *Minutes.*

PRACTICE. Defcribe the *Circle a e b c,* draw the two *Diameters a b* and *e c* at *Right Angles,* and the *Circle* will be divided into four equal Parts; make *a g, a n,* each equal to *a d,*

Fig. XXVIII.

as

as also *c m, c k, b l, b h, e i,* and *e f,* then will the *Circum-*
ference be divided into *twelve* equal Parts, each containing
thirty Degrees: Divide *a f, a m, &c.* each into three equal Parts,
and then will the *Circle* be divided into thirty six, each containing ten Degrees. Laſtly, divide each of thoſe Diviſions
into ten equal Parts, by the preceding Problems of Sect. I.
and the *Circumference* will be divided into *three hundred* and
ſixty equal Parts, as required. *Q, E. F.*

PROBLEM IV.

TO *find the Center of a Circular Arch, and the whole*
Diameter of the Circle, of which the given Arch is a Part
or Segment.

Fig.XXIX   Practice. Let *a b c* be the *Circular Arch* given ; aſſume
three Points therein, as *a, b, c,* and by Prob. XIII. Sect. I. find
the *Center, &c. Q. E. F.*

PROBLEM V.

A Circle being given, to find its Center.

Fig.XXX.   Practice. Let *a b c* be the *Circle* given ; aſſume therein
three Points, as *a, b, c,* and by Prob. XIII. Sect. I. find the
Center, &c. Q. E. F.

PROBLEM VI.

TO *deſcribe an Ellipſis* (a e l b k h,) *to any Length given,*
(a c d b.)

Fig.XXXI.   Definition. An Ellipsis (*Greek*) is a Geometrical Figure,
comprehended in one only Line, but that not circular, nor having all its Parts equally reſpecting the Center, but two *Focus*
Points, as *c, d.*
   An Ellipsis is generated by an *oblique Section* of a *Cone,*
and is to be deſcribed divers Ways, as following:

PRAC-

PRACTICE. Divide *a b*, into three equal Parts, at *c* and *d*, with the Interval *a c* ; on *c* defcribe the Circle *a e d b*, and on *d* the Circle *l b k c*; from *o*, through *c* and *d*, draw *o d l*, and *o c e*; alfo from *n*, through *d* and *c*, draw *n d k*, and *n c b*; extend your Compaffes from *n* to *b*, and defcribe the Arch *b k*, and with the fame Diftance on *a* the Arch *e l*; and thus is the *Ellipfis compleated* as required.

PROBLEM VII.

TO defcribe an Ellipfis a different Way from the pre-ceding.

PRACTICE. Divide the *Diameter x y* into four equal Parts Fig. XXXII. at *e i m*, with the Radius *x e*; on *e* defcribe the Circle *e x i*, and on *i* the Circle *i e n m*, and on *m* the Circle *m i y*; at *i* draw *n f* at Right Angles to *x y* : From *f*, through *e* and *m*, draw the Right Lines *f m b*, and *f e a*, alfo from *n*, through *e* and *m* the Lines *n m d* and *n e c*: With the Interval *f g*, on *f* defcribe the Arch *g n b*, and on *n* the Arch *w f k*, and the *Ellipfis* will be *compleated* as required.

PROBLEM VIII.

TO defcribe an Ellipfis according to any Length and Breadth Fig. XXXIII. g iven, as h and i.

PRACTICE. Make *a d* equal to *h*, bifect *a d* in *g* by *e f*, at Right Angles ; make *f e* equal to *i*, and *f c*, *f b*, or *e c*, *e b*, equal to *g d* or *g a*; fo fhall *b c* be the Umbilque, or two *Focus* Points; upon which two *Pins, Nails, &c.* being faf-ten'd, and about them put a *String*, whofe Ends faften toge-ther in the Point *e*, this *String* being moved about the two *Pins* with a *Blacklead Pencil, &c.* will defcribe the *Ellipfis*, whofe *Length* and *Breadth* fhall be equal to the two given Lines *h i*. *2. E. F.*

PROBLEM IX.

To describe the same Ellipsis a different Way.

Fig.
XXXIV. PRACTICE. Make *a l* and *m b* equal to *s* and *t* at *Right Angles*, as in the preceding; make *l x* and *a y* each equal to *h b*, or *h m*; divide *x h* into three equal Parts, and make *x i* equal to one of those Parts; make *h c* equal to *h i*; with the Interval *i c*, on *i* describe the Arches *t t* and *w w*, and on *c* the Arches *v v* and *z z*, interfecting the former in *g* and *f*; from *f*, through *i* and *c*, draw the Right Lines *f i r*, and *f c q*, as also from the Point *g* the Right Line *g c p*, and *g i h*; On *c*, with the Interval *c a*, describe the Arch *o a o*, and on *i* the Arch *d l d*; extend you Compasses from *f* to *m*, and on *f* describe the Arch *o m d*, as also on *g* the Arch *o b d*, which will compleat the *Ellipsis* as required.

PROBLEM X.

To find the Center and two Diameters of any Ellipsis.

Fig.
XXXV. PRACTICE. Within the *Ellipsis* draw at Discretion *two parallel Right Lines*, as *e f* and *g h*; bisect these *Parallels* in *i* and *k*, and draw the Right Line *i k*, which bisect in *l*, the *Center* of the *Ellipsis*, whereon with any *Radius* describe *a Circle*, as *m n o*, interfecting the *Ellipsis* in *p* and *q*; join *p q*, and bisect it in *r*, and draw *r l* to *t* and *s*, which is the longest *Diameter*; through *l* draw *e d*, parallel to *p q*, and 'tis the lesser *Diameter*. *Q. E F.*

PROBLEM XI.

To describe an Ellipsis according to any Length and Breadth given, without knowing the Focus Points, or by Segments of Circles, as by the preceding Problems.

Fig.
XXXVI. PRACTICE. Let *d c* be the longest *Diameter*, and *a b* the shortest; at the Distance of *h b* draw *f i* and *e g* parallel to *c d*, and *e f* and *g i* parallel at *a b*, at the Distance of *h c*, cut-

ting

ting the former in *e f g i*. Divide *a e, a g, b f, d e, d f, c g*, and *c i*, each into equal Number of Parts; the more, the more exact; draw Right Lines from the Divisions of *a e*, to thofe of *e d, &c.* as by Prob. I. hereof, and their Interfections will defcribe the Ellipfis required. *Q. E. F.*

Note, That the longeft Diameter of an Ellipfis is called, the Conjugate; and the fhorteft, the Tranfverfe Diameter.

PROBLEM XII.

To defcribe a Figure, call'd an Egg Oval, equal to any Breadth given, as h n.

Practice. Make *a c* equal to *h n*, and bifect *a c* in *b*; whereon, with the Diftance *a b*, defcribe the Semicircle *a d c*; on *a*, with the Interval *a c*, defcribe the Arch *c e*, and with the fame Opening on *c*, the Arch *a f*, croffing the former in *g*, completing the *Oval* required. *Q. E. F.* Fig: XXXVII.

N. B. That the Figure thus defcrib'd, is vulgarly called an *Egg Oval*, tho' in fact, it is not; becaufe the Arches *c e* and *a f* interfect each other, and conftitute an Angle at *g*, which is contrary to the *Curvature* of an *Ellipfis*. Therefore to defcribe an actual Egg Oval, proceed as follows, *viz.* Having defcribed the Figure according to the preceding Way, draw the Line *b g*, which divide in *l*. On *l* with the Opening *l g*, defcribe the Arch *o g h*, and on *g* the Arch *p l k*, interfecting the former in *r* and *i*. Laftly draw *l i*, cutting the Arch *c e* in *m*, *l r* cutting the Arch *a f* in *s*, and on *l*, with the Opening *l m*, defcribe the Arch *m z s*, which will complete the true *Egg Oval*, as required.

PROBLEM XIII.

To defcribe an Equilateral Triangle.

Definition. A *Triangle* is a plain Geometrical Figure, bounded with three Sides, conftituting three *Angles*, and therefore

D   fore

fore called a Triangle. When a Triangle hath all its Sides equal, 'tis called an *Equilateral Triangle*, as *e a b*. That Triangle as hath two Sides equal, and the third unequal, is called an *Iſoceles Triangle*; and that Triangle whoſe three Sides are unequal, as *b o i*, is called a *Scalenum Triangle*.

Note, That what is here delivered in relation to the Names of Triangles, is only with reſpect to their Sides; therefore, when Triangles are mentioned with regard ro their Angles, they are diſtinguiſhed as following, *viz*. *A Right-angled Triangle*, is that which has one Right Angle and two Acute Angles, as *g b l* right-angled at *g*, and acute-angled at *b* and *l*. All Angles are meaſured by an Arch of a Circle, whoſe Center is the Angular Point; and the Number of Degrees contained in ſuch an Arch, is the Quantity of the Angle.

If the Quantity of the Angle is ninety Degrees, as the Angle 1, 2, 5, 'tis called a *Right Angle*; and when leſs than ninety Degrees, 'tis called an *Acute Angle*, as the Angle 3, 2, 4; but when the Angle is greater than a Right Angle, containing more than ninety Degrees, ſuch an Angle is called an *Obtuſe Angle*.

Figg. XXXVIII. An *Amblygonium Triangle* is that as hath one Obtuſe Angle, and two Acute Angles, as *b o i*. An *Oxigonium Triangle* is that as hath all its Angles acute, as *a b b*. In every plain Triangle, *the Sum of the three Angles are always equal to* 180 *Degrees*. In every Triangle, any two of the Lines being taken for two Sides, the other remaining (be which it will) is called the *Baſe*; therefore any Side of a Triangle may be made the *Baſe*.

In all right-angled Plain Triangles, that Side as is oppoſite to the Right Angle, is called the *Hypothenuſe*, and the other two Sides its *Legs*; and ſometimes one of the Legs is called the Baſe, and the other (*Cathetus*, a *Greek* Word for) Perpendicular.

PRACTICE. Make *e b* equal to *f g*, and on *e* and *b*, with the Interval *f g*, deſcribe the Arches 1, 1, and 2, 2, croſſing in *a*; join *a b* and *a e*, the Triangle required; for as *a b*, *b e*, and *e a*, are Radius's of equal Circles, therefore the Triangle is Equilateral. *Q. E. F.*

P R O B-

PROBLEM XIV.

Fig.
XXXIX.

TO *make an Iſoceles and Scalenum Triangle.*

PRACTICE. (1) Draw *z x* equal to *v,* and with the Interval *w,* deſcribe Arches croſſing in *y*; join *z y*, *y x*, and 'twill complete the *Iſoceles Triangle* required.

(2) Draw *n p* equal to *l,* and with the Intervals *m c*, on *p* and *n* deſcribe Arches croſſing in *o*; join *n o*, and *o p*, and the *Scalenum Triangle* will be completed as required. *Q. E. F.*

PROBLEM XV.

TO *deſcribe a Geometrical Square on a given Line,*
   (z x.)

DEFINITION. A GEOMETRICAL SQUARE, is a Figure which Fig. XL. hath four equal Sides, and the Angles right, as *n m z x.*

PRACTICE. From *x* erect a Perpendicular *x m*, equal to *z x*, and on *m* and *z*, with the Interval *z x*, deſcribe Arches croſſing at *n*, join *n z* and *n m*. *Q. E. F.* For *z x* is equal to *x m*, equal to *m n*, equal to *n z*, and *m z* is common; therefore the Triangles *x m z*, and *m n z*, are equal angled; therefore the Angle *x* is equal to the Angle *n ;* but the Angle *x m z* is equal to the Angle *x z m*, and *n m z* equal to *n z m*, each equal to forty five Degrees; therefore *m* and *z* are right-angled, and the oppoſite Sides are parallel. *Q. E. D.*

PROBLEM XVI.

TO *deſcribe a Parallelogram* (z x y n,) *equal in Length and*
   Breadth, to two given Lines, p, q.

DEFINITION. A PARALLELOGRAM is a Quadrilateral Figure, Fig. XLI. whoſe oppoſite Sides are parallel; from the Words *Parallel* and *Gramma,* a Figure or Letter.

PRAC-

PRACTICE. Draw *z x* equal to *p*, and erect the Perpendicular *x y* equal to *q*, with the Intervals *q* and *p*, on *z* and *y* describe Arches crossing in *n* ; join *n y* and *n z*, and the Parallelogram will be completed. *Q*, *E. F.*

PROBLEM XVII.

TO *describe a Rhombus on a given Line* xy.

Fig. XLII.   DEFINITION. A RHOMBUS is a Geometrical Figure of four equal Sides, but the Angles are unequal; two opposite ones being Acute, and the other two Obtuse: 'Tis called *Rhombus*, from the *Greek* Word *Rhumbos*, a Fish, called the Turbot, or Glass Quarrels in a Window.

PRACTICE. On *y*, with the Interval *x y*, describe the Arch *x z n*, make *x z* and *z n* equal to *x y*, and join *x z*, *z n*, and *n y*, the *Rhombus* required. *Q. E. F.*

PROBLEM XVIII.

TO *describe a Rhomboides, equal to the given Lines* a n *and Angle* m.

Fig. XLIII.   DEFINITION. A RHOMBOIDES is of the same Derivation as the *Rhombus*, and is a Figure between a *Parallelogram* and a *Rhombus*; from the one it takes its Correspondency of Sides, from the other Proportion of Angles, and therefore is called a *Rhomboides*.

PRACTICE. Draw *b f* equal to *n*, and (by PROB. IV. SECT I.) the Angle *d f b* equal to *m*, making *f d* equal to *a*; on *b* and *d*, with the Intervals *a n*, describe Arches crossing in *c*, join *c d* and *c b*, the *Rhomboides* required. *Q. E. F.*

PROBLEM XIX.

TO *describe a Trapezia, equal to the given Lines* a b c d *and Angle* c.

DEFI·

DEFINITION. The Word *Trapezia* feems to come from the Fig. XLIV.
Greek Trapeza, a Table: 'Tis an irregular Geometrical Figure
of *four unequal Sides*, were neither the Sides nor Angles equally correfpond.

PRACTICE. Draw *fg* equal to *d*, and the Angle *fg i* (by
PROB. IV. SECT. I.) equal to *e*, and make *g i* equal to *c*; on
f and *i*, with the Intervals *b* and *a*, defcribe Arches croffing
in *b*; join *b i*, and *b f*, the *Trapezia* required. *Q. E. F.*

PROBLEM XX.

TO frame or make a regular *Pentagon* upon a Line given.

DEFINITION. A PENTAGON (*Greek*, from *Pente*, five, and Fig. XLV.
Gonia, an Angle,) is a Geometrical Figure of five Angles,
and all equilateral, and thereby its Sides are all equal, as the
Figure *a c b d e*.

PRACTICE. Divide *e d* in the Middle at *n*, from which
erect the Perpendicular *n b*, equal to *e d*, extend *b e* to *f*, fo
that *e f* may be equal to *e n*; upon the Bafe *e d*, make the
Triangle *d c e*, each Side equal to *b f*; on *c* and *d*, with the
Interval *e d*, defcribe Arches croffing in *b*; as alfo with the
fame Interval on *e* and *c*, defcribe Arches croffing in *a*; join
e a, *a c*, *c b*, and *b d*, and the Pentagon will be compleated as
required. *Q. E. F.* *Pentagons* may be defcribed by PROB. II.
hereof. By defcribing a Circle, and dividing its Circumference
into five equal Parts, (as there fhewn,) and then to draw
Lines from one Divifion to another, will frame a Pentagon as
required.

PROBLEM XXI.

TO make a regular *Hexagon* on a Line given, (d e.)

DEFINITION. A HEXAGON is a Geometrical Figure, confifting of fix Angles, from *Hex*, fix, and *Gonia*, an Angle.

Fig.XLVI. PRACTICE. On *de* (by PROB. XIV. hereof,) make the Equilateral Triangle *dh e*, and on *h e* the Equilateral Triangle *h f e*, and on *h f* the Triangle *h a f*; continue *e h* to *b*, and *f h* to *c*, making *h c* equal to *f h*, and *h b* equal to *e h*; laſtly, join *a b*, *b c*, and *c d*, and the *Hexagon* will be compleated as required. *Q. E. F.*

PROBLEM XXII.

To deſcribe a Heptagon on a given Line (H I.)

DEFINITION. A HEPTAGON is a Geometrical Figure of ſeven Angles, from the *Greek Hepta*, ſeven, and *Gonia*, an Angle,

Fig. XLVII. PRACTICE. Biſect H I in C, and from thence raiſe the Perpendicular C M; with the Interval H I, on I deſcribe the Arch 1 2 3 4 5; divide this Arch into ſix equal Parts, and make A B equal to A 1; on B, with the Radius B I, or B H, deſcribe the Circle I C H *m*; laſtly, take the Line H I in your Compaſſes, and ſet off that Length from H to K, from K to L, from L to *m*, from *m* to N, N to O, and join the Right Lines K H, K L, L *m*, *m* N, N O, and O I, they will compleat the *Heptagon* required. *Q. E. F.*

PROBLEM XXIII.

To deſcribe an Octagon, whoſe Sides ſhall be each equal to a given Line (E C.)

DEFINITION. An OCTAGON is a plain Geometrical Figure, conſiſting of eight equal Sides and Right-equal Angles, from *Octo*, eight, and *Gonia* an Angle.

Fig. XLVIII. PRACTICE. Biſect E D in C, whereon raiſe the Perpendicular *c n*; on D, with the Interval D E, deſcribe the Arch B E, which divide into ſix equal Parts, as before; make B A equal to two of thoſe Parts, and on A, with the Interval A D, deſcribe the Circle D E I F G H L M, wherein ſet round E D, eight Times, and drawing the Right Lines E I, I F, F G,

3 G H,

G H, H L, L M, and M D, will compleat the *Octagon* required. *Q. E. F.*

PROBLEM XXIV.

TO defcribe a Nonagon, or Enneagon, whofe Sides fhall be each equal to a given Line, (D L.)

DEFINITION. ENNEAGON, from the *Greek*, a Regular Polygon, or Geometrical Figure, confifting of nine equal Sides, and the like Angles.

PRACTICE. Bifect D L in C, and thereon raife the Perpendicular C H; on L, with the Interval L D, defcribe the Arch D B, which divide into fix equal Parts, as in the preceding; make B A equal to three Parts of the Arch B D; on A, with the Interval A L, defcribe the Circle L, D, E, F, G, H, I, K, and therein fet off the Diftance D L, from D to E, from E to F, &c. *Q. E. F.* Fig. XLIX.

N. B. That the fecond Problem hereof may be ufed when 'tis required, to infcribe a regular *Polygon* within a Circle, &c.

N. B. That *Regular Polygons* of any Kind may be infcribed by the following Rule, *viz.*

Divide the Circumference of the Circle three hundred and fixty Degrees, by the Number of Sides in the Polygon, and the Quotient will be the Number of Degrees contain'd in each Side: As for Example,

Let the *Polygon* be a *Decagon*, which is a Geometrical Figure of ten equal Sides, and the like Angles.

PRACTICE

PRACTICE. Divide 360 by 10, the Number of Sides in the *Decagon*, 10) 360 (36, the Quotient or Number of Degrees contain'd in each Side as required.

Having now exemplified all the moſt uſeful Definitions and Problems abſolutely neceſſary to be well understood by every good GARDENER, I ſhall in the next Part lay down the true Management and Ordering of *Fruit* and *Foreſt-Trees,* *Evergreen* and *Flowering Shrubs.*

NEW

NEW

PRINCIPLES

OF

GARDENING.

PART II.
Of FRUIT-TREES.

SECT. I.

Demonſtrating the Variety of Gardens, their Situation for Fruit, the Nature of Soils, and their ſeveral Improvements by Manures.

HE Productions of *Gardens* being greatly different, are therefore divided into divers *Claſſes*: As, Firſt, the *Kitchen Garden*, whoſe Products is all Manner of *Sallets, Herbage, Roots,* &c. neceſſary for the *Kitchen.* Secondly, the *Fruit Garden*, which ſupplies the Table every Month in the Year, with

E

the

beſt of Fruits. Thirdly, the *Flower Garden,* which gratifies the *Sight* and *Smell* with its Flowers. Fourthly, the *Market Garden,* which produces all Sorts of *Pulſe,* as *Peaſe, Beans, Roots, Sallets, Herbage,* &c. (as the Kitchen Garden,) for the Service of *Cities, Towns,* &c. Fifthly, *Nurſery Gardeners,* or *Nurſery Men,* who raiſe all Sorts of *Trees, Shrubs, Plants,* &c. for the Plantation of *Fruit Gardens, Parterres, Wilderneſſes, Groves,* &c. And Sixthly, the *Phyſick Garden,* wherein is cultivated all *Medicinal Plants* for Phyſical Uſes.

Theſe Varieties of Gardens affords no leſs Employment for *Gardeners;* and therefore they are diſtinguiſhed according to that Part of Gardening in which they are employ'd, as the *Kitchen Gardener,* the *Fruit Gardener,* the *Flower Gardener,* or *Floriſt,* the *Market Gardener,* the *Nurſery Gardener,* (or *Nurſery Men,*) and laſtly the Phyſick Gardener; to which Variety may be added, the compleat *Groundworkman* and *Planter,* who *ſurveys, deſigns, lays out,* and *plants* Gardens in general.

I having in the preceding Parts exemplified the Manner of deſcribing all Kinds of Geometrcial Lines and Figures, abſolutely neceſſary to be well underſtood by every Gardener, ſhall now proceed to Directions for raiſing and planting all Sorts of Fruit, Foreſt, and Timber-Trees, Evergreens, and Flowering Shrubs, as alſo the Time and Manner of Grafting, Inoculating, Pruning, Nailing, Gathering, and Preſerving all the beſt Sorts of Standard, Dwarf, Eſpallier, and Wall-Fruits.

The firſt Thing to be conſidered for the Propagation of Trees, is the *Nature* and *Situation* of the *Soil,* wherein they are to be planted, as *Rapin* obſerves, Book iv. Page 178.

> *Though to all Plants each Soil is not diſpoſed,*
> *And on ſome Places Nature has impoſed*
> *Peculiar Laws, which ſhe unchang'd preſerves ;*
> *Such ſervile Laws* Great Britain *ſcarce obſerves.*

The adapting of Fruit-Trees to their proper Soils they moſt delight in, cauſes them to thrive infinitely better, than if they were planted in a Soil, wherein they delight not.

All

All Grounds not all Things bear : The Alder-Tree
Grows in thick Fens ; with Sallows Brooks agree ;
Aſh craggy Mountains ; Shores ſweet Myrtle fills.
And, laſtly, Bacchus *loves the ſunny Hills.*

'Tis obſervable, that the Apple called the Kentiſh-Pippin, will thrive better in *Kent*, than any other kind of Apple ; as alſo Codlins, when in divers other Places, neither of thoſe Fruits will thrive, but are ſoon deſtroyed by the Canker ; and even amongſt Pear-Trees, I have obſerved, that Summer-Pears will thrive in Land, where Winter-Pears will not.

In order to attain the Knowledge of what Species of Fruits are moſt natural to the *Soil*, where we intend to raiſe or plant our Trees, I adviſe, that Obſervation be made of the different Growth of Trees in the neighbouring Parts, and of Experiments on Variety of Kinds planted in our own Garden.

For various Plants, what Air and Soil is good?
And that, which hurts them, muſt be underſtood.
Warm Air and Moiſture is by Apples *loved;*
But, if to ſtony Hills they are removed,
You muſt not blame them, if they then decay :
Through a crude Soil the Fig *will make its Way.*
If it be not expoſed to the Rude North,
A humid Sand will make the Peach *bring forth.*
The Pear *when it has Room enough to ſpread,*
Where it has Warmth ſufficient over Head,
If it be ſeconded by the wet Ground,
With ſwelling Fruits *and* Bloſſoms *will be crowned.*
The backward Mulberry *chuſes to be dry,*
For conſtant Moiſture is its Enemy ;
And a wet Soil the Apple *vitiates ;*
The Cherry *deeply rooted, propogates*
It ſelf with Freedom, as in Italy
The thriving Olives *every where we ſee.*
A milder Ground the Lemon *moſt deſires :*
One more ſevere the yellow Quince *requires.*
It is not fit that Apricots *ſhould ſtand*
In a hot Mold ; and Cherries *love not Sand,*

E 2   *No*

No more than Strawberries; *which laſt if ſet*
In Earth that's well ſubdued, if to the Heat
Of the warm Sun expoſed, they ſoon abound
With Juice, their Berries *then grow plump and round.*
Thoſe Hills, which favour BACCHUS, Lemons *ſtarve,*
And Melons, *which a gentler Clime deſerve.*
When a warm Situation Plums *obtain,*
They quickly recompence the Gardener's *Pain.*

RAPIN, Book iv. Page 202.

The beſt Situations for Fruit-Gardens, are the *South*, and thoſe as declines from the South towards the Eaſt, to forty five Degrees. An exact *Eaſt Wall* is not to be diſpiſed; for though the Bud is checked or kept back in the Spring by the Eaſterly Winds, yet it has the Advantage of the whole *Anti-Meridian Sun* in *Summer* and *Autumn*, which diſperſes the cold Dews early in a Morning, and by its Poſition, is defended from the South-Weſt Winds that blows in the *Autumn*, oftentimes *deſtructive to Fruit*. Beſides, the Fruit ripens very well, and oftentimes better than that of a South (Wall or) Situation; for the *Morning Sun* in the *Summer* is the very beſt; and although the Sun departs there, from about Eleven in the Morning, yet the Air being warmed by the Sun, is fully ſufficient in the remaining Part of the Day, to preſerve and continue the ſame Heat, without the Sun-Beams. The Accidents attending this Expoſition, is the *North-Eaſt* and *Eaſterly Winds*, which blaſt *Peach* Trees, and kills other Fruits at the Time of their knitting or ſetting for Fruit. The *South Expoſition* receives the Sun ſoon after Six in the Morning after the Tenth Day of *March*, and continues till near Six at Night.

Its Accidents are the *Eaſt and by South*, &c. Winds which often blight *Peaches, Apricots*, &c. as is ſaid before of the Eaſt Expoſition. The *Weſt Expoſition* is bleſt with the *Sun's Rays*, when it has paſſed the *Meridian*, and continues till it deſcends the *Horizon*: The Fruit not receiving the early Warmth of the *Sun*, is generally ten or twelve Days later in ripening, and are ſeldom ſo good as thoſe of the Eaſt Expoſition, but always in greater Abundance, being defended from the *North-Eaſt*; *Eaſt* and *Eaſterly Winds*, which often *blow* in the *Spring*, deſtroying the *Bloom* and *Tender Fruits* of Eaſtern

Expo-

Expositions more than thofe of the Weſt. The *Accidents* attending this Expoſition are *high* and *turbulent Winds*, generally happening at the End of the Summer, as I obſerved before.

The *North Aſpect* is of all others the *moſt cold*, and expoſed to the *North-Weſt, North*, and *North-Eaſt Winds*, which are *deſtructive* to Fruit; and although this Expoſition is ſo openly expoſed, yet it produces *Morella - Cherries*, divers Kinds of common *Plumbs*, and even *Duke-Cherries* alſo, at a Seaſon when all others are gone, and in very great Perfection.

Theſe Expoſitions being thus explained, it now remains to ſpeak ſomething of the *Nature of Soils*, proper for Plantations of Fruits; for the diſtinguiſhing whereof there are many Rules; but for ſuch that cannot change their Situation or Dwelling, muſt be ſatisfied with their own Soil, which, if bad, may be improved, as hereafter directed.

I ſhall not here aſſign certain Depths of Soils, wherein we are to *plant*, ſeeing that oftentimes we are obliged to uſe what we can find. 'Tis certain that the deeper Land is in Goodneſs, the better it is for the Trees planted therein.

Some Soils hold *two Foot*, and *two Foot* and *half*, and others one *Foot*, or *nine Inches* in Depth. When Land is very *ſhallow*, that is, when its Depth is leſs than *twenty Inches*, which is a ſufficient Depth for Fruit-Trees, it muſt be raiſed with good Earth brought from other Parts. There are divers Kinds of Land, wherein Trees thrive: As, Firſt, a *light Sandy Land:* Secondly, a *ſandy Loamy Soil*, with *Brick-Earth* at Bottom: And, laſtly, *ſtiff, cold*, and *wet Clay*. And beſides all theſe, there are many other Kinds of Lands, as *Marſh Lands, Heaths, Boggy Grounds*, &c. wonderfully different in their Qualities and Compoſition; ſome being a perfect *Rock* of *Gravel*, others *Clay, Chalk, Quagmires*, &c. and ſome of all Kinds mix'd together: But above all, for our Purpoſe, the ſecond Kind mention'd, namely, the *ſandy Loamy Soil*, of a *brown Colour*, with a ſtrong *holding Bottom*, is of all others the very beſt for *Fruit* and *Foreſt-Trees*. Of this Sort of Land are the moſt Parts of *Twickenham, Iſleworth, Brentford*, and other Parts adjacent thereunto.

Chuſe

Chuſe a rich Soil *when you intend to plant,*
Not that which heavy Sand *has render'd faint.*
Avoid low Vales, *which lie between cloſe Hills,*
Which ſome thick Pool *with* noiſome Vapours *fills ;*
Where pithy Miſts, *and* hurtful Steams *aſcend,*
Leaſt an ill Taſte *they to your* Fruit *may lend.*
Learn that t'avoid, where deep in barren Clay
The ſpeckled Euts *their yellow Bellies lay ;*
Where burning Sand *the upper Hand obtains,*
Or where with Chalk *unfruitful* Gravel *reigns :*
And leſt th' external Redneſs of the Soil
Deceive your Labours, and deſpiſe your Toil,
Deeply beneath the Furrows thruſt your Spade ;
Outward Appearance many hath betrayed.
Earth under the green Sward may be encloſed
To a rough Sand, or burning Clay *diſpoſed.*
Still fly that Place where Auſter *always blows,*
And for your Trees that Situation chuſe,
Where in the open Air, *on a Deſcent,*
To bleſs their Growth, *more gentle Winds conſent.*

Rapin, Book iv. Page 179.

Soils being different in *Contexture, Colour,* or *Site,* I
have reduced them into three Sorts, *viz.* As, Firſt, *Light, San-*
dy, and *Gravel:* Secondly, *Mellow, Loam,* and *Brick-Earth :*
And, laſtly, *Stiff, Cold Land,* and *Clay.*

The *Manures* proper for thoſe ſeveral Kinds of Soils are
as follow : Firſt, For a *looſe ſandy Soil* take of *Mud,* ſcoured
out of *Ponds,* &c. and of *ſtrong Loam* an equal Quantity;
to which add a third Part of good *Horſe-Dung,* well mix'd
together, and it will make an *excellent Compoſt* for *ſandy*
or *light Land.* All *Compoſts* may be made in any Quantity;
ſo that the Proportion of the Quantities of each Sort is carefully obſerved, and well mix'd.

When that you have mix'd a ſufficient Quantity, caſt it into
the Form of a *Leſtal,* and let it be turned three or four
Times in the Year, and always kept clean from Weeds; for
they exhauſt the *vital Parts* thereof, and at the End of one
Year 'twill be fit for Uſe. If to one Rod of Ground be
allowed

allowed one *Load* of *Compost*, 'twill be a very good Allowance.

Marle (of the blue Kind) is a good *Manure* for *light sandy Land*; which, if laid on with Discretion, will last fifteen or twenty Years: For where *Marle* is used, the *Poorness* and *Depth* of the *Ground* is to be always considered. On tolerable good Land may be laid eighty or an hundred Loads to an Acre; and on that as is *barren* and deep, from two hundred to four hundred Loads each Acre.

Clay of the lighter Sort is good Manure for *light shelfy Gravel*, or *sandy Land;* but Care must be taken that the *Clay* is not digged in too deep. If an equal Quantity of *Clay* and *Sand* be equally mix'd together, the Compost will be a very good Loam.

Cow-Dung is an *excellent Soil* for *hot Lands*, as also *Deers, Sheep, Hogs,* and *Bullocks Dungs.*

Sandy Loams are some of the very best Lands for *Gardening*, and require but little Help ; yet notwithstanding, *Time* doth eraze out all the Signs and Marks of their *Strength*, which may be restored, or greatly improved as follows:

To one Load of *Horse-Dung* (well rotted) add a Quarter of a Load of *Sea-Sand*, (if to be had easy, if not, other Sand,) the same Quantity of *Lime slacked*, as also of *Pigeon Sheep-Dung*, and *Cow-Dung*, half a Load of *Chalk*, beaten small, and half a Load of *Marle*; mix them proportionally together, and it will be a good Compost, fit for immediate Use.

Chalk and *Marle* makes a good *Compost :* To every seven Load of *Marle* add ten Load of *Chalk :* If you allow *Marle* in greater Quantity, 'twill make Lands too luxurious.

Secondly, The *Manures* proper for *mellow Loamy* Land, whose Bottom is inclinable to *Brick-Earth*, is *Horse-Dung* well rotted, with some *Sea-Coal Ashes*, mix'd with it, well known to most Gardeners.

This kind of Soil is the most natural for *Gardens, Plantations*, &c. and requires little Help or Improvement, it being *strong* in its *own Nature*, and needs nothing more than the Spade to ridge it in the Winter, to bring it into *Order* and *Culture.*

Thirdly, and *lastly, stiff* and *cold Clay Lands* are help'd by divers *Composts.* To three Load of the *natural Mold* add

two

two Load of good *rotten Dung*, one Load of *Sand*, two Load of the firſt Spit of a *rich Turf, Meadow,* or *Graſs-Ground,* half a Load of *Street-Dung,* or *Sea-Coal Aſhes,* with a ſmall Quantity of *Pigeons Dung;* mix theſe proportionally together, and lay the Compoſt in a Heap, obſerving to turn it once a Month for the Summer Seaſon, and in Winter it will be fit for Uſe. *Pigeons-Dung,* caſt thin upon *cold Lands* early in the *Spring,* is very helpful, eſpecially for *Corn* and *Meadow* Lands: Five Load will dung an Acre. *Sea* and *Drift Sands* are very good Compoſts for *Clay Lands,* making way for the Roots to ſhoot; as alſo doth *Sea-Coal Aſhes.*

Rubbiſh of *Buildings* is very good for the Roots of Trees in *cold Land;* and *Chalk,* broken ſmall, is a good Compoſt: The ſoft *fat Chalk* is the beſt.

Lime is another good Compoſt for *ſtiff Clays,* its Heat cauſing a Fume, and its Tenderneſs makes way for the Roots, to fetch home their Nouriſhment. The *Lime* uſed herein muſt be ſlacked, and as its Heat is great at firſt, therefore muſt be uſed with Diſcretion.

Cold and *ſhallow Land* is ~~beſt manured~~ by the following Compoſt: Take one Load of the *natural Mold,* two Loads of good *rotten Horſe-Dung,* one of *Sand,* or *Sea Coal Aſhes,* and one of *Chalk,* which mix proportionally together, and 'tis fit for Uſe.

N. B. that the oftner *Clay Lands* are dunged, and the *leſs* you lay on at a Time, is the *better*; for Clay is of ſuch a *greedy Nature,* that it ſoon *eats* out the *Dung,* and oftentimes *binds* it, ſo that 'tis of no Uſe.

And beſides the aforeſaid Compoſts, *ſtiff Lands* and *Clays* may be improved by their being *ridged early* in the Winter, by the Help of *Froſts, &c.* which will ſo melorate the Ridges, that they will fall down like Aſhes. Beſides, the Winter's Air greatly ſweetens the Soil, by exhauſting and diſperſing the *cold* and *raw* Vapours, which are fully expos'd to the Air, by its being thrown up in Ridges. To explain the Manner of *Ridging, Digging,* and *Trenching* of Ground, is needleſs, ſince 'tis well known to every *Gardener,* and *Gardener's Labourer.*

When

When *cold* or *Clay Lands* are troubled with Water, dig Drains to convey it away, with a Defcent, that the Water may pafs; and inftead of *Arches, &c.* of *Brick Work,* fill them up fix or eight Inches with *large Stones,* and over them lay fmall *Brufh Green-wood,* and thereon the *Mold.* Thofe Drains fo made will convey away the Water, and drain the Lands as defired.

Of all Sorts of Land for Plantations, none is fo bad as the *Clay,* efpecially the *ftrong Blue, ftrong White,* or *ftrong Red;* but when naturally mix'd with Stones, not fo bad.

Befides the preceding Soils, *viz. Sand, Loam,* and *Clay,* there are in many Parts two Sorts of *Land,* called *Ruffet-Grays,* whofe Temper is between *Sand, Loam,* and *Clay;* of which one Sort is very *ftrong* and *heavy,* and the other more *lighter,* coming near to the Nature of *Sand.* The *ftrong* and *heavy* may be melorated, as the *Clays,* and the *lighter* by the following Compofition. To one Load of *rotten Dung* add one Load of *Street Cleanings,* one Load of *Lime,* and half a Load of *Coal Afhes,* or *Drift Sand,* with a fmall Quantity, or Sprinkling of *Pigeons Dung,* which being well mix'd, is a very good Compoft; and if to it you add *old Rags, Pot-Afhes, rotten Leaves, &c.* 'twill greatly improve it. This Compoft being turned once a *Month,* for *four Months,* will be an excellent Manure.

N. B. That the beft Time to make Compofts is in *September,* to be ufed in *February;* for thereby there is but little of the *volatile Parts* exhaufted away by the *Sun's Heat,* or Growth of *Weeds,* which Compofts naturally produce.

This laft Sort of *light Gray-Ruffet Land* hath two different Situations; the firft is, when it lies high, (for which the foregoing Compoft is to be ufed,) and the other, when it lies *low* and *wet,* which requires a Manure or a *more lively Nature* than that as lies high: Therefore, for fuch *fandy wet Lands,* take the following Manure, (*viz.*) To one Load and a half of *Sea-Coal Afhes* or *Sea Sand* add one Load of *rotten Horfe-Dung,* one Load of *Street Dung,* with half a Load of *Sheep* and *Pigeons Dung*; mix thefe well together,

F   and

and they will make an excellent Compoft for fuch Lands. About eighty Loads is a good Allowance for one Acre.

Thefe Directions being fufficient for the manuring any Sort of Lands, 'twill not be amifs to fay fomething in relation to their *Bottoms*, which are either *advantageous* or *prejudicial* to the Roots of Trees. *Firft, Advantageous*; and fuch are *Gravel, Chalk,* and *fhelly Rock,* mixed with *Earth,* which always abounds with *nitrous Particles*, as nourifhes and improves their Roots. *Secondly, Prejudicial*; as a *barren Sand or Clay*; the one *drinking* the Nourifhment away from the Roots, and the other *retaining* it too long. *Chalk Bottoms* are very good; they produce Fruit *wonderful fweet,* and in great Plenty.

I fhall now conclude this *Section* with fome ufeful Obfervations on good and bad Lands, known by their natural Productions. *Firft,* then, fuch Lands as naturally produce *Mallows, Docks, Hemlock,* and other Weeds of the like Nature, are generally good and fruitful; for fuch Weeds love fat deep Land. For 'tis ever to be obferved that fuch Land as produce Weeds, or Grafs, naturally ftrong, is undoubtedly *very rich* and *fruitful.*

Land, as naturally produces Weeds, &c. of a fmaller Growth, as *Dazies, Plantane, Clover, &c.* is often very good; but feldom fo good as the preceding.

Barren Earth is to be known divers Ways: As, Firft, when inftead of good green *Grafs,* and a *plentiful Crop,* be a *pale fmall Grafs,* inclinable to a *blewifh Colour*: Secondly, *Broom, Furze, Heath, Mofs, &c.* denotes *barren Land,* efpecially if they be fmall. Lands fituated near the Sea Coaft, is often barren, being poifoned and ftarved by the *ill Vapours* and *Storms* proceeding from thence, which is alfo deftructive to Trees and Plants.

Mountanous and *rocky Lands,* extream *hot* and *dry,* are generally *barren*; fo alfo is *extream cold* and *moift Lands,* as *ftrong Clays,* whofe *tough* and *Binding Nature* in the Winter will not admit the *Rain* or *Snow* to foak into it, and in the Summer locks up the *Grain* or *Roots* within itfelf, that they have not *Liberty* to fhoot or fprout forth.

Sands

Sands upon *mountainous rocky Places* producing fmall *moffy* and *yellow Grafs*, are generally barren.

Black moorifh Sands produce *four* unwholfome Grafs; and *white* or *yellow Sand*, a fhort *blewifh moffy Grafs*.

Gravelly, gritty, loofe Sand, is alfo *barren*, caufed by *Cold*, the *Gravel* wanting *good Mold*, to warm that as grows in it.

Barren Lands always require much more Manure than better Lands, notwithftanding 'tis confumed in half the Time; for in *Clay Lands* the *Toughnefs* of the *Clay* is fo great, the Soil cannot *incorporate* with it.

Great Rains is the Caufe of Barennefs in *hollow hungry Sands*, as well as *great Droughts*: For the *Sun* exhales the *Moifture* and *Heart* of the Soil, which the Rains produce; fo that *light fandy Lands* are deprived of their *vital Juices* both Ways.

Land may be fit for *Fruit-Trees, Corn, &c.* but not for *Timber-Trees;* fuch whofe Depth is one Foot, or fifteen Inches, and its Bottom a *cold wet Gravel*, which is very difagreeable to their Roots.

Note, when I fpeak of *Timber-Trees*, I mean *Oak, Afh*, and *Beach*, and not *Abeals, Elms, &c.* of the *Aquatick* Tribe.

The like Depth of Ground is oftentimes found lying on an *undivided Rock*, or *Quarry* of *Stone, Marble, &c.* of a large Extent; alfo improper for Timber-Trees; and although the *Afh* is a Tree that naturally runs fhallow, yet 'tis generally a *Pollard*, and decays before it comes to any Perfection for Timber.

S E C T. II.

Of the Manner of raising Stocks from Kernels, &c. and Time of Grafting and Inoculating Fruit-Trees; with Observations thereon.

FRUIT-TREES are raised from *Kernels, Suckers, Layers, Cuttings, Seed, Grafts,* and *Inoculation.* (1.) Those from *Kernels,* are *Apples, Crabs, Pears, Peaches, Almonds, Cherries, Abricots, Plumbs, Walnuts, Chesnuts,* and *Filberts.* (2.) By Suckers, are the *Plumb, Quince, Medlar, Filbert, Codlin, Gooseberries, Currants,* and *Rasberries*; as also *Paradise-Stocks.* (3.) By Layers, are *Vines, Figs, Quinces, Mulberries, and Cornelion-Cherry.* (4.) By Cuttings, the *Vines, Codlings, Mulberries, Pomgranates, Barberries, Figs, Quinces, Genitings, Paradise-Stocks, Gooseberries,* and *Currants.* (5.) By Seed, the *Service* and *Mulberry.* (6.) By Grafting, and Budding, or Inoculating on Stocks of *Plumbs, Peaches, Cherries, Crabs, Pears,* all the Sorts of *Peaches, Abricots, Nectorines, Almonds, Plumbs, Cherries, Apples, Pears,* &c.

To raise young Stocks for *Grafting* and *Budding,* you must prepare a Border, (or many, if you sow much,) of good mellow fresh Land, about three Feet in Breadth each, and thereon sow your *Kernels,* (not too thick;) after which, with your Spade, turn them in about four Inches deep, and then rake and finish your Border, not forgetting to set *Traps for Mice,* as will visit them in the Winter.

The Time for sowing of Kernels is from the Time as the Fruit is ripe, until the Spring following, *viz. February* or *March.*

If you are careful in keeping them clean from Weeds, and that they be watered now and then, they will be greatly
encou-

encouraged, and thrive thereby. *N. B.* The Sorts of *Kernels* to be fown, are the *Crab, Apple, Pear, Cherry,* and *Filbert :* The others, as *Peach-Stones, Almonds, Apricots, Plumbs, Wall-nuts,* and *Chefnuts,* muft be fown or dropp'd in *Drills* made with a Hough, about four or five Inches in Depth, and about two Foot and half afunder: The *Kernels* muft be placed in the *Drills,* at the Diftance of *nine* or *ten Inches* afunder, becaufe they will not be removed before they are made Trees by *bud-ding* or *grafting.* Thefe *Kernels* delight in a *light rich Land,* and love to be *clear* of Weeds, and kept *moift* by Waterings in very *dry* Seafons.

In *Autumn* when the Seedlings has done growing, trench a Piece of *frefh mellow Land,* and therein plant all the largeft, leaving the weak ones till the next Autumn.

The Rows you plant them in muft be two Foot and a half afunder, and the Stocks Diftance in the Line, about one Foot.

You muft alfo obferve, to prune of the *Tap-Root* of every Plant, and thereby they will have good Roots in Plenty, which otherwife would be but one, and that very bad for tranfplant-ing. When your Plantation has feen two or three Years, and the Plants arrived to the Bignefs of a Man's Thumb towards their Bottom, you may begin to *graft* or *inoculate* them with fuch *Fruits* as you think beft, which being grown a Year or two after their *Inoculation* or *Grafting,* will be fit to tranf-plant againft any *Wall, Efpallier,* &c. Perhaps it may be expec-ted that I fhould, according to the vulgar Way, defcribe and explain the Method of *grafting* and *inoculating* Fruit-Trees; but knowing that 'tis familiar with every *Gardener,* and is what cannot be well underftood by bare Theory only, without the *Practice,* therefore I advife every one as is a Lover of *Curiofi-ties* in *Art* and *Nature,* and is defirous to well underftand thofe two *Philofophical* Entertainments, to be fully informed therein by the Help of fome *Nurfery-Man* or *Gardener* at the proper Seafons for thofe Works, of which I fhall now deliver every ufeful Obfervation to be made therein.

Firft, in *Grafting,* which is performed four feveral Ways, *viz.* (1.) *Whip-Grafting,* generally ufed on fmall Stocks for *Cherries, Pears, Apricots,* &c. (2.) *Stock-Grafting,* ufed in grafting *Apples* on *Crabs,* or *Pears* on *Quinces,* or any other Fruit, whofe Stocks are large. (3.) *Rind-Grafting,* ufed for the
graft-

grafting of *large Stocks* or *Trees*, as are too large to cleave, as in *Stock-Grafting*. And, laftly, *Inarching* or *Grafting* by *Approach*, ufed chiefly for *Oranges, Lemons, Citrons,* &c.

The Time or Seafon for Grafting, is all *February, March,* and about one Week in *April.* The firft you begin with muft be *Cherries* and *Plumbs,* they being forward Fruits, after them *Pears,* and, laftly, *Apples.*

In the Choice of *Cions* or *Cuttings* for *Grafting,* you muft obferve to take them from fuch Trees as are *good Bearers,* and from fuch Parts of the Tree, as is *truly vigorous* and *healthy,* and fuch Shoots as are fulleft of Buds. *Note,* that the *laft Years Shoot* is what you are to ufe, and not thofe of two or three Years

And further obferve, that 'tis beft to cut off your *Cions* or *Grafts* a Month before you ufe them, and lay them in Earth, half buried, during that Time ; but obferve to lay the *Bottom End* in the Ground, inftead of the Top.

By *Midfummer* your *Stock* and *Graft* will be grown together ; and then they require to have their *Bandage* taken away, that they may have free *Liberty* to *thrive* and profper.

Secondly, Inoculation, (called by *Gardeners, budding* ;) by which is raifed *Peach-Trees, Nettorines, Apricots, Cherries, Plumbs, Pears, Apples,* &c.

The Seafon for this Work, is from the Beginning of *June,* to the Middle of *Auguft* ; and 'tis beft performed *very early in a Morning,* in the Cool of an *Evening,* or in *cloudy Weather,* for hot Weather is *very prejudicial* to the *Buds* and Bark of the Stocks, during the Operations.

Great Care muft be taken to *unbind* the *Buds* in due Time, which may be known by the Swelling of the Stock, above and below the Bud. Thofe Trees, as you bud early, may be unbound at fixteen or eighteen Days after *Inoculation* ; and thofe, as you you *bud* late, fomewhat longer. In the *Spring* following you muft cut off the Heads of the Stocks, about one Inch and half above the Bud, after which your Bud will fprout out, and make a handfome Tree. *N. B.* It is ufual to put in two or three Buds in each Stock, at proper Diftances, in a fmooth Part of the Stock, for Fear of a *Mifcarriage,* and bud them fuch a Height above Ground, as to leave Room underneath, to bud them again the next Year, in Cafe they mifs the firft. There are divers Sorts of *Peaches* as takes very well, and *others very diffi-*

difficult: As for Inftance, an *Old Newington* takes very well, and a *Minion* very difficult; therefore that ye may not be wholly difappointed, when you bud a Stock with a *Minion,* put in alfo over it a Bud of an *Newington;* for if the *Minion* miffes, 'tis ten to one but the *Newington* takes, (which is one of the *beft Peaches* we have;) and provided that they both take, then when you head your Stock down, cut away the *Newington Bud,* and the Remains is the *Minion;* and the like of other *eafy and difficult Fruits* in general.

When among other Seafons of the Year,
The Time of Grafting *comes, do not defer,*
In proper Stocks young Cions to inclofe;
Then Buds *between the cloven Bark difpofe:*
And if your Fruit *be bad, as oft it will,*
Make Choice of better, and remove the ill.
By thefe Improvements, greateft Praife you get,
And thus your Gardens Honour you complete.
Into your Stocks the Foreign Pears *admit,*
And far-fetch'd Apples *place within the Slit.*
Hence fprings a nobler Race and greater Store
Of hopeful Offfpring than you had before.
The Plants you want the Gardeners *will give:*
If not from diftant Countries them derive.
Greece *firft fought Plants in barb'rous Climes, and then*
She civilized the Trees as well as Men.
Thefe ftill at Home, fhe fortunately plac'd,
And by Tranflation did correct their Tafte.

When Plants *of a corrected Tafte are found,*
And Stocks *are chofen which are young and found;*
The Grafter *then th'adoptive Bough muft bring*
Into thofe Stocks: Of this the Means I fing.
Which though they are diftinct, you learn with Eafe
How to graft fruitful Slips in barren Trees.
Some cut down Trunks which bore a lofty Top,
And hollow them above, thus Woodmen lop
The talleft Oakes, and cut out four fquare Stakes;
But firft of all a Wedge its Paffage makes.

This

This done, the Cions *may defcend downright
Into the* Cleft ; *and with the Stock unite.
Though others in the Rind, betwixt each Bud,
Make an Incifion, and the Graft include ;
Which, by Degrees, is afterwards inclin'd
T'incorporate it felf with the moift Rind.
Some like a flender Pipe the Bark divide,
Or like a Scutcheon, flit it down the Side,
Or the hard Trunk, which a fharp Anger cleaves,
Into its folid Part the Graft receives :
Mean while, with Care, the Branches which are joined,
You with a feven-fold Cord muft ftrongly bind,
And all the Chinks with Loam and Bafs defend ;
For if the* cruel Air *fhould once defcend
Into the Cleft, it would impede their Juice,
And to the Plant its Nourifhment refufe.
But if thefe Dangers it has once endured,
When the adopted Branch is well fecured.*

   By their Conjunction, *Trees there Nature loofe ;
That which was* wild ~~before, more~~ civil *grows.
Unmindful of their Mother, they forfake
The Tafte, which they from her at firft did take.
From yellow* Quinces *and* Cornelians *rife
Fruits, which are differenc'd by various Dies ;
The* Pear *thus mends ; the* Slow *affords good* Plums *;
And the bad* Cherry *better now becomes.*

   *From diff'rent Boughs diftinguifh'd Species fhoot ;
But now I tell how you muft mix your Fruit,
What Branches with each other you may join,
What Sorts will beft in Amity combine.*

   All Kind of Pears *the* Quinces *entertain,
And then receiv'd with their own Tincture ftain.
The hoary* Pears *their Tafte to* Apples *give,
They with the Shrubby* Willow *too will live.
The* Fig *would love the* Mulberry, *if that
Its blacker Hue would fomewhat moderate.*
Cherries *with* Laurels *blufhes will compound ;*
Apples *with* Apples *do their Tafte confound.*

They

They of Auvergne, *in Willows, Fruits inclofe* ;
'Tis true, at firft their Colour grateful fhows:
But by this Marriage they degen'rate are,
And tafte but ill, although they look fo fair.

RAPIN, *Lib.* iv. *Page* 194.

SECT. III.

Of the Time and Manner of Planting all Sorts of Fruit-Trees, in any Kind of Land, as Clay, Loam, Sand, Gravel, &c.

FIRST, I advife, that in the Spring you provide ten, twenty, &c. Loads of the *firft Spit* of fome *wafte Common* or *Grafs Ground,* whofe *Soil* is a *fandy Loam,* where *Cattle* has been continually *fed,* and has not been broke up or *till'd in the Memory of Man,* which being done, throw it up into the Form of a *Leftal,* obferving to bury the *Turf* as much as poffible; or it may firft be pared thinly off, before the Earth is digged, and afterwards mix'd with Difcretion. The Mould thus prepared muft be turn'd once a *Month* till *October,* at which Time it will be fit for Ufe. If your Land be of the *Clay Kind,* mix *Drift Sand* or *Sea-Coal Afhes* with your Mould, to prevent its being converted to the *Native* Soil, *viz. Clay.*

It is almoft impoffible to exprefs, how *agreeable* this Compoft is to the *Roots* of *young Trees*; therefore the *more* you can afford them, the better 'tis for their future Growth and Profperity.

To plant Fruit-Trees in a *ftiff Clay,* &c. proceed as follows :

Firft, Dig your Holes *four* or *five Foot fquare,* and about *twenty Inches* or *two Foot deep*; carry away the native Earth, and fill up the Holes with good Mould and Dung well rooted, and mix'd together; or if you have Plenty of the foregoing Compoft to ufe that inftead, 'twill add much to their Growth,

G it

it having a *very strange* and *uncommon Fertility* in it, more than any other Compost of Made-Earths whatsoever. Before you fill up the Hole, *pave* the Bottom with broken *Tiles, Brick-Bats,* &c. to prevent the Roots getting into the *poisonous* Clay.

If your Land be a *sharp hot Sand* or *Gravel,* mix *fresh Mould, Cow-Dung, Horse-Dung,* well rotted, and a *mild Clay,* together in a Compost, which if made in the Spring, and turn'd monthly in the *Summer,* may be used in *October.*

When you plant in a very *good sandy Loam,* 'twill not be amiss to mix your Earth with the Compost of *fresh Earth,* before prescribed, for 'tis of *admirable* Service.

In the planting of Fruit-Trees, the following Methods are to be observed :

First, That the *Earth* be truly prepared as before directed.

Secondly, If your Land be not cold and wet, plant in *October, November,* or *December* at latest, for thereby, during the *Winter,* the Roots will be *swelling* and preparing themselves to to put forth their tender *Fibres* and *Strick-Root* early in the *Spring.*

But if your Land is *naturally cold, wet,* and *heavy,* 'tis best to plant in *February,* when the *Spring* is making its *Entrance,* and the *Earth* growing warm, which *nourishes* the Roots of Trees; whereas, was they planted in *October* or *November,* the *wet* and *cold* might have kill'd their Roots.

To *plant* Trees *late in the Spring,* as *March* or *April,* in *light Soils,* is very *dangerous*; 'tis too often seen, that the *parching Winds* and *dry Weather* prove fatal to them.

Thirdly, That you don't plant the Trees *too deep*; for thereby, in four or five Years, the *Roots* will be got below the good Earth, which will throw the Tree into a *sickly decaying Condition.*

If the *upper Roots* of any Tree be six or seven Inches below the Surface, 'tis sufficient, for all the *best Juices of the Earth* lies near to the Surface

Fourthly, That Fruit-Trees be not planted too near; for after five or six Years, they crowd one another, and cause many Branches to be nailed near a Perpendicular, which will lessen the Fruit, and soon *ruin the Tree,* especially *Peach* and *Apricot-*

cot-*Trees*, whose Bark is thick, and will not admit young Shoots to come where great Wood is cut away: Therefore always keep Trees thin of Wood in the Middle, that their Branches may have Room to spread *Horizontally*, and thereby be kept in a bearing Condition.

This *Misfortune* of too near planting is not the only one; for by the near Distance, their Roots soon meet, and rob one another of their proper Nourishments, and deprive the Borders of their *Fertility*, which, when once lost, is never to be recovered again; but by destroying the first planted Trees and planting others therein of different Kinds.

If *Fruit-Trees* against *Espalliers, Walls,* or for *Dwarfs,* be planted at eight, nine, ten, twelve, or fourteen Foot distance, 'twill be found to do very well, *viz. May Cherries* at eight Foot; *Peaches* and *Nectarines,* when without *Vines* between them, at nine or ten Foot; when with *Vines,* at twelve Foot; Plums, Duke-Cherries, and Apricots, at twelve or thirteen Foot; and *Pears* at fourteen or fifteen Foot; as also *Apples,* except such as are grafted on *Paradice-Stocks,* which need not exceed seven or eight Foot Distance.

> *You who the Beauty of your Trees design,*
> *To each along the Walls its Seat assign.*
> *Cherries with Cherries, Figs with Figs may meet,*
> *The* Syrian *and* Crustumian *Pears are fit*
> *To mingle with the* British, *but we find,*
> *That Apples and red Plums must not be join'd.*
> *All that are of a Sort together plant,*
> *They must succeed, if they no Culture want:*
> *And when Affairs of greater Moment cease,*
> *To set their Stations be your Bus'ness;*
> *For if they have not ample Room to spread,*
> *They then both Strength and Nourishment will need.*
>
> Rapin, *Lib.* iv. *Page* 215.

N. B. I do advise, that those Borders wherein your Fruit-Trees are planted, be kept clean from Weeds, and that there be neither Pease or Beans *sown or planted* in them, as is common, or any edging of Box, *&c.* to exhaust the Richness and Humidity of the Soil from the Fruit-Trees, which is oftentimes

the

the *Death* or *Ruin* of them. And that the upper Part of the Wall may be useful for the first three or four Years, 'tis very frugal and commendable to plant tall *Standard-Cherry*, *Plumb*, and *Apricot-Trees*, (if the last be *budded* on a *Muscle-Stock*, and be of the *Bruxel* Kind,) in the intermediate Spaces between the other Wall-Trees, by which Means both Top and Bottom will be filled together, and with good Care, may be done in three Years Time. As the lower Trees comes up, the upper ones are to be cut away, to give Room, and at length, taken quite away, and transplanted as Standards in the Orchard or Kitchen-Garden.

Vines are often planted in those intermediate Spaces, and soon get to the Top, producing Fruit the third or fourth Year.

In the placing of a Wall-Tree, at Planting observe, that the Bud or Graft is from the Wall, as also the best Roots, and that 'tis placed inclining at the Distance of eight or nine Inches at Bottom, and two or three at the Extremity of the Head; for if you plant your Tree close to the Wall, when it has arrived to be large at Bottom, it will naturally grow from it, so that you cannot keep them in good Order; and besides, the the Wall gauls them, and they soon *die* ; or otherwise are render'd *very weak,* and worth nothing.

'Tis a common Practice in the pruning of the Roots of *Trees*, to reduce them both in *Number* and *Length*, but for what Reason I cannot imagine, excepting such small, tender, fibrous Roots as are killed by the Wind, presently after the Tree is taken up, which is absolutely necessary to be done, and such Roots as are inclinable to grow downwards, which we call *Tap-Roots*. 'Tis evident, that the more Roots is left to Trees, (so as they are not over and above large in Number and Quantity,) the greater Quantity of *Juices* such Trees are capable of receiving, and consequently a greater Nourishment. In a Word, the only Reason for so doing is, that Trees will live being so pruned, and much less Trouble in Planting.

If you plant *Peach, Nectorine,* or *Apricot*-Trees in the *Autumn*, leave their Heads on till the *Spring* following before you head them, at which Time cut them off at about six or seven Inches above the Bud, and observe, that the *Cut* is towards the Wall. The Time for this *Work* is *March*.

Before

Before I proceed any further, I fhall mention an *Abufe* which moft *Fruit* and other *Trees* receive as are bought of *Nurfery-Men*, which is the *cutting* and *bruifing* their *Roots* in taking out of the *Nurfery*, and *breaking* them in *packing* up: A Crime unpardonable.

If by Tranfportation the Roots of Trees are very dry, 'tis good to lay their Roots (but not Top alfo) in a Pond for twenty four Hours before you plant them.

When *Trees* are above Ground, and their being planted prevented by *Froft*, 'tis beft to put them in a *Cellar*, cover'd clofe from the *Air*, &c. and when the Froft is gone, *foak their Roots* in Water, as before directed.

The Diftances before deliver'd for *Wall Trees* holds good in *Dwarfs* and *Efpalliers*; as *Efpalliers* and *Wall-Trees* are planted with an Inclination to the *Efpalliers* or *Walls*, fo on the contrary, *Dwarf* and *Standard* Trees muft be planted *exactly perpendicular*.

The Height of *Dwarf Trees*, when firft planted, muft be regulated to the Land wherein they are planted. If the Land is *dry*, fix Inches above the *Graft* is a good Height; but if a *moift Land*, about eight or nine.

Standards in any Land whatfoever fhould be *headed* at fix or feven Foot at moft, except where particular Trees are required for high Walls, &c. that People may not eafily come at the Fruit, &c.

When *Standard* or *Dwarf Apple-Trees* are planted, the *Place* of Grafting fhould be placed even with the Surface of the Ground, if it does not caufe the *Roots to be too deep*, which muft *always be avoided*.

Where any *Fruit-Tree* decays having grown long in that Place, plant another of a *different Species* in its Place, and *not one of the fame*; for the *old Tree* having exhaufted thofe Juices appropriate to its own Kind, will *ftarve* your new-planted Tree, when at the fame Time another of a different kind will thrive, and profper very well.

Hence it appears, that every Plant hath its peculiar Juice, by which 'tis fupported; and therefore the Earth contains as great a Variety of Juices as of Plants, &c.

But

But Nature never ſhew'd more Wantonneſs,
Then when ſo many Shapes ſhe did impreſs,
From Wardens to the Pears which leſſer grow,
And did to each its proper Juice allow.

RAPIN, Lib. iv. Page 218.

Trees of the *firſt Year's Graft* or *Bud,* are always the beſt; which to make choice on in a Nurſery, obſerve that their *Bark be ſmooth,* and free from *Canker, Gauls, &c.* that their yearly Shoots be *ſtrong* and *vigorous,* and that they be *well rooted*; ſuch Trees as have but one *Stem,* or two at moſt, are the beſt for planting.

When you prune the Root of a Fruit-Tree for planting, obſerve to cut away all dead *fibrous Roots,* all bruiſed Parts committed by the Spade in taking up, which perform with a *Knife, &c.* as cuts *ſmooth* and clean.

When you prune a Tree, hold it in your *Left-Hand,* with the *Head* behind you; the Cuts at the End of every Root will be downwards when planted, which is the right Way of pruning Roots.

To plant Trees in the Summer Seaſon, as muſt of Neceſſity be removed, (otherwiſe 'tis beſt to leave them till *November,*) take of the Compoſt I directed for the planting young Trees with, and an equal Quantity of *Cow-Dung;* mix theſe well together, and put to them as much *Water* as will make it into Pap, which is performed in the following Manner:

The Compoſt of *Earth* and *Cow-Dung* being well mix'd together, you muſt provide a *Bearing-Tub,* wherein mix the mix'd Dung and Earth with Water: The Inſtrument with which 'tis ſtirr'd in mixing, is ſuch as *Brewers* uſe in *ſtirring* their *Malt* in the Marſh-Tun.

When this Mixture is of ſuch a Thickneſs, as to ſupport the Stirrer from falling, being put upright in the Tub, 'tis fit for Uſe. The *Pap* being thus prepared, and the Hole digg'd of ſuch a Magnitude as is neceſſary, *viz.* if in bad Ground, *&c.* to be made good with freſh Land and Compoſt, as before directed, which being done, fill all the Sides of the Hole up with good Mold, leaving in the Middle ſufficient Room

for

for the Root of the Tree, then place your Tree therein, and with your Hands place or fpread all fuch Roots as are necef-fary, in a *horizontal Pofition,* pouring thereon the Pap before prepared, and putting frefh Mold about the outward Part thereof, till it has caufed the Pap to rife and mix itfelf with every Root in general, and flows out above the Crown of the Root, treading it now and then very gently to force it up in the hollow Parts of the Roots ; then fill up the Hole, making a Cup about it, which fill up with rotten *Horfe-Dung,* and in two Hours the Tree will be fix'd. This Way of planting is very good for *Tews, Holleys,* and all other *fibrous-rooted* Trees. 'Tis alfo an *excellent Method* for planting very large Trees; and according to this Manner of planting, that *celebrated* Planter the Honourable JAMES JOHNSTONE of *Twickenham,* has planted fome Thoufands of *Fruit, Foreft-Trees,* and *Ever-Greens,* with great Succefs.

Laftly, To preferve the Roots of new-planted Trees from the Cold of the Winter, and Heat of the Summer, lay about the Stem of every Tree good *rotten Horfe-Dung,* without *long Litter, Fern, &c.* for that breeds *Worms, Ants,* and other Vermin injurious to Fruit-Trees.

Let the Thicknefs of the Dung be about four Inches, or not quite fo much, covering it thinly with a little Mold ; and if your Land be dry or hot, form the *Dung* and Mold in the Form of a *Difh* or *Cup,* to receive the *Water,* which muft be carefully given during all dry *Seafons,* both of *Spring* and *Summer.*

SECT.

SECT. IV.

Of the several Kinds of Earth proper for all Sorts of Fruit-Trees.

FIRST then, *Pears*, *Apples*, *Plumbs*, and *Fig-Trees*, will thrive in any kind of Land as is *deep*, be it moderately *hot* or *cold*.

In *hot*, *dry*, and *light sandy Land* the *Peach* must be budded on a *Peach-Stock*, and in *wet* and *strong Land* on a *Muscle*, or *White Pear Plumb-Stock*.

Almonds love a *light Land*, when raised from their own *Kernels*; but if *grafted* on a *Plumb*, a *strong Land*.

When *Almonds* or *Peaches* are budded on their own *Stocks*, and planted in *strong Land*, they are too subject to *Gum*, which impairs their Health.

Quinces will not thrive in *light Land*, delighting more in *strong*, *wet*, *heavy* Lands.

Pears grafted on *Pear-Stocks* delight in a *dry Soil*; and when grafted on a *Quince-Stock* in a moderate *wet strong* Soil.

Cherries thrive well in *light Lands*, but better in a good *sandy Loam*.

Vines produce the *best Grapes* when planted in *dry light Lands*, as *chalky, sandy, gravelly, rocky, &c.* Lands, and the Exposure warm.

Peaches budded upon *Almonds* thrive best in *dry hot Lands*.

The *Winter Bouchretien Pear* produces the fine Colours of *Yellow* and *Carnation* when *grafted* on a *Quince*, which it will not do when *grafted* on a *Pear-Stock*.

> *Now, that the Plant may with the Mold comply,*
> *What Fruits it most approve you first must try:*
> *Whether the Vine thrives best upon the Place,*
> *Or other Trees; for there can be no Grace*

In

In any Ground that's forced *againſt its Will*
To bring forth Fruit; *therefore remember ſtill*
Never with NATURE *any Force to uſe;*
For 'tis injurious, *if ſbe ſhould refuſe.*
  When once the Land is levell'd and prepared,
Let it in equal Diſtances be ſhared:
Appoint the Seats in which your Trees ſhall ſtand,
Then chuſe a Quince *from a ſelected Band:*
And having cut *the woody Part away,*
Into warm Mold you then the Plant may lay:
Nor think it unworthy of your Hand
To make the Furrows hollow, *or t'expand*
The Earth *about the Roots; for ſtill we find,*
That he who does the Law of Planting mind,
He who from Parent Stocks *young Branches cuts,*
And then in Trenches the ſoft Layers *puts,*
Seldom repents theſe neceſſary Pains,
But rather Profit by his Care obtains.
  While Fortune waited on the Perſian State,
CYRUS, *who from* Aſtyages *the Great,*
Himſelf derived, himſelf his Gardens *till'd;*
How oft aſtoniſh'd IMOLUS *has beheld*
Th' Induſtrious PRINCE *in planting* Trees *and* Flowers,
And watering them, employ his vacant Hours?
How oft ORONTES *ſtopp'd his* haſty Flood,
And gazing on the Royal GARDENER *ſtood.*
  The Sabine Valleys *heretofore have known*
When nobleſt Romans *have forſook their Town;*
When they their Pomp *and* Glory *laid aſide,*
And to the RAKE *and* PLOW *themſelves apply'd.*
  And this Employment warlike FABIUS *choſe,*
When he return'd from vanquiſhing his Foes.
He *who in open Senate made Decrees,*
Manures his *Ground, and now gives Laws to* Trees.
No longer o'er his Legions *he commands,*
But ſows the Earth with his *victorious Hands:*
The Glebe, by this triumphant Swain ſubdued,
Repay'd his Pains with timely Gratitude:

Became

Became more fruitful than it was before,
And better Plants *and larger* Apples *bore.*
   Thus MASSINISSA *when he won the* Day
And made false Syphax *with his* Troops *obey :*
In tilling of his Ground he spent his Time,
And try'd t'improve the barb'rous Libian *Clime.*
   Illustrious GEORGE, *who carefully attends*
His Kingdom Government *sometime descends*
From his high THRONE, *and in the Country deigns*
To please himself, and slack his Empire's Reins.
He thinks not that he makes his GLORY *less*
T' improve his Ground; his Servants round him press,
Thousands *with* Fruits, Thousands *with* Flowers *strive*
To fill the Place; the Water *some derive*
Into the Gardens, *while with watchful Eye,*
He oversees the Work, and equally
To ev'ry Labourer his Duty shews,
And the same on all the Field bestows.
Nor does the King *these Arts in vain approve;*
The grateful Earth *rewards his* Royal *Love.*
   But why should I such great Examples name;
Our Age wants·nothing that should more inflame
Its Zeal; for since the greatest Men now please
Themselves in cultivating of their Trees;
Since 'tis their Praise to do it, why should you
Refuse this sweet Employment to pursue.
If Fruit *of your own raising can invite,*
If in your Villa *you can take delight,*
Or can the Country love, to that apply
Yourself and to your Plants *no Pains deny.*
The Stars if kind, or Goodness of the Soil,
Help not so much as never-ceasing Toil.
Then let the Earth *more frequent Tillage know;*
The stubborn Globe *is vanquish'd by the* Plow.
When Rain *or stormy* Winds *pernicious are,*
When the Sun's Influence or intemperate Air,
Injurious proves, the Tiller's Industry,
And Culture all Defects will soon supply.
   That this is true, a Marsian *Clown has shewn,*
Who in a little Garden *of his own,*

Which

Which he himself manured, had Store of Fruit,
While all the Country elfe was deftitute :
The ftanding Corn *you on his Ground might view,*
And Apples broke the Boughs *on which they grew.*
  His Neighbours quickly envied his Succefs,
He by his Theffalian *Arts his Ground did drefs ;*
They faid, and haftened on his early Corn
By Herbs *upon the* Marfian *Mountains born,*
Or Magical Infufions ; *then repleat*
With Rage *and* Envy *to the Judgment-Seat.*
They haul the blamelefs Swain, *where his Defence*
He makes with Pain *and rural Eloquence.*
His Sickle *he produces, and his* Spade,
And Rake, *which by long Ufe were brighter made.*
See here, faid he, the Crimes which I have done ;
If Tools *by* Time *and* Ufage *bright, are one :*
Thefe are my Magick Arts, *thefe are my* Charms:
Then ftretching forth his Labour-ftiff'ned Arms,
His Sabine Dame, *and Daughter's brawny Hand,*
Inur'd to work, *and with the Sunbeams tann'd.*
Thus by his Induftry *his Caufe he gains ;*
So much a Field *improves by conftant Pains.*
Hence comes good Corn, *and hence the* Trees *are crown'd*
With heavy Boughs ; *hence 'tis that they abound*
In their choice Fruits, *in each of which we find*
A Colour *proper to* itfelf *affign'd.*

RAPIN, Book iv. Page 181.

S E C T. V.

Containing a Catalogue of all the best Wall, Espalier, *Dwarf,* and *Standard* Fruits *now growing in* England; *with General Rules for their pruning.*

I. OF *Peaches* and *Nectorines,* budded on the *Peach, Muscle, Plumb,* or *Almond* Stocks,

Of Peaches: *The best are,*

White and Red Magdalenes,
Mountabon,
Bourdine,
Minion,
Early Admirable,
Old Newington,
Yellow Alberge,
Anne,
Bell Chevreux,
Rambollion,

Nivet,
Perfique,
Peach Royal,
Swalsee, *introduced by the Lord* Peterborough,
Hative,
Swifs,
Flanders,
Nobles,
Albemarle.

Ripe in the great Season of Peaches, *viz.* from about *July* 20. to *August* 20.

Their Expositions to be full *South,* or declining to the *East,* forty five Degrees at most.

Of Nectorines: *The best are,*

Newington,
Roman,

Temple, *ripens late,*
Elrouge,

Ripe in *August.* Their Exposition as the preceding.

The

The late Peaches are,

Late Admirable,
Catherine,
Malegotune,
Burdock,
Peach-Poe,
Man-Peach,

Pourpree,
Wimbleton,
Bellgard,
Late Purple,
Murry Nectorine.

All which ripens in the End of *August* and *September.*

For thefe late Fruits, a *Full-South* Expofition is of all others the very beft.

The Goodnefs of *Peaches* is judg'd by the *Nature* and *Goodnefs* of their *Taftes*; the beft having fine *musky, fugar'd, vinous, excellent, noble,* and *delicious Juices*; and thofe of a *bad Kind, dry, watry,* and *infipid.* The *Pulps* of *Peaches* have two different *Qualities*; the one when *ripe,* cleaving *faft* to the *Stone*; and the other coming *clear* from it. Thus faith *Rapin,*

Some of a thicker Subftance ftick faft on,
While others which are thinner quit the Stone.
Thefe laft with Juice and dewy Moifture fwell,
And all the other Sorts by much excel.

II. Of *Pears* grafted or budded on *Pear* or *Quince Stocks:* Of which there be *three Kinds,* viz. *Summer Pears, Autumn Pears,* and *Winter Pears.*

The beft Summer Pears are,

Citron D'camus, *ripe Middle of*
  July; *afterwards comes*
Primite,
Jargonel,
Petit Mufcat, *July,*
Sugar Mufcat,
Green Chizel,
Goofeberry Pear,
St. Magdalene,

Quire-Song Pippin.
Vermillion,
Mouille Bouche,
Windfor,
Summer Bouchretien, *Aug.*
Cyprus,
Royal Bergamot, *ripe in the*
  Beginning of Auguft.

After

After which comes the

Summer Buree,
Orange Bergamot,
Summer Bergamot,
Grofs Rouffellet,
Petit Rouffellet,
Petit Blanquet, *July*,

Grofs Blanquet,
Blanquet Mufque, *July*,
Rozate,
Caffolet, *Aug.*
Rouffellet.

The beft Autumn Pears are,

Vert-longuee, *Oct.*
Buree du Roy,
Autumn Bouchretien,
Petit Oing,
Rouffellet, *Aug. Sept.*
Doyenne, *Sept. Oct.*

Greenfield,
Lovisbon,
Deagoe,
Meffire John, *Oct.*
Cuiffe Madam, *July*,

Autumn Pears,

Craffan, *Oct. Nov.*
Bizidery, *Oct. Nov.*
Swan's Egg,
Lanfac, *Nov.*
Salladin,

Roy Musk,
Hambden's Bergamot,
St. Michael,
St. Andrew.

The beft Winter Pears are,

Winter Bouchretien, *ripe in Feb. March.*
Golden Bouchretien, *Jan. Feb. March.*
Spanifh Bouchretien, *Nov. Dec.*
Colmar, *Nov. Dec. Jan. Feb.*
Sir Germaine, *Dec. Jan.*
Ambret, *Nov. Dec. Jan.*
Virgoulee, *Nov. Dec. Jan.*
Lachafferie, *Nov. Dec. Jan.*

Amadote, *Nov. Dec.*
Winter Thorn, *Nov. Dec. Jan.*
Salviati,
Royal D-hyver,
La Marquis,
Grey Buree,
Winter Buree,
Satin Pear,
Martin See, *Nov.*

The

The best Baking Pears are,

Pickering,
Spanish Warden,
English Warden,
Perkinson's Warden.

Black Pear of *Worcester,*
Pound Pear.
Cadilliac.

III. *Apricots* grafted or budded upon *Plumb-Stocks,*

The best Kinds are,

Masculine,
Bruxelles,

Orange,
Turky.

Which last is an excellent Fruit, but a very tender Tree, and a bad Bearer.

IV. *Figs* raised by *Layers* or *Suckers,*

The best Sorts are,

Fig-Flower, or large white Fig, *with a short Stalk,*
Fig-Flower, or large white Fig, *with a long Stalk,*
Little Marseilles white Fig, *a good Bearer.*
Black Madera Fig,
Grey Fig,
Brown-Purple Fig,
Genoa Fig,
Vernisingue Fig,
Green Fig,

Yellow Fig,
Flat Violet,
Long Violet,
Melinga Fig, *of a Violet Colour,*
Brugeotte Fig, *of a Violet Colour,*
Dwarf Fig, *of a Violet Colour,*
Bouriageotte Fig, *a deep Violet,*
Little Mignionne Fig, *a brownish Violet.*

Figs in general delight in much *Sun*; their Season of ripening is in *August* and *September.*

V. *Plumbs* grafted or budded on *Plumb Stocks.*

The

The best Sorts are,

Musk Perdigon,
Purple Perdigon,
White Perdigon,
St. Catherine,
Roche Corbon,
Green Gage,
Reineclaude,
Maitreclaude,
Queen-Mother,
Violet,
London Plumb,
Fotheringham,
Drapdor,

Blew Diapree,
White Matchlefs,
Cerney Perdigon,
Imperatrice,
La Royal,
Damazine,
Mogul, *good for baking,*
Plumb Ordin,
Morocco,
Orleaince, *or* Orline, *an excellent Bearer, and a good Fruit on a South Wall.*

The Goodnefs of all thefe Fruits deferves a *South Wall,* but will do very well on an *Eaft* or *Weft* Wall, or any Decliner to the South.

VI. *Apples* grafted upon *Crab Stocks,*

The beft Kinds are,

Non Pareill,
Golden Pippin,
French Pippin,
Holland Pippin,
Kentifh Pippin,
Kirking Pippin,
Winter Pearmain,
Autumn Pearmain,
Summer Pearmain,
Pome Roy,
Ruffeting,
Golden Ruffeting,

Corpendue Rennet,
Golden Rennet,
June Apple, *fo called, becaufe 'twill keep till* June,
Quince Apple, *excellent for the Kitchen,*
Jerufalem Apple,
Api,
White Calvil,
Red Calvil,
Monfterous Rennet.

VII.

VII. Of *Grapes* raifed by *Layers* or *Cuttings*.

The beft Kinds for this Climate are,

July Grape,	White and Black Fronteniacs,
Black Currant Grape,	Claret Grape,
Early Sweet-Water Grape,	Burgundy Grape,
Mufcat,	Black Clufter Grape,
French Sweet-Water Grape,	White Raifin Grape, *for Tarts*.
White and Black Mufcadines,	

> *To Plumbs and Grapes juft Commendations yield,*
> *If on the Wall they are by Nails upheld.*
> *Mufcat and Purple Vines, which both obferve*
> *Their wonted Seafons, may our Praife deferve.*
> RAPIN, *Lib.* iv. *page* 219.

VIII. Of *Cherries* grafted or budded upon the *Black-Cherry Stocks.*

The beft Kinds are,

May Cherry, *its being early,*	White *and* Black-Hearts,
Holman's Duke,	Caroon,
May Duke,	Carnation,
Lukeward,	Flemifh,
Early Flanders,	Englifh,
Clufter Cherry,	Morella,
Bleeding Heart,	Common-Black.

IX. Of *Goofeberries* raifed from *Cuttings*, or by *Suckers*.

The beft Kinds are,

Red and Green Champains,	Walnut,
Old Red,	Damfon,
White Dutch,	Black hairy Goosberry.
Amber,	

X. Of *Currants* raised by *Cuttings* or *Suckers.*

The best Kinds are,

Large white and red Dutch, || Black Medicinal Currant.

XI. Of *Rasberries* increas'd by *Runners,* or *Suckers.*

The Kinds are,

Purple, || White.
Red,

XII. *Strawberries* increas'd by *Runners.*

The Kinds are,

Scarlet, || Hautboy,
Wood, || Great White Strawberry,

XIII. The *Barberry* raised by *Suckers,* or *Layers.*

The Kinds are,

Berberry *with Stones,*   Berberry *without Stones.*

XIV. Of *Nut* or *Shell-Fruit.*

The Kinds are,

English *and large* French Wal- || White and Red Filberts, *of*
   nuts, *best for pickling.*   *which the Red is the best.*
Chesnut,

XV. The *Quince* raised by *Layers,* or *Cuttings.*

XVI. The *Mulberry* raised by *Layers, Cuttings,* or *Seed.*

XVII.

XVII. The *Cornelion Plumb* or *Cherry*, raifed by Layers, Slips, and Stones, often lie *two Years* in the Ground before they fpring.

XVIII. And Laftly, the *Medlar*, which is increafed by grafting on the *White-Thorn*, *Quince*, or *Pear-Stock*, and the *Service* by young Sets from the Woods, or by fowing their Seeds.

I having in the former Part of this *Section*, explained the Manner of *preparing* and *planting* of *Fruit-Trees* in general, and have now delivered a *Catalogue of the beft Fruits*, and how *propagated*, either by *Grafting, Inoculation*, &c. I fhall in the next Place proceed to lay down fome general Rules to be obferved in their *pruning*, and afterwards explain the Culture and Management of every Sort particularly.

General Rules to be obferved for pruning Fruit-Trees.

I. The nearer Branches are laid to a *Horizontal Pofition*, the *more apt* they are to produce Fruit.

II. The nearer Branches are laid to a *Perpendicular Pofition*, the *lefs apt* they are to produce Fruit, but *Wood* in great Plenty.

III. That the Middle of *Fruit-Trees* be kept clear of *great Wood* or *thick Branches*, efpecially *Peaches* and *Apricots*.

IV. That the Quantity of Wood left after Pruning, be in fome Degree of Proportion to the *Strength* and Condition of the Tree, not to crow'd in more Wood than *Nature* can well fupply.

V. That the Branches of *ftrong* and *vigorous* Trees be left *longer* than thofe as are *weak*, and to cut away all as grow forward from the Wall.

VI. That Branches be not laid a-crofs each other, except on a very great Occafion, &c.

VII. In the pruning young-planted Trees, of one Year's Shoot, obferve, That if a Tree has *one* or *two vigorous*, or well-difpofed *Branches*, with two or three weak ones, prune them all to an equal Length, of about five or fix Inches, leaving but two of the weak, with thofe two as are ftronger; but this is never to be done, but when the Shoots are placed regular, *viz.* a ftrong Branch and a weak one on one Side, and the like on the other.

Therefore if all the weak Branches be on the one Side of the Tree, and the ſtrong ones on the other, diſplace one of the ſtrong Shoots entirely, and leave one ſtrong Branch only with the other two as are weaker. If the Poſition of the two weak Shoots ſhould be both above the ſtrong ones, and they not on one Side; then at ſuch Times 'tis beſt to cut away the two weak Branches intirely, and form the Tree with thoſe Shoots as will proceed from the Buds of the remaining Branches.

VIII. *Weak* or *decaying Trees* ſhould have their Wood pruned much ſhorter than thoſe as are in perfect Health, and the Shoots preſerved muſt be fewer in Number.

IX. When Trees of one Year's Growth produce ſeven or eight Shoots, chuſe out three, or four at moſt, of the middling Wood, and diſplace all the others.

X. When either young or old Trees produces ſtronger Branches towards the Bottom than the Top, 'tis a Sign that its upper Part is in an ill State of Health; therefore at ſuch Times 'tis beſt to cut away the weak Part entirely, and form a new Tree with the ſtrong and healthy Branches remaining.

XI. When Trees of any Age produce weak Branches at Bottom, and vigorous ones at Top, 'tis beſt to cut down that Tree to the weak Branches, and thereby they will be ſtrengthened, and the Tree proceed upwards in an equal State of Health.

XII. To nail in bearing Branches over-thick, ſtarves the Bloom, cauſes the Fruit to be ſmall and inſipid, and at length ruins the Tree. Therefore avoid thick nailing; for of the two Extremes, 'tis beſt to prune and nail too thin, rather than too thick; for as I ſaid before, that thick nailing ruins a Tree, ſo on the contrary, thin nailing cauſes fine Fruit and good Wood, &c.

XIII. When you prune Dwarf-Trees, obſerve that the Bud you prune at ſtand outward, and not inward, or Side-ways, and thereby the Tree in its natural Growth will form itſelf, without the Aſſiſtance of Hoops, &c. to extend out their Branches to form the Tree.

> *You cannot be ſo often put in Mind*
> *Of that Advantage which your Plants will find:*
> *By being* prun'd, *the Boughs will thus obey,*
> *And by your* Tool *are faſhion'd any Way:*

3

Though tough with Age, they ftoop to your Command,
Nor can the crooked Pruning-Knife withftand :
And when the Trees thus cut revive again,
When from their Wounds they borrow Courage, then
Oft exercife your Power, and fo reftore
Beauty to that which was deform'd before.
Youth unadvis'd doth in Defire exceed,
And would without all Moderation breed.
The Pruner's Care muft fuccour each Defect ;
He with his Knife their Vices muft correct ;
Superfluous his Servants may reprefs ;
Deftructive Pity makes them more increafe.
   But in what Part they muft be cut, and how
From the Experienc'd you will better know : ·
Always untouch'd the chiefeft Branches fave,
From whom you hope a future Race to have.
   Now if the Seafon proves reciprocal,
You may behold your Fruit upon the Wall :
Your Garden's Riches then will make you glad ;
Nor think that any Thing can Colour add,
Or Bignefs to them, but that Influence,
Which on their Ranks kind Phœbus does difpenfe.
Nature your Wifhes then will fatisfy
If with thefe Methods only you comply.
And though we Ripenefs to our Fruits impart
By Heat on Walls reflected, yet this Art,
By the Reports of dark Antiquity,
In the Records of Time is fet more high.

                    RAPIN, Lib. iv. Page 220...

                                 SECT.

S E C T. VI.

Of the Native Place, Name, Exposition, and Culture of the Peach and Nectorine-Trees.

I. **I**TS Native Place is *Persia*, whofe extreme Parts, (*North* and *South*,) differ about ten Degrees of *Latitude*, which Difference is fuppofed to be the Caufe of their feveral Kinds being ripe at divers Seafons.

That is, 'tis fuppofed, that our early *Peaches* were Natives of the *Northern*, and our lateft of the *Southern* Parts.

The mean Latitude of *Perfia* is about thirty five Degrees North, its Extremes being, the one thirty, and the other forty Degrees Latitude.

II. Its *Name*. In *Greek* 'tis called πισκὴ μηλία ῥοδ́μηνα; in *Latin*, *Malus Perfica*; in the *Arabian* Language *Sauch*, or *Chauch*; in *Italian Perfiche*; in *Spanifh Pexigos*; in *Dutch Perceboom*; in *French Pefche*; and by the *Germans Pfefich-baum*.

III. The *South* and *South-Eaft Expofitions* are certainly the very beft; but *Peaches* will do very well on a South-Weft, and oftentimes on a Weft Wall, which ripens its Fruit, juft as that of the South Wall is gone. *Peaches* ought not to be planted on a *cold wet Soil*, their Fruit are always *watry* and *infipid*.

IV. In the *Culture* of *Peach-Trees* great Care muft be had, to *well* and *timely* pruning, *&c.* In which obferve

When *Peach-Trees* haften to bear very foon, 'tis a Sign of *Decay* or *Weaknefs*; and the beft Help for them is, to dif-burden the Tree of its Bloom, and prune it to fhort Wood.

When *Peach-Trees* are *vigorous*, cut out fuch large Wood as appears to be ufelefs, and nail in the Remains at a long Length, as twelve or fourteen Inches. In making *Choice of Shoots*,

Shoots, always chufe the *middling Wood,* as are full of *fwelling double Buds*; for thofe produce Fruit which the *flat fingle Buds* do not, their Product being *Wood* and *Leaves* only.

The beft *Time* to prune *Peach-Trees* is in *March,* when all the hard *Frofts* are over: You muft obferve in pruning to cut out all *dead* Wood, all *Autumn Shoots,* and *yellow faplefs* Branches; to cut your Shoots to about fix or eight Inches in Length, and to lay in the Branches at a moderate Diftance, as three Inches, *&c.*

In *May* you muft carefully and difcreetly thin your *Peach-Trees* of their fuper-abundant Fruit, leaving them not too thick, which will caufe all the Fruit to be fmall, and good for nothing; one good Peach is better than a thoufand bad ones.

About *Midfummer* top the Shoots with Difcretion, and nail them to the Wall, without any great Regard to the Order, becaufe at the next Pruning they will be all alter'd ; and about this Time you may begin to introduce the *Sun* to your Fruit; but do it gradually, which will give it its *natural Colour,* and *Maturity* likewife.

When *Peach-Trees* have their Branches nailed, or placed *horizontally,* the *Sap* is retarded, and the *Bloffoms* will not fall from the Trees, by being, as it were, ftrangled by the *Superfluity* of *Sap,* which often happens in Trees whofe Branches are *perpendicular,* or near thereunto: Therefore Regard hereunto fhould be had, as I have before faid, that the Branches fhould be nailed *horizontally.*

Be careful to difplace all *Suckers* as may rife from the Roots or Bottom of the Trees, and carefully keep all Side-Branches nail'd up, cutting, or rather rubbing off all Buds or Branches as grows forwards from the Wall, and alfo cutting away all Shoots infected by *Blights, Infects, &c.*

If the *Summer* be *hot* at the Time of your Fruit ripening, make a *Bafon* over the *Roots,* and give them Plenty of Water, fo as not to over-do it, and the Fruit will be wonderfully augmented thereby. If the Mowings of *Grafs-Plots, &c.* be laid in thofe Bafons, it will prevent the *fcorching Rays* of the *Sun* from *drying* away the *Moifture.*

The

The firſt *Peach* ripe is the *Nutmeg*, at the End of *July*; after which follow the reſt in Order, in the Months of *Auguſt* and *September.*

N. B. That *Peaches* are infinitely better when gather'd three or four Days before they are eaten. When you gather *Peaches* take care they are not bruiſed, and lay them on *Vine-Leaves,* with their Heads downwards in your *Fruittery,* till they are eatable, always remembering that if a *Peach* is laid on its Side, 'twill immediately be rotten.

When you prune new-planted *Peach-Trees* of the firſt Year's Shoot, (which ſhould be done in *March,*) do not leave *too much* Wood, nor cut it all away, as many do; but diſcretionally proportionate the ſame to the *State* of the *Tree,* as I have before mention'd.

In the *pruning* of Fruit-Trees in general, obſerve when you prune off the End of a *Shoot,* that you cut it off a little above a *Leave-Bud,* the Slope cut at the Back thereof. The more any Tree is pruned, the more it will ſhoot.

When you deſire a Fruit-bearing Tree to produce new Wood, which of itſelf is not inclinable to do, rub off the Bloom, (or moſt of it,) and *prune* the Shoots to *half* their uſual Length, and the Tree will break out into Plenty of Wood, which muſt be govern'd as I have before directed.

The *Nectorine* being a *Kind* of a *Peach,* or at leaſt one of that *Tribe,* is to be managed in all Reſpects as the *Peach.*

If Mr. *Bra - - l - - y's* Report of the Peaches in *Italy,* (mentioned in his *General Treatiſe for the Month of* December, *Page* 133.) growing to ſixteen or eighteen Foot high in two or three Years after planting, without Walls, be actually true, 'tis evident that they love a warm Expoſition; and therefore we muſt allow them the beſt Wall our Garden affords.

S E C T.

S E C T. VII.

Of the Native Place, Name, Expofition, and Culture of the Pear-Tree.

I. THE native Places from whence Pears were original-ly brought, were *Alexandria, Numidia, Greece,* and *Numancia,* as appears by their feveral Names.

II. Its Name. The *Arabians* call it *Humeeth;* the *Italians. Pere;* the *Arabs Cirmetre,* or *Kemetri;* the *Germans Bir, Bi-ren,* and *Piren;* the *Spaniards Pyras;* the *French Poire;* and the *Dutch Berre.*

III. The beft Sorts of Winter Pears (all which the Catalogue. confifts of) deferve the very beft Wall and Afpect you can give them. *N. B.* They will not be ripe, till fome Time after they are gather'd. All Baking-Pears may be planted againft *North-Eaft* or *North-Weft* Walls, as alfo the *Roufellet, Orange, Ber-gamot, Catherine,* and other Summer and Autumn Pears.

The Soil wherein Pears delight, is a rich, fandy, deep Loam, as the Reverend Mr. *Lawrence,* in his *Pleafure and Pro-fit of Gardening improved,* Vol. I. Chap. 7. obferves, " That a " rich, deep, fandy, mix'd Earth, in fifty four Degrees of Lati- " tude, will do more towards accelerating the ripening of the " beft Fruit, then a ftiff cold Clay will do in fifty one " From which it appears, that the fo-much celebrated Mr. *Bradley* is very much miftaken in his *New Improvements of Planting and Gardening,* Part III. Page 30. Where, fayshe, " The Soil which " the Pear chiefly delights in, is a wet Earth, inclining to Clay." (And further adds, in the following Words) " Nay, I have feen " this Kind of Tree profper extremely in the ftrongeft Sort of " blew Clay, which is accounted the worft of Soils; fo that " this Sort, no more than the Apple-Tree, delights in what we " call rich Earth." Now 'tis true, that Pear-Trees will grow. in cold wet Earths, and in Clay alfo ; but, alas! the Fruit they.

K   preproduce is *watry* and *infipid,* and confequently good for nothing, even in the beft of Seafons. And as an Inftance to prove that Pears do delight in what Mr. *Bradley* calls rich Earth, (by which is to be underftood, a good *mellow,* fandy, *deep, holding Loam,*) let any Perfon go to the Honourable Mr. *Johnftone's* at *Twicken-ham,* where they will fee, on his Terrafs, are growing the very *beft Pears* in *England,* and in the greateft Perfection, whofe Soil is a fine, rich, holding Loam, fomething inclinable to a Brick-Earth. I could inftance divers other Places to prove the Miftake; but in regard to its coming from a Gentleman, and not from a Gardener, I will modeftly forbear, only adding, that inftead of its being inclinable to Clay, he meant Brick-Earth.

When the Situation and Nature of Soils are inclinable to too much *Cold* or *Wet,* let the Holes be prepared as I directed in the former Part of this *Section,* and therein plant the *Lachaffe-rie, Winter-Thorne, Virgoulee, St. Germain,* or *Amadot,* which are very fine in their Kinds, and will do on a South Afpect tolerable well.

Pears upon *Quince-Stocks,* are beft for *low Walls, Dwarfs,* or *Efpalliers,* and efpecially in wet Lands. Thefe Stocks doth effectually cure too great a Luxuriancy in the Pear, and caufes it to produce Fruit much fooner than when on a Pear Stock; but then on the other Hand, it has this Evil attending it; it is a fhort-lived Tree.

The feveral *Bonchretien* Pears, being grafted upon a *Quince,* and planted in a warm Soil, produce much better and larger Fruit than on a Pear-Stock.

When young new-planted Pear-Trees (and indeed any other) are too vigorous, running altogether into fruitlefs Wood, take them up with Care, and immediately plant them again in the fame Place without pruning: This Removal will put a Stop to their *luxuriant Growth,* and caufe the Tree to profper very well.

The beft Seafon for pruning Pear-Trees, is at the Fall of the Leaf, in which Care muft be taken, to cover all large Wounds with a Mixture of *Rofin, Mutton-Suet,* and *Bees-Wax,* as foon as the Branch is cut off. The laft Year's Shoots may be pruned to nine Inches, a Foot, or eighteen Inches in Length, according to the Strength of the Shoot; always obferving to cut out all

falfe

falfe Branches, called Water-Shoots, known by the extraordinary Diftance of their Buds, and to lay in no more Wood, then the Roots may be reafonably fuppofed capable of fupplying with fufficient Juices.

In *Nailing* of *Pear-Trees*, always remember to place the Branches *Horizontally*, otherwife they will foon come to Ruin: *Perpendicular* Branches are ever deftructive.

To diftinguifh the proper Branches which produce Fruit from thofe as produce Leaves only, obferve the following Account, *viz.* There be few Pear-Trees as produce Fruit before they are three Years old, or their Wood of the like Age, that is, fuch Shoots as are produced this Year, are preparing themfelves all the fecond Year to produce Fruit in the third. Hence it appears, that Pear-Trees have their bearing Buds in three feveral States, continually fucceeding one another. The blowing Buds of three Years old difcover themfelves at the Fall of the Leaf, who, whilft the Fruit preceding them was growing and ripening, they were preparing to fucceed them the enfuing Year.

Thefe Buds of three Years Growth are known by their being very full, and larger than any others, in a feeming Swelling impatient State of breaking out into its beautiful Drefs of delightful Bloom. The next preparative Buds of two Years, are of a fharp conical Form, and Red-ruffet Colour, growing very near to the fruitful Bud before defcribed: And laftly, the Junior Bud of one Year is a very fmall one, but full above the Bark, and always breaks out very near to that of two Years Growth: And befides all thefe, there is another wonderful Work of Nature, which is the Preparation of fmaller Buds as are continually forming themfelves within the Bark, to break out, and fucceed thofe their next Seniors of one Year's Growth, and fo on, *ad infinitum:* And in Confideration that this wonderful Work of Nature was never explained by any one, therefore, for the Ufe of the Curious, and all others concern'd in Gardening, I fhall foon communicate an entire, new, and general Syftem of the beft Fruits now extant in *England*, wherein the true Form of their Buds, Branches, Leaves, Bloffoms, and Fruits, are truly reprefented, as they appear in their feveral Stages or Degrees of Growth: With Obfervations on their Progrefs, and proper Directions for their Managements, *&c.*

explain'd,

explain'd, and curiouſly engraven on Copper Plates, as large as the Life itſelf.

Prune *Luxuriant Trees* very late, and cut away one of the largeſt Roots, eſpecially a *Tap-Root*, if any be; which will retard its haſty Growth, and cauſe it to bear.

Suffer not any *Snags* or Branches pruned ſhort, from which good Fruit comes; to projeƈt from the Wall more than two Inches at moſt.

In *May* begin your Summer Pruning, obſerving to cut all *forward* and *luxuriant* Branches to an *Inch and a half,* or *two Inches,* from the Place they ſhoot from. This ſhortening will check the Courſe of the Sap, and cauſe a good bearing Branch (or more) to come in its Place, or break out into bearing Buds itſelf, and produce Fruit in the progreſſive Manner before deſcribed.

N. B. That what I have ſaid here in reſpeƈt to ſtopping the *luxuriant Growth* of Pear-Trees, the ſame is to be underſtood of all other Fruits, the *Vines* and *Figs* excepted.

The *Summer Bonchretien* ſhould be always pruned in *May,* obſerving to nail in the Shoots at full Length; for they produce their Fruit at the Extremities of the Branches.

Both *Summer* and *Winter Bonchretiens* ſhould be planted againſt *high Walls,* as *Houſes, &c.* They want more Room to extend themſelves than any other Pear; and if they are confined by Pruning, immediately grow full of *Knots,* and produce but little Fruit: A warm Soil is beſt for them.

When a young *Pear,* or any other Fruit-Tree, as a *Peach* or *Apricot*-Tree, breaks out with Shoots on the one Side, and not on the other, Care muſt be taken to timely lead ſome of the tender Shoots to the barren Side, that thereby both Sides may be filled. The bending of thoſe Branches are not any wiſe hurt thereby, but rather helped, by reaſon that early Check cauſes them to bear Fruit very ſoon.

If in *July* your Pear-Trees are over-vigorous, and break out with forward Shoots, cut them off cloſe, and nail in all Branches as lie fluſh with the Wall, ſtill obſerving that 'tis beſt to rub off the Buds of ſuch Branches when they firſt appear. Suffer no Suckers to grow at the Roots of your Trees, any more than Weeds, *&c.*

At

At the End of *Auguſt*, and Beginning of *September* the *Autumn Pears* are fit to gather, which Work ſhould be done in the Middle of the Day, when the Fruit is perfectly dry.

They are not ripe, or fit to be eaten till ſome Time after they are gathered, as a Week, ten Days, and ſome a Month.

All *Winter Pears*, as Bonchretiens, Colmar, St. Germain, Virgoulee, Lachaſſerie, Ambret, *&c.* muſt not be gathered till *Michaelmas*, or Middle of *October*; at which Time (as I ſaid before) great Care muſt be taken to gather them perfectly dry; if otherwiſe, they will grow moldy, and be preſently rotten.

About the End of *November* the Winter Pears begin to ripen, as the Lachaſſerie, Virgoulee, Ambret, Colmar, Craſan, St. Germain, *&c.* which, with Care, moſt of them will laſt all *January*, and Part of *February*, and the *Winter Bonchretien* till *May*.

In the *Autumn*, when the Pears begin to drop from the Trees, as the *Winter Pears* will do when their Time for gathering is come, lay under every Tree the *Mowings of Graſs*, for the Fruit to *fall* on, and carefully take them away as they fall, to your Conſervatory, leaſt others fall upon the firſt, and bruiſe them. The Manner of preſerving Winter Fruit I will exemplify at the latter End hereof.

In *March* prune young Pear-Trees of one Year's Shoot with Diſcretion, not for to take but litttle from them, or to take all away, (as is too often done by many.)

This Month of *March* is the proper Seaſon to retard the luxuriant Growth of Trees, by (what Mr. *Lawrence* calls) *Plaſhing*, that is, cutting the luxurious Part near to whence it ſhot, ſomething more than half through; which checks its vigorous Growth, and thereby is ſooner diſpoſed to bear Fruit. If by Miſmanagement Fruit-Trees have many perpendicular Branches as are unfruitful, 'tis beſt to plaſh them, as before directed.

N. B. But this Way of Plaſhing is not to be practiſed on any Trees but Wall-Trees, Peaches excepted, and very low Dwarfs, whoſe Branches are ſecured by Stakes ; for was Standards to be cut in that Manner, the Winds would ſoon break off thoſe Branches.

3

The

The beſt Pears for *Eſpaliers* and *Dwarfs*, are the *Citron, d'Camus, Primit, Sugar Muſcat, Jargonel, St. Magdalen, Quire-Song Pippin, Vermillion, Mouille Bouche, Gooſeberry Pear, Green Chizel, Cyprus, Orange Bergamot, St. Germain, Ambret, Spaniſh Bonchretien, Virgoulee, Colmar, Lachaſſerie,* and indeed all others, with good Care, the *Summer* and *Winter Bonchretiens* excepted for Dwarfs, but very well for *Eſpaliers*, where they have Room to extend themſelves.

Your *Eſpalier* and *Dwarf Pears* being planted in the *Autumn*, at the Fall of the Leaf, as I before directed, at their proper Diſtances, *&c.* in *May* following pinch off the Tops of perpendicular luxuriant Branches, within half an Inch from whence they ſhoot, and 'twill cauſe others to break out as will be good Wood. At this Time you may diſcern what Buds will be ſerviceable in filling up empty Places, or for Fruit, and all others ſhould be diſplaced. This Work being now done, the Sap immediately heals the Wounds.

The Proportion laid down for the Diſtance of Eſpaliers from Walls, and their Height, by the Reverend Mr. *Lawrence*, is very good, *viz.* as Eight to Twenty, that is, if the Diſtance of the Eſpalier from the Wall be twenty Feet, the Height muſt be eight Feet, *&c.*

The ſeveral Kinds of uſeful Wood in a Winter Pear-Tree are three, *viz.* Wood with Fruit; Wood preparing itſelf for Fruit, which is doing a Year beforehand; and laſtly, the yearly Shoot; ſo that that Shoot as is made this Year, is ſwelling and knotting itſelf in the ſecond Year, to produce Fruit in the third Year; but yet there be ſome Summer Pears as produce Fruit the ſecond Year: Therefore Care muſt be taken every Year to lay in young Wood to ſucceed the Place of the old, which muſt be cut out when grown barren of fruitful Buds, *&c.*

SECT.

SECT. VIII.

Of the Native Place, Name, Expofition, *and Culture of the Apricot.*

I. ITS native Place is *Epira, Epire,* or *Epirus,* a Province in *Greece,* firft founded by the *Romans,* and therefore was called *Mala Epirotica.*

II. The *Apricot* by the *Greeks,* is called μελα αρμενιακα; in *Latin, Malus Armenica;* in *Arabick, Mex,* and *Mermex;* in *Italian, Armoniache, Moniache, Bachofe,* and *Grifomele;* in *Spanifh, Albiricoques, Alvaricoques,* and *Alberchigas;* by the *Germans, Sir Johan Pfferfick;* and the *French, Abricot,* or *Carmaignoles.*

III. Their Expofition is beft when *South;* but will do on *South-Eaft, South-Weft,* or *Eaft* and *Weft Walls* very well.

IV. Their *Culture,* wherein obferve (after the Tree is planted, as before directed,) to *prune* and *nail* them according to the Manner directed for the *Peach,* to keep the Trees clear of *Suckers* and *Weeds,* and to cut away all *blighted Branches,* or others infefted by *Infects, &c.* to thin the Fruit with Difcretion in *May;* and when it is fully grown, to gradually expofe it to the Sun, which in its Ripening will give its natural Colour and Tafte.

'Twill not be amifs, if at the Time of your Fruits ripening, that you make a Bafon over the Roots of the Trees, and give them Water plentifully, if the Seafon be very *hot,* and to lay the Mowings of *Grafs* therein, to prevent the *Sun* from drying away the *Moifture* as is neceffary for the Trees.

About the End of *May,* or Beginning of *June,* the *Mafculine Apricot* is ripe; and towards the Middle of *July* the *Orange* and *Turky;* which laft, is a Fruit of an excellent Flavour.

Apricots gather'd one Day before they are eaten, gives them an excellent delicious Flavour.

3   The

The true *Bruxelles Apricot* is an excellent Fruit, and will profper very well on *Efpaliers*, *Dwarfs*, or *Standards*.

N. B. The Method laid down for *plafhing* of Pear-Trees, &c. is not to be practifed on the *Apricot* at *no other Time* but the *Month* of *May*, the *Sap* being then capable to heal the Wound inftantly.

In *March* prune all young-planted Trees of one Year's Shoot, which perform with Difcretion, not to leave more Wood than is neceffary, nor to lay in the Branches over long; and laftly, not to prune them too fhort, to add new Vigour, as fome call it, too often to the Deftruction of good Trees.

S E C T. IX.

Of the Native Place, Name, Expofition, and Culture of the Fig.

I. **I**TS Native Place: The *Fig* is an Native of *Barbary*, long fince introduced into many Parts of *Europe*, as *France*, *Spain*, *Italy*, *England*, &c. where, by Length of *Time*, and divers *Improvements*, the feveral *Sorts* are become as numerous as *Peaches*, *Apples*, &c.

II. Its Name, in *Greek*, is called σῦκον; in *Latin*, *Ficus* ; in *Arabick*, *Sin*, *Tin*, or *Fin*; in *Italian*, *Fichi* ; in *French*, *Figue*; in *Dutch*, *Feigen* ; in *Spanifh*, *Hygos*; and by the *Germans*, *Feighen*.

III. This *Favourite Fruit* delights beft in a *South Expofure*, where its Soil is *dry* and *ftony*, like unto the *Vine*.

IV. In the Cultivation of the Fig, you muft obferve, that it doth not delight in being much prun'd, or often digg'd about. The beft Seafon to *plant* the *Fig* is in *March* or *April*, when all the *cold Frofts* are gone and over; and if the Spring prove dry, never forget to give them *Plenty of Water*; 'twill greatly add to their Growth. In *March* take off the *Suckers* of *Figs*, and tranfplant them where required,

and

and at the fame Time lay down the *Layers*; which take off, and tranfplant the *March* or *April* following: You muft not cut or prune the *Tops* or *Heads* of either *Suckers* or *Layers* of *Figs*; 'tis *immediate Death* to them, when fo cut.

The beft Seafon to prune *Fig-Trees* is in *June*; at which Time you muft obferve, that you leave all the Shoots with their Tops on, becaufe thofe extream Parts, (*viz.* the three laft *Buds* or *Eyes*) produce the Fruit the enfuing Year.

Cut out all large Wood, as is too much, which always cut off as near the Ground as may be, and cover the Wound immediately with the Mixture of *Mutton-Suet*, *Rozin*, and *Bee's Wax*, as I before mention'd. The *largeft*, or *ftrongeft Shoots* of the *laft Year* are what *produces* the *Fruit*; all fmall weak Shoots are now to be cut away.

Admit not *Suckers* at the *Roots* of your Trees, except that an *Increafe* is required.

If in *June* you *pinch* or *nip* off the End-Buds of the young Branches, 'twill ftop the over and above Courfe of the Sap, and caufe the Fruit to come much earlier, and in greater Perfection: *Sand*, *Lye-Afhes*, &c. laid at the Roots of *Fig-Trees*, greatly accelerates the Ripening of the Fruit. At the Pruning of *Fig-Trees*, obferve to nail up, or confine to the Wall, all the large Branches; but let the young Shoots, which produce Fruit, be at free Liberty: The Fruit will ripen much better than when confined to the Wall. But in *November* following it will be beft to nail them clofe to the Wall, the better to preferve them from the Winter's Frofts.

And although the common Practice in *England* has been to plant this Fruit againft Walls only, yet 'tis to be underftood, that *Figs* will profper, and produce good Fruit in great Plenty, when planted *Dwarfs* or *Standards;* as may be feen in the Gardens of that *great Encourager* of Planting, the Honourable *James Johnfton*, of *Twickenham*. The *beft Figs* as I know of now in *England*, as are really good, are the White and long Purple Figs, ripe at the End of *Auguft*: The others, mention'd in my Catalogue, are of *France;* of which fome are, and others might be alfo cultivated in *England*, with as much Eafe as the Purple and White; and that my Reader may be informed of their feveral Qualities, take the following Defcription: The *Figs* mention'd in my Catalogue, are either *White*, *Black*,

3   L   *Tellow*,

Yellow, Grey, Green, Brown, Purple, or *Violet colour'd,* confifting of fixteen different Kinds. As, firft, Of *White Figs,* which are three in Number, *viz.* the *Flower of Figs,* the firft ripe, called by the *French Figue Fleru,* having a fhort Stalk fomething flat. The fecond is of the fame Name with a long Stalk; and the third, called the fmall *Marfeilles Fig,* of a flat Make, and very fruitful Kind.

All thefe three Sorts bear twice a Year, *viz.* Spring and Autumn; and their Fruit are richly fugar'd, have but few Seeds, and are melting.

II. *The Black Fig,* or *Madera Fig,* called by the *French le Figue de Madere,* is a black large *Fig,* of a long Make, a very great Bearer, and requires a very warm Expofition to ripen its Fruit, as well as a very high Wall to extend it felf.

III. *The Yellow Fig,* called by the *French Incarnadine,* or *Incarnation,* is a very large *Fig,* like unto the *White Flower of Figs* : 'Tis a great Grower, bears twice a Year, *Spring* and *Autumn*; it feldom produces much Fruit in the *Spring,* but generally in *September* great Quantities: It is of a *Reddifh Colour* within Side, and a very good Fruit.

Befides this Yellow Fig, there is another called the *Golden Fig,* and by the *French Figue Dorée:* 'Tis a large flat Fruit, its Skin breaks in Ripening, and produces a much better Crop in the *Autumn* than in *Summer.*

IV. *The Grey Fig,* called by the *French la Figue de Grife,* a large Fig of a long Make, greyifh on one Side, and a little blewifh on the other, an indifferent good Bearer, and a tolerable good Fruit.

V. *The Green Fig,* called in *French Figue Verte,* and by fome *La Verdalle,* or *Figue d' Efpagne, Spanifh* Fig, by the *Italians Verdone,* is a plump round Fruit, always green without, and when ripe, very red within Side.

'Tis a very *hardy Tree,* and produces a better and larger Crop in *September* and *October,* than in *Summer,* and is a very good Fruit.

VI. *Brown-Purple Figs*; of which there are two Sorts, *viz.* the *Genoa Fig,* called by the *French Figue de Gennes,* or *la Figue Fievre,* the *Treaver Fig.* It is an excellent fine flavoured *Fig,* and produces Fruit larger than any other: Its *Shape* is

long,

long, and Colour a *brownish Purple*, and withal an excellent Bearer, when in a warm Expofure.

The other Kind of *Brown-Purple Figs*, are called *Vernifingue*; it is an excellent good Fruit, of a brownifh Purple Colour, and delights in a warm Expofition.

Laftly, Violet Figs, of which there is *fix Sorts:*

As, 1ft, The *long Violet Fig*, called by the *French Figue Violette longue, Figue Poire, Pear Fig*, and by fome *Figue de Bourdeaux*, the *Bourdeaux Fig:* 'Tis a very large Fruit, a great Bearer, ripe in *September*, when no other Fig is in Seafon; 'tis very full of large Seeds, and its Pulp fomewhat dry.

2dly, The *flat Violet Fig*, called by the *French Figue Violette plat:* 'Tis a plentiful Bearer in the *Autumn*, but not in the *Spring*; of a middling Size, a fine *delicious melting Tafte*, and indeed is one of the very beft Sort of *Figs*.

3dly, The *Bouriageotte Fig*, ripe in *September*, of a *light Violet* Colour, a very large Fruit, a plentiful Bearer in the *Autumn*, but not at *Midfummer;* and withal an excellent good Fruit.

4thly, The *Melinga Fig*, called by the *French Figue de Melingue*, an excellent delicious Fruit, of a *Violet* Colour without, and *Red* within; its Form is long and thin, and when near ripe, is fubject to drop its Fruit: It loves a very warm Expofure, and will not admit of any pruning for many Years after planting.

5thly, The *Dwarf Fig*, called by the *French Figuier Nain:* The *Buds* of this Tree are very clofe fet, and its Shoots fhort; its Fruit is large, and of a *Violet Colour* without, and *Red* within; 'tis a plentiful Bearer, and a very good Fruit.

6thly, The *Burgeotte Fig*, an excellent Fruit in Tafte, *large* and flat in Shape, of a *Violet Colour* without, and *Red* within, and a very good Bearer in *Autumn*.

Laftly, The fmall *Mignionne Fig*, called by the *French Petite Figue Mignionne:* Its Fruit is of a *brownifh Blew* without, and *very Red* within, but fmall, being not much larger than the *Carnation Cherry*, and is a very good Bearer.

N. B. If *Figs* are planted in Tubes, as *Oranges* are, and in the *Winter* fhelter'd in a *Green-Houfe* from the *Cold, &c.* they will oftentimes produce Figs ripe in *May*.

N. B. That when any Kind of Fig at its Ripening, is obferved to have a *Drop* hanging at its *End*, 'tis then in greateft *Perfection*, and fhould be immediately gather'd.

L 2　　　　　　　　　　　　　　*N. B*

N. B. There are fome *Figs* as do not difcover their Ripening by a *Drop*, therefore when ever they are obferved to *decay* or *flag* at the *Stalk*, you may depend upon their being ripe.

Figs muft *not* be gather'd in the *Heat* of the *Sun*, therefore 'tis beft to gather them in a *Morning* after the *Dew* is gone, and before the *Heat* of the Day is come on; and being kept in the *Fruitry* one Night after gathering, caufes them to eat *much finer* than when firft gather'd.

SECT. X.

Of the Native Place, Name, Expofition, and Culture of the Plumb.

I. THE native Places of the *Plumb-Tree* is *Armenia*, whofe Latitude is about fourty two Degrees, and *Damafcus* (formerly a Town of *Syria*) fituated in thirty five Degrees Latitude, from whence they were firft brought into *Italy*.

II. A *Plumb*, in *Latin* is called *Prunus*, or *Prunum ;* in *Arabick Anas, Avas,* or *Hagias*; in *Italian Prune,* or *Succine ;* in *Spanifh Prunas, Andrinas,* or *Amexeas ;* in *Dutch Pruym*; in *French Prune ;* and by the *Germans Pflaumen.*

III. Altho' *Plumbs* will produce excellent Fruit from Dwarf, Efpallier, or Standard Trees, yet there be many *good Sorts* as delerves even the beft Wall the Garden affords; as the *Perdigon, Greengage,* &c. nay, all in general are vaftly helped thereby.

IV. Its *Culture.* The *Plumb* delights in *good Land*, inclining to be *rather ftrong* and *wet*, than *light* and *dry*; and will ripen very well againft *Eaft, Weft, North-Eaft,* or *North-Weft* Walls.

The

The *Seafon* for pruning is *January*, or *February* at furtheft, and the Manner the fame as that of the Pear.

When *Plumb-Trees* are *vigorous* and *luxuriant*, 'tis beft to *plafh* or prune them very late, and if need be, both Operations may be ufed.

Carefully mind to deftroy all Manner of *Weeds, Suckers, &c.* in the *Spring*, and to nail up all ufeful Branches.

In *July* pick off the Leaves, and *let in the Sun*; but do it by *Degrees*, and thereby they'll receive their natural *Colour* and *Tafte*.

About the End of *July*, the *London-Plumb, Plumb-Mordin, &c.* are ripe, after which comes all others in order, and continues till *September*.

Plumbs gather'd a Day or two before they are eaten, and kept in *Nettles*, eat much finer than when firft gather'd.

S E C T. XI.

Of the Native Place, Name, Expofition, and Culture of the Apple-Tree.

I. ACCORDING to the Obfervation of Sir *William Temple*, on the Conqueft of *Africk, Greece, Afia Minor*, and *Syria*, it appears, that foon after that Conqueft the *Romans* brought into *Italy* all Sorts of *Mala*, which we call *Apples*, and from thence were fent into divers other Parts, and *propagated* as other Fruits, *&c.*

Amongft the great *Variety* of *Englifh Fruits*, there is none fo *univerfal* as the *Apple*; for be *Land* of a *hot* and *dry, wet* and *cold* Nature, one or other of the Sorts will produce Fruit; and where Land is good, in very great Quantity.

The Excellency of the Liquor extracted from this Fruit, *is a* fufficient Encouragement for its Propagation, exclufive of its profitable Ufes at Table, in the Kitchen, *&c.*

Apples

Apples are increas'd, being *grafted* on *Crab-Stocks*, as before deliver'd; and are generally planted *Standards*, *Espaliers*, or *Dwarfs*, and best when the Land is a *fresh strong Loam*, with a good Bottom of *Brick-Earth*.

If *Apples* are grafted on *Paradise Stocks*, they will bear Fruit the *second* or *third Year*, and are best for *Dwarfs* or low *Espaliers*. 'Tis a common Practice amongst most *curious Gardeners* to plant small *Apple-Trees* grafted on *Paradise Stocks*, in large *Flower Pots*, or Tubes, wherein they produce Fruit very plentifully, being kept in small *Open Heads*, or *Dwarfs*; which are very great *Embellishments* of *Entrances*, *Partares*, *Cabinets*, &c.

The *Codlin* is a Kind of *Apple*, increas'd from *Suckers*, taken from its Root in the latter End of *October*, or Beginning of *November*, and is an excellent Fruit, both for its Earliness of ripening, and *good Services* in a *Family*. It may also be increas'd by *Cuttings*, cut off in *March*, and planted under a *North Wall*. The *Apple-Tree* does no Ways delight in being pruned in the *Winter* with a *Knife*, the Canker being commonly the next as takes Place, which soon kills the Tree; therefore, I advise, that in *May* and *June* you carefully observe to *rub* or *pinch* off all *luxuriant*, &c. Branches, and tie in others fit for Use, and thereby your Trees will be preserved from that Distemper.

The *best Season* for planting this Fruit is, when its Leaves are just fallen, *viz.* in *October*, at which Time 'tis best to plant the Cuttings of *Paradise Stocks*, under a *North Wall*, which being kept clean from Weeds, and water'd in the *Spring*, if very dry, will be fit to graft on in three Years. Their native Place is *France*.

If *Golden Pippins*, *Nonpareils*, *Holland Pippins*, *French Pippins*, &c. were planted against an *East Wall*, and their pruning perform'd in *May* and *June* by *pinching*, as I before directed, their *Fruit* would not only be *much finer* in Taste, but wonderfully *larger* and beautiful.

The *Kernels* of *Apples*, saved from such Fruit as were grafted on *Crab-Stocks*, and sown, most commonly produces a much worse Kind of Fruit then the *Mother-kind*, and very often perfect *Crabs* and *Wildings*. If you sow the *Kernels* as are saved from *Apples*, produced by a Seedling without grafting, the
Fruit

Fruit they produce are feldom either *Crab* or *Wilding*, but are often as good as the *Mother-Fruit*, and fometimes (tho' very feldom) better.

S E C T. XII.

Of the Vine; its Names, Culture, &c.

THIS *Glorious Plant* the VINE, when cultivated, is called by the *Greeks* ἄμπελ@ οἰνοφόρ@ ; by the *Latins Vites, Vinifera, Sativa,* and *Culta*; by the *Arabians Karin, Karni,* or *Harin*; by the *Italians Vite Venefera*; by the *Dutch Wiingaert,* or *Wiinftacke*; by the *French Vigne*; by the *Germans Weinreb*; and by the *Spaniards Vid,* or *Parm.*

'Tis propagated by *Layers,* or Cuttings, which Works are to be done in *October* : And in the Operation you muft obferve, that three or four *Buds* at leaft be in the Ground; for 'tis from them their Roots put forth. In the Choice of Cuttings obferve to take thofe as are of the laft Year's Shoot, *ftrong* and *vigorous,* which cut to fixteen or eighteen Inches long, and plant under an Eaft Wall, leaving but two Buds out of Ground, in Rows, about a Foot or fifteen Inches afunder ; and in the Rows, at the Diftance of eight Inches. When your Cuttings are thus planted, cover the ground between them with *Horfe-Dung,* about five or fix Inches thick, and if the *Spring* prove very dry, you muft now and then give them Water, fo as to keep them moift, which a Vine requires at its ftriking Root; and if your Land be warm and light, in two Years Time will be fit to tranfplant.

If the *Cuttings of Vines* be planted in the open Air, without the Help of any Shade, and are about two Foot, or two Foot and a half in Length, and all buried, two Buds excepted; fuch Cuttings kept *moift* in the *Spring,* will grow and thrive very well; but in this Operation, you muft obferve, that you lay the Cuttings in *floping,* the loweft Part

3

not to exceed ten Inches, or a *Foot* in Depth, and to bend the
upper Part in such a Manner, as for the two Eyes or Buds as
are left out of the Ground to stand Perpendicular.

The warmest *Exposure* is the *best* for the *Vine,* and therefore should be always defended by *Woods, Hills, &c.*

The best Soil for *Vines* is a *rich warm Loam,* mix'd with
fresh *hot Sand,* or *Gravel,* or instead thereof, *Sea-Coal Ashes,
Wood Ashes, Brick-Rubbish, Lime,* or *Drift Sand.* When
you prepare Borders of this Mixture, they need not be
more than four Foot in Breadth, or deeper than one Foot;
for those Juices of the Earth as nourishes the *Vine,* lies very
near to the Surface of the Ground.

The best Season for *planting Vines* is *October,* or Beginning
of *February,* if the Weather be open; but of the two, I recommend the *Autumn* Planting before that of the *Spring.* When
Vines are remov'd from a *Nursery, &c.* great Care must be
taken to *preserve the Roots* from the *parching Winds,* and that
they be not very dry at Planting. So soon as *Vines* are taken
out of the Ground, they should be packed up with *wet Moss,*
or *wet Hay,* and closely bound in *Mats,* which will preserve
their Roots a long Time if need be.

When you plant *Vines,* prune the Ends of their Roots with
Discretion, and to the Top or Head of the Plant leave but
two or three Joints at most; and when in *April* they begin to
shoot, make choice of the two strongest Shoots, which preserve, and the others displace; as also other small Shoots at
all Times, that thereby those two Branches may have the
whole Nourishment, which will enable them to produce *Fruit*
much sooner than had they been weaken'd by other Branches as
would have robb'd them of their Strength.

To plant *Vines* at such Distances as they will fill in Time,
as eighteen or twenty Feet, (their Branches being laid in a
horizontal Position,) is losing the Use of a great deal of Wal-
ling for several Years; therefore, to prevent such Losses, I advise that you plant your Vines at ten Foot apart; and when
they meet, and want Room, to cut away so much of the intermediate Vine (*viz.* the middlemost of every three) as will
give sufficient Room for the others to extend themselves. And
although Mr. *Lawrence* discommends the Practice of now and
then laying down Branches to *strike Root, &c.* yet I cannot
but

but *commend the Practice*; for thereby, as *old Wood*, or *Plants fails*, they are immediately fucceeded by thofe new ones, and the Wall kept full of Wood. The Objection made by Mr. *Lawrence* againft thofe *Layers*, being directed perpendicularly, is but for the firft Year; for the Shoots afterwards produc'd by them, may be led *horizontally*, or otherwife, as the *Pruner* pleafes.

'Tis true, that the *horizontal Nailing of Trees* greatly checks the *Sap*, and caufes the Branches of many Trees to bear much fooner; but for *Vines*, I am certain that although they are luxuriant, and nail'd exactly perpendicular, will in many Places produce wonderful Grapes, and in very great Quantity; witnefs the South-Wall of the honourable Mr. Johnstone at *Twickenham*, next the Road leading to *Richmond* in *Surry*; whofe Grapes are ever in the greateft Perfection, both for Goodnefs and Quantity, and are always nailed perpendicularly. I could mention divers other Places, who nails in the fame Manner with great Succefs, but for the prefent let the preceding fuffice.

The vigorous Nature of a Vine is fuch, that though the Branches are led up a Wall of twelve or fourteen Feet in Height, yet the Fruit at the Top hath fufficient Quantity of Juices for its Nourifhment, and is not inferior to that as grows within three or four Feet of the Ground. To plant *Vines* againft low Walls of four or five Foot high, as Mr. *Lawrence* directs, at his Diftance of fix or feven Yards, and not to make good with Layers, &c. would prove in the End to be a very great *Lofs* and Difappointment to the Planter, which *Experience will prove*.

'Tis good to have your young *Vines* out of *rich Nurferies*, that is richer than wherein they are to be planted, that thereby at firft Planting they may receive a fmall Check; for too great Vigour at firft Planting is always bad.

The beft Seafon for the *general pruning of Vines* is at the *Fall* of their *Leaf*; but if then neglected, not to exceed the Middle of *February* at lateft. The moft vigorous Branches are thofe as produce the Fruit, which muft *carefully be preferved*, and the fmall fruitlefs Branches cut entirely out.

M   Such

Such Branches as are very ftrong may be allowed two Foot in Length ; and others of lefs Vigour, to be fhorter, as a Foot, fifteen Inches, *&c.* according to their Strength and Vigour.

In the Cutting of a *Vine,* obferve that you cut about an Inch above the *Bud,* and that the Cut be on the *Back* thereof; fo that when the *Sap* moves in the *Spring,* it by running may not *hurt* or *damage* the *Bud;* and obferve further, that 'tis beft to make choice of fuch Buds were you top a Branch, as will admit of the Cut or Slope-Part to be next to the Wall, as well as behind the Bud; for when the Cut is vifible, it is not only more expos'd to the Prejudice of Weather, but is alfo a difagreeable Sight; therefore, if you make choice of fore-right Buds, they will anfwer the End.

In the Nailing of Vines, or any other Fruit-Tree, *never make ufe of Leather* for *Shreds;* the beft is, *Lift,* or *Cloth,* and obferve that you do not nail the Shred tight about the Branch, but leave room for it to fwell in its Growth. The Diftance that you nail the Branches of Vines one from the other, muft not be lefs than nine Inches, nor more than one Foot.

The Fruit of *Vines* is always produced by the laft Year's Wood, at one or more of the three firft Buds from the old Wood; therefore when *Vines* are once got in a *fruitful State,* you need not leave their Shoots more than four or five Buds in Length at moft.

For the well *Management* of *Vines* in *Summer,* obferve this Rule, That no Kind of Branch be fuffer'd to grow, as is not fit and perfectly neceffary for Wood, Fruit, or Shelter.

Therefore in *May* be diligent to pick off all fmall weak Shoots, which will put out in many Places, and if not difplaced, rob the Fruit of its Nourifhment; alfo nail in all ufeful Branches, and in your *Vineyards* tie up the leading Shoots to Stakes. In *June* (not in *May,* as Mr. *Bradley* directs in his *New Im-provements of Planting and Gardening,* as he calls them, *pag.* 8.) is the beft Time to ftop the *luxuriant Growth* of the *Vine,* by nipping off the Branches at two or three Joints beyond the Fruit, and to make choice of fuch vigorous Branches as are required to fill empty Places, to be nailed in, without be-ing ftopp'd by *Nipping* or *Pinching,* except they are of very

great

great Lengths: Alfo nail clofe to the Wall all Branches with Fruit, and difplace all weak ones when they appear as before directed; but obferve that the Fruit is *not* thereby *laid open* to the *Sun*, which will now either *deftroy* or fpoil its Growth.

N. B. *The beft Grapes are always produced by vigorous Branches at the fourth or fifth Joint.*

In *July, Vines* are in their *full Strength and Vigour*; therefore keep them carefully pruned of falfe Wood, as is faid before, that the Fruit may not be deprived of its proper Heat and Nourifhment; and about the Middle of this Month examine all vigorous Shoots pruned at *Midfummer,* whereon you'll find fecondary Shoots from their feveral Buds, which difplace, the uppermoft excepted, prun'd off at one or two Buds Length, to admit Nature's exerting herfelf in its laft Shoot of *Autumn*, and to preferve the Lofs of Fruit or Wood from thofe Branches.

'Tis abfolutely neceffary that ftrict Regard be had to *Summer Pruning,* that a fufficient Number of vigorous Shoots be laid in to *fucceed* fuch *old ones* as will be cut out in the *Winter;* and although *Vines* will produce *Grapes* from *Knots of old Wood*, yet they are *never fo good* as thofe produced from *ftrong and vigorous* Branches.

Great Care muft be taken to tie up all ufeful Branches of *Vines* planted againft *Efpaliers,* or in *Vineyards,* and alfo to difplace by *Pinching* all ufelefs weak Branches, as directed for Vines againft Walls.

In *Auguft* give them the laft Pruning, and keep the Fruit *clofe* to the *Wall,* difcreetly fhaded with Leaves, fo as to partly expofe them to the *Sun,* and preferve them from the *cold* Nights.

In *September* the *Vine* produces its *delicious Fruit,* which muft be very dry when gathered, otherwife they foon grow moldy and rotten.

Grapes gather'd dry, and preferved from the Froft, will keep a long Time; but 'tis beft to gather them a little before they are ripe, and to hang them on a Line, with the End of the Stalk feal'd with Sealing-Wax.

SECT. XIII.

Of the Cherry, its Name, Culture, &c.

I. IT appears by the Obſervation of Sir *William Temple,* that the *Cherry* is a Native of *Pontus,* a Province in *Aſia Minor,* firſt brought from thence *Ann. Rom.* 683. by *Lucullus* into *Italy;* and about *one hundred Years* after 'twas introduced into *England.* Its Name in *Greek* is κεράσℴ; in *Arabick, Seraſic* ; in *Latin, Ceraſus,* or *Ceraſum*; in *Spaniſh, Ceraſas,* or *Guindas*; in *Italian, Ciregie*; in *Dutch, Kriken* ; in *French, Ceriſes,* or *Guines ;* and by the *Germans, Kirſen,* or *Kirſchen.*

Amongſt the ſeveral Kinds of *Cherries,* the *May Duke, Holman's Duke,* and *Lukeword,* deſerve a Place againſt the *beſt Wall*; the others will do very well *Dwarfs, Eſpaliers, half* and *whole Standards,* the *Morella Cherry* excepted, which is beſt againſt a *North-Wall,* and if preſerved on the Trees till the End of *Auguſt,* becomes a *rich* and *noble Fruit* for the Table; for by its long hanging, loſes moſt of its *Acidity,* or Sourneſs.

All *Cherries* are propagated from the *Black Cherry,* by being either *budded* or *grafted* thereon, and delight in a light rich Loam.

The leſs *Cherries* are pruned, the better they like it ; but however, where weak or luxuriant Branches happen, they muſt be govern'd by the Knife; as alſo the Ends of leading Shoots, which muſt be ſhorten'd to eight or nine Inches. The beſt Time for this Work is *October.*

When *Cherry-Trees* take to *bear very early,* and grow but little, 'tis beſt to *pull* off *moſt of the Bloom,* and ſhorten the Branches, which will cauſe the Tree to *ſhoot* with freſh Vigour; or if your Trees are Bark-bound, what ſome call Hidebound, 'tis beſt to *ſlit* open the *Bark* of the Body from Top to Bottom, and its large Branches alſo, with the Point of your

3   Knife ;

Knife; but obferve to do it on the Side, and not in the Front of the Tree: Be careful to difplace Suckers, and cut away all Tops of Branches infected with the *Black Fly, &c.*

In the End of *May* the *early* fmall *May-Cherry* is ripe, after which comes the *Early Duke, Holman's Duke,* and all others; of which the laft are the *Englifh, Carnation,* and *Morella.*

If *Duke Cherries* were planted againft *North-Eaft, North-Weft,* and *North Walls,* they would produce Plenty of Fruit when thofe of the *South-Wall* were all gone; but they muft be *covered* in the *Spring,* when in Bloom, during the Time of *cold Winds.*

N. B. *That the Morella, and Early fmall May-Cherry produce their Fruit at the very Ends of their Shoots; fo that they muft not be topp'd in Pruning, as other Cherries are.*

S E C T. XIV.

Of Goofeberries, their Culture, &c.

GOoseberries, are a kind of Fruit as were formerly ufed for *Sauce* to *Green Geefe,* and for that Reafon, by the *Antients,* were called *Goofeberries.*

This Fruit is fo agreeable in its Nature, as to be contented in any Soil wherein the *Cherry, Pear,* or *Apple* grows, and will live under their *Shade* with great Pleafure.

The beft Kinds are thofe mention'd in my Catalogue of Fruit, which would be greatly improved, was they bred up in *little Dwarfs,* as we do *Apples, Pears, &c.* and the Branches not fuffer'd to run a-crofs each other, or any to rife in the Middle; and befides the Improvement gain'd in the Goodnefs of the Fruit, they make a very agreeable Figure to the Eye, on which Account I place them in the Borders of the Fruit-Garden.

N. B. They are increafed by *Suckers,* or *Cuttings.*

SECT.

SECT. XV.

Of Currants, their Culture, &c.

THE feveral Sorts of *Currants* are three, (*Vide the Ca-talogue,*) which are in general increafed by *Suckers,* and delight in the fame Land as the *Goofeberry.*

If Currants were alfo bred in fmall Dwarfs, as I before mention'd of the Goofeberry, the Fruit would be greatly im-proved, both in Size and Tafte, and their Forms very hand-fome in open Borders.

If the large *White* and *Red Dutch Currants* are planted and nail'd againft a Full *South-Wall,* and the Wood kept thin, they will produce wonderful pleafant Fruit, and very large; fo likewife if they are planted againft a *North Wall,* they will produce good Fruit till the Middle of *December.*

In the Management of both *Goofeberry* and *Currant,* Care muft be taken to keep them free from *old Wood*; for the beft Fruit is produc'd by the *young Wood,* which ripens in *July.*

SECT. XVI.

Of Rasberries, their Culture, &c.

OF *Rasberries* there be three Kinds, *viz.* the *Red,* the *Black,* or *Purple,* and the *White*; all which delight in good ftrong rich Land.

They are in general increafed by *Suckers,* or *Runners,* and fhould be planted in fingle Rows at three Foot and a half Di-ftance each Row from the other, and in the Rows at a Foot or fourteen Inches afunder.

The

The beft Time to plant them is *November*, (and not *March*, as Mr. *Bradley* directs in his third Part of *New Improvements, Page* 50. for the drying *March* Winds would greatly hurt their Roots:) Neither will Rasberries fucceed very well, as he fays they do, when planted in beds, each having three Rows at a Foot and a half Diftance from each other; for by their being fo thick planted, they cannot be digged every Winter to let in Nourifhment, *&c.* nor can they be helped with good Dung, or kept to fingle Roots, as they fhould be, to fucceed (as he calls it) very well.

'Tis beft to plant *Suckers*, or *Runners*, of one *Summer's Growth*, and to prune off the very fmall fibrous Roots, leaving the large Roots to about five or fix Inches in Length, and the Top ten Inches, or one Foot.

When you prune the *Roots* and *Tops*, as before directed, take Care that you do not break off that Bud at the upper Part of the Root, as is to produce Wood for the next Year; for if that Bud is broke off, 'tis in vain to plant the Plant; therefore, as you plant Rasberries, be fure that every Plant hath its *leading Bud* at Bottom, and then there may be Hopes of Succefs.

The firft Year they will produce Branches or Shoots about two Foot and a half high, which in the *Autumn* (if not prevented) will produce Fruit at their extreme Parts, which I believe is no wife advantageous to them; therefore I advife that fuch Shoots be topp'd as foon as the Bloom appears, except that the Curious is inclin'd to preferve the Fruit for the fake of its Novelty, more than its Goodnefs.

The fecond Year they will fhoot with greater Vigour than the firft; and the third Year greater than the fecond, *&c.* You muft be very careful in deftroying the Suckers, not only between Row and Row, but alfo between Plant and Plant in the Rows, and thereby you will have the Fruit in great Perfection.

Every Year's Wood makes its *Exit* immediately after it hath produced its Fruit, which *dead Wood* is beft broken out in the *frofty Weather* of the approaching Winter.

The fucceeding Shoots being now got up, are to be *topp'd in March*, cutting off all the upper Part as appears weak, fo that the Remains will be about three or four Foot high.

N. B.

N. B. Before I conclude the Difcourfe of the *Rasberry*, I muft admonifh you not to plant this Fruit in Land, as is troubled with the Weed called *Vervine*, or *Bearvine*, which is of the climbing Tribe, and will actually fmother and fpoil both Fruit, Root, and Branch, in a very fhort Time. *Couch-Grafs* is alfo a *very bad Weed* to difplace, when once got amongft the Roots of your *Rasberries. N. B.* The *Rasberry* ripens in *July*, and continues for three Weeks or a Month, and fometimes longer, when on *rich ftrong Land*. Note alfo, that *Horfe* or *Cow-Dung*, well-rotted, is very good for *Rasberries*; but *Sea-Coal Afhes*, if dry Weather comes on them, is *prefent Death*; therefore Care muft be taken to avoid that Manure.

S E C T. XVII.

Of Strawberries, their Culture, &c.

OF STRAWBERRIES there be divers Kinds, as the *Scarlet*, the *Wood*, the *Hautboy*, the *Green*, and the *White*; which two laft are not fo preferrable as the preceding three, whofe Culture I am now to explain. 1. The *Scarlet Strawberry* is a great Bearer, and an excellent Fruit; it delights in a moift, frefh, mellow Land, and loves much Water when in Bloom. The beft Seafon to plant *Strawberries* in, general is at *Bartholomew-Tide*, if the Weather permits, or as foon after as poffible; and by this early Planting they will produce half a Crop the firft Year.

N. B. *The wonderful Difcovery of Mr.* Bradley's, *of his making Plantations of Strawberries in* April *and* May *with good Succefs, and to gather Fruit from them, fo prodigioufly foon after, as the fecond* June *following, is very furprizing.*

I cannot conclude the Culture of this Plant, without mentioning, that I have made Plantations of them (even) in *June* (when the Fruit has been near ripe on the Plants) with good Succefs;

and

and foon afterwards gather'd very good Fruit from them. And what then? why nothing; for 'tis, and has been for many Years paſt, a common Practice, to my certain Knowledge, amongſt divers Gard'ners to plant at that Time, their Multitude of Buſineſs nota dmitting of planting ſooner. But to return:

Strawberries in general, do not love *rich Land* equally; therefore that Preparation of Soil as will ſuit this Kind, will *deſtroy* or *ruin* another; as for Inſtance, *Land* richly dung'd produces the beſt *Wood* and *Hautboy-Strawberries*; and if *Scarlet-Strawberries* be planted therein, the Product will be nothing but an *Infinite Quantity of Leaves*, with little or no Fruit; and on the contrary, if *Scarlet Strawberries* be planted in freſh mellow Land without Dung, they will produce Fruit in great Plenty. Hence it appears, that the judicious Mr. *Bradley* knew nothing of the Culture of Strawberries, when he ſo much depended upon the ſuppoſed Practice of the *Hammerſmith Gardeners*, whoſe Rules, as he calls them, he hath preſcribed to the World, for the Management of Strawberries, without taking the leaſt Notice of the different Soils they delight in. *Vide* his *New Improvements,* Part III. Page 48.

His Directions there given is general, *viz.* the ſame Land for the *Scarlet* as for the *Wood* and *Hautboy,* which muſt be *dung'd* too with *Horſe-Dung* and *Sea-Coal Aſhes,* and digg'd or trench'd in the Ground in *February,* and then to plant the *Strawberry Plants* or *Runners* (by him called *Slips,* a new Term) therein, at about *eight Inches* apart. Now all Mankind as are *Gardeners,* knows that the *Scarlet-Strawberry* and *Hautboy* are never planted nearer than a *Foot* one Way, and *fifteen Inches* the other, at leaſt, and very often *eighteen Inches:* But for *Wood-Strawberries* his Diſtance of *eight Inches* is very right, and his Preparation of Land alſo, if they have no other Strawberries at *Hammerſmith,* than Woods and Hautboys. I own I have made a long Digreſſion, and it is high Time to return to ·to the Culture of Strawberries in general, which is the Subject that led me into it.

Scarlet-Strawberries muſt be planted in Rows, about fifteen or eighteen Inches apart, and their Diſtance in the Rows one Foot. They muſt be carefully *ſtring'd* all *Summer,* and *digg'd* between in the *Winter*; and being thus kept in ſingle Roots, will

N   pro-

produce wonderful fine Fruit very early, for the Space of four or five Years, but not longer. If this Kind of *Strawberry* be admitted to run thick in a Bed, they will produce fine coloured Fruit, but not so *soon* as the *single Roots* by a Fortnight; and in dry Seasons are very apt to burn up.

The *Hautboy* hath the same Duration and Management as the *Scarlet*, it differing only in the Goodness of Land.

The *Wood-Strawberry* delights in a very rich Land, and are planted in Beds, somewhat more than three Feet wide, their Rows from each other being about eight Inches; and as the *Scarlet* and *Hautboy-Strawberries* are generally kept to single Roots, these are let run together in their Beds all in a Mat, and the Alleys between them digg'd in the Winter.

N. B. That when you plant *Wood-Strawberries*, 'tis best to plant the Runners as are got from Woods, where the Land as they grow in is very poor, and not such Runners as may be had from old planted Strawberries of the Guarden, for they degenerate in six Years Time.

I cannot by any Means commend the Practice of the *Hammersmith Gardeners* (as mention'd by Mr. *Bradley*, Part III. Page 49.) of their planting *Savoys* and *Cabbages* for *Winter* in the *Alleys* of the *Strawberry* Beds, whose Roots doth very much exhaust the Goodness of the Ground; and beggar the *Strawberries* growing on the Sides of each Bed.

Wherever Plantations of *Strawberries* are made, great Care should be taken to have *Plenty of Water* very easily whilst they are in *Bloom*, and during the Ripening of their *Fruit* also; otherwise in dry Seasons, for Want of Water, the *Crop* will soon be over.

If *Strawberries* of three Years Growth be planted in Flower-Pots, and placed in a *gentle Hot-Bed*, about the Middle of *January*, they will produce Fruit in *March*.

You must observe in their Management, that they are *not over-heated*, that they are not confin'd too much, and *destroy'd by the Steam*, but give them enough of *Air*, so as not to let in *Frosts*, *cold Winds*, &c. that they have *moderate Waterings* with warm Water when in Bloom, and not stifled for want of *Air*.

SECT.

S E C T. XVIII.

Of *Barberries, their Culture*, &c.

OF BARBERRIES there are *two Kinds*, the one with *Stones*, the other *without Stones*; which laſt is eſteem'd the beſt. The Soil it delights in, is a good mellow Loam: 'Tis increas'd by *Suckers* or *Layers*, and makes a beautiful Hedge. The Bloom of this Fruit appears very *beautiful* in the *Spring*, as well as its Cluſters of *Red Berries* towards the *Autumn*, which muſt then be gather'd for Uſe when the *Dew* is off, and are perfectly dry.

S E C T. XIX.

Of *Walnuts, Cheſnuts, Philberds,* and *Hazel.*

(1.) OF WALNUTS there be divers Kinds, as the *Bird-Walnut*, whoſe *Kernel* is the exact *Shape of a Bird*, and therefore ſo called. (2.) The *French Walnut*, a Fruit of a very large Growth, thick ſhell'd, its Kernel but ſmall, and very inſipid, and therefore much better for pickling than for the Table. (3.) The common *Engliſh Walnuts*, of which ſome are very good, others good for nothing, *&c.* as 'tis in all other Fruits in general. But their Culture is all the ſame.

In

I. In order to obtain good *Walnuts*, I advise, that you make Choice of the very best you can find, both for Goodness of *Kernels* and *Thinness* of *Shell*.

The *Mother-Tree* being pitch'd on, gather its *Nuts* when they are observed to fall from the Tree, and lay them by till their *Green Husks* cracks; at which Time peel them off, and dry them in a convenient Place, keeping them *turn'd* every Day, and be sure that no Water comes near them at any Time, for that will destroy the Kernel. Your Nuts being dry'd, put them into a Bed of *moist Sand* placed in the *Green-House*, *Tool-House*, &c. where *no Wet* can come to them.

About the Beginning of *January*, if the Weather be open, *moisten the Sand* moderately, which will cause them to prepare themselves for planting in the Beginning of *February*, at which Time they are to be placed in good fresh Land that is *not hot* and *dry*, at the square *Distance* of *six Inches*, and about *three Inches* in Depth.

'Tis the Practice of many to plant or sow them in their *Husks*, and to *soak* or steep them in Water; which I can no wise commend; for, to my Loss, I have had the Experience.

During all the first and second Years (for so long they must remain in the Seed-Bed) keep them very clean from Weeds, and in very dry Seasons let them have moderate Waterings; 'twill greatly advance their Growth.

At the End of two Years take them out of the Seed-Bed, and prune of all *Tap* or *Downright Roots* and Side Branches, but *never* touch the *leading Shoot*; then plant them out in the *Nurse-ry* in Rows at three Foot apart, and the Plants in the Rows, at eighteen Inches asunder, keeping them clear from Weeds, and digg'd every *Winter*, to keep the Ground mellow, and let the Winter's Rains to their Roots. When your Trees are got to be five or six Foot high, they may be *inoculated* with any Kind you approve off, which will cause them to bear much sooner. When you plant a *Walnut-Tree*, observe to prune the End of every Root, to cut away all as are inclinable to grow downwards, to place every Root as near a *Horizontal Position* as you can, and as shallow as conveniently may be; for 'tis the *want* of *Horizontal Roots* as occasions their long Growth before they bear Fruit; and that you prune off all Side Branches, but never prune or top the Head or leading Shoots. And the same must be observed

ferved in the Chefnuts, and all other Trees as have a large Pith.
N. B. I advife, that *Walnut-Trees* be forthwith planted with
all poffible Expedition after taking up, for their Roots are of fuch
a *fpongy Nature,* that they are prefently *mouldy* and *dead;*
therefore till they are planted, preferve their Roots from *Winds,*
Sun, and *Air.*

The proper Seafon for planting the *Walnut* is *October.* It delights in a very *deep Soil* of a *dry rich Nature,* on a gravelly
Bottom. 'Twill alfo thrive on a *Gravel* mix'd with *Loam,* or
on *Clay* naturally *mix'd* with *Stones* or *Chalk,* but will *not* profper in *fhallow Land,* or on a *ftiff Clay.*

II. The *Chefnuts,* both *Spanifh* and *Horfe-Chefnuts,* are Trees
as covet much Room to extend themfelves, and are very beautiful Trees, efpecially in their Time of Bloom.

For the Propagation of thefe Plants, Care muft be taken to
procure the *Nuts* at the Time of ripening, and to take their
Husks off, as directed for the *Walnut;* that they be perfectly
dried, and put into *Sand* a little moift, where they muft remain
till the Beginning of *February,* not forgetting to give them a
little Moifture about *Chriftmas,* or Firft of *January,* to prepare
them for planting at that Time. The Manner of planting them
is exactly the fame as the *Walnut,* and delights in the fame Soils.
This Tree is very fubject to put out many Side-Branches near
the Bottom, which will grow if laid in the Ground, but never
makes fuch good Trees as thofe raifed from Seed.

N. B. That you do not fteep the Nuts in Water, (as many
do;) for fuch Nuts as thefe as are not of a quick Growth, are
killed thereby, the Water caufing the Kernel to fwell to haftily,
and crack before the *leading Bud* has prepared it felf; and befides,
it often *mouldies* and rots the Kernel entirely. Therefore have
fpecial Regard to all Seeds as are not of a quick Growth, that
they have not too much Wet at the firft fetting out.

III. Of *Hazel* or *Philberds,* which are excellent Fruit in their
Seafon.

They are increas'd by *Nuts,* as the preceding, or by *Suckers*
or *Layers*: They will thrive in moft Kinds of Soils, provided
they

they are not too *wet*, but beſt on *dry Ground*; therefore I recommend them for *Hedges*, planted on dry Banks.　There is
two Kinds of *Philberds*, *viz.* the *White* and the *Red*, of
which the Red is the moſt valuable.

S E C T. XX.

Of Quinces,　their Culture, &c.

AMONGST all the ſeveral Fruits for the *Kitchen* and
Conſervatory Uſes,　none are more *delicate* than the
Quince.

Of *Quinces* there are ſix Sorts, *viz.* the *Portugal Apple-Quince*,
the *Portugal Pear-Quince*, the *Barberry-Quince*, the *Engliſh-
Quince*, the *Lyons-Quince*, and the *Brunſwick-Quince*.

1ſt, The *Portugal Apple-Quince*, a fine, large, yellow
Fruit, tender, and ſoon boiled, and is eſteemed the very beſt.

2dly, The *Portugal Pear-Quince*, as good as the former,
but different in Shape, it being of the Form of a Pear.

3dly, The *Barberry-Quince*, an excellent Fruit, but ſmall.

4thly, The *Engliſh-Quince*, the very worſt of all: 'Tis a harſh
Fruit, and covered with a Coat of *Down* like *Cotton*.

5thly, The *Lyons-Quince*, a fine, large, yellow Fruit.　And,

6thly, The *Brunſwick-Quince*, a fine, large, white Fruit.

N. B. That the four *laſt* are all inferior to the two *firſt*.

The *Quince* (as many of the preceding Fruits) hath great
Variety of Names:　In *Greek*, 'tis called μηλέα κυδωνία; in
Latin, *Malus Cydonia*, or *Malus Cathonea*, from an Iſland in
the *Grecian Sea*, from whence 'tis ſaid to have been firſt
brought:　But *Pliny* affirms, that it received its Name of
Malus Cydonia from *Cydone*, a Town in *Certe*:　The *Arabians* call it *Seffargel*; the *French*, *Pome de Coing*; the *Spaniards*, *Membrillio*, and oftentimes *Marmello*; the *Italians*,

Melo-

Melocotognio; the *Germans, Kuttenopffel;* and the *Dutch, Que-Apple.*

This Fruit is raifed either from *Layers, Suckers,* or *Cuttings,* and delights in a *moift Soil.* 'Tis beft when grafted, although it is a natural Fruit; for by the Check given to the Sap thereby, it produces Fruit much fooner.

N. B. That the Cuttings, or Cions, muft be taken from an old bearing Tree, as is of the beft (or at leaft a very good) Kind.

The Seafon for planting this Fruit-Tree is *October, November, &c.* as for other Fruit-Trees.

SECT. XXI.

Of the Mulberry-Tree, its Culture, &c.

OF *Mulberries* there are two Kinds, *viz.* the *Black* and the *White:* The *Black Mulberry* is a Tree of a very flow Growth; but its Fruit is *excellent,* and 'tis a very great Bearer. This Kind delights in good mellow Land; and is beft increas'd by Layers; wherein obferve, that you let the Layers remain upon the Stools, or Mother-Plant, for *two Years* after laying, but beft when three Years; for the Roots are not perfected in the firft Year; and therefore if you take them up (as is ufual) at one Year's End, 'tis very feldom that ever one in ten comes to any Thing. The Time to lay them down is in *March;* but 'tis beft to plant them at the *Fall of their Leaf,* and to well mulfh them with *Horfe-Dung* afterwards, to pre-ferve their Roots from the *Winters Frofts.* In the training up this Plant, you muft obferve the very firft Year of its Shoot-ing, to place a ftraight *Stake* perpendicular by its Side, againft which the Shoot muft be tied with *Baft, Mat, &c.* For the Nature of this Tree is fuch, that if this Care is not taken, 'twill grow very crooked and deformed, as they generally are when young in moft Places. If *Cuttings* of this Plant are put

in.

in the Ground in *March*, and not taken up again till two Years after, they will make good Plants,   But obferve in the Operation, that the Cuttings be *two Foot at leaft* in Length, that they be placed *floping* in the Ground, fo as not to be in any Part deeper than one Foot at moft, leaving but *two Buds* out of the Ground ; and though the *Mulberry* is of fuch a flow Growth, as never to produce (or at leaft very feldom) Shoots of one Year, two Foot in Length, yet that is not to be regarded: The two and three Years Wood, under the laft Year's Wood, is as good for this Purpofe as any. 'Tis faid, that this Plant is raifed from Seed alfo; but I never faw the Practice, and therefore can fay nothing thereof.

The *White Mulberry* is of a much more vigorous Growth than the *Black*: It delights in good Land as the other, and is increafed by *Seed* or *Layers ;* but its Fruit is *very infipid*, and 'tis a bad Bearer; fo that upon the whole, I cannot recommend this Plant, except 'tis for Variety's fake, and to help fill up the Quarters of a *Wildernefs*, or for the Ufe of its Leaves for the Silkworms. I cannot but acknowledge that I am of the fame Opinion as the ingenious Botaniſt Mr. *Bradley*, who, in his *New Improvements, Part* iii. *Page* 19. believes, That if the *Black Mulberry* was either *grafted, budded,* or *inarched,* upon the *White Mulberry,* much finer Trees might be raifed, and in much lefs Time than by Layers, Cuttings, or Seed, the common Way.

S E C T. XXII.

Of the Cornelion Cherry.

THIS Kind of Fruit is very *beautiful* in a Wildernefs ; 'tis increafed either by *Layers* or *Seed, viz.* its *Stones,* which oftentimes lie two Years in the Ground before they fpring. The Layers are to be laid down in *February*; and the Stones to be fowed in a Bed of fine Mold, cover'd about two Inches thick, as foon as the Fruit is ripe.

S E C T.

S E C T. XXIII.

Of Medlars.

MEDLARS are a pleafant Fruit, whereof there are feveral Kinds, *viz.* the *Common Englifh*, a fmall Fruit; the *Dutch Medlar*, a large Fruit, and a good Bearer; and the *Neopolitan Medlar*, a Fruit without Stones, very plentiful in *Italy*, and but a Stranger to our *Englifh Climate*. They in general love a rich Soil, and are propagated by being either grafted on the *White* or *Hawthorn* in *March*, or inarch'd in *May*, or budded in *July*.

S E C T. XXIV.

Of the Service-Tree.

THE SERVICE makes a glorious Tree, and is very beautiful when planted in Walks; they produce fine Clufters of Fruit in *September* and *October*, which, when ripe, are as if they were *rotten*, though not fo. This Tree is propagated by *Suckers* or *Seed*. If you increafe them by Seed, when the Fruit is ripe rub off the Pulp, by rolling them in Sand; after which dry the Stones or Seed in the *Sun* or *Air*, and put them into *Sand*, as directed for the *Walnut*, and in *January* fow them in a moift Border, covering the Seed about two Inches thick with fine Earth.

When they have been *two Years* in the Seed-Bed, tranfplant them into a *Nurfery*, (as the *Walnut*,) always minding to keep them clean from Weeds; and if your Border has an *Eaft Expofition*, 'tis much *better* than to be fully expos'd to the *South Sun*.

O

Sun. It delights in rich ſtrong Ground, and when grown to *ſix Foot high*, ſhould be *budded*, with Buds taken from a Tree, as is known to be of a *good Kind:* They will produce Fruit *much ſooner*, in *greater Plenty*, and much finer in Taſte.

COROLLARIES, *or additional Directions.*

I. WHEN at any Time 'tis ſaid that a particular Fruit is beſt againſt a *South*, *Eaſt*, or *Weſt Wall*, it is not to be underſtood that thoſe Walls muſt be *direct* to thoſe *Cardinal Points*, but to be within the *Declination of ten Degrees*, or *fifteen* at moſt, either *Eaſtward* or *Weſtward* of South *Walls*, or to the *South* of *Eaſt* and *Weſt* Walls.

II. The *Eaſt Expoſition* is better than the *Weſt*, becauſe the early Rays of the *Sun* diſperſes the *cold Dews* from off the Fruit in a Morning, which the *Weſt* is chill'd with, being not diſperſed till late in the Day.

III. If Borders for Fruit-Trees be well prepared with freſh *untried Earth*, (ſuch as is mention'd in the Section of Planting,) and made *ſix Foot broad*, and *fifteen Inches* in Depth, 'tis ſufficient for any Fruit-Tree.

IV. Obſerve that the Earth wherein young Trees are planted, be not mix'd with new *Dung* of any Kind; for 'tis *Poiſon* to the Roots of every Tree, and very often preſent Death.

V. *Gravel-Walks*, *Brick-Pavements*, &c. before Walls reflects an additional Heat to them, and greatly helps the Ripening of the Fruit.

VI. *Brick-Walls* are the beſt for Fruit, as well as the moſt beautiful: Their Height above Ground ſhould not exceed *ten Feet* at moſt. 'Tis much better for all Wall Fruit in general to be planted thin, extending themſelves *horizontally* to a good Length, than to be planted thick, and be carried *perpendicularly*, and in a ſmall Time *rob* each other of their proper Nouriſhment, as has been obſerved before.

VII.

VII. If *poſſible*, keep all new-planted Trees well water'd, during the *Months* of *April, May, June,* and *July.*

VIII. All Fruit-Trees planted for to make *Dwarfs*, muſt have their *perpendicular Shoots* pinch'd off in *Spring*, that thereby they may break out into *Side* or *Horizontal Branches*, and form the Tree deſired.

IX. *Apples*, when in *Dwarfs* or *Eſpaliers*, muſt have the ſame Pruning as the Pear.

X. All Kind of *Dwarf-Trees* muſt be kept open, entirely free from Wood, as are not *horizontal*, and their Height ſhould never exceed five Foot.

XI. To preſerve Fruit in its Bloom, place *Pannels* of *Reed* (of the Height of your *Wall*, and about four Foot in Breadth) at about twenty Yards Diſtance from one another; but don't fix them ſquare to the Wall, for that will rather confine the Winds than diſcharge them: If the acute Angle be about thirty five or forty Degrees, the Wind will ſlide away eaſily, which otherwiſe, when very ſtrong, would tear them all to Pieces, and eſpecially thoſe of a *South* Wall, when the Wind is at *Eaſt* or *Weſt*.

XII. To preſerve *Fruit* from *Winds*, whoſe Courſe is not parallel, but rather oppoſite to a Wall, 'tis beſt to cover the *Trees* with *Mats*, or *Sale-Cloths*, old *Blankets, &c.* and alſo in Time of *Froſts:* But always obſerve to uncover them in the Day-time, if it does not *freeze*, or *cold cutting Winds blow*, which muſt always be guarded againſt, be it *Night* or *Day*, 'tis the ſame, all ought to be cover'd.
N. B. *When you nail up thoſe Coverings, be ſure that you ſecure them by Nails, that the Wind don't blow them looſe, and by beating and flapping againſt the Wall, knock off moſt of the Bloſſoms.*
The ſeveral Inventions lately publiſh'd of *horizontal Shelters, &c.* are of ſome Uſe in ſtill Nights; but when the Tree is preſerved, as aforeſaid, which by divers *Experiments* I have

found

found to be the very beft Way, they are of no Ufe: Neither do *Dews* or *Rains* always fall perpendicular, (tho' 'tis their natural Courfe fo to do;) for by the Situation of *Winds* are obliged, when they blow, which is almoft always, to fteer fuch Courfes as they direct, and thereby affect the Wall-Fruit *in an Oblique*, and not a *perpendicular* Pofition *always*, as fuppofed.

And befides, 'tis evident, that although Dews are prejudicial when frozen on Trees in the Spring, yet when the Frofts are gone, they are a very great Nourifhment to Fruits ; and as Mr. Lawrence *did but only receive a Hint of thofe Horizontal Shelters from an ingenious Gentleman, of or near* Chel-fea, *who firft mentioned them to him, 'twas fomething very odd, that the Practice thereof fhould be recommended before it had been proved.*

XIII. 'Tis too often feen that many Fruit-Trees are planted in a Soil as they do not delight in; therefore at fuch Times obferve what Fruits do agree beft with fuch a Soil, and convert your Tree to the fame by *Grafting, Inoculation, &c.*

XIV. There is nothing fo much *adds to*, or *fubftracts from*, the Goodnefs of Fruit, as the Goodnefs or Badnefs of *Soils*.

XV. *Hot* and *dry Summers* caufes Fruit to ripen before its *natural Seafon*, and *wet* and *cold Summers* the contrary; therefore when Fruits have not their natural Seafons, they cannot have their *true rich Taftes*.

XVI. A *dry Summer* caufes Trees to bear Plenty of Fruit the fucceeding Year, and a *wet Summer* caufes a great Production of *Wood*, and but little Fruit.

XVII. When a Tree grows *crooked,* or inclining downwards, cut or fcore the Bark *horizontally* in divers Places in the confined or hollow Part of the Tree, and in a fhort Time, if the Tree be young, 'twill become *ftreight*, and grow upright.

XVIII. To prevent tempeftuous Winds from injuring new or old Plantations of Fruit-Trees, you muft plant fubftantial and lofty Efpalier Trees and Hedges, on the Weft and North Parts of your Gardens.

The

The Kinds of Trees neceſſary for this Work are Cheſnuts, Walnuts, Limes, Elms, Pine, *Scotch* Fir, &c. (whoſe Manner of Planting, &c. follows in its proper Place of Foreſt Trees in the ſucceeding Part.)

This Work ought to be firſt done, that when the Fruit-Trees are planted, they may be defended from all ſuch Injuries.

The proper Places to plant theſe Eſpaliers of Defence in, is without the utmoſt Walls at about fifty nine or ſixty Foot Diſtance from the Wall, in Rows tolerably thick, *viz.* at the Diſtance of ten or twelve Foot in the Row; and 'twill be beſt to plant two Rows at leaſt, or three, at the ſame Diſtance from one another in ſuch a Manner, as for the Trees in the ſecond Line to ſtand oppoſite to the intermediate Spaces of the firſt, and thereby every three Trees will conſtitute an equilateral Triangle, and the Heads of the ſecond Line cloſe thoſe of the firſt, and the like of the third to the ſecond, &c.

When you plant three Rows of Trees for an Eſpalier, obſerve that thoſe of the talleſt Growth are placed in the back-moſt Line, thoſe of the middling Growth in the middle Line, and moſt of the ſhorteſt Growth in the firſt Line; and if the Bottom be filled up with Lawrel, 'twill make an admirable good Eſpalier of Defence.

Eſpaliers of this Kind checks the Violence of tempeſtuous Winds, much better than a Brick-Wall, which being cloſe and compact, reflects back the Winds, and oftentimes deſtroy or greatly injure tender Plants; but when ſuch Tempeſts beat againſt theſe Eſpaliers, they eaſily comply with its Force, without a direct Repulſe, (as a cloſe Wall muſt do,) or prejudice any Tree which they are planted to defend.

XIX. When Walls are built againſt Terraſs-Walks, they ſhould be built double, that is, that Wall as ſupports the Weight of Earth, muſt ſtand about eighteen Inches backward behind that, againſt which you plant your Fruit-Trees; and when thoſe Walls are brought up near to their Height, an Arch muſt be turn'd from one to the other, in which, at every fifty or ſixty Foot, 'tis good to leave ſmall Air-Holes, to let out the Damps, whoſe ill Effects would injure the Fruit-Trees.

N. B.

N. B. That moſt of thoſe Fruits mentioned in the Catalogue are now growing in the Gardens of the Honourable *James Johnſton* at *Twickenham*, in the County of *Middleſex*, Latitude 51 Degrees, 32 Minutes, whoſe great Perfections plainly demonſtrate the indefatigable Care and Judgment of the ingenious Mr. *John Lee*, Senior, Gardener to that worthy and much honoured Gentleman, by whoſe judicious Management all thoſe Fruits are now arrived to the greateſt Perfection of Beauty, Strength, and Fertility, as Art with Nature are capable to produce.

I cannot well conclude this Section, without taking notice of the great Happineſs a Gentleman poſſeſſes, when he is ſo well fix'd with a skilful induſtrious Gardener, by whoſe Judgment and Care he is daily enjoying the Pleaſures and Advantages of the beſt Fruits, Herbs, Sallets, &c. in the greateſt Perfection, which Recompence is all as can be receiv'd for the Expences and Labours thereof. And on the other Hand, how unhappy it is for a Gentleman to have an unskilful Perſon deſcended from the Tail of a Coach, Stable, &c. who taking upon him, firſt a blew Apron, and then the Name of a Gardener, aſſumes the Government of choice Trees committed to his Care, becauſe he has been much acquainted with cleaning Knives, ſweeping Stables, &c. which he thinks are neceſſary towards their Pruning, as well as making Hot-Beds, &c. without conſidering that thoſe Trees and Plants were obtained with much Labour, long Time, and great Expence, which by his unskilful Hand ſhall in one or two Years Time be totally ruin'd, to the great Loſs of his Maſter, and his eternal Shame.

I ſay where Misfortunes of this Nature happen, which is too frequent, 'tis a very great Loſs and Diſappointment, and a Crime unpardonable; and therefore I cannot but take the Liberty to ſay, that a good Gardener deſerves a much greater Reſpect and Encouragement than that of Stewards, Butlers, &c. who oftentimes undeſervedly poſſeſs a much larger Share thereof.

SECT.

SECT. XXV.

How to preserve Winter Fruit after Gathering.

IN the Gathering of all Kinds of Fruits, as I obferved before, great Care muft be taken that they are perfectly dry, otherwife they will rot prefently; and that they hang upon the Trees their full Time; for if Fruit be gather'd before, 'twill fhrink and become good for nothing. To know when it has hung its full Time, obferve when the Fruit naturally drops of it felf, now and then one, *&c.* alfo when Fruit will drop by an eafy Touch, 'tis fully grown.

As you gather Fruit, be careful to place it in the Basket, that none be bruifed, for Bruifes caufe them to rot inftantly; as alfo, that you do not mix your gather'd Fruit with that that has naturally fell of it felf, or by Winds.

That your fine Winter Pears may not be deprived of any Part of their Beauty, take Care in gathering to preferve their Stalks.

To prevent Fruit as is choice, from being bruifed, in forting the fmall ones from the large ones, let two Perfons be appointed to gather it, the one gathering the large and beft, and the other the fmall; or one Man may perform the whole, by gathering the beft firft, and the fmalleft at laft.

When your Fruit is gather'd lay it in your Fruitery, in middling Heaps, wherein they will fweat for a confiderable Time, which muft be obferved; and when over, lay them on your Shelves with clean Wheat-Straw underneath them, or, for want of Shelves, upon the like Straw on the Ground, and of fuch a Thicknefs as to be eafily examined, and the rotten ones pick'd out as they happen, which muft be minded with great Diligence, at leaft, every third Day.

Your Fruit being thus plac'd, cover it up very clofe with clean Wheat-Straw, as is not in the leaft mufty, &c. which will caufe the Fruit to be the fame; as alfo ftop all Chinks, Holes, &c. to keep the external Air entirely out.

When hard Frofts happen, you muft be very careful to keep out the Froft, and to cover clofe all your Fruit in general.

In fhort, the clofer and warmer your Fruit is kept, the longer 'twill keep, and the better 'twill be.

N. B. That oftentimes Fruit is deftroyed by Mice, Rats, &c. therefore guard againft thofe Vermin by Traps, Cats, &c.

S E C T. XXVI.

Of the Planting Fruit-Gardens in a more grand and delightful Manner than has been done before.

I Having in the preceding Sections fully demonftrated the Management of Fruits in general, I fhall now proceed to inform you how to lay out and plant a Fruit-Garden, in a more delightful and advantageous Manner than has been practifed, or perhaps thought on by any.

The Form which I here offer is a Paralellogram, whofe Dimenfions are twenty Pole by fix Pole, and its Quantity one hundred and twenty Rods, or three Quarters of an Acre exactly.

And as I before have plainly demonftrated that a South or South-Eaft Wall is of all others the very beft, therefore to that End I have placed the Wall P Q, within the Bounds of my Plan, whereby I receive the Benefit of the South-Side, as alfo the like of the Wall D E, for the Advantage of its North-Side.

The Difpofition of the Whole is as following, *viz.*

I. The Line A B fituated at the Parallel Diftance of twelve Foot, from the North-Side of the Wall D E, is compofed of

3   Standard

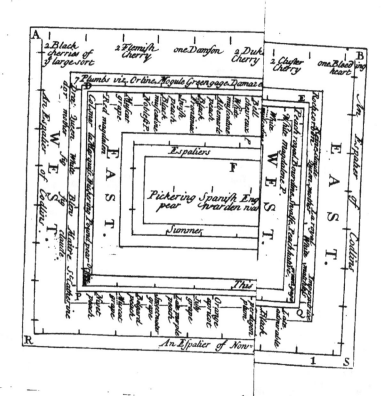

Plate II against Page 110

Standard Cherries, Damſon, and Mulberries; which Kinds of Cherries therein are ſo elected as to ſucceed thoſe againſt the South Wall D E, and to continue the whole Seaſon in great Plenty.

The Kinds and Number of Cherries therein planted, are, two Duke Cherries, two Early Flanders, two White Hearts, two Black Hearts, two Caroons, two Lukewards, one Bleeding Heart, two Cluſter Cherries, two Engliſh Cherries, two Flemiſh Cherries, two Carnation Cherries, two Black Cherries of the large ſort, with one Damſon, and four Black Mulberries.

(2.) The Wall D E, hath on its North-ſide, Firſt, ſeven ſorts of Plumbs, *viz.* The Orline, White Mogul, Greengage, Damazen, Maiter Claude, Plumb Mordin, and Violet, which ſucceeds others planted againſt South-Eaſt and Weſt Walls. Secondly, eight Morella, and ſeven Duke Cherries; which laſt, if their Bloom be preſerved in the Spring by covering, will produce Cherries when thoſe of the South and other Walls are gone.

The South-ſide of this Wall is planted with all the beſt Peaches, Grapes, Cherries, Summer Pears, and Figs, whoſe Number and Kinds are as following, *viz.* Firſt, of Peaches, one Red Magdalen, one Nobleſt, one Swiſh Peach, one Albemarle Peach one Belcheverux, one Ann Peach, one Yellow Alberge, one Old Newington, one Early Admirable, one Minion Peach, one Montabon, and one White Magdalen; in all twelve. Secondly, of Grapes, one Muſcat, two black Muſcadines, two black Frontiniacs, two white Muſcadines, one Cluſter Grape, one Claret Grape, and one white Frontiniac; in all ten. Thirdly, of Cherries, one early May Cherry, one Holman's Duke, and one Lukeward in all three. Fourthly, of Figs, the White and the Blue; in all two. Fifthly, of Summer Pears, one Buree, one Summer Bonchretien, one Groſs Rouſellet, one Vermillion Pear, one Royal Bergamot, and one Autumn Bonchretien; in all ſix.

(3.) The Wall P Q hath on its North-ſide twenty two Morella Cherries, which, with the eight of the other Wall makes thirty exact, and are what I ſuppoſe ſufficient for the Service of any Family to preſerve for Uſe in Tarts, Beer, Brandy, &c.

The South-ſide is planted with all the beſt late Peaches, the firſt exceped, Grapes, Apricots, Plumbs, and Winter Pears, whoſe Number and Kinds are as follow, *viz.* Firſt, of Peaches, one Nivet Peach, one Bellgard, one late Purple, one late Admirable, one Catherine, and one Malecotune; in all ſix.

P

Secondly,

Secondly, of Grapes, one black Currant Grape, one Burgundy Grape, one July Grape, one Sweet-water Grape, and one Muſcat Grape; in all five. Thirdly, of Apricots, one Turkey Apricot, and one Orange Apricot; in all two. Fourthly, of Plumbs, one Blue Perdigon, one white Perdigon, one Greengage, and one Musk Perdigon; in all four. Fifthly, of Nectorines, one Newington Nectorine, and one Roman Nectorine. Sixthly, of Winter Pears, one Winter Bonchretien, one Golden Bonchretien, one Spaniſh Bonchretien, one Colmar, one St. Germaine, one Winter Thorne, one Lachaſerie, and one Virgoulee; in all eight.

(4.) The Wall E Q, is planted on its Eaſt-fide with Plumbs to ſucceed thoſe of the South; the Number and Sorts are as follow, *viz.* one Rochcorbon, one Reine Claude, one Queen-Mother, one La Loyal, one White Matchleſs, and one Imperatrice.

And againſt its Weſt-fide, four Peaches and one Plumb, to ſucceed thoſe of the South Wall, *viz.* one Peach Royal, one Bourdine, one Swalſe, and one Hative Peach, with one Greengage Plumb.

(5.) The Wall D P is planted on the Eaſt-fide, with one Colmar Pear, three Baking Pears, *viz.* The Pickering, La Marquis, and Pound Pear, with one Orlin Plumb; and its Weſt-fide with Plumbs in general, two Figs excepted, *viz.* one Drapdor, one Queen-Mother, one White Fig, one Blue Fig, one Maitre Claude, and one St. Catherine.

(6.) The Wall G H is planted with the Satin, Ambret and Lanſac Pears on the Eaſt-fide, and with two Orange and one Turky Apricot on the Weſt-fide.

(7.) The Wall L O is planted on its Eaſt-fide, with one Virgoulee, one Royal d'Flyver, and one Lachaſerie Pears; and on its Weſt-fide with one Perſique Peach, one Temple Nectorine, and one Rambollion Peach.

(8.) The Eſpaliers A R and B S are planted with ſixteen Codlings, and the Eſpalier R S with twenty eight Nonpareil, Golden Pippins, French Pippin, Holland Pippins, Kentiſh Pippins, and Kirton Pippens; of which the two firſt are to be ten of each and of the four laſt two of each Kind.

(9.) The Quarter F is encompaſs'd with an Eſpalier of Summer Pears, ſixteen in Number; as alſo is the Quarter I, with an Efpalier of Autumn Pears, fixteen in Number; as alfo the Quarter K, with an Efpalier of the like Number of the beft Winter Pears.

(10.) Within the Quarter F is four Dwarfs, all Baking Pears; as alfo is in the Quarter K, *viz.* the Pickering Pear, Spanifh Warden, Englifh Warden, Perkinfon's Warden, Black Pear of *Worcefter*, Pound Pear, Cadilliac, and Donvil.

(11.) The four Dwarfs in the Quarter I, to be White Figs.

N. B. That the Diftance of the Efpaliers from the Walls are fifteen Feet, therefore their Height muft not exceed fix Feet; all other Parts may be meafur'd by the Scale annex'd.

Having thus explain'd to you the Manner and Nature of the Fruits being planted, fo as for every Fruit to have its true Expofition and Succeffion, &c. I fhall in the next Place draw up a Catalogue of the feveral Fruits planted therein.

I. Of the feveral Kinds of Cherries.

Early May,
May Duke,
White Heart,
Black Heart,
Carroon,
Early Flanders,
Bleeding Heart,
Clufter Cherry,
Lukeward,
Carnation,
Flemifh,
Englifh,
Large Black Cherry,
Morella.
Number of Kinds is fourteen.

II. Of Peaches.

White Magdalen,
Montabon,
Minion,
Early Admirable,
Old Newington,
Yellow Alberge,
Ann Peach,
Belchevereux,
Albemarle,
Swifh Peach,
Nobleft, Red Magdalen,
Perfique,
Rambollion,
Peach Royal,
Bourdine,
Swalfe,
Peach Hative,
Late Admirable,
Catherine,
Malecotune,
Late Purple,
Belgard,
Nivet.
Number of Kinds is twenty four.

P 2   III.

III. Of Nectorines.

Temple Nectorine,
Newington Nectorine,

Roman Nectorine.
Number of Kinds is three.

IV. Of Apricots.

Turky,
Orange,

Bruxelles.
Number of Kinds is three.

V. Of Pears.

Buree,
Summer Bonchretien,
Grofs Roufellet,
Vermilion Pear,
Royal Bergamot,
Autumn Bonchretien,
Virgoulee,
Royal-d'Hyver,
Lachaferie,
Satin Pear,
Ambret,
Lanfac,
Colmar,
La Marquifs,
Pickering,

Pound Pear,
Cadilliac,
Donvil,
Black Pear of *Worcefter,*
Spanifh Warden,
Englifh Warden,
Perkinfon's Warden,
Winter Bonchretien,
Golden Bonchretien,
Spanifh Bonchretien,
St. Germaine,
Winter Thorn.
Number of Kinds is twenty
  feven.

VI. Of Figs.

White and Blew. In Number two.

VII. Of Grapes.

White Mufcadine,
Black Mufcadine,

White Frontiniac,
Black Frontiniac,

Claret

Claret Grape,
Cluster Grape,
Muscat,
Black Currant,

Burgundy,
July Grape,
Sweet-water Grape·
Number of Kinds is eleven.

VIII. Of Plumbs.

Orlin,
White Mogul,
Greengage,
Damazeen,
Maitre Claude,
Plumb Mordine,
Violet,
Rochcorbon,
Reine Claude,
Queen-Mother,

La Royal,
White Matchless,
Imperatrice,
Drapdor,
St. Catherine,
Blew Perdigon,
White Perdigon,
Musk Perdigon,
Damson.
Number of Kinds is nineteen.

IX. Of Apples.

Codlins,
Nonpareil,
Golden Pippin,
French Pippin,

Holland Pippin,
Kentish Pippin,
Kirton Pippin.
Number of Kinds is seven.

X. Of Mulberries.

Black Mulberry. In Number one.

This being done, I will now sum up the whole in general :

1*st*,	Of Cherries there are in Kinds	14
2*dly*,	Of Peaches	24
3*dly*,	Of Nectorines	3
4*thly*,	Of Apricots	3
5*thly*,	Of Pears	27
6*thly*,	Of Figs	2
7*thly*,	Of Grapes	11
8*thly*,	Of Plumbs	19
9*thly*,	Of Apples	7
10*thly*,	Of Mulberries	1

Total   111   And

And all of different Kinds, and excellent good; to which we may add nine other Sorts of Summer, Autumn, and Winter Pears, as are to be planted in the Espaliers, about the three Quarters F I K, which requires forty eight Trees; so that the Sum of our Variety of good Fruit may be placed at 120 different Kinds at least.

The Number of Trees of each Kind, is

Cherries	26
Peaches	24
Nectorines	3
Apricots	5
Pears	86
Morella Cherries	30
Figs	8
Grapes	15
Plumbs	17
Apples	28
Codlins	16
Mulberries	4
Total	262

And every one at its proper Distance.

N. B. If any one thinks that the Number of Pears are too great, 'tis very easy to introduce other Fruit in their Stead; but for my Part, I can't but recommend them, seeing that they are all good Fruit, and ripen in such Order, as to furnish our Table nine Months in the Year plentifully.

N E W

NEW
PRINCIPLES
OF
GARDENING.

PART. III.

Of Foreſt-Trees, their Culture, &c.

SECT. I.

Of the ſeveral Methods by which Foreſt-Trees are raiſed.

 Oreſt-Trees are raiſed either by **Cuttings, Seed, Suck-**
ers, or Layers. (1.) By *Cuttings,* as the Sallow, Alder, and all the Kinds of Oziers and Willows ; of
which the *French* Kind is of great Uſe in the nailing of Wall-Trees, and of all other Willows the
moſt tougheſt.

(2.)

(2.) By *Seed*, of which is raifed the Oak, Afh; Beach, Horn-Bean, Horfe and *Englifh* Chefnut, Walnut, Philberd, Quick-Beam, *Scotch* and Silver Fir, Pinafter, Holly, Yew, Elm, Lime, Service, Wild Cherry, Wild Pears, Crab, Maple, Syca-more, and Hawthorn.

(3.) By *Suckers*, fuch are the Elms, Poplars, Abeal, Maple, Birch, and Hazel, or Philberd.

(4.) By *Layers*, as the *Englifh*, *Dutch*, and Witch Elms, Lime, Abeal, Platanus, Maple, Sycamore, and Philberd.

The feveral Kinds of Soil wherein Foreft-Trees moft delight in, are as follow, *viz.*

ALDER in boggy, drain'd, or dry poor Land.

ASH in the fame, as alfo in chalkly Ground, moift Clay, crag-gy or flinty Ground, Gravel mix'd with Loam, or a good Thicknefs of Mould.

ABEAL on dry poor Land, hungry Gravel, and on wet ftrong Loam.

BEECH in fome dry barren Soils, in chalky, dry, rich, fandy, hot, or flinty Land, Gravel mix'd with Loam, or deep in Mould.

BIRCH in fome dry, barren, boggy, drain'd, or dry, fandy, hot Lands.

CHESNUTS in moift Clay, black, fat, or dry, rich Land, and on moift Gravel.

ELM on chalky and flinty Ground, Gravel if well mix'd with good Loam, a moift Gravel, and in any good loamy Land whatfoever, be it ever fo rich; but it will not do on a hungry Gravel.

FIRS in fome barren mountanous Lands, a frefh, moift, gravelly Soil, mix'd with Loam, and in a rich fandy Loam alfo.

HOLLY on a dry poor Soil, and a Gravel when mix'd with a tolerable Thicknefs of Mould, and in fandy rich Loam alfo.

HORNBEAN on dry rich Land.

JUNIPER in chalky Land.

LIME on moift rich Land, or a very fat Soil, but not dry, fan-dy, or hot Ground, for that caufes them to drop their Leaves much fooner than other Trees.

MAPLE on dry, poor, clear Soil, and good rich Mould alfo.

OAK

OAK in black fat clayey, moist clayey, craggy, dry, rich, flinty Gravel, with Loam or Mould, and moist gravelly Lands, but not in a hungry Gravel.

PINE the same as Fir.

POPLAR on some dry, barren, chalky, dry and poor Lands.

SALLOW in moist Clay, dry and poor Land.

WALNUT in chalky, dry and poor, dry and rich Lands, or in Gravel mix'd with Loam.

WILLOW in boggy, drain'd, moist clayey, and moist gravelly Lands.

YEW in dry barren Soils, and those as are very rich also, especially a rich sandy Loam.

N. B. That although many of the above mention'd will grow and thrive in many poor and barren Lands, yet you are to understand that almost all sorts of Forest-Trees are much improved by a fresh fat Soil, or what we call a rich sandy Loam, if not mix'd with Dung, except 'tis well consum'd.

Therefore always beware of fresh Dung coming near the Root of any Tree, for 'tis perfect poison, and oftentimes present Death.

N. B. That Trees intended for flinty Lands, are best raised by their Seed sown therein, such as Oak, Ash, Beech, &c.

N. B. That Poplar will not thrive in chalky Ground; Abeals not on Clay; Willows not on dry poor Soils; Elm not on dry sandy hot Lands; Oak, Elm, Walnut, and Ash, not on a hungry Gravel; and none of the Aquaticks on any kind of Gravel, except that as is very moist.

N. B. That clayey Land produces the toughest Oak; and that in very strong Clay few Trees will live.

I having now explain'd by what Methods Trees are raised, and the several Soils they delight in, I shall in the next place lay down Rules and Directions to be observ'd in the several operations thereof.

First, Of raising Trees from Cuttings.

Trees rais'd by Cuttings are the Alder, Poplars, Willows, &c. wherein observe that the Ground wherein you plant them be of a moist Nature; that you take your Cuttings from the most healthy Branches; that their Thickness be not less than

Q   half

half an Inch, nor more than an Inch Diameter; for when they are lefs than half an Inch, they are very weak, and have too much Pith for their Bignefs, which oftentimes take wet and kill the Cutting; and when they are larger than one Inch 'tis long a healing over at top, and therefore longer expofed to the wet lying thereon; therefore at fuch Times 'tis beft to put a little Wax on the Cut. That their Length be about three Foot, of which one third to be above Ground.

When you plant Willows, &c. for to make Pollards, they may be of a greater Size, as nine, ten, or twelve Foot long; but the preceeding is beft for Hedges, Wood, &c. The beft Seafon for planting them, is *October*, and in the planting obferve, that you don't ftrip up the Bark at bottom, that the Bottom is not fplit or fhaken by cutting, as alfo the Top, and that the Earth be well clofed about it, and kept water'd the firft Summer.

> *Others no Roots require; the Lab'ror cuts*
> *Young Slips, and in the Soil fecurely puts.*
>
> DRYDEN.

And then again,

> *Some Trees their Birth to bounteous Nature owe,*
> *For fome without the Pains of Planting grow :*
> *With Oziers thus the Banks of Brooks abound,*
> *Sprung from the watry Genius of the Ground.*
> *From the fame Principles green Willows come,*
> *Herculean Poplar, and the tender Broom.*
>
> DRYDEN.

Secondly, *Of raifing Trees from Seed.*

Wherein obferve that the Seed be not gather'd too foon before it has got its full Maturity, which will caufe it to fhrink; or too late, when it has fuftain'd Damage by Rain, Froft, &c. Therefore when it appears dryifh and pretty hard, it may be fafely gather'd; and be fure to preferve it from wet, till 'tis fow'd, for that will caufe it to mould and rot. Their be divers Kinds of Seeds, as will not come up after fowing till the fecond Spring, as *Yew-Berries, Holy-Berries, Afhen-Keys, Hornbeam, White-Thorn,*

Thorn, &c. which ſhould be kept the firſt Year in *Sand*, or Mould, to prevent their being deſtroyed by Vermine, &c. The beſt Land for raiſing all Trees from Seed, is a light freſh Sandy Loam, which ſhould be trenched two Spit deep, levelled, raked, and divided into Beds of four Foot, and their Alleys between them about two Foot wide.

The beſt Seaſon for ſowing Seed of Trees, is as ſoon as they are ripe in *October*, in which obſerve to ſow ſuch Seed as are of a quick Growth, as *Aſh, Lime, Maple*, &c. thinner, than thoſe of a ſlow Growth, ſuch as *Holly, Yew, Hornbeam, Beach*, &c.

After you have ſown your Seed, tread all your Beds over, to fix the Seed into the Earth, and cover it over with good fine Mould about three or four Inches thick.

When Froſty Weather approaches, 'tis neceſſary to cover your Beds with Horſe-Dung to keep out the Froſt, which take away at the Change of Weather; and be ſure that Traps are ſet to deſtroy Mice, &c.

N. B. That ſuch large Seed as *Cheſnuts, Acrons*, &c. are beſt to be planted with a *Dibber*, as Beans, or ſow'd in *Drills*, like Peaſe: But 'tis beſt to plant Cheſnuts at ſix or ſeven Inches Square; and the Acrons to be dropp'd in the Drills, at about five or ſix Inches Diſtance.

The better your Land is, and the cleaner 'tis kept, the more your Oaks and Cheſnuts will thrive, and indeed all other Seeds in general.

When the Weather in the Spring and Summer prove very dry, you muſt not forget to water your Seed-Beds, and to take ſpecial Care that the Force of the Water, in watering, do not hurt or break the tender Shoots.

At *Michaelmas* ſift amongſt the young Plants, ſome rich Mould, ſuch as old decayed Hot-Beds, &c. which the Winters Rains will waſh in, and greatly ſtrengthen their Fibrous Roots.

In *February* following, take out of your Seed-Beds all the the largeſt and ſtrong Plants, leaving ſuch as are weak till the next *Autumn* or *Spring*, and plant them out in Beds in Lines about four or five Inches apart, and the like Diſtance in the Rows, always obſerving to cloſe the Earth very firm to their Roots, and that the Land be good mellow holding Land, free from Stones, Weeds, &c. *N. B.* I adviſe that they be planted in a

Q 2   chop'd

chopp'd Trench with the Spade, by the Side of the Line, and not with a Dipper, as is common; for if their is not very great Care taken with a Dipper, it will leave the lower Part of the Hole unclofed, which undoubtedly caufes the Plant oftentimes to perifh.

The beft Expofure for Seed-Beds, and thefe tranfplanted, is the *Eaft*; for in the Afternoon, they will be free from the *fcorching Sun*, which oftentimes being too hot, prevents their Growth.

If you have the Conveniency of Water, 'tis good to keep them always moift; 'twill add greatly to their Growth. In *April*, *May*, and *Auguft*, 'tis beft to water them in a Morning, but in *June* and *July*, in an Evening.

Chefnuts and *Walnuts*, muft ftand three Years in the Seed-Bed, becaufe they will not endure often tranfpanting.

> *But fome from Seeds, inclos'd in Earth arife;*
> *For thus the Maftful Cheftnut mates the Skies.*
> *Hence rife the branching Beech, and Vocal Oak,*
> *Where Jove of old oraculoufly fpoke.*

Thirdly, Of raifing Trees by Suckers.

To raife Trees from the Spawn or Exuberance of the Roots of others, fuch as *Elms, Abeal, Poplars*, &c. obferve that Care be taken to prevent Cattle from cropping them, that they be taken up at *Michaelmas*, and planted out in Beds as directed for thofe raifed from Seed, and let them remain therein two Years before they are planted out in the Nurfery, always obferving to keep them moift in the *Spring* and *Summer*, and clear from Weeds.

> *Some from the Roots a rifing Wood difclofe,*
> *Thus Elms, and the Savage Cherry grows:*
> *Thus the green Bays, that binds the Poets's brows,*
> *Shoots and is fhelter'd by the Mother's Boughs.*
>
> DRYDEN.

Fourthly

Fourthly, Of raifing Trees by Layers.

This Method of raifing Trees, is applicable to fuch that cannot be raifed from Seed, as *Elms, Platanus,* &c. and even many as may be raifed from Seed alfo, as the *Lime,* &c.

The firft Work to be done herein is to make choice of a Piece of frefh Pafture, &c. as is very good and rich in Nature, and beft when inclinable to, or is a fandy Loam.

Secondly, That the Ground be carefully trench'd two Spit and Crum in Depth, and in very fmall Spits, wherein plant Mother-Plants (by *Gardeners* call'd Stools) of *Elms, Limes, Platanus, Alder, Abeal, Poplar, Philberd,* &c. in fuch Quantity as will be capable to produce the Number of Trees defired.

If your Stools are made of very large well grown bodied Trees, each will produce Yearly about thirty Layers, or Plants, fo that you may proportionate your Number of each fort, to the Nature of your Soil wherein you intend to plant, and the Magnitude of your Plantation intended.

The beft Time to plant your Stools is *October*; and if your Land be very frefh and rich, they may be planted, at leaft eight Foot from each other, both in the Row, as well as one Row from the other, and it matters not what the Form of the Trees are, as the Stools are made off, whether they be ftraight or croocked, fo as their Bodies are but large and well rooted.

In *February* following, or rather *January,* of the two Months, is the Time to lay down thofe Branches produced the laft Year.

To every Stool you will have fix or feven principal Branches; which you muft plafh at their Bottom, that they may comply with being laid down the eafier; which done, twift all the Side-Shoots at fuch a convenient Place, as will admit of the twifted Part to be about eight Inches deep, which may be let in with a Trowel or Spade, and the extream Part of every Shoot, to be fhorten'd to five or fix Inches, or more, if need be, always obferving to leave three Buds at leaft above Ground; to place your Layers upright; and that they are not too thick, whereby they will be all fmall, and hardly worth the Trouble of planting out.

In *October* following, if the Seafon permits, take off the Layers, and prune away all the Parts of thofe principal Branches be-

3

fore plaſh'd, to give Room to thoſe other Shoots as are to to ſucceed them; which muſt be laid down in like manner the Spring following; and ſo the like every Year.

> *Some bow their Vines, which buried in the Plain,*
> *Their Tops in diſtant Arches riſe again.*
>
> DRYDEN.

SECT. II.

Of the Manner of planting Nurſeries and their Government.

IN order to have a proſperous Nurſery, good Choice muſt made of a proper Piece of freſh mellow Land, ſuch as are deep, and with a good Bottom of ſtrong Loam or Brick-Earth, rather than Sand or Gravel.

Your Ground being determin'd, Trench it as ſoon after *Michaelmas* as the Weather will permit, and divide it into convenient Quarters for the Reception of the ſeveral Trees as are to be tranſplanted therein.

The beſt Seaſon for to remove your young Trees is *October* or *November*, which muſt be planted in Rows about four of five Foot apart, and their Diſtance in the Rows, two Foot or more, as the Nature of your Plants requires; for thoſe or a quick Growth, intended for Hedges, extend their Side-Branches more than thoſe of a ſlow Growth. In *May* following you muſt Viſit your new planted Nurſery, and diſplace all the Side-Buds, or Shoots of the leading Shoots, of ſuch Trees as you intended for Standards, and not refer that Work as is commonly done till *Michaelmas*, when thoſe Side-Branches have robb'd their Leader of as much or more Strength and Quantity as they themſelves contain. The Objection made to this

3   Practice

Practice is bare Theory only, *viz.* 'Tis fuppofed that when Trees are thus train'd up, they will grow taper and weak, which when admitted to diftribute part of their Sap to their Horizontal or Side-Branches, caufes the Tree to be much thicker in Proportion to its Height, and confequently much ftronger. Now in order to prove this, I have made the Experiment on Limes and Dutch Elms, which are both of a quick Growth; and that I might not be deceived in the Goodnefs of the Land, I disbudded every other Tree of each Kind in feveral Rows, and at the *Michaelmas* following I pruned the others, whofe Buds I had left on in the Spring, according to the common Way.

In the next Spring afterwards, as the Buds began to project out, I difplaced them, leaving the other Trees with theirs on, as I did the Year before, and in the like Manner I proceeded till the *Michaelmas* following; at which Time I not only found thofe Trees, as I had fo often disbudded, much larger and ftronger Plants, but their Bodies were all fmooth and clear from Knots and other Deformities, as the Knife is the Caufe off.

The only Caufe of Trees being weak and flender, and hardly capable of fupporting themfelves, is the too near planting them in the Nurfery, not having fuch Quantity of Air as is neceffary for their Support.

And that this may not be efteem'd bare Theory only, let any but compare the Growth of the outfide Plants of any Nurfery, as is of fix or feven Years Growth, with thofe of the inward Parts, and the prodigious Difference of their Growth and Strength will be a fufficient Demonftration to prove the Truth of what I have afferted.

When your Trees have been thus managed for three Years, they muft all be taken up, and replanted again in their fame Places, carefully obferving to prune away all Tap-Roots and others, as are bruifed by the Spade. This Removal caufes them to ftrike frefh, whereby they get fine fibrous Roots, which had they not been moved, could not have had. If Trees ftand long in a Nurfery, 'tis feldom that they have any more than very large Roots without Fibres, and therefore for want of them are fubject to Mortality. And on the contrary, if Trees are removed in the Nurfery every three, or four Years at longeft, 'tis very feldom one in fifty dies.

When

When your Nurfery has feen three Years paffed over its Head, 'twill be high Time to lend a helping Hand, by giving it a good Dreffing of Dung well confumed, but beft when mix'd with frefh Earth, and turn'd four or five Times in the Summer before 'tis ufed; at which Time Care muft be taken that 'tis not digg'd in too deep, but rather turn'd in, for 'tis better for the Trees to have the Salts of the Dung wafhed down to their Roots, than to have it laid clofe to them, which oftentimes canker and kill their tender Fibres.

If your Land was not frefh and hearty at your firft planting, it will be beft to give a Dunging in the Manner before delivered the fecond Year, inftead of ftaying untill the third.

S E C T. III.

Of the Oak.

OF Oaks there are divers Kinds, which were they to be diftinguifhed by the Difference of Leaves, Shoots, Acorns, &c. would admit of as great Varieties as Pears, or any other Fruit whatfoever.

The beft Kinds are what Mr. *Bradley* calls the upright and fpreading Oak, which generally grow to a very large Stature, and even fo very large, (if his Report is true,) that the Timber alone of one Tree has been fold for upwards of fifty Pounds. *Vide* his *New Improvements*, Part I. Page 42.

This very large Sum to be paid for one fingle Tree, obliges me to make fome near Calculation of the Quantity of Timber as muft be contain'd in fuch a Tree, to amount to fo great a Sum.

Admit that fuch a Tree was fold at four Pounds a Load, which is a very great Price, and feldom or ever given for Oak, it muft contain twelve Load, twenty five Foot equal to fifteen Tun and a half, and upwards; and if the Tree was fold at fifty Shillings *per* Load, which is a cuftomary and very great Price, its Quantity muft be twenty Load, equal to twenty five Tun, which,

is

is very furprizing. The great Advantages arifing from large Plantations of Oak, is fo well known to this Nation, that I need not trouble my Reader with telling him of its great Ufe in Civil and Naval Architecture, or its Bark when peel'd in *April,* (for Tanners Ufe,) which is the proper Time to fell this Tree; or that its Acorns is excellent Food (as Mr. *Bradley* calls it) for Hogs, well known to every old Woman.

I fay the Excellency of this noble Plant is fo univerfally known, that to offer any Thing in order to encourage its greater Increafe, would be needlefs, feeing that all our *Englifh* Gentlemen of Fortune are not only good Judges of its great Ufe, *&c.* but at this Time are principally devoted to the Pleafures and Profit of Planting in general, wherein the Oak has a Place not inferior to any.

This noble Tree is raifed from an Acorn, which fhould be fowed immediately after its falling from the Tree, and is always beft when the Acorn is planted in the Place appointed for its future Growth; but when it cannot be fo order'd, they muft be fown in a Seed-Bed. In the removing of young Oaks from the Seed-Bed to the Nurfery, or to the Spot where they are to remain, be careful to prune off their Tap-Root, and head them down to two Buds only, which alfo obferve to do again the next Spring after, and then let one leading Shoot arife to form the Tree.

The Reafon of heading down this Plant twice, is to enable its Root to throw forth a ftrong Shoot the third Year, which never fails of making a handfome Tree. And during the Time as the Oak is in the Nurfery, Care muft be taken every Spring and Summer to difplace all the Side or Horizontal Buds, as I have once before directed, that the leading Shoot may receive all the full Nourifhment as the Earth produces, and be free from Knots, Wounds, *&c.* which muft happen, if thofe Buds are admitted to grow, at the Time of pruning.

Every third Year they muft be tranfplanted as before directed in the Management of Trees planted in the Nurfery; at which Time prune their Roots, but not their leading Shoots, always remembring that if you cut off, or only top an Oak, it ever afterwards is but a Pollard, and will never become a Timber-Tree.

To have good Oaks, or at leaft as good as can be, on wet Clays or dry Banks, *&c.* 'tis beft to plant the Acorns therein,

R

rather

rather than to plant large Trees from the Nurſery, whoſe former Life were not acquainted with the different Juices of ſuch
Soils, which thoſe young Trees raiſed from the Acorns will digeſt, being by Birth naturalized thereunto; and the like of gravelly, flinty, and rocky Lands.

A good ſtrong Land, like unto a light Brick-Earth, or a
a Loam inclinable to Clay, produces the beſt and tougheſt Oaks,
and the ſooneſt of all other Soils.

Gravel will produce Oaks of a noble Stature, very ſtreight,
and a fine Grain, but they ſoon decay.

If at any Time the Heads of your young Oaks ſhould be too
heavy for their Bodies, and thereby be inclinable to hang down
and be crooked, cut away thoſe Side-Shoots of their Heads as is
the Cauſe; but 'tis beſt to lead them up, tied to ſtraight Stakes
plac'd on Purpoſe, which if practis'd, and the Side-Buds always rubbed off, the Timber produc'd by ſuch Trees would be perfectly ſound
and clear from Knots, which renders it of much greater Value
than that which is otherwiſe.

The proper Diſtance as Oaks ſhould be planted from one another, in Woods, Groves, Parks, &c. ſhould never be leſs than
thirty five Feet.

And thus the Means of raiſing Woods I ſing ;
Tho' from the parent Oak young Shoots may ſpring,
Or may tranſplanted flouriſh, yet I know
No better Means than if from Seed they grow.
'Tis true this Way a longer Time will need,
And Oaks but ſlowly are produc'd by Seed :
Yet they with far the happier Shades are bleſt,
For thoſe that riſe from Acorns, are the beſt,
With deep-fix'd Roots beneath the Earth deſcend,
So their large Boughs into the Air aſcend.
Perhaps becauſe, when we young Sets tranſlate,
They looſe their Virtue, and degenerate ;
While Acrons better thrive, ſince from their Birth,
They have been more acquainted with the Earth.
Thus we to Woods by Acorns Being give :
But yet before the Ground your Seed receive,
To dig it firſt employ your Labourer,
Then level it ; and, if young Shoots appear

Above

Above the Ground, sprung from the cloven Bud,
If th' Earth be planted in the Spring, 'tis good
Those Weeds by frequent Culture to remove,
Whose Roots would to the Blossoms hurtful prove;
Nor think it Labour lost to use the Plow,
By Dung *and* Tillage *all Things fertile grow.*
  Whether you plant young Sets, or Acorns sow,
Still Order keep; for so they best will grow:
Order to ev'ry Tree like Vigour gives,
And Room for the aspiring Branches leaves.
  When with the Leaf your Hopes begin to bud,
Banish all wanton Cattle from the Wood.
The browzing Goat *the tender Blossom kills;*
Let the swift Horse *then neigh upon the Hills,*
And the free Herds *still in large Pasture tread,*
But not upon the new sprung Branches feed;
For whose Defence Inclosures should be made
Of Twigs, or Water into Rills convey'd.
When ripening Time has made your Trees dilate,
And the strong Roots do deeply penetrate,
All the superfluous Branches must be fell'd,
Lest the oppressed Trunk should chance to yield
Under the Weight, and so its Spirits loose
In such Excrescences; but as for those
Which from the Stock you cut, they better thrive,
As if their Ruin caus'd them to revive;
And the slow Plant, which scarce advanc'd its Head,
Into the Air its heavy Boughs will spread.
  When from the fasten'd Root it springs amain,
And can the Fury of the North sustain;
On the smooth Bark the Shepherds should indite
Their rural Strifes, and there their Verses write.
  But let no impious Ax prophane the Woods,
Or violate their sacred Shades; the Gods
Themselves inhabit there.   Some have beheld
Where Drops of Blood from wounded Oaks distill'd;
Have seen the trembling Boughs with Horror shake:
So great a Conscience did the Antients make
To cut down Oaks, *that it was held a Crime*
In that obscure and superstitious Time.

For Dryopeius *Heaven did provoke,*
By daring to deſtroy th' Æmonian Oak;
And with it, but included Dryad too,
Avenging Ceres *here her Faith did ſhew :*
To the wrong'd Nymph, while Ereſichthon *bore*
Torments as great as was his Crime before.
Therefore it well might be eſteem'd no leſs
Then Sacriledge, when ev'ry dark Receſs,
The awful Silence, and each gloomy Shade,
Was ſacred by the Zealous Vulgar made :
Whene'er they cut down Groves, or ſpoil the Trees,
With Gifts the antient Pales *did appeaſe.*
   Due Honours once Dodona's *Foreſt had,*
When Oracles were through the Oaks convey'd;
When Woods inſtructed Prophets to foretel,
And the Decrees of Fate in Trees did dwell.

Rapin.

S E C T. IV.

Of the Beech; its Culture, &c.

THE *Beech* is a Tree well worth our Eſteem, and highi-ly deſerves the greateſt of Encouragement for its Im-provement, on Account of its great Uſes, not only for the noble *Shade* and *Shelter* for *Cattle,* or *Maſt for Deer,* but for its great Services: Firſt, To *Carpenters, Joiners, &c.* whoſe Plains in general are made of this Wood, and many other In-ſtruments alſo: Secondly, To *Mill-Wrights,* for making the *Rimbs of Wheels* for *Corn-Mills, Water-Engines, &c.* and for *Mud-Cills, Conduit-Joice, &c.* Thirdly, For Keels of *Ships,* and other Parts belonging thereunto: For this noble Timber is of ſuch a Nature, that if it's kept always wet, or always dry, 'twill laſt for many Ages; but if it happens to be often wet and dry, 'tis pre-

ſently

fently rotten and ufelefs. Fourthly, For *Firing:* Of which the City of *London* deftroys many thoufand Loads every Year, being cleav'd into Billets for that purpofe. And befides all this, 'tis of prodigious great Ufe in many other Services, as to *Turners*, *Upholfters*, &c. which to mention here is needlefs, fince 'tis well known to all our Country Workmen in general.

This Tree is propagated from its Seed, call'd *Maft*, which muft be gather'd about the middle of *September*, when it will begin to fall; and when gather'd, and well dried, it muft afterwards be preferved in Sand till *January*, then fowed in the Seed-Bed, and order'd in every Refpect as the *Oak*, with whom it greatly delights to grow.

'Tis obferved that the Land it delights moftly in, is *Mountains*, *chalky* Hills, &c. as before defcrib'd.

The Diftance that thefe Trees are to be planted from each other, fhould be never lefs than forty Foot: It makes a ftately Tree, and well deferves to be planted in our *Avenues*, inftead of thofe ufelefs Trees, the *Lime* and *Dutch Elm*.

Thefe Trees when planted young, at about two Feet apart, and fuffer'd to throw out their Side-Shoots, makes very beautiful Hedges in *Gardens*, *Wildernefs*, &c.

When this Tree is intended to be propagated on poor Lands, 'tis beft to fow the Maft, rather than plant the Tree from the Nurfery, as is before faid of the Oak.

When e'er you plant, through Oaks *your* Beech *defufe;*
The hard Male Oak, *and lofty* Cerrus *chufe:*
While Efculus *of the Maft bearing kind,*
Chief in Ilicean Groves *we always find:*
For it affords a far extending Shade;
Of one of thefe fometimes a Wood is made.
They ftand unremoved, though Winters do affail,
Nor more can Winds, or Rain, or Storms prevail.
  To their own Race they ever are inclin'd,
And Love with their Affociates to be join'd.
When Fleets are rigg'd, and we to fight prepare,
They yield us Plank, *and furnifh Arms for War,*
Fuel to Fire, to Ploughmen Plows they give,
To other Ufes we may them derive.

But

But nothing muſt the ſacred Tree prophane ;
Some Boughs for Garlands from it may be ta'n :
For thoſe whoſe Arms their Country Men preſerve,
Such are the Honours which the Oaks *deſerve.*
　We know not certainly whence firſt of all,
This Plant did borrow its Original ;
Weather on Ladon, *or on* Mænalus,
It grew, if fat Chaonia *did produce ;*
It firſt, but better from our Mother-Earth,
Then Modern Rumours, we may learn their Birth.
When Jupiter *the World's Foundation laid,*
Great Earth-born Giants Heaven did invade ;
And Jove *himſelf, (when theſe he did ſubdue,)*
His Lightning on the factious Brethren threw.
Tellus *her Sons Misfortunes does deplore,*
And while ſhe cheriſhes the yet warm Gore,
Of Rhacus, *from his Monſtrous Body grows,*
A vaſter Trunk, and from his Breaſt aroſe
A hardned Oak ; *his Shoulders are the ſame,*
And Oak *his high exalted* Head *became :*
His hundred Arms which lately through the Air,
Were ſpread, now to as many Boughs repair.
A ſeven-fold Bark his now ſtiff Trunk does bind ;
And where the Giant ſtood a Tree we find :
The Earth to Jove *ſtrait conſecrates this Tree,*
Appeaſing ſo his injur'd Deity ;
Then 'twas that Man did the firſt Acorn eat :
Although the Honour of this Plant be great,
Both for its Shade, and that it ſacred is,
Yet when its Branches ſhoot into the Skies.
Let them take heed, while with his brandiſh'd Flame,
The Thund'rer rages, ſhaking Nature's Frame.
Leſt they be blaſted by his pow'rful Hand,
While Tamarisks *ſecure, and* Mirtles *ſtand.*

Rapin.

SECT.

SECT. V.

Of the Ash; its Culture, &c.

THE *Ash* is a very useful Tree, on many Occasions; as for Watermens Boats-Staves, Oars, &c. Coach and Cart-Wheels, Plows, and many other Works in Trade, and therefore ought to be as much increased, as any other Tree whatsoever,

This Tree is a very free grower, and is increased from its Keys, which are thorough ripe about the End of *October*, or the Beginning of *November*, at which Time they are to be gather'd. In the gathering of *Ashen-Keys* for an Increase, you must observe, that those Trees from which you gather them, be straight thriving Trees, and not of a small Stature, or any ways decaying. After your Keys are gather'd, let them be dry'd, and put into Sand, wherein let them remain till *January*, at which Time they should be sown in the Seed-Bed, as before directed, &c.

The first Year after sowing, they lie in the Earth, and the next *Spring* come up. Therefore for the first Year, the Ground wherein they are sown, may be sow'd with a Crop of *Barley*, *Oats*, or any other Crops of the like Nature.

But the most advantageous Way is to keep them the first Summer after gathering in Sand, and to sow them in the Spring following, *viz.* about the middle of *January*.

During that Time as you keep them in Sand, observe that the Sand be kept indifferently moist, and that the Air may have free Access to them, and in the laying them therein, be careful that they don't lie in Lumps, or too thick, but in such a Manner as for the Sand to encompass every Key.

In the Spring, when you sow them, first prepare the Bed wherein they are to be sown; and as soon as that is done, sow them of a reasonable Thickness, and immediately cover them with

3   fine

fine Earth, about two Inches in Thickneſs; for if they lie long in the Air before they are cover'd, 'twill be a Prejudice to them, as alſo will the Weeds, if they are ſuffer'd to grow amongſt them. The Firſt Year they ſhoot but little, to what they will the ſecond after which they muſt be traſplanted into the Nur-ſery, as before directed, &c.

When you tranſplant an Aſh Tree, young or old, obſerve to prune its Side-Branches; but never meddle or cut off the leading Shoot.

Aſhes, in general, are of ſuch a Nature, as to extend their Roots to a very great Diſtance from the Bodies to which they belong, and entirely deprive all other Trees of their proper Nouriſhment; and, indeed, even Corn, and all other Vegitables of the like Nature, will languiſh and pine away to nothing.

And ſeeing that this Tree is pernicious to all others, there-fore I adviſe that Plantations of Aſh be by themſelves, that nothing may be wrong'd by their ravenous Nature, and their Diſtance from each other be about twenty five Foot.

Thus in ſome even Fields the Aſb delights,
Where a good Soil the gen'rous Plant invites:
For from an Aſb which Pelion *once did bear,*
Divine Achilles *took that happy Spear,*
Which Hector *kill'd, and in their Champion Fate*
Involv'd the Ruin of the Trojan *State.*
The Gods were kind, to let brave Hector *die*
By Arms as noble as his Enemy.
Aſh, *like the ſtubborn* Hero *in his End,*
Always reſolves to break rather than bend.

RAPIN

SECT.

S E C T. VI.

Of the Elm ; its Culture, &c.

OF *Elms* there are three Kinds, *viz.* the *English*, the *Dutch*, and the *Witch Elm*, of which the Englifh is the moft profitable, as well as the moft beautiful.

They all delight in one and the fame Soil; which fhould be a good Loam, to have them in the greateft Perfection; not but they will do on other Lands, as before deliver'd. Thefe Trees are increafed by Layers or Suckers, which laft fhould remain in the Bed two Years before they are tranfplanted into the Nurfery.

Of all the feveral Kinds of Foreft or Ever-green Trees, there's none makes fuch Beautiful Hedges in Gardens, Groves, Wildernefses, &c. as the Englifh Elm; and although 'tis a Tree of a flow Growth, yet if 'tis grafted upon the Dutch Elm, 'twill advance to a large Stature in a fmall Time.

The great Ufe of the Elm to *Wheel-Wrights, Mill-Wrights, Pipe-Borers, Pump-Makers,* &c. is fo well known that it needs no manner of Difcription, to exemplify the Excellency thereof.

And in the *Park* 'tis delightful, being planted in open Avenues, where its noble Shade and Verdure demonftrates its Grandure and Glory: Witnefs that matchlefs Spot of Ground, *Greenwich Park,* whofe delightful Walks are chiefly adorn'd with this beautiful and moft advantagious Plant.

And befides, 'tis one of the moft Hofpitable Plants growing for 'till admit of fuch under Shrubs, as *Afh*; and divers other Trees will not.

With Rows of Elm, your Garden or your Field
May be adorn'd, and the Sun's Heat repell'd.
They beft the Borders of your Walk compofe ;
Their comely Green ftill ornamental fhows.

S   *On*

On a large Flat, continued Ranks may rise,
Whose Length will tire our Feet, and bound our Eyes;
Where endless Walks the pleased Spectator views,
And ev'ry Turn the verdant Scene renews.
  The sage Corycian *thus his native Field;*
Near swift Oobalian Galesus *till'd;*
A thousand ways of planting Elms he found;
With them sometimes he would inclose his Ground:
Oft in directer Lines to plant he chose;
From one vast Tree a num'rous Offspring rose.
Each younger Plant with its old Parent vies,
And from its Trunk like Branches still arise.
They hurt each other, if too near they grow;
Therefore to all a proper Space allow.
  The Thracian Bard *a pleasing Elm-Tree chose,*
Nor thought it was below him to repose;
Beneath its Shade, when he from Hell *return'd,*
And for twice lost Enrydice *so mourn'd.*
Hard by cool Hebrus Rhodop *does aspire;*
The Artist, here, no sooner touch'd his Lyre,
But from the Shade the spreading Boughs drew near,
And the thick Tree a sudden Wood appear:
Holm, Withy, Cypress, Plane-Trees *thither prest;*
The prouder Elm *advanc'd before the rest:*
And shewing him his Wife, the Vine, *advis'd,*
That nuptial Rites were not to be dispis'd.
But he that Counsel scorn'd, and by his hate,
Of Wedlock, and the Sex, incurr'd his Fate.

N. B. That the Distance to plant Elms at, is thirty or thirty-five Foot from each other, or rather so much square.

The Difference which in planting each is found,
Now learn; since th' Elm *with happy Verdure's crown'd.*
Since its thick Branches do themselves extend,
And a fair Bark does the tall Trunk commend.

RAPIN.

SECT.

SECT. VII.

Of the Lime-Tree, by some call'd the Linden-Tree; its Culture, &c.

THE *Lime* is a beautiful Tree in the Spring, but 'tis of a very small Duration, if the Land wherein it grows be hot, as a *Sand* or *Gravel*, &c. 'Tis a Tree of a quick Growth, raised from *Seed* or *Layers*; it makes very fine *Espaliers*, or Hedges, and indeed is conformidable to any shape whatsoever: Its Leaf is of a fine light Green, makes a pleasant Shade, and is one of the very first as welcomes in the Spring with its beautiful Leaves: 'Tis a very useful Tree for an immediate Shade, and for *Avenues, Wildernesses*, &c. in such Places were future Profit by Timber is not regarded. But for my part, I should rather make Use of them, to fill up the Quarters of a Wilderness, than to plant them in *Avenues*, where no Tree is so Beautiful and Profitable as the English Elm.

But then again, altho' the Elm is an advantageous Tree, when full grown, if fell'd and fold, and will fetch a great Price; yet 'tis supposed that a Lover of Gardening values those beautiful Trees, when they are in their Prime, at a much higher Rate, than to destroy them for the sake of their Timber, and thereby ruin grand Avenues, Walks, &c. to the great Prejudice of a noble Seat. Suppose that *Greenwich Park* had been planted with the View of cutting down the Elms when grown to their full Maturity, what would have been the Consequence? Why, the Destruction of the most beautiful Spot of Ground in the Kingdom, and the Ruin of the Town also. And since every Gentleman, is willing to possess the utmost Pleasure of such Trees Durations, which when they decline are no more than Fire-wood, why may not the Lime-tree be admitted in loamy holding Lands, interspersed with the Elm, &c. seeing that when either of their Beauty is over, and decaying, the

Goodness

Goodnefs of their dying Bodies are of equal Value for the Fire.
'Tis certain that the Elm makes an excellent Shade, and a beautiful Tree, but not handfomer than that of the Lime, whofe curious natural Shape exceeds all that Art can produce: Witnefs
thofe noble Trees before *Ham-Houfe*, oppofite to the Seat of the
Honourable *James Johnfton's at Twickenham*, Middlefex; and
thofe in *Bufhy* and *Hampton-Court Parks*, whofe beautiful
Forms is not Inferior to any growing.

This Tree is of a very long Duration, and often of a large
Magnitude. Mr. *Evelin*, in his Difcourfe on *Foreft-Trees, Chap.*
xxix. *Page* 82. makes mention of a *Lime-Tree*, growing at
Depenham in *Norfolk*, ten Miles from *Norwich*, whofe Circumference at bottom, was fixteen Yards and half, and its perpendicular Altitude about thirty Yards, which to me appears to
be more ftranger than Mr. *Bradley's* Report of the Oak. However, though every Lime does not arrive to that prodigious
Magnitude, yet they never fail of a proportionate Size.

The Nature of this Tree is to grow taper and ftreight ;
to conftantly keep its pyramental Form; to have Plenty of Leaves,
whereby it makes a good Shade; to preferve its felf by its tough
Bark from the violent Winds; to produce good Quantity of Roots,
from which the Head is plentifully fupp.ied; to fend forth fla-
grant Flowers or Bloffoms in the Spring; produces Branches,
whofe Wood is of a Beautiful red gloffy Colour; foon heals
over its Wounds by a Knife, &c. and therefore is preferved from
the wet, fo that 'tis very feldom they gow hollow; its Wood is
of great Service in Carving, and is a very fweet kind of Fuel.

In the pruning of their Roots, obferve that you cut away all
their fmall woolly Fibrous Roots; for they are prefently dead
after taking up; and befides they hinder the Earth from getting
to the principal Roots: But for their Heads, 'tis beft to leave
them on, pruning off all Side or Horizontal Branches clofe to the
Body of the Tree, without leaving on Side-Snags as is common.

The Seed of this beautiful Tree is ripe in *October*; at which
time it muft be gather'd, and in a fine dry Day if poffible; after which lay it to dry in an open Room; for the Space of fix
feven Days, and then it being very dry, put it into Sand as was
directed for the *Afhen-Keys*, and in the middle of *February* following, muft be fown in the Seed-Bed, which would be beft if
under

under an *Eaft* or *North* Wall, &c. After they have continued two Summers in the Seed-Bed, tranfplant them in the Autumn following to the Nurfery, as before directed.

When Limes are planted to make an Efpalier or Hedge, they are planted at three Foot Diftance in the Lines; in which obferve, that whenever you plant Hedges of *Lime, Elm,* &c. to plant one low or fhort Plant between every two of the higheft, and thereby your Hedge will be full at the Bottom, which otherwife very rarely happens. Lime-Trees planted for fhady Walks, may be at ten, twelve, or fixteen Foot a-part; but for thofe in large Avenues, not nearer than thirty five or fourty Foot.

N. B. That Hedges of Limes, or of Elms, fhould at firft planting be cut down within four Foot of the Ground, and all their Side or Horizontal Branches fhorten'd, 'twill add very much to their Improvement.

The beft Lime-Trees for Standards, are thofe of fix or feven Years Growth.

High fhooting Linden *next exacts your Care;*
With grateful Shades to thofe who take the Air.
When thefe you plant, you ftill fhould bear in Mind
Philemon *and chafte* Baucis: *Thefe were join'd*
In a poor Cottage, by their pious Love,
Whofe facred Ties did no lefs lafting prove,
Then Life it felf. They Jove *once entertain'd,*
And by their Kindnefs on him fo much gain'd;
That, being worn by Times devouring Rage,
He chang'd to Trees their weak and ufelefs Age.
Tho' now transform'd, they Male and Female are;
Nor did their Change ought of their Sex impair.
Their Timber chiefly is for Turners good;
They foon fhoot up, and rife into a Wood.

N. B. That the *Platanus-Tree* is propagated as the Lime-Tree, by Layers: Its Leaves are very large and beautiful. 'Tis a Tree of a quick Growth, delights in good Land; but 'tis late in the Spring before its Leaves comes out, and in fome hot Summers drop very early.

S E C T.

S E C T. VIII.

Of the Maple; its Culture, &c.

THE *Maple-Tree* is very proper to be cultivated in our *Gardens,* in regard to its being a very free Grower, and thickens the Quarters of *Wildernesses, Coppices, Woods,* &c. when train'd up as a *Shrub* or *Bush,* and not as a Standard Tree. This Plant is very subject to receive a Sort of *Honey-Dew* on its Leaves, which being wash'd off by Rains, is prejudicial to all such Plants as it falls on; therefore for that Reason 'tis best to cut them down near to the Ground, that they may break into divers Branches, and make a Thicket from the Bottom.

Or if they are train'd up in Hedges, they make a very handsome Appearance, and will thrive under the Drip of other Trees although others cannot endure long under the Drip of them.

The Soil this Tree delights in, is a dry Ground, or Bank; 'tis increas'd by Seed, Suckers, or Layers; and its Seed lies a Year in the Ground before it comes up; therefore 'tis best to keep it the first Year in Sand, as the Ash, &c.

> *Respect is likewise to the Maple due,*
> *Whose Leaves, both in their Figure, and their Hue,*
> *Are like the Linden; but it rudely grows,*
> *And horrid Wrinkles all its Trunk inclose.*

3   RAPIN.

S E C T.

S E C T. IX.

Of the Sycamore; its Culture, &c.

THIS Tree is moſt proper for a Wood or Coppice, rather than a Wilderneſs or Garden, on Account that
its Leaves are ſubject to receive and retain ſuch *Honey-*
Dews, that it draws to them ſeveral Kinds of *Flies,* which are
very troubleſome to People when walking near them.

Of *Sycamore-Trees* there is two Sorts, the one with plain
green Leaves, and the other *varigated.* 'Tis a Tree as makes a
fine Shade, a very quick Grower, of a beautiful Colour and
Leaf.

'Tis a Tree as grows to a tolerable good Stature, its Timber
is of good Services in divers Affairs, and is very eaſy propagated from Seed or Layers. The Seed ſhould be ſow'd as ſoon as
ripe, which is known by the Time of its falling, and will
come up the Spring following.

It thrives beſt in a light and dry, rather than a wet and ſtiff
Land.

S E C T. X.

Of the Hornbeam; its Culture, &c.

THE *Hornbeam* is a Plant that will make a Standard,
but not over and above large ; yet for Variety's ſake,
'tis proper to have ſome of them in our Wilderneſs.
'Tis beſt for Hedges, which of thoſe as ſhed their Leaves yearly,

ly, none is fuperior to it. It *is* raifed from Seed, which lies
one Year in the Ground before it comes up, or otherwife, as long
in Sand as the Afh, and fhould be fown in the fame Seafon and
Manner. It makes a very beautiful Thicket for the Entertainment of Birds in the Quarters of a Wildernefs, &c. and very
often holds on its Leaves all the Winter, till they are difplaced
by the young ones in the Spring.

> *If any Plain be near your Garden found,*
> *With* Cyprus, *or with* Hornbeam, *hedge it round;*
> *Which in a thoufand* Mazes *will confpire,*
> *And to Receffes unperceiv'd retire :*
> *Its Branches, like a Wall, its Paths divide,*
> *Affording a frefh Scene on every Side.*
> *'Tis true, that it was honour'd heretofore;*
> *But Order quickly made it valued more,*
> *By its fhorn Leaves, and thofe Delights which rofe*
> *From the diftinguifh'd Forms in which it grows.*
> *To fome cool* Arbour *by the Way's Deceit,*
> *Allur'd, we hafte, or fome oblique Retreat,*
> *Where underneath its* Umbrage *we may meet*
> *With fure Defence againft the raging Heat.*

RAPIN.

SECT. XI.

Of the Hazel, its Culture, &c.

THE *Hazel* is a very fine Plant for the thickening of a
Wildernefs, and its Fruit is no lefs diverting to the young
Men and Maids in the Nutting-Seafon. 'Tis a very
profitable *Coppice-Wood,* and is propagated from its Nuts, or by
Suckers: When by Nuts, they fhould be fown foon after they
are gathered, which fhould not be, until the Kernels have re-

3   ceived

ceived their full Growth; and the Soil as they will thrive in, is poor, fandy, dry, or cold Lands, &c. but when better, 'tis better ftill.

When they have feen three Years over their Heads, in *January* cut them down, leaving about fix or eight Inches above Ground; and the Spring following they will break out into divers Shoots, which in five Years, or thereabouts, will be fit to make Hurdles, &c. or if let growing until eight or nine Years, will make fine *Hop-Poles, Hoops, Fire-Wood,* &c.

I cannot but recommend thofe propagated from Seed, before thofe from Suckers, being fown as aforefaid, kept clean from Weeds, and kept at the Diftance from one another of about three or four Foot.

But if you plant Suckers, the proper Time for that Work is *October,* at which Time you muft prune them down as before directed, *viz.* within fix or eight Inches of the Ground.

N. B. That as this Plant may be eafily propagated by *Layers,* laid down from the Mother-Plant, or Stool, as *Elms, Limes,* &c. 'tis more fafer to plant the Layers as are well rooted, which one Year will perform, than to run the Hazard of planting Suckers, which often fail.

> Hafle *difpers'd in any Place will live :*
> *In ftony Grounds* Wild Afh, *and* Cornel *thrive;*
> *In more abrupt Receffes thefe we find,*
> *Spontaneoufly expos'd to Rain and Wind.*
>
> RAPIN.

T   S E C T.

S E C T. XII.

Of the Birch; its Culture, &c.

IN Confideration that the Services of the *Birch-Tree* is of the fmalleft Number of any *Foreft-Tree*, therefore 'tis contented to live in the worft of Soils; and altho' this Tree is but of fmall Ufe, befides its terrible Afpect to Children, &c. yet 'tis a very beautiful Plant, and highly deferves a Place in the Quarters of our Wildernefs. And befides, its Faculty of attracting and preparing from the Earth, that pleafant and healthy medicinal Liquor, is a fufficient Reafon, that it highly deferves a due Encouragement as well as other Foreft-Trees.

And although the making of Birch-Wine is known to fome People, yet I cannot but think, that if I infert it in this Place, it may oblige others, without any Difpleafure to any.

The Method that I fhall lay down, is the fame as Mr. *Evelyn* makes Mention of in his learned Difcourfe on Forreft-Trees, Page 77.

In the Beginning of *March* cut an oblique Hole, or rather a Slit, under the Branch of a well-fpreading Birch-Tree, which keep open by a fmall Wedge or Stone put therein. To this Hole, or Slit, fix a Bottle to receive that clear Water or Sap as will extill it felf out of the Aperture into the Bottle, which muft be taken away when full, and others fix'd in its Place, &c.

Having in this Manner obtain'd a fufficient Quantity of the Sap or Birch-Water, put to every Gallon thereof, a Quart of Honey well ftirr'd together, and boil it almoft an Hour, with a few Cloves and a little Lemmon Peel, being kept well fcummed.

When it is fufficiently boil'd, as before, and become cold, put to it two or three Spoonfuls of good Ale, which will caufe

it

it to work like new Ale, and when the Yeaſt begins to ſettle, bottle it up as you do other Liquors, as Wine, &c. and in a competent Time 'twill become a moſt brisk and ſpiritous Wine, and a very great Opener. *N. B.* That if you don't like Honey, (it being diſagreeable to ſome) inſtead thereof, you may allow one Pound of the beſt double-refin'd Sugar, or it may be dulci-fied with the beſt of *Malaga* Raiſins; which laſt will make it a wonderful fine Wine.

And altho' this Wine is very gentle and harmleſs in its Ope-ration within the Body, yet 'tis ſo ſtrong in the common Stone-Bottles, that they cannot preſerve its Spirits. This Wine is very good for the Phthiſick, diſſolves the Stone in the Bladder, and exceedingly ſharpens the Appetite, being drank *ante Paſtum.*

S E C T. XIII.

Of the Quickbeam.

THE *Quickbeam*, called by ſome *Wickey*, or *Wicking*, and by others Wild or *Spaniſh Aſh*, is a moſt beau-tiful Tree for a Wilderneſs, not only for its pleaſant Leaves and Straitneſs of Shoots, but for its delightful Bloſ-ſoms in the Spring, and curious Cluſters of red Berries in the Autumn.

'Tis raiſed from its Seed, and requires the ſame Culture as the Aſh.

S E C T. XIV.

Of the Alder, Poplar, Withy, Willow, Sallow, and Ozier; their Culture, &c.

(1.) THE *Alder*, an amphibious Plant, who greatly delights in wet boggy Lands, River-Sides, *&c.* is increas'd by large Cuttings, as before directed. The Shoots of this Plant should be cut down every third or fourth Year, at longest; for if they are suffer'd to grow a longer Time, the Wounds will be so very large, that with the Wet, *&c.* they will soon rot, and become hollow, and thereby instantly decay.

The best Time to cut or head down this and all other Aquatick Trees, is in *February*; for by the immediate Flowing of the Sap, their Wounds are soon heal'd.

(2.) Of *Poplars* there are four Kinds, *viz.* First, the large White Poplar, commonly called *Abeal*, with a large, pale, green Leaf, and white underneath. Secondly, the small White *Abeal*, whose Leaves are somewhat smaller, but of the same Form and Colour as the preceding. Thirdly, that Kind of *Poplar* as is called the *Aspen* or *Asp-Tree*. Fourthly, the other Kind is the *Water-Poplar*; its Leaf is of a pale Green, as the large White, but in Form like the *Aspen*. The young Shoots is of a yellowish Green, and delights to grow by River's Sides. The best Use these Trees can be applied to, is for the breaking of Westerly and Northerly Winds, and to be planted in dry or wet Lands, where no other Tree will thrive; for the Advantage as will arise from its Timber, *&c.* for Fuel, Posts, Rails, Stiles, *&c.* is many Times better than that from the Willow.

This

This laft is increafed by large Cuttings, in the Manner as directed for Willows, &c. in the firft Section hereof; which when planted for Stumps, to cut or lop, and thofe for Pollards, may be planted five, fix, or eight Foot high, of any Thicknefs not exceeding three Inches (or little more) Diameter.

In the Planting thefe large Cuttings, be careful that neither of the Ends be fplit in cutting; and that the Bark is not difplaced in any Part. Plant them about eighteen or twenty Inches deep; and the beft Seafon is *October*, if your Land is not very wet, or *February* if otherwife.

Thefe Sorts of Trees, well managed, may be lopp'd every five Years, and will turn to a very good Account.

Into your Foreft, fhady Poplars bring,
Which from their Seed with equal Vigour fpring.

RAPIN.

(3.) The *Withy:* It delights in Land that is not over moift or dry; as Banks of Rivers, Hills, &c. wherein fmall Springs fpew out, or Banks in Morifh Lands, and may be lopp'd every fifth Year.

(4.) The *Willow* delights in the fame Soil; and both are increafed by large Cuttings, as before directed.

I fhall not trouble my Reader with the feveral forts of Willows, feeing that they are all propagated by the fame Method; and therefore fhall only add, that no Gentleman fhould be without the fmelling Willow, which is a Plant of a quick Growth, bears a fine fhining broad green Leaf, with beautiful Flowers, delightful to Bees; and the fine French yellow Willow, which is of as tough a Nature as Whitleather, and of great Ufe in nailing Fruit-Trees, and other fuch-like Works in a Garden.

(5.) Of *Oziers* there are feveral Sorts, and all raifed as the preceeding. They love a more Moift or Moorifh Land than the Willow or Sallow.

The proper Diftance to plant *Oziers* is about two Foot and half, or three Foot, mixing Stumps and Pollards together; and the beft Seafon to plant them, is in *February*. 'Tis a Plant of great Service for Baskets, &c. and therefore highly deferves our Notice.

3

(6.) The

(6.) The *Sallow* is a Plant as delights on moiſt Banks: 'Tis increaſed by *Seed, Layers,* or *Cuttings.* There are three Kinds common ; of which the Round-leaf Sallow delights beſt in moiſt Banks, as aforeſaid, and the others in wetter Lands, as Moors, &c.

> *Alder, and Witby, chearful Streams frequent,*
> *And are the Rivers only Ornament.*
> *If antient Fables are to be believ'd,*
> *Theſe were Aſſociates heretofore, and liv'd*
> *On fiſhy Rivers in a little Boat,*
> *And with their Nets their painful Living got.*
> *The Feſtival approach'd; with one Conſent,*
> *All on the Rites of* Pales *are Intent:*
> *While theſe unmindful of the Holy Day,*
> *Their Nets to dry upon the Shore diſplay.*
> *But Vengeance ſoon th' Offenders overtook;*
> *Perſiſting ſtill to labour in the Brook,*
> *The angry Goddeſs fix'd them to the Shore,*
> *And for their Fault doom'd them to work no more.*
> *Thus to Eternal Idleneſs condemn'd,*
> *They felt the Weight of Heaven, when contemn'd.*
> *The Moiſture of thoſe Streams by which they ſtand,*
> *Endues them both with Power to expand*
> *Their Leaves abroad; Leaves, which from guilt look pale,*
> *In which the never ceaſing Frogs bewail.*
>
> RAPIN.

N. B. That the proper Seaſon to fell the *Oak* is in *April;* the Elm, Cheſnut, and Walnut, from *October* to *February* ; and the *Beech, Aſh, Willow, Abeal,* &c. may be lopp'd in any part of the ſame Months.

SECT.

SECT. XV.

Of the Black Cherry-Tree.

ALTHOUGH the *Black Cherry-Tree* is not directly a Forest-Tree, yet in Regard to its being a beautiful Tree in a Wilderness, I could not pass it by without taking some Notice thereof.

The Soil as is most natural to it, is a dry Soil, with a gravelly Bottom, not but they will do very well in most Kinds of Loam.

They are increased from the Stones of the Fruit, which when ripe should be gather'd, and the Pulp got off, either by rowling them in dry Sand under a Plank, &c. which must afterwards be put into Sand, not too thick so as to heat, and in the *February* after, may be sown in a Seed-Bed, as already described.

This Tree makes a glorious Appearance in the Spring, when in Bloom, and is no less pleasant when its Fruit is ripe: 'Tis a Tree as draws great Quantity of Birds to it, who are the most delightful, and beautiful Embellishments, as a wild and rural Garden can be adorn'd with ; and besides, its Bloom gives great Relief to the most industrous Bee.

If the aspiring Plant large Branches bear,
And Cherries with extended Arms appear ;
There near his Flocks upon the cooler Ground
The Swain may lie, and with his Pipe resound
His Love ; but let no Vice those Shades disgrace,
We ought to bear a Reverence to the Place :
The Boughs, th'unbroken Silence of a Wood,
The Leaves themselves demonstrate that some God
Inhabits there, whose Flame might be so just,
To burn those Groves which had been fir'd by Lust.
But through the Woods while thus the Rustick sport,
Whole Flights of Birds will thither too resort ;

Whose

Whose different Notes and Murmurs fill the Air :
Thither sad Philomela *will repair;*
Once to her Sister she complain'd, but now
She warbles forth her Grief on ev'ry Bough,
Fills all with Tereus *Crimes, her own hard Fate,*
And makes the melting Rocks, compassionate.
Disturb not Birds which on your Trees abide,
By them the Will of Heav'n *is signified :*
How oft from hollow Oaks the boading Crow,
The Winds and future Tempests do foreshow.
Of these the wary Ploughmen should make use ;
Hence Observations of his own deduce,
And so the Changes of the Weather tell,
But from your Groves all hurtful Birds expel.

The riper Cherries are, when gather'd, the founder are the Kernels; and if they are sown as before directed, they will come up in the following Spring. But if they lie long out of Sand, &c. to be very dry, after the Pulp is taken off, they will not come up till the second Spring, and sometimes never.

The Fruit is ripe in *July*, and in many Places they are very large, and of an excellent fine Taste.

The Tree is naturally of a very large Growth : And Mr. *Cook*, in his *Treatise* of *Forest Trees*, tells us, that at *Casbiobury*, he measured the Height of one Black-Cherry-Tree, and found it to be eighty five Foot, five Inches.

S E C T.

SECT. XVI.

General Directions for planting Forest Trees, &c.

WHEN your Trees in the Nursery are arrived to a proper Bigness, fit to be transplanted in the *Park, Forest, Wilderness,* &c. they are to be transplanted in the following Manner, *viz.*

If your Ground is not in general to be trench'd, which should always to be done for the Planting of *Wildernesses, Coppice,* &c. then first set out the Distance as each Tree is to stand, as is before directed, and dig for each Tree a Circular Hole of ten Foot Diameter, and about two Foot deep at most, observing to lay the first Spit of Earth by it self, which afterwards must be cast into the Bottom of the Hole; and if 'tis a Meadow, &c. as you plant in, the Turf must be well chopp'd to Pieces with the Spade before the Tree is planted thereon.

Your Hole being thus prepared, the next Work to be done is the pruning of the Tree, wherein observe that you don't head any Tree, and especially the *Oak, Walnut, Chesnut, Ash, Elm, Beech,* &c. and that you prune away all matty Fibrous Roots, and such as are dead by the Winds, as will hinder the Earth's getting to the larger: Also mind that your Knife is very Sharp, that you cut clean, that you prune the End of every Root, and cut away all that are bruised.

Your Tree being thus pruned, place it in the Hole as 'tis to stand, and fill in the Earth equally about its Roots, and be careful to see that every Root is well inclosed therewith, not to be hollow, &c. which causes the Tree to perish ; the Earth being firmly placed to the respective Roots, the Tree must be

U   secured

secured by Stakes; that the Winds do not displace it, and if you pile up a great deal of Earth over their Roots, 'twill be a Means of keeping the Tree fast, and preserve them from the Scorching Heat of the Sun.

But, as I said before, take care that you don't plant to deep, and especially in wet and cold Lands.

NEW

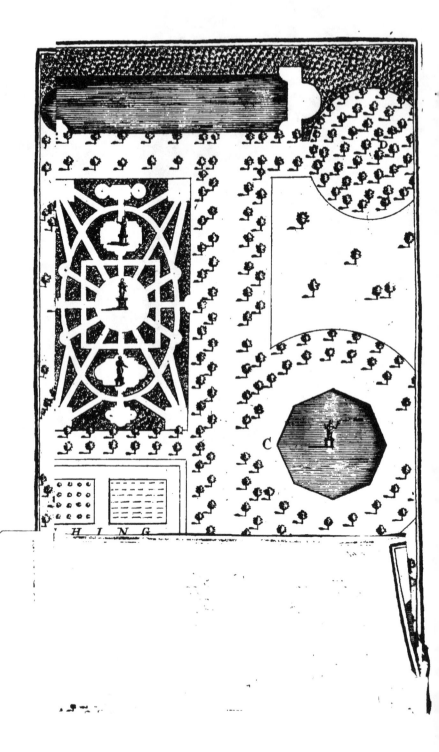

NEW
PRINCIPLES
O F
GARDENING.

PART. IV.

Of Ever-Greens; their Culture, &c.

SECT. I.

Of the feveral Methods by which Ever-Greens are raifed.

VER-GREENS are propogated by *Seed, Cuttings, Layers, or Suckers.*

(1.) By *Seed*; as the Fir, Pine, Ever-Green, Oak, Holly, Yew, Bay, Box, Laurel, Phillyrea, Juniper, Piracantha, Arbutus, Italian Green Privet, Cyprus, Cedar of Labanus, &c.

(2.) By

(2.) By Cuttings; as the Yew, Laurus-tinus, Bay, Box, Laurel, Phillyrea, and Piracantha.

(3.) By *Layers*; as the Holly, Yew, Laurus-tinus, Bay, Box, Laurel, Phillyrea, Alaternus, Piracantha, and Arbutus.

(4.) By *Suckers*; the Bay, Box, Laurel, and Phillyrea.

In the Propagation of some Ever-Greens from *Seed,* as Yew, Holly, *&c.* you muſt obſerve that their Seeds, don't come up till the ſecond Spring after gathering. Therefore 'tis beſt to preſerve them the firſt Summer in Sand, as directed for the Beech, Hornbeam, *&c.* and to ſow them in Seed-Beds the Spring afterwards in the ſame Manner.

To raiſe *Ever-Greens from Cuttings,* 'tis beſt to do that Work in *October,* placing the Cuttings in Chopp'd Trenches about a Foot Diſtance from one another, and in the Rows three or four Inches aſunder. The Length of Cuttings ſhould never exceed fifteen Inches, and muſt be planted about eight or ten Inches in Depth, and between each Row ſo planted, 'tis beſt to lay in a moderate Thickneſs of Horſe-Dung, which preſerves their Roots, *&c.* from the Froſt of the Winter, and keeps them cool in the following Spring and Summer, at which Times, in dry and hot Weather, they muſt be plentifully water'd.

The Method of increaſing Ever-Greens by Layers, is perform'd in the very ſame Manner as that of Foreſt-Trees; in which you are to obſerve, that 'tis beſt to let the Layers of the Arbutus, and ſuch hard-wooded Trees, remain on the Stools at leaſt two Years before they are taken off.

SECT. II.

Of the Pine-Tree; its Culture, &c.

THIS ſtately Tree deſerves a much greater Reſpect than of late it has receiv'd; but I believe 'tis only owing to the great Miſtake of planting it in a wrong Seaſon, which oftentimes cauſes it to miſcarry, to the great Loſs and

Diſcouragement

Difcouragement of fuch Gentlemen as would gladly give it its due Encouragement.

The Seafon for planting this Tree is the End of *March,* or End of *Auguft;* and not in *October, November, December, January,* or *February,* as has been the Cuftom hitherto, to the great Prejudice and Lofs of many fine Plants. This Noble Tree delights in a frefh gravelly Soil, mix'd with Loam ; but mortally hates Dung of any kind.

At the planting of thefe Trees, good Care muft be taken to fecure them with Stakes, that the Winds do not difturb them in ftriking Root.

And whereas I advife you in the planting of Foreft-Trees, to cut off their Fibrous Roots at planting, you are now to obferve the contrary Rule, which is to preferve all their Fibrous, and other larger Roots, feeing that their bruifed Ends are cut clean, and all broken Roots taken quite out. The beft Method of planting this, and all other Ever-Greens in general, to be certain of Succefs, is to make ufe of that fure and ingenious Manner of Planting, mention'd in SECT. 3. PART II. firft, difcover'd by the Honourable Mr. Secretary *Johnftone* of *Twickenham ;* and whereas the Roots of this Tree do naturally run far from the Body in few Years, therefore they don't delight in being removed when grown large, and for that Reafon I advife that they be planted for good, when but three or four Years of Age ; and that they be fafely preferv'd from Cattle, 'till they have Strength to preferve themfelves from fuch Injuries.

This glorious Plant is moft proper to be planted in *large Avenues* of *boundlefs Views,* to environ *Canals, Bafons, Bowling-Greens,* &c. and in the Quarters and other Parts of a *Wildernefs, Grove,* &c.

'Tis raifed from Seed fowed in *February,* or Beginning of *March,* in a Seed-Bed, as was directed for Foreft-Trees, &c.

N. B. That if you keep the Side-Branches prun'd off, as they break out, 'twill greatly add to their Growth: But always remember that Pines, Firs, &c. muft not be headed at any Time whatfoever.

The Pine, *which fpreads its felf in every Part,*
And from each Side large Branches does impart,

Adds

Adds not the leaft Perfection to your Groves;
Nothing the Glory of its Leaf removes.
A noble Verdure ever it retains,
And o'er the humbler Plant it proudly reigns.
To the God's Mother dear; for Cybele
Turn'd her beloved Atys *to this Tree.*
On one of thefe vain-glorious Marfyas *died,*
And paid his Skin to Phœbus *for his Pride.*
Away of boring Holes in Box be found,
And with his artful Fingers chang'd the Sound.
Glad of himfelf and thirfty after Praife,
On his Shrill Box he to the Shepherds plays.
With thee, Apollo, *next he will contend;*
For thee all Charms of Mufick do defcend.
From the bold Piper foon received his Doom;
(Who ftrive with Heaven never overcome.)
A ftrong made Nut their Apples fortifies,
Againft the Storms which threaten from the Skies.
The Trees are hardy, as the Fruits they bear,
And where rough Winds the rugged Mountains tear,
There flourifh beft; the lower Vales they dread,
And languifh if they have not room to fpread.

S E C T. III.

Of Fir-Trees; their Culture, &c.

OF *Fir-Trees* their are divers Kinds, as the *Scotch Fir,* the *Silver Fir,* the *Spruce Fir,* and the *Norway Fir.*

The *Scotch Fir* is a beautiful Plant, and highly deferves our Notice; 'tis eafily propagated by Seed as is before faid of the Pine, and delights in good Land alfo. The *Spruce Fir,* is not fo fine a Plant as the *Scotch Fir,* nor likewife the *Silver Fir.* However, they are both Beautiful Trees,

3   when

when promiscuously planted in a *Wilderness, Grove, &c.* The *Norway* Fir is an excellent fine Plant for to make Hedges, it being a very close thick Grower, and of a beautiful Green: And the only Nursery, that I know of, as has this Tree, with all other Ever-Greens, Fruit and Forest-Trees, Flowering Shrubs, &c. in their best Perfection, is that of the ingenious Mr. *Peter Mason*, Nursery-Man at *Isleworth* in the County of *Middlesex*, who I dare to affirm, has one of the best Collection of *English* Fruits of any Nursery-Man in *England*; and on whom every Gentleman may safely depend of having, not only every Kind of Fruit exactly of the right Kind desired, but the very best Growth, and at reasonable Rates.

> *Let lofty Hills, and each declining Ground,*
> *(For there they flourish) with tall Firs abound.*
> *Layers of these cut from some antient Grove,*
> *And buried deep in Mould, in Time will move*
> *Young Shoots above the Earth, which soon disdain*
> *The Southern Blasts, and launch into the Main.*
>
> RAPIN.

SECT. IV.

Of the ILEX, *or* Ever-green Oak; *its* Culture, &c.

THIS Kind of Oak is to be valued for the great Services of its Timber, as well as the immediate Beauty of its Form and delightful Leaves, which are green all the Winter, &c. 'Tis a Tree of a quick Growth, and is naturally very large. 'Tis increas'd from its Acorn, and is as much inclinable to have Tap-Roots as the common *English* Oak. The Time of planting the Acorns is in *February*, when they should be planted in a Bed, about five Inches square off one another, and the Mould very fresh and good, always observing to keep them clean

from

from Weeds, and to water them in dry Seafons, &c. Their Continuance in the Seed-Bed muft be two Years; after which Time, they fhould be tranfplanted at proper Diftances where they are to remain, at two Foot and a half, when to make Hedges, and if for Standards, not nearer than thirty Foot: They love a deep, loamy, moift Land. In the Gardens of that beautiful grand Seat of the late Earl of *Dyzart* at *Ham*, near *Richmond* in *Surry*, are many fine Hedges of this Plant, as well as a wonderful large Standard growing at the End of the Terrace, next to the Melancholy Walk, from whofe Acorns thofe Hedges were raifed.

The Obfervation of Mr. *B-d-y*'s in his *New Improvements*, Part I. Page 50. on the Tap-Roots of Trees, is entirely wrong; where he fays, " If we confult the Anatomy of Plants, we " ought to be very careful, not to injure their Tap-Roots, which " are always anfwerable to the leading Shoot on the Top of the " Tree; it is therefore reafonable to believe, that a Plant by " lofing of that downright Root, is in Danger of lofing alfo the " Top-Shoot, which is fed from it. And although a Tree may " ftrike frefh Roots after the Amputation of this leading Root, " yet we may find by Experience that the Sap will then pufh " forth Branches in the Side of the *Stem*, and difcontinue its up- " right Growth."

Now, when a Man writes to the World with a Defign to inform Mankind, 'tis abfolutely neceffary, when he fays, *I know, or have found this or that Thing by Experience, &c.* that he at the fame Time fhould mention where, and when, and in what Manner he made thofe Experiments, with Demonftrations to prove the Truth thereof, which Mr. *B-d-y* has omitted. About ten Years ago, I planted a Wildernefs of *Oaks, Elms, Limes, Platanus, &c.* for the late Honourable *Thomas Vernon*, at his Seat in *Twickenham-Park*, where in feveral Parts thereof, I made Experiments on divers Oak-Trees planted therein; part of which had their Tap-Roots carefully preferved, and others pruned off; and the Confequence was thus, *viz.* altho' thofe with Tap-Roots were planted near to thofe without, and in divers Parts of the Wildernefs, whofe Land differ'd very much in refpect to its Goodnefs, yet in every different Kind of Land, thofe Trees whofe Tap-Roots were cut away, growed with much greater Vigour, and produced finer Perpendicular Branches than thofe whofe Tap-Roots were not difplaced; and indeed many of

thofe

thofe with their Tap-Roots dwindled away, and in three Years
Time died; whereas thofe whofe Roots were pruned, that is,
their Tap-Roots cut off, growed away with Strength and Vigour, and foon became ftately Trees; fo that the above Doctrine
of Mr. *Bradley*'s, of the Tap-Roots of an Oak being cut away,
'twill continue its upright Growth, appears to be like the Horizontal Shelters of Mr. *Laurence*'s, *viz.* an Imagination or
Self-Conceit only.

SECT. V.

Of *the Holly, its Culture*, &c.

THE Wild or Green Holly is generally raifed from its
Berries, which muft be gather'd when ripe, and afterwards fweated before they are put in Sand, as I have already directed: In which Operation Care muft be taken, that
they do not heat over much in their Sweat, for thereby it o'ten
happens, that they become ufelefs, which greatly difappoints the
diligent Planter. The Soil that this Plant delights in, is a fandy gravelly Ground, and is much inclining to have Tap-Roots, which
muft be prevented by being often tranfplanted, at leaft every
three Years, as before directed for Fruit and Foreft-Trees.

The beft Time to remove this Plant, is in *April* or *Auguft*,
being planted in that Manner as directed for the Pine-Tree. If
that you would graft or bud any of the varigated Kinds on the
Green Holly, you muft provide your felf with Cuttings of fuch
Kinds as you like, which may be grafted on young Stocks, of five or
fix Years Growth in *April*, or budded, if your Grafts fhould
mifs, in *July*. And in the Operation of grafting you muft obferve, that the Leaves of the Cutting be carefully cut off, the upper one excepted; that they be exactly placed Bark to Bark; that
they be carefully tied with Baft, and well loam'd, that the Wet
or Air do not get in at the Top, or any Part thereof, which will
immediately kill the tender Graft or Cutting, and thereby difap-

X   point

point you of the Succefs defired. The Bark of this Plant produces Bird-Lime, which may be made divers Ways, but none
better than that prefcrib'd by Mr. *Bradley* in his *New Improvements,* Part II. Page 11.

This Plant makes an excellent Hedge in either Garden, Wildernefs, or common Field, and a good Fence againft Cattle :
'Tis a Tree as will grow in the Drip or Shade of Foreft-Trees,
and is a beautiful Plant in the Quarters of a Wildernefs or Thicket : Its Leaves are always beautiful, and the Berries afford a moft
delightful and agreeable Profpect in moft Months of the Year.
Befides this Green Holly, as produces red Berries, there is another
Kind of Green Holly, that produces yellow Berries, and is a
very beautiful Plant in a Wildernefs, as aforefaid.

The feveral Kinds of Varigated or Bloach'd Hollies, are only
beautiful when promifcuoufly planted amongft the Green Hollies
in a Wildernefs, in fuch a wild Manner as if placed there by Nature.

And alfo when planted in Hedges, to environ an open Com-
partment, Cabinet, Grove, &c. in a Wood or Wildernefs, but never fo fine when train'd up in thofe ftiff Forms of round-headed
Plants, or what the Gardeners call *Pediments,* meaning *Pyra-
ments* or *Cones.* For a Holly is a Plant that loves Liberty, and is
always in its greateft Beauty, when fufer'd to grow wild,
without the Trouble of clipping by Sheers, &c. If Gentlemen
did but compare the mean Afpect of their ftiff clipp'd Hollies,
with the Beauty of thofe free Growers on wild Commons, &c.
they would never after fuffer thofe fine Plants to be fo often injur'd by the unthinking Gardener.

The pretty Invention, as called by Mr. *Bradley* in his *New
Improvements,* Part II. Page 15. of planting Ever-green Hedges
with *Columns* and *Pilafters,* or Varigated Hollies fet in them
at proper Diftances, is entirely wrong; for the Nature of
a Holly is fuch, that it cannot be pruned into thofe nice Members
that are contain'd in the Bafes and Capital of *Columns* and *Pilafters.* I could fay much more on this Head, but at prefent fhall
forbear, feeing that it did not come from an *Architect* any more
than from a *Gardener*; and therefore do advife, that where Hedges of Holly are to be planted, good Choice be made of fuch kind
of Varigated Hollies as naturally grow thick, which mix in the
Hedge-Lines in an irregular Manner with the Green Holly, juft

3

as

as if Nature had been the Planter or Director thereof, and by this Means you will have the moſt beautiful Hedges that Art can produce.   Of this kind of Holly-Hedge are many now grow-ing in the delightful Gardens of Sir *Matthew Decas,* at *Richmond* in *Surry.*

I cannot well conclude this Section, without taking Notice of thoſe wretched Figures many Nurſery-Men and Gardeners breed up their Hollies and other Ever-Greens in, as the Forms of Men on Horſeback, as againſt *Hyde-Park* Gate by *Kenſington;* when they know no more of the Anatomy or Proportion of thoſe Fi-gures, than they do of the beautiful Proportions of Architecture, which they ignorantly attempt to execute, when they breed up Yews, Hollies, *&c.* in the Forms of Balluſtrades, Pedeſtals, *&c.* with the moſt deform'd Body plac'd thereon, by them call'd a round or ſquare Column, which hath neither Baſe, Shaft, or Ca-pital, or indeed any one Thing in them as is beautiful or plea-ſing.   And ſeeing that our *Britiſh* Nation does at this Time con-ſiſt of the moſt noble grand Planters and Encouragers of Gardening of any in *Europe,* 'tis to be hoped, that, for the future, better Rules will be obſerved therein, that is, ſuch as are conſiſtent with Reaſon, Art, and Nature; and that ſuch Plants as have received ſuch former Injuries, may be reſtored to their proper and natural Shapes as ſoon as Time can operate the ſame.   To mention the ſeveral Gardens wherein theſe Abuſes have been executed, would be endleſs; and therefore I ſhall only add, that moſt of the Ever-Greens now growing in the Parterres of his Majeſty's Roy-al Gardens at *Kenſington* and *Hampton-Court,* are of thoſe diſ-proportion'd Forms, *viz.* Columns placed on Pedeſtals, without any Sort of Order, wherein the Beauty of a Column conſiſts, *&c.*

To conclude: When any Part of an entire Order of Columns in Architecture, as a Pedeſtal, Column, or Entablature is juſtly executed, nothing is of ſo grand and beautiful an Aſpect.   And on the contrary, when perform'd by an unskilful Hand, nothing appears ſo diſagreeable.   Hence it is that the Beauty and very Life of Architecture depends on good Proportions.

X 2   S E C T.

S E C T. VI.

Of the Yew-Tree; its Culture, &c.

THE *Yew-Tree* is produced of Seed, or raifed from Cuttings or Layers. Its Seed muft be order'd as the Holly,
becaufe it will not come up till the fecond Spring after
gathering.

'Tis a Tree of a very flow Growth, it loves a light fandy
Soil fomething moift: It makes a beautiful Hedge, as well as
fine Standards, to be mix'd with other Trees in Groves of Ever-
Greens, and to grow wild in the Quarters of a Wildernefs. To
make any further Complaints of the Mifapplication of this Tree
in fet Forms would be needlefs, feeing that the fame has been fufficiently demonftrated in the laft Section.

The beft Seafon to remove this Plant in, is *Auguft* or *April*,
and fhould be planted in the Manner as directed for the Pine-
Tree.

'Tis a Tree that generally has great Plenty of fibrous Roots, if
order'd in the Nurfery, by digging about them every Year, and
being tranfplanted every third, as before directed. The Diftance
they fhould be planted in the Nurfery, muft be in the Rows
about three Foot afunder, and the Rows from each other two
Foot and a half.

S E C T. VII.

Of the Bay-Tree; its Culture, &c.

THE *Bay-Tree* is a beautiful Tree, and may be bred Standards, to be planted in an open Grove of Ever-Greens. 'Tis encreafed from Seed, Layers, Suckers, or Cuttings. It delights in a gravelly, moift, fhady Soil, and therefore beft in a Grove or Wildernefs. It muft (as all other Trees) be kept well water'd after planting, which is to be done in *April* or *Auguft*. To raife this Tree from its Seed or Berries, you muft obferve, that they are not gather'd before they are quite ripe, that afterwards you lay them thin, in a dry Place to fweat, which being over, put them into dry Sand, and keep them therein till the Middle of *February* next enfuing, and then fow them in a Bed of fine Earth, as directed for the Afhen-Keys, &c. When they have ftood three Years in the Seed-Bed, you muft tranfplant them into the Nurfery, obferving to prune off their Roots, and keep them digg'd every Year, free from Weeds, and tranfplanted every third Year, till they are planted out in the Places where they are to remain. Amongft all the Kinds of Ever-Greens, I know none more beautiful than the Bay-Tree, provided that its luxuriant Branches are pruned with a Knife, and not barbaroufly mangled with Sheers. To increafe this Plant from Cuttings or Layers, you muft obferve to perform thofe Works in *October*, in the Manner as before directed. In fome very hard Winters, the fevere Frofts will difcolour them, and the only Way to recover fuch Plants, is to head them down to found and healthy Wood.

The *Dutch Bay-Tree* is more tender than our *Englifh Bay-Tree*, and therefore requires to be fhelter'd in the Green-Houfe during the Severity of the Winter. Of this Kind of Bay-Tree, the fineft, that I ever faw, are thofe in the Gardens of the *Royal Palace*

3

Palace at Kenſington, and ſome others at the *Lodge-Gardens* in *Windſor Great-Park,* and in many *Noblemen* and *Gentlemen's Gardens* at *Twickenham* in the County of *Middleſex.*

> *In watery Vales where pleaſant Fountains flow,*
> *Their fragrant Berries lovely Bay-Trees ſhow.*
> *With Leaves for ever green; nor can we gueſs,*
> *By their Endowments, their Extraction leſs.*
> *The charming Nymph liv'd by clear* Peneus *Side,*
> *And might to* Jove *himſelf have been ally'd,*
> *But that ſhe choſe in Virtue's Path to tread,*
> *And thought a God unworthy of her Bed.*
> Phœbus, *whoſe Darts of late ſucceſsful prov'd*
> *In* Python's *Death, expected to be lov'd;*
> *And had ſhe not withſtood blind* Cupid's *Power.*
> *The fiery Steed and Heaven had been her Dower.*
> *But ſhe by her Refuſal more obtain'd,*
> *And loſing him, immortal Honour gain'd,*
> *Cheriſh'd by the* Apollo, *Temples wear*
> *The Bays, and ev'ry clamorous Theater,*
> *The Capital itſelf; and the proud Gate*
> *Of great* Trapeian Jove *they celebrate.*
> *Into the* Delphick *Rites, the Stars they dive,*
> *And all the hidden Laws of Fate perceive.*
> *They in the Field, (where Death and Danger's found,*
> *Where claſhing Arms, and louder Trumpets ſound,)*
> *Incite true Courage: Hence the Bays, each* Muſe
> *Th' inſpiring God, and all* good Poets *chuſe.*

RAPIN.

S E C T.

SECT. VIII.

Of the Laurel; its Culture, &c.

THE *Laurel* is a noble Ever-Green, and a Tree of a quick Growth. It delights in the Shade, and is a great Embellishment to the Parts of a Wilderness. 'Tis a Tree that loves Liberty, and therefore very improper for headed or pyrament Plants. It makes a beautiful Hedge, being carefully pruned with the Knife, and not with its great Enemy the Sheers. 'Tis propagated from the Berries, Cuttings, or Layers; and when bred up as Standards, is wonderful pleasant in Groves of Ever-Greens, and within the Quarters of a Wilderness, its Cover is delightful to all Kind of Game, as Hares, Pheasants, Woodcocks, &c. and will thrive in any Land as is not over hot.

SECT. IX.

Of the Laurus-Tinus; its Culture, &c.

THE *Laurus-Tinus* is both an Ever-green and Flowering Shrub, and is all the Winter the most beautifullest Plant of any in the Garden.

'Tis increas'd by Layers or Cuttings, and is a very quick Grower, but never makes a large Tree. The Soil it delights in, is a moist sandy Loam, and in a shady Place. The best Form that this Tree appears in, is in either that of a Cone, or quite wild in a Wilderness. Also Hedges of this Plant is

wonderful

wonderful fine, if their Beauty is not deſtroyed by the un-
ſkilful Hand of the Gardener, in clipping them at the ſame
Seaſon as he does Yews, Hollies, &c.   The proper Seaſon for
to prune this Plant is, when all its Bloom is gone, which is in
the Spring; juſt before they begin to ſhoot out their young and
tender Branches.

It is beſt to lay down the Layers, or plant the Cuttings in
October, and to tranſplant them in *Auguſt* following; as before
directed for the Pine-Tree.

Of Laurus-Tinus there is two Sorts: The one, which
blows very early; and the other, (called the black ſhining
Laurus-Tinus,) as blows late in the Winter, which continues
until the end of *May*, and of the two, is the moſt beautiful.

S E C T. X.

Of the *Phillyrea*; its Culture, &c.

THE ſeveral Kinds of *Phillyrea's* are five, *viz.* The
True Phillyrea, the Plain Phillyrea, the Bloach'd Philly-
rea, the Dutch Silver-leafed and the Dutch-guilded
Phillyrea.

Theſe Kinds of Phillyrea's, in general, are beſt increaſed from
Layers. They delight in a light Soil, and ſhould be laid down
in *September*, or *October* at lateſt, and planted the *Auguſt*
after.

The true *Phillyrea* is a very ſlow grower; but makes a moſt
beautiful Tree, and eſpecially when bred up in the Form of
a Cone.   It will endure hard Weather, and values not the
Inſults of Winds.

The other four Kinds are leſs able to engage the Violence
of a Storm, or to endure great Colds; therefore are beſt againſt
a Wall, or in Thickets of Wilderneſſes, &c.

Let

Let Phillyrea on your Walls be plac'd,
Either with Wire, or slender Twigs made fast.
Its brighter Leaf with proudest Arras *vies,*
And lends a pleasing Object to our Eyes.
Then let it freely on your Walls ascend,
And there its native Tapestry extend.

RAPIN.

S E C T. XI.

Of the Arbutus, *or* Strawberry-Tree *; its Culture,* &c.

THIS beautiful Plant produces Blossoms twice a Year, and its Fruit is ripe in the Winter: 'Tis a Plant that greatly adds to the Beauty of a Garden, Wilderness, &c. but will not admit of being clipp'd as most other Ever-Greens are; 'tis a very great Ornament to a Wilderness, and makes the most agreeable Hedge as can be desired: The Leaf is of a very agreeable Form, and of a pleasant lively Green ; 'tis increased from Seed or Layers, which last, should be laid down in *September*, and remain upon the Stool two Years at least, to be well rooted, being always water'd in dry and hot Seasons. The Fruit is ripe about *Christmas*, whose Form is very like that of a Strawberry; but its Taste is like unto that of Service. When the Fruit is gather'd, let it dry ; then break them to Pieces, which put into Sand, where they must remain until the End of *March*, or Beginning of *April*, at which time they must be sow'd in a Bed of fine Earth, cover'd about half an Inch with fine Mould sifted thereon.

Your Seed being thus sown, you must be careful to keep the Earth moist ; and when you water it, take care that the Water's Force do not disturb the Earth, whereby the young Seedlings may be prejudiced. *N. B.* If you were to sow the Seed on a decay'd Hot-Bed, 'twould greatly help the Germination of the Seeds.

Y

S E C T.

SECT. XII.

Of the Piracantha; its Culture, &c.

THIS Ever-Green is increafed from Layers, or its Berries, which are to be order'd as thofe of the Yew, Holly, &c. becaufe they do not grow, or at leaft come up, till the fecond Spring after they ripen.

The Perfections of this Plant are many; as, firft, 'tis a free Grower, and with good Care will make a large Tree; fecondly, its Leaves are of a very beautiful Form, and a pleafant Green; thirdly, its fine Bunches of white Bloffoms, produced in *May*; and, laftly, its beautiful Clufters of red Berries which hang all the *Winter*.

'Tis a very proper Plant for a Hedge, in refpect to its Thorns, and is very beautiful in the Quarters of a Wildernefs.

Its Wood is of a very hard Nature; and therefore the moft tender Branches of the laft Years Shoot, are thofe you muft lay down for Layers; which fhould be done in *October*, and remain upon the Stools two Years, before they are taken off, and in that time they will be well rooted, and fit to tranfplant; which may be done in *Auguft* or *April*. Its proper Soil is a dry Gravel; but it will thrive in moft loamy Lands, that are not very wet or cold.

SECT. XIII.

Of the Box-Tree; its Culture, &c

OF Box-Trees there are two Kinds; the one plain, and the other varigated; which are both raised from Slips, Layers, or Seed.

Their natural Soil is chalky mountanous Lands, but will grow very well in moſt loamy Soils. 'Tis a Tree that will grow to a very large Size, of which Box-Hill in *Surry* is a good Evidence.

It is a very pleaſant Tree, to be mix'd with other Standards in a Grove of Ever-Greens: It makes fine Hedges, and is very beautiful in the Quarters of a Wildernefs. 'Tis a Tree of a very ſlow Growth; but its Wood is of great Service for the making of Sectors, Quadrants, and other Mathematical Inſtruments; and will endure the hardeſt Froſts our Winters produces. Its Leaf is very ſmall, and of a beautiful light Green, and is never ſo diſagreeable as ſome makes it, in reſpect to its Smell.

Dutch Box is of a much leſſer Growth, then the preceeding, being only uſed for the Edging of Borders, inſtead of Bones, Border-Boards, &c. and is of all others the moſt cheapeſt, handſomeſt, and laſting Edging; but the moſt improper to Edge ſuch Borders with wherein Fruit-Trees are planted, except they are very broad, and the Roots of the Box cut away every Year, on that ſide that is next to the Fruit-Trees, by a Spade, or the like, at the Time when thoſe Borders are digg'd; for you muſt underſtand that this kind of Box grows more in its Roots, than its Top, and is an open Robber of every Plant or Shrub that grows near it.

S E C T. XIV.

Of the Juniper ; its Culture, &c:

OF this Kind of Ever-Green we have two Sorts, *viz.* the common *English* and *Swedish* Juniper ; which are both hardy Plants. They are of a beautiful Green, and makes a very fine Variety, being planted wild amongst other Ever-Greens in a Wilderness Thicket, *&c.* They both delight in a dry poor Soil ; but are improved by a good sandy Loam.

They are increased from their Berries sown in *March,* in dry light Ground, and will come up in six Weeks or two Months after sowing. They must remain in the Seed-Bed two Years before they they are transplanted, during which Time they must be carefully kept clean from Weeds, and water'd in a very dry Season. *N. B.* That the oftner these Sorts of Trees are transplanted, the better they will be rooted ; and in the pruning of them, observe to cut off their Tap-Roots, and in planting to place their other Roots, in a Horizontal Position. I will not here undertake to describe the several Virtues belonging to that so much celebrated Liquor as is distill'd from the Berries of this Plant, because 'tis already known to every old Woman ; but for such as are curious herein, I believe, may be fully inform'd in the *Ladies Diary,* not long since published, or other such Books of the like Nature.

S E C T. XV.

Of the Italian Green-Privet.

THIS kind of Privet, is increased from its Berries, sown in *March* on a Bed of light Earth, inclinable to a Gravel, which is the Soil it most delights in, covering the Berries about an Inch thick with fine Earth sifted over them, obſerving in dry Weather to keep them frequently water'd, and always clear of Weeds.

When they have ſtood two Years in the Seed-Bed, they ſhould be tranſplanted into Hedges, or the Quarters of a Wilderneſs; which in both Places are very beautiful.

This Plant is of a very quick Growth; and altho' 'tis a Fóreigner, yet 'twill endure the Violence of our Winters Froſts, &c. without any kind of Prejudice to its Verdure.

This ſort of Privet was brought from *Italy* by the ingenuous Mr. *Balle* of *Kingſington*, which by the *Italians* is called *Olivetta*, becauſe its Leaves are not unlike thoſe of the Olive.

S E C T. XVI.

Of the Cyprus, Lignum-Vitæ, and Cedar of Lebanus ; its Culture, &c.

AMONGST all the Ever-Greens hitherto treated off, none make a more grander Appearance in a Garden, than the *Cyprus*, and *Cedar* of *Labanus* ; neither is any Tree ſo eaſy to be cultivated; for their Ordering has no ſort of Difference from that of an *Ever-Green, Oak, Pine,* &c.

I have obſerv'd in ſeveral old Gardens, divers fine Walks of thoſe Trees, far exceeding all others I ever ſaw of any kind, which of late have been deſtroy'd ; to the great Shame of thoſe as were the Inſtruments of their Death.

I am not inſenſible of diſpleaſing ſome People herein ; but that regard not, ſince my Abilities are capable to prove the Truth of what I have aſſerted; and indeed, amongſt all thoſe Sacrifices, I can't but ſay, that I was heartily ſorry to hear of the Deſtruction of that old and grand Walk of Cyprus Trees, not long ſince growing in the Gardens lately in the Poſſeſſion of the *Lady Humble* at *Twickenham.* However, for the future, I hope to ſee theſe Trees flouriſh, and be kindly received in the

moſt

most grand Parts of our Plantations, wherein they are a very great Enrichment.

Though Cypresses contiguous well appear,
They better shew, if planted not so near.
And since to any Shape with Ease they yield,
What Bounds more proper to divide a Field?
Repine not Cyparissus then in vain,
For by your Change, you Glory did obtain.
*   Silvanus and this Boy with equal Fire,*
Did heretofore a lovely Hart admire:
While in the cooler Pastures once it fed,
An Arrow shot at random struck it dead.
But when the Youth the dying Beast had found,
And knew himself the Author of the Wound;
With never-ceasing Sorrow he laments,
And on his Breast his Grief and Anger vents.
Silvanus mov'd with the poor Creature's Fate,
Converts his former Love to present Hate,
And no more Pity in his angry Words,
Than to himself th' afflicted Youth affords.
Weary of Life, and quite oppress'd with woe,
Upon the Ground his Tears in Channels flow:
Which having water'd, the productive Earth,
The Cyprus first from thence deriv'd its Birth,
With Silvan's Aid; nor was it only meant,
T' express our Sorrow, but for Ornament.
Chiefly when growing low your Fields they bound,
Or when your Garden's Avenues are crown'd,
With their long Rows, sometimes it serves to hide,
Some Trench declining on the other Side.
Th' unequal Branches always keep that green;
Of which its Leaves are ne'er devested seen:
Though shook with Storms, yet it unmov'd remains.
And by its Trial greater Glory gains.

RAPIN.

NEW

...es of Trellis Work for the enter... *Plate*

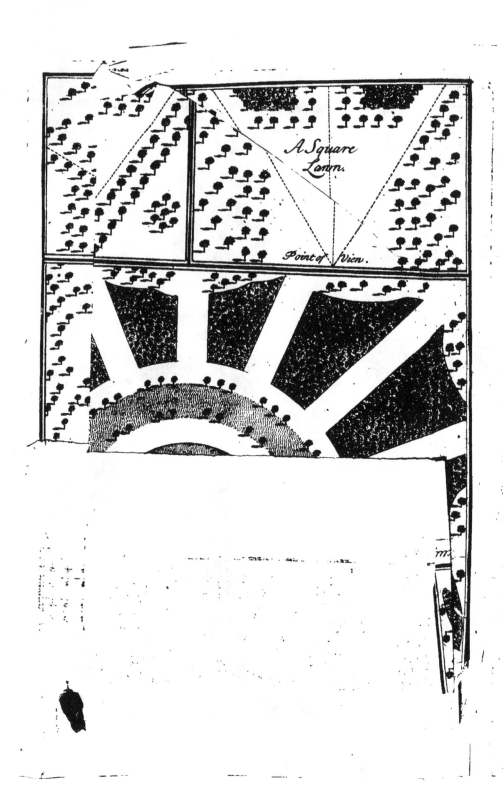

A Square
Lawn.

Point of View.

NEW
PRINCIPLES
OF
GARDENING.

PART. V.

Of Flowering-Shrubs ; their Culture, &c.

SECT. I.

Of the several Methods by which Flower-ing-Shrubs are raised.

FLOWERING-SHRUBS are propagated from *Layers, Suckers, Cuttings,* or *Seed.*

(1.) Those propagated from Layers, are the Jessamine, Honey-Suckles, Lilacs, Roses, Senna, Pomegranate, and Althea Frutex. (2.) From *Suckers,* are the Lilac, Spiræa Frutex, Syringa, and Guilder-Rose. (3.) From Cuttings, are Jessamine, Honey-

Honey-Suckles, and Pomegranate. And, laſtly from Seed, are the
Tulip-Tree, Maracock, or Paſſion-Flower, Spaniſh Broom, Laburnum, Bladder Senna, Scopion Senna, Arbor Judæ, and Mezerion.

I need not here repeat the Method of laying down the Layers, planting the Cuttings, or ſowing the Seeds, of the moſt common Sorts, becauſe that the ſame Method is to be obſerved
herein, as directed for the Ever-Greens, &c. But for the uncommon Kinds, as the Tulip-Tree, &c. I ſhall be more particular therein.

S E C T. II.

Of the Tulip-Tree; its Culture, &c.

THIS beautiful Tree, though rank'd amongſt the Shrubs,
in regard to its Flowers, yet 'tis a Tree of a very
great Growth.

In the Lord *Peterborough's* Wilderneſs, at *Parſon's-Green,*
near *Fulham* in *Middleſex,* is growing a moſt beautiful and
ſtately Tree of this Kind, and of as great a Height as moſt
Timber-Trees. 'Tis an Inhabitant of the Wood, which is demonſtrated by its not thriving in an open Expoſure, and is a
beautiful Tree to compoſe Part of a Grove of Foreſt Trees.
The Leaves are like the Maple, and of a pleaſant Green; and
its Flowers like unto a Tulip, from which 'tis called the
Tulip-Tree, which are produced at the Ends of the Branches.

The Petals of the Flower are mighty beautiful, being of a
yellow Ground, varigated with a delightful Red.

The Fruit which ſucceed thoſe curious Bloſſoms, are of a conical Form, but never ripens in England.

And as this noble Tree is a Native of *Carolina* and *Virginia,*
(at which Places its Seed ripens very well,) 'tis from thence
we muſt receive the Seed that we propagate our Plants from in
England

England. But if we fuffer young Shoots to break out at bottom, or cut down the Plant as a Stool, and the young Shoots being laid down, as Layers of Lime, *&c.* they will ftrike Root, and grow very well. The Soil it delights in, is a fandy warm Loam: Its Seed muft be fown in *Auguft* at lateft, in Pots fill'd with the aforefaid Soil, which muft be fheltered all Winter; and in the Spring they will come up: At which time keep them clean from Weeds, and do not fuffer them to be over dry for want of Water.

When your young Nurfery, has lived two Years in the Seed-Pots, they muft be tranfplanted into larger Pots fingly, wherein they muft remain for eight or ten Years, being fheltered every Winter, and taken up, and replanted again in the fame Pots, to create good Roots, every third Year; which will fupport its Trunk when planted out, with fufficient Plenty of Juices, and gaeatly add to its future Growth.

S E C T. III.

Of the Maracoc, or Paffion-Plant.

ALTHOUGH there may be many Kinds of Paffion-Trees in other Parts abroad, as in *Amfterdam* Phyfick Gardens, *&c.* as mention'd by *Tournefort* in his *Elements of Botany,* p. 206. yet we have but one that will refift the Severity of our Winters. This Flower was firft difcover'd by the *Spanifb* Friars, in the Weft-Indies, of which Plaee 'tis an Inhabitant: The Magnitude of each Flower, when full blown, is generally about four or five Inches Diameter, wherein are ten Petals, divers ftaminous Threads, and other Particles; which together, the Friars fuppofed was an Epitome of our Saviour's Paffion, and therefore called it the Paffion-Flower. *Vide Bradley's Improvements, Part* II. *Page 52.*

The Soil it beft delights in, is a very moift cool Soil, well mix'd with Cow Dung: 'Tis increafed from Layers or Cuttings; the firft laid down in *March,* towards the Beginning of the

Z   Month,

Month; and the latter planted in the End of *May*, or Beginning of *June*. 'Tis a Plant of a quick Growth, beft againft a Wall, and is a very great Embellifhment to the Pleafure-Garden.

S E C T. IV.

Of the Spanifh-Broom; its Culture, &c.

THIS is a beautiful Shrub for a Wildernefs, being mix'd amongft other Plants: Its Leaves are of a delightful Green, and its Flowers of a pleafant Yellow, which put forth in *June* and *July*. 'Tis generally increafed from its Seed fown in *March*, on a Bed of light Earth; but it may be increafed from Layers, laid down with a Twift as an Elm, or being cut at a Joint as a July-Flower.

S E C T. V.

Of the Laburnum, its Culture, &c.

THIS delightful Shrub is of a quick Growth, and of great Beauty in a Wildernefs, when it produces its beautiful Clufters of yellow Bloffoms in *May* and *June*. Its Nature is very agreeable to either Shade, or open Expofure; but beft when mix'd with Foreft-Trees, as Platanus, Elm, Lime, *&c.* 'Tis propagated from its Fruit, or Seed, which is ripe in *September*, and very like unto young Peafcods, juft before ripe. The Time to fow this Seed is in *March*, and muft remain in its Seed-Bed for two Years; after which, it may be tranfplanted at Pleafure, when other Trees are planted.

S E C T.

SECT. VI.

Of Senna ; its Culture, &c.

OF this Kind of Shrub, there are two Sorts, *viz.* the Blad-der-Senna, and the Scopion-Senna ; of which, the laſt is the moſt beautiful. They both delight in a good loamy Soil, and may be propagated by Seed ſown about the Middle of *March*, or by Layers laid down in *October*, or *April*. They are Lovers of the Shade, and are mighty beau-tiful in the Quarters of a Wilderneſs. The latter of the two produces Bloſſoms, as well in the Autumn, as in the Spring; that are very delightful.

SECT. VII.

Of the Arbor Judæ; its Culture, &c.

THIS Shrub is naturally a *Weſt-Indian*, and has not long been brought into *England.* 'Tis of a large Growth; it delights in a loamy Soil; produces beau-tiful Cluſters of Bloſſoms in *March, April,* and *May ;* it reſiſts the Severity of our Climate; 'tis propagated from Seed ſown in *March ;* and is a beautiful Plant in a Wilderneſs.

Z 2 SECT.

S E C T. VIII.

Of the Mezerion; its Culture, &c.

OF Mezerions there are two Kinds, *viz.* the White Mezerion, and the Red Mezerion; of which, the laft is
the moſt common. They are both of a ſmall Growth,
and therefore are rather more proper for open Borders, than the
Quarters of a Wilderneſs.

In *January*, the Air is perfum'd with the delightful Odour
of their Bloſſoms, which cover their Branches long before their
Leaves come out, and continue a long Time in Bloom. When
their Bloſſoms are gone, they ſtill appear no leſs beautiful, being adorn'd with their Vermillion Berries, mix'd amongſt their
beautiful Leaves, which makes a moſt delightful Compoſition.

They are increaſed from their Berries ſown in *March*, and
love a ſandy Loam.

S E C T. IX.

Of the Jeſſemine and Honey-Suckle, their Culture, &c.

THESE Flowering Shrubs are not inferior to any of the
preceding, in regard to thoſe moſt pleaſant (I may
ſay heavenly) fragrant Odours which perfume the Air,
even into its diſtant Atmoſphere, produced by their beautiful
Bloſſoms.

(1.) JESSEMINES;

(1.) Of Jessemines, there are three Kinds, *viz.* the White, the Yellow, and the *Perfian*. The common White Jeffemine is a free Grower, and refifts the Severity of our Winters: It produces its beautiful fragrant Flowers in *June*, and continues in Bloom till *September*: 'Twill grow in any loamy Land, and is increafed from Layers laid down, or Cuttings planted in *September*; wherein obferve, that in Confideration of their Roots ftriking at their Joints, therefore be careful to bury two or three in the Ground to either Layer or Cutting, and they will fucceed to your Defire.

The Beauty of this Plant is fo great, that in my humble Opinion, a Garden cannot well have too many of them. And as this is a Plant of Liberty, it muft therefore be planted at the Bottom of Standard-Trees in Groves, Walks, &c. and even in Hedges alfo, wherein 'twill interfperfe itfelf with its delightful Bloffoms, and plea'ant Odour.

And altho' it has been the Practice of Breeding this Plant up in headed Plants, yet I cannot commend it, feeing that it naturally hates to be either confined, or ftump'd with Sheers.

The *Spanifh* White Jeffemine may be grafted on this common White: 'Tis a fweet delightful Flower; as alfo are the *Italian* and *Portugal* Jeffemines, whofe Bloffoms are very large and beautiful.

The *Perfian* Jeffemine is a beautiful Shrub: Its Flowers are Purple, and will endure the Winter's Frofts.

The Yellow Jeffemine, is alfo a very agreeable Shrub, and will endure the Severity of our Climate.

(2.) Honey-Suckles; of which, there are feveral Kinds, as the Ever-green, the Early-red, the Late-White and Red, and the Scarlet-flower'd Honey-Suckles. They, in general, are increafed from Layers, or Cuttings, as the Jeffemine. They are all Lovers of Liberty, and when bred up in headed Plants, make a moft terrible Figure all the Winter.

They delight in the Shade, and love to clamber on other Trees. They are Natives of the Woods, of a quick Growth, but incapable of fupporting their own Bodies, and therefore borrow the Ufe of their neighbouring Trees to affift them therein.

And as their Bloffoms perfume the Air with their delight-Odours all the Summer, 'tis impoffible that a Garden can have too many, being carefully planted, fo as to run up Standard-Trees, Hedges, &c. as before is faid of the Jeffemine.

Thus

Thus fays Rapin of the Gardener.

Nor knows he well to make his Garden shine
With all Delights, who fragrant Jessemine
Neglects to cherish, wherein heretofore
Industrious Bees laid up their precious Store.
Unless with Poles you fix it to the Wall,
Its own deceitful Trunk will quickly fall.
These Shrubs, like wanton Ivy, still mount high,
But wanting Strength, on other Props rely.
The pliant Branches which they always bear,
Make them with Ease to any Thing adhere.
The pleasing Odors which their Flow'rs expire,
Make the young Nymphs and Matrons them desire,
Those to adorn themselves withall; but these
To grace the Altars of the Deities.

RAPIN

SECT. X.

Of the Lilac; its Culture, &c.

THE Lilack is a very handfome flowering Shrub; of which there are two Sorts, *viz.* the White, and the Blue, whofe Flowers are very beautiful: 'Tis a great Embellifhment to a Wildernefs, and is a Shrub of a large Growth; they are both raifed by Layers laid down in *March,* or by Suckers taken off and planted in *September* or *October*: And love a light Soil.

SECT.

S E C T. XI.

Of Roses; their Culture, &c.

OF Roses we have a very great Variety, which are in general, very pleafant and delightful; as, *Firſt*, the Monthly Rofe, that blows fingly, and that which blows in Clufters. 'Tis beſt to have fome of this Sort planted againſt a South-
Wall, which will caufe them to blow early, as at the End of
March, or Beginning of *April*, and continue till the Middle of
June. Thofe of the fame Kind, planted in open Borders,
will not produce their Bloom till the Middle of *May*, and will
continue till the Beginning of *Auguſt*. And you muſt obferve
as foon as their Bloſſoms are gone, to top their Branches; which
will caufe a fecond Bloom in the Autumn, that will continue till near unto *Chriſtmas*.

Secondly, The Cinnamon Rofe, a forward Blower, and a
fine Flower.

Thirdly, The Damask Rofe, of an excellent pleafant Odour:
It blows in *May*, and will laſt for fix or feven Weeks.

Fourthly, The Cabbage Rofe.

Fifthly, The *Rofamundi*, or *York* and *Lancaſter* Rofe.

Sixthly, The Province Rofe.

Seventhly, The White Musk-Rofe.

Eighthly, The Red Rofe.

Ninthly, and *laſtly*; The Yellow Rofe.

All which are propagated from Suckers or Layers: The laſt
laid down in *September* or *October*, and the firſt planted in
October. They are, in general, beautiful Ornaments in a Grove;
Wildernefs. or any other Part of the Garden, and highly deferves our Notice, much more than they have had hitherto.

S E C T. XII.

Of the Pomegranate ; its Culture, &c.

OF this Plant there are two Kinds, *viz.* the Single, and the Double-bloſſom'd Pomegranate, whoſe Bloſſoms are of a beautiful Vermillion Red. Of which, the firſt frequently produces Fruit, and ſometimes ripens with us. Theſe Plants delight in a light Soil, and are propagated from Cuttings, planted in *Auguſt* or *September*, on an Eaſt Border; or from Layers laid down at the ſame Time, or in *March*. They are both beautiful Plants, and are beſt for a Wilderneſs, rather than for headed Plants, which, by being often clipp'd, ſoon proves their Ruin: 'Tis a hardy Plant, and will endure the Winter Froſts, cold Winds, &c.

S E C T. XIII.

Of the Altheæ Frutex ; its Culture, &c.

THIS Plant is uſed chiefly to adorn the Quarters of a Wilderneſs: Of which, there are two Sorts, *viz* the White, and the Purple-flower'd: They are both propagated from Suckers, or Layers, laid down in *September*; or from the Seeds, ſown in the Middle or End of *March*. Their Bloſſoms are very beautiful, which do appear in great Plenty in *Auguſt*. They afford a good Proſpect; and will thrive in any Kind of ſandy Loam, or other Soil whatever, Clay excepted. The Time for Planting this Shrub, is *October*.

S E C T.

SECT. XIV.

Of the Syringa ; its Culture, &c.

THIS Shrub is of great Beauty in a Wildernefs, producing fine Bunches of fragrant Bloffoms in *May,* whofe
Odour is very pleafant, and not unlike that of Orange
Bloffoms. It delights in fuch Part of a Wildernefs as is not entirely fhaded, or quite open. 'Tis propagated from Suckers
taken off, and planted in *October,* and is a very free Grower.

SECT. XV.

Of the Guilder-Rofe; its Culture, &c.

AMONGST all the Flower-Tribe hitherto mention'd,
none makes a more grand Appearance in *May,* than the
Guilder-Rofe, whofe beautiful Bloffoms are produced in
great Clufters; and each Flower a perfect Globe of three or
four Inches in Diameter. 'Tis a Plant that will rife twelve or
fourteen Foot high, and is very beautiful and pleafant in a Wildernefs. The Soil it delights in, is a good ftrong Loam; and
it is propagated from Suckers taken from the Mother Plant, and
planted in *October.*

SECT. XVI.

Of the Almond; its Culture, &c.

THE Almond-Tree is a very beautiful Tree during the Time of its Bloom in the Spring, and highly deferves a Place in our Wildernefs. 'Tis propagated from the Kernels fown in *March*; or it may be grafted on the Plumb-Stock in *February*, or budded thereon in *July*. The Soil proper for this Plant, is a fandy Loam, if raifed from its Kernel; and when grafted or budded on the Plumb-Stocks, on a ftronger Land.

SECT. XVII.

Of the Mirabalon Plumb, and Double-Bloffom'd Cherry.

THESE two Plants produce great Quantities of Bloom in the Spring, and continue their Bloffoms a long Time. They are wonderful beautiful, when mix'd in a Wildernefs amongft Almond-Trees, and will thrive in moft Soils: They are both propagated by being grafted, the firft on a Plumb-Stock, and the latter on a Cherry-Stock.

SECT.

S E C T. XVIII.

Of the Sweet-Brier ; its Culture, &c.

ALTHO' the Sweet-Brier is not directly a flowering Shrub, yet its fragrant Odour highly obliges us to plant it in all Parts of our Gardens and Wildernesses, and especially for Hedges, and at the Bottoms of Standard-Trees, *&c.* And besides this common Sort, there is another Kind of it called *Eglantine,* which produces a fine red Flower, with broad Leaves, that perfumes the Air very strongly with its pleasant Odours. The first Kind hereof is raised from Berries sown in *February* ; and the latter propagated from Layers laid down in *September.* This last Kind makes very beautiful headed Plants, which are very proper to be raised in Pots, to adorn the Ladies Chimneys, and perfume the Air of their Chambers with its pleasant and most delightful Odours.

S E C T. XIX.

Of the Furze-Bush, and English Broom ; their Culture, &c.

THE Beauty of these two Shrubs, seems to be valued much after the very same Manner as a curious Tulip, Auricula, Julyflower, *&c.* is by Florists, when 'tis become common, and in every Garden. Whilst on the other Hand, if they chance to have a Seedling whose Blossom is an indifferent good one, and not near so good as that which is

common;

common; yet the Seedling shall carry the Bell, and that which far exceeds it, be not regarded: Which indeed is the Case of these two Shrubs; for were they not common, they would be valued, and cultivated with as much Eagerness as any Ever-green or Shrub whatsoever; for, in Fact, the Furze is capable of any Form required, but much finer when let grow in its own rural Manner as Nature directs. If the Beauty of this Shrub, that is, its fine green Leaves, which serve for a proper Ground to cast forth the Beauty of its yellow Flowers, with which it abounds in all Seasons of the Year, was compar'd with that of the long-esteem'd Yew, whose Aspect is melancholy, and the true Image of Sadness; 'twould not only be found to be much the finer Plant of the two, but more deserving the Gardener's Care.

For to speak the naked Truth, the Yew-tree is never better placed, than when planted in a Church-yard as an Emblem of Mortality, which is its true Representation, and, in my humble Opinion, very improper for a delightful Garden.

But to return to the Culture of these Plants; observe that they are both raised from Seed sown in *February* or *March*, but are difficult to remove; therefore transplant them the *October* next after Sowing, in such Places where they are to remain. They both make good Cover for Game; and the Furze makes a most beautiful Hedge, wherein many Birds take great Pleasure to build their Nests, which is not a small Ornament to either Garden or Wilderness.

SECT. XX.

Of the several Months of the Year, when Flowering Shrubs are in Blossom, and their Duration.

THE first blowing flowering Shrub is the *Mezerion*, which presents its *beautiful Blossoms* in *January*, and continues in Bloom to the Middle of *February*.

In *February*, the *Furze* opens its golden-colour'd Bloom, which continues till *October*.

In

In *March*,⎫
In *April*,⎬ the *Arbor Judæa*, and holds till *May*.

In *May*, the *Lilac, Syringa, Guilder-Rofe, Laburnum*, and *Honey-Suckles*; of which, the feveral Kinds of the laft keep blowing till *September*; but the others, about fix or feven Weeks at moft.

In *June*, the *White Jeffemines*, and *Spanifh Broom*; the firft till *September*, and the laft till *Auguft*.

In *July*, the *Tulip-tree*, which continues till *Auguft*.

In *Auguft*, the *Althæa Frutex*, which lafts till *September*.

The *Senna's* blow twice a Year, *viz.* Spring and Autumn; and foon after them comes that beautiful Ever-green and flowering Shrub, the *Laurus-tinus*, which is not only a Grace to the Garden all the Winter, but in the Spring alfo, till the Beginning of *March*.

This being a fufficient Information of their feveral Seafons of Bloom, from which a Garden may be fo planted, as to have one or other of the feveral Kinds always in Bloffom throughout the whole Year; I fhall, in the next Section, inform my Reader in what Manner they are to be difpofed of, fo as to receive a beautiful and grand Appearance, as well from thofe whofe Growth is fmall and low, as from them of a large and higher Stature.

SECT. XXI.

Of the Manner of Difpofing and Planting Flowering Shrubs in the proper Parts of a Wildernefs.

BEFORE we can come to the Planting of thefe beautiful Shrubs, we muft confider the Nature of their Growth, in refpect to Stature; and alfo the great Variety of their Colours, which ought to be fo intermix'd, as for every Flower to be an Oppofite or Ground to throw forward the Beauty of the other.

The

The several Statures of these Plants may be reduc'd to three Sizes, *viz.* those of the tallest Growth; those of the middling Growth; and those of the lowest Growth.

First then; Those of the highest Growth are the double-blossom Cherry, Lilac, Guilder-Rose, *Spanish* Broom, Laburnum, Mirabalon Plumb, Tulip-tree, White Rose, and Almond.

Secondly; Those of a middling Growth are the Syringa, Damask Rose, Musk Rose, Spira Frutex, Arbor Judææ, Senna's, Althæa Frutex, Almond, being grafted a half Standard, as also the Mirabalon Plumb, and double-blossom Cherry.

Thirdly and *lastly*; The low Tribe are the Mezerion, the Furze, the Red Rose, the Cabbage Rose, the Province Rose, the Monthly Rose, the Mundi Rose, the Cinnamon Rose, the Yellow Rose, the Almond, being grafted low; as also the double-blossom Cherry, and Mirabalon Plumb, into which Class I introduce the Sweet-Brier.

Having thus divided them into their several Classes, we must next consider their several Colours, that we may thereby dispose of them in the best Manner, so as to cause the greatest Variety; and in order thereto, we'll begin with those of the first and largest Class.

First, then, of those the double-blossom Cherry, the White Lilac, the Guilder-Rose, the Mirabalon Plumb, and the White Rose, are all entirely White Blossoms. The other Kind of Lilac blue, the *Spanish* Broom, and Laburnum, yellow; the Tulip-tree, a mix'd Colour; and the Almond, a Peach Colour; so that the Colours produced by this Class are white, blue, yellow, a mix'd, and a Peach Colour. The several Sorts of White are five; of Yellow, two; of Blue; Mix'd; and Peach-Colour; of each, one only. Their several Colours being thus distinguish'd, we must now come to their Planting; wherein, first, observe, that these of the highest Rank must be planted backward from the View, to give Room for the others to come before them, in such Manner as to form, by the Difference of their several Growths, a perfect Slope of beautiful Flowers.

But to the Purpose: Let the first Plant be the double-blossom Cherry; the second, an Almond; the third, the Mirabalon Plumb; the fourth, a Blue Lilac; the fifth, a Guilder-Rose; the sixth, a *Spanish* Broom; the seventh, a White Lilac; the eighth, a Laburnum; the ninth, the White Rose; and the tenth, a Tulip-tree; and then beginning again with the double-blossom Cherry,

Almond,

Almond, Mirabalon Plumb, Blue Lilac, Guilder - Rofe, *Spanifh* Broom, &c. you will have placed them in fuch a Manner, as to be always beautiful. And altho' they are not all in Bloom at one Inftant, yet one or other of them are: And even thofe as have no Bloffoms, are extremely beautiful, in refpect to the great Variety of Colours contain'd in their Leaves and Shoots.

The fecond Clafs, which is to be planted immediately before the firft, muft have its feveral Colours difpofed of in the like Manner; wherein always obferve, that you never place a Flower-Shrub that is white, yellow, &c. before a Plant of the firft Clafs which is of the fame Colour, or Kind, always regarding to follow the Steps of Nature as near as poffible.

The third and lowermoft Clafs being to be order'd in the fame Manner, I need not fay any more thereof; but that if Sweet-Brier was judicioufly intermix'd in this Plantation, 'twould add a great Grace to the whole; and when the Standard-trees planted in the Hedge-lines of Walks, and Hedges alfo, which fhould never be fuffer'd to grow very high, are fill'd with the feveral Kinds of Jeffemines and Honey-fuckles to run up and about them in a wild and rural Manner; the Whole muft then make a moft agreeable Compofition, being alfo back'd with the great Varieties of Foreft-trees, planted in the Midft of the Quarters.

Having thus laid down the moft agreeable and pleafant Manner of difpofing and planting of flowering Shrubs in a Wildernefs, they being proper for fuch Plantations only; I fhall, in the next Place, proceed to the Confideration of fuch odoriferous Flowers, whofe Smell and Afpect are both curious and delightful.

SECT.

S E C T. XXII.

Of odoriferous, or sweet-smelling Flowers, that are truly beautiful; their Use in Groves, Wilderness, Cabinets, open Plains, &c.

IN the twelve Months of the Year, there are eight which will produce Flowers, both grateful to the Eye, and pleasant to the Smell; as

In *January*, the several Kinds of *Polyanthos.*

In *February*, the Polyanthos, Hyacinths, and Violets.

In *March*, the Polyanthos, Hyacinths, Stock July-Flowers, and Violets, Roses, if against a South Wall.

In *April*, the Hyacinths, Stock July-Flowers, Wall-Flowers, Auriculas, Junquils, Roses, white Narciffus, and Narciffus Polyanthos.

In *May*, the Wall-Flowers, white Narciffus, Lillies, and double flower'd Rocket, Roses.

In *June*, the sweet William, Lillies, Primrose Tree, Pinks, Roses, and Carnations.

In *July*, the Sweet William, Pinks, Carnation, and Tuberose, and lastly,

In *August*, the Pink, and July-Flowers, commonly called Carnations.

The Odours of these Flowers being extreamly pleasant, are therefore to be planted in every Walk, and of each an equal Quantity; that thereby they may always be adorn'd with one or other according to their natural Succeffion.

S E C T.

S E C T. XXIII.

Of such Perennial, Bulbous-rooted, and Annual Flowers, as are truly beautiful and proper to adorn the most noble and rural Parts of a delightful Garden.

THESE Kinds of Flowers are only pleasant to the Eye, and may be so disposed of, as to adorn our Gardens every Month in the Year, *viz.*

In *January*, Snow-drop, Winter Aconite, Hepatica.

In *February*, Snow-drop, Crocus, Hepatica, Dazies.

In *March*, Crocus, Tulips.

In *April*, Tulips, Ranunculus, Anemonies.

In *May*, Tulips, Ranunculus, Lillies, Crown Imperials, Martagons, White Hellebore, Valerian, Monkshood, *African* Marigold, *French* Marigold, Double Poppies, Lupines, Scarlet Beans, Annual Stock, *Venus* Looking-glass, *Candy* Turf, Heart's Ease, Foxglove, Thrift.

In *June*, Lillies, Martagons, Foxglove, Valerian, Monkshood, Rosechampion, Batchelor's Buttons, Scarlet Lychnis, *African* and *French* Marigolds, Female Balsam, Larkspur, Double Poppies, Lupines, Annual Stock, *Venus* Looking-glass, *Candy* Turf, Heart's Ease.

In *July*, the Hollyhocks, Campanula's, Rosechampion, Batchelor's Buttons, Scarlet and White Lychnis, *African* and *French*

B b

Marigolds,

Marigolds, Capcicum Indicum, Marvel Peru, Female Balfam, Larkfpur, Double Poppy, Scarlet Beans.

In *Auguft*, Hollyhocks, Sun-flowers, Campanula's, Colchicum, Saffron Crocus, *African* and *French* Marigolds, Capcicum Indicum, Marvel Peru, Female Balfam, Larkfpur, Double Poppies, Scarlet Beans.

In *September*, Anemonies, Colchicum, Saffron Crocus, *African* and *French* Marigolds, Capcicum Indicum, Marvel Peru, Female Balfam, Larkfpur, Scarlet Beans.

In *October*, Starwort.

In *November*, none worth our Notice. And, laftly,

In *December*, the Black Hellebore.

I fhall not, under a Pretence of Difcovery, offer any Directions, that Flowers of the higheft Growth, ought to poffefs the Middle of a Border; while thofe of the loweft Rank, the extream Parts; and them of a mean Growth, a Medium Place between the two Extreams: Becaufe that every Gardiner is perfectly acquainted therewith; and 'tis what they have practifed many Years before Mr. *B--d--y*, in his *New Improvements*, Part II. Page 135. gave himfelf the Trouble to publifh the Difpofition of Flowers in a Border, as a new Thing; which every one long before knew as well, as that feven Days make one Week, or twenty four Hours, a natural Day, *&c.*

But as thefe Flowers do not afford pleafant Smells, which thofe of the preceding Section do; 'tis therefore that I advife that thofe which are both grateful to the Smell and Eye, be the Inhabitants and only Poffeffors of Borders in general; and that the others which are contain'd in this Section, or the greateft Part thereof, be the Inhabitants of the inward Parts of an open Wildernefs, *&c.* planted promifcuoufly in the Quarters thereof; but not in regular Lines, as has been the common Way: But, on the contrary, in little Thickets, or Clufters, feemingly without any other Order than what Nature directed, which, of all others, is the moft beautiful.

N. B. That in the Difpofition of thefe Clufters of Flowers, Care muft be taken to mix the feveral Sorts in fuch a Manner, as for every Part to be equally adorn'd throughout the whole Year.

Perhaps

Perhaps it might be expected here, that I should demonstrate the Culture of Flowers in general; which I have here omitted, because I shall communicate that in another Volume; wherein I shall not only demonstrate the true and genuine Practice thereof, but also the several great Errors of many late Authors. Together with a Parallel of the Theorical or Paper Botanist, with the Practical and Experienc'd Planter and Gardiner.

S E C T. XXIV.

Of the several Sorts of Flowers proper to adorn Chimneys, &c. during the Seasons of Spring, Summer, and Autumn.

HAVING, in the several Parts of this Work, demonstrated the true Practice of Ordering Fruit and Forest-Trees, Ever-Greens, and Flowering-Shrubs; with proper Directions for the several Sorts of Flowers to adorn a beautiful Garden, &c. I shall now lay down exact Rules for the Adorning the Chimneys of Halls, Chambers, &c. with such fragrant Flowers as are most suitable, *viz.* Truly Innocent, Beautiful, and Pleasant.

In Order to truly execute this Work in the best Manner, we must, first, be furnished with beautiful Flower-Pots of *Dutch* Ware, *China*, &c. wherein other Garden Flower-Pots must be placed, in which our Flowers are to grow.

These

Thefe being provided, we muft, in the next Place, confider which of the feveral Sorts of Flowers are beft for our Purpofe, that are, as I faid before, Truly Innocent, Beautiful, and Pleafant.

Firft then, to begin the Year, prepare fome indifferent good Mold, with which fill as many Pots as are fufficient for your Chimney; and in the Middle of each Pot, plant a very large Root, or two, of Snow-Drops, of the double Kind, which environ with a Circle of the feveral Sorts of Crocus. This Work being done at the Time when Snow-Drops and Crocus have done Blowing, will, in the *January* following, make a glorious Appearance, and grace their Places of Abode, wherein they then are placed.

The Polyanthos prefents its beautiful Flowers in *February*, as alfo the Hepatica, Hyacinths, and Violets; all which being planted in the like Manner, will fucceed the preceding, and be very entertaining.

In *March*, we have Stock-July-Flowers, Hyacinths, and Violets; and if they are all planted together in one Pot, *viz.* the Stock-July-Flower in the Center, and the Hyacinths and Violets about it, they will make a very beautiful Appearance, and their fweet Odors be very agreeable.

The moft beautiful Flowers of *April*, are Hyacinths, Stock-July-Flowers, Wall-Flowers, Tulips, Ranunculus, Anemonies, Jonquils, Narciffus, and Auricula's; which are thus to be difpofed of, *viz.* In the Center of fome Pots plant a Wall-Flower; in others, a Clufter of Tulips, or Jonquils, becaufe they both grow indifferent high; and in Order to have them in the greateft Beauty, let every Tulip in each Pot be of a different Colour; and that they may make their beft Appearance, place a handfome Flower-Stick in the Center of each Pot, with a gilt Head, to which tie up every Flower with Thread, &c. but in a free loofe Manner, fo as not to reprefent a ftiff Bundle of Flowers, void of Freedom, in which the Beauty of every Thing confifts. The Jonquils muft be encompaffed with a Circle of Ranunculus; the Tulips, with a Circle of Hyacinths; the Stock-July-Flowers, with Anemonies; and the Wall-Flowers with Narciffus.

N. B.

N. B. If Care is taken to plant Tulip, Ranunculus, Anemonies, Narciflus, Hyacinths, and Jonquil Roots, at different Seafons of the Year; they may be fo order'd as for their Blooms to be divers Times repeated, *viz.* as foon as the firft Bloom of Tulips, *&c.* is over, which were in the firft Pots for *April,* they fhall be fucceeded with a fecond Bloom of the fame Kind of Flowers, in other Pots, which fhall endure the Month of *May*; and after them a third, for the Month of *June*; and fo on.

The Manner of performing this, is by Planting their Roots in the Autumn, at feveral Times, *viz.* about fix Weeks diftant from the Time of the firft Planting, to that of the fecond, and the fame from the fecond to the third, *&c.*

In *May*, the White Lillies, and Crown Imperials are in their Beauty, which being planted as aforefaid, and environ'd with a Circle of Double-White Narciffus, are very beautiful. If the Roots of Lillies and Crown Imperials, are kept out of the Ground the whole Month of *February,* in a moift Place, where the Sun and Air cannot deftroy them, and planted again in Flower-Pots at the Beginning of *March,* they will produce fine Flowers in *June,* which being environ'd with Pinks, yield a very graceful Afpeft, and pleafant Odor.

In *June* and *July,* our beft Ornaments are, the feveral Kinds of Pinks, Carnations, Amaranthus, Tricolor, and Coxcomb, Lychnis, Campanula's, Tuberofe, Larkfpurs, Sweet-Williams, and Sweet-Bazil; all which are beft to be planted fingly, being tied to a handfome Flower-Stick placed in the Center of each Pot.

In *Auguft* and *September,* the Amaranthus's, Pinks, July-Flowers, Campanula's, Marvel Peru, Female Balfam, Capcicum Indicum, and Larkfpurs: To which may be added, the White and Red Calvills, and other beautiful Sorts of Apples grafted on Paradice-Stocks; as alfo round-headed Plants of the large Sweet-Brier, White Jeffemine, and Honey-Suckles, for the feveral Months of their Blooming.

In the Months of *October, November, December,* and indeed *January* alfo, a good Fire is the beft Ornament for Chimneys; excepting fuch where little Ufe is made of the Rooms, whofe beft Furniture is fmall Hedge Laurus-Tinus Plants, planted in large Flower-Pots, as direfted for Flowers, *&c.*

Having

Having thus deſcribed the ſeveral Sorts of Flowers fit for this Purpoſe; I don't doubt, but that the diligent Gardiner will find a very great Satisfaction therein, who muſt always obſerve to remove away ſuch as are fading, and introduce freſh ones in their ſtead, that thereby there may be a continued Series of Pleaſure and Delight, free from a Mixture of diſagreeable fading Objects.

NEW
PRINCIPLES
OF
GARDENING.

PART VI.

*Of the Situation and Disposition of Gardens
in general.*

SECT. I.

Of Situations.

THE moſt noble and pleaſant Situation of all others, is that on the Top of a Hill, as *Richmond* Hill in *Surry, Harrow* in *Hertfordſhire, &c.* where the Air is fine and clear, with noble Views.

The greateſt Misfortunes attending theſe noble Situations, is their open Expoſure to all Kinds of Weather, and the great Want of that moſt uſeful and pleaſant Element, Good Water.

And,

And, on the contrary, where Situations are low, they often abound in too great a Plenty of Water, which, when ſtagnant, or of a ſlow Motion, is very unhealthy.

All Kinds of Fenny, Boggy, Marſhy Lands, &c. whence Fogs and noiſome Vapours ariſe, are always to be avoided.

Bogs, &c. on the North Side of a Houſe or Garden, are unhealthy; for they being interpoſed between the Sun and the Bogs, &c. receive the noiſome Vapours, as they are exhaled by the attractive Power of the Sun.

Situations on the South Side of a Hill are to be preferr'd before thoſe at the Top; for altho' their Views are not ſo extenſive, yet they are well guarded from the Northern Winds, and generally abounds with a much better Soil, and Plenty of Water.

The beſt and moſt healthy Soil to dwell on, is that whoſe Surface is a fine ſandy Loam, with Brick-Earth underneath, and a Gravel at Bottom, wherein are generally good Springs for Houſhold Affairs.

Theſe are the moſt general Cautions to be obſerved, when Situations are to be choſen: But when they happen to be unalterable, every one muſt be contented; and therefore I ſhall conclude this Section with the Advice of RAPIN.

> *If on thy Native Soil thou doſt prepare*
> *T' erect a* Villa, *you muſt place it there,*
> *Where a free Proſpect does itſelf extend*
> *Into a Garden; whence the Sun may lend*
> *His Infl'ence from the* Eaſt; *his radiant Heat*
> *Should on your Houſe through various Windows beat:*
> *But on that Side which chiefly open lies*
> *To the North Wind, whence Storms and Show'rs ariſe,*
> *There plant a Wood; for, without that Defence,*
> *Nothing reſiſts the Northern Violence,*
> *While with deſtructive Blaſts o'er Cliffs and Hills*
> *Rough* Boreas *moves, and all with Murmurs fills;*
> *The Oak with ſhaken Boughs on Mountains rends,*
> *The Valleys roar, and great* Olympus *bends.*
> *Trees therefore to the Winds you muſt expoſe,*
> *Whoſe Branches beſt their pow'rful Rage oppoſe.*

S E C T. II.

Of the Difpofition of Gardens in general.

ON this very Point depends the whole Beauty or Ruin of
a Garden, and therefore every Gentleman fhould be
very cautious therein; I muft needs confefs, that I have
often been furprized to fee that none of our late and prefent
Authors did ever attempt to furnifh Gentlemen with better Plans
and Ideas thereof, than what has hitherto been practifed.

The End and Defign of a good Garden, is to be both profitable and delightful; wherein fhould be obferved, that its Parts
fhould be always prefenting new Objects, which is a continual
Entertainment to the Eye, and raifes a Pleafure of Imagination.

If the Gentlemen of *England* had formerly been better advifed in the laying out their Gardens, we might by this Time
been at leaft equal (if not far fuperior) to any Abroad.

For as we abound in good Soil, fine Grafs, and Gravel,
which in many Places Abroad is not to be found, and the beft
of all Sorts of Trees; it therefore appears, that nothing has
been wanting but a noble Idea of the Difpofition of a Garden.
I could inftance divers Places in *England*, where Noblemen and
Gentlemens Seats are very finely fituated, but wretchedly
executed, not only in refpect to difproportion'd Walks, Trees
planted in improper Soils, no Regard had to fine Views, &c.
but with that abominable Mathematical Regularity and Stiff-
nefs, that nothing that's bad could equal them.

Now thefe unpleafant forbidding Sort of Gardens, owe their
Deformity to the infipid Tafte or Intereft of fome of our Theo-
orical Engineers, who, in their afpiring Garrets, cultivate all
the feveral Species of Plants, as well as frame Defigns for Situations they never faw: Or to fome Nurfery-Man, who, for
his own Intereft, advifes the Gentleman to fuch Forms and
Trees as will make the greateft Draught out of his Nurfery,

C c   without

without Regard to any Thing more: And oftentimes to a Cox-comb, who takes upon himfelf to be an excellent Draughtfman, as well as an incomparable Gardener; of which there has been, and are ftill, too many in *England,* which is witnefs'd by every unfortunate Garden wherein they come. Now as the Beauty of Gardens in general depends upon an elegant Difpofition of all their Parts, which cannot be determined without a perfect Knowledge of its feveral Afcendings, Defcendings, Views, *&c.* how is it poffible that any Perfon can make a good Defign for any Garden, whofe Situation they never faw?

To draw a beautiful regular Draught, is not to the Purpofe; for altho' it makes a handfome Figure on the Paper, yet it has a quite different Effect when executed on the Ground: Nor is there any Thing more ridiculous, and forbidding, than a Gar-den which is regular; which, inftead of entertaining the Eye with frefh Objects, after you have feen a quarter Part, you only fee the very fame Part repeated again, without any Variety.

And what ftill greatly adds to this wretched Method, is, that to execute thefe ftiff regular Defigns, they deftroy many a noble Oak, and in its Place plant, perhaps, a clumfey-bred Yew, Holley, *&c.* which, with me, is a Crime of fo high a Nature, as not to be pardon'd.

There is nothing adds fo much to the Pleafure of a Garden, as thofe great Beauties of Nature, *Hills* and *Valleys,* which, by our *regular Coxcombs,* have ever been deftroyed, and at a very great Expence alfo in Levelling.

For, to their great Misfortune, they always deviate from Na-ture, inftead of imitating it.

There are many other Abfurdities I could mention, which thofe *wretched Creatures* have, and are daily guilty of: But as the preceding are fufficient to arm worthy Gentlemen againft fuch Mortals, I fhall at prefent forbear, and inftead thereof, proceed to General Directions for laying out Gardens in a more grand and delightful Manner than has been done before. But firft obferve,

That the feveral Parts of a beautiful Rural Garden, are *Walks, Slopes, Borders, Open Plains, Plain Parterres, Avenues, Groves, Wildernefses, Labyrinths, Fruit-Gardens, Flower-Gar-dens, Vineyards, Hop-Gardens, Nurferies, Coppiced Quarters,*
Green

Green Openings, like Meadows: Small Inclofures of *Corn*, *Cones* of *Ever-Greens*, of *Flowering-Shrubs*, of *Fruit-Trees*, of *Foreſt-Trees*, and mix'd together: *Mounts, Terraces,* Winding *Valleys, Dales, Purling Streams, Baſons, Canals, Fountains, Caſcades, Grotto's, Rocks, Ruins, Serpentine Meanders, Rude Coppies, Hay-Stacks, Wood-Piles, Rabbit* and *Hare-Warrens, Cold Baths, Aviaries, Cabinets, Statues, Obelisks, Manazeries, Pheaſant* and *Partridge-Grounds, Orangeries, Melon-Grounds, Kitchen-Gardens, Phyſick* or *Herb-Garden, Orchard, Bowling-Green, Dials, Precipices, Amphitheatres,* &c.

General DIRECTIONS, *&c.*

I. THAT the grand Front of a Building lie open upon an elegant Lawn or Plain of Graſs, adorn'd with beau‹ tiful Statues, (of which hereafter in their Place,) terminated on its Sides with open Groves.

II. That grand Avenues be planted from ſuch large open Plains, with a Breadth proportionable to the Building, as well as to its Length of View.

III. That Views in Gardens be as extenſive as poſſible.

IV. That ſuch Walks, whoſe Views cannot be extended, terminate in Woods, Foreſts, miſhapen Rocks, ſtrange Precipices, Mountains, old Ruins, grand Buildings, *&c.*

V. That no regular Ever-Greens, *&c.* be planted in any Part of an open Plain or Parterre.

VI. That no Borders be made, or Scroll-Work cut, in any ſuch Lawn or plain Parterre; for the Grandeur of thoſe beautiful Carpets conſiſts in their native Plainneſs.

VII. That all Gardens be grand, beautiful, and natural.

VIII. That ſhady Walks be planted from the End-Views of a Houſe, and terminate in thoſe open Groves that encloſe the Sides of the plain Parterre, that thereby you may enter into immediate Shade, as ſoon as out of the Houſe, without being heated by the ſcorching Rays of the Sun.

Without a Shade no Beauty Gardens know;
And all the Country's but a naked Show.

Cc 2 IX. That

IX. That all the Trees of your fhady Walks and Groves be planted with Sweet-Brier, White Jeffemine, and Honey-Suckles, environ'd at Bottom with a fmall Circle of Dwarf-Stock, Candy-Turf, and Pinks.

X. That all thofe Parts which are out of View from the Houfe, be form'd into Wilderneffes, Labyrinths, &c.

XI. That Hills and Dales, of eafy Afcents, be made by Art, where Nature has not perform'd that Work before.

XII. That Earths caft out of Foundations, &c. be carried to fuch Places for raifing of Mounts, from which, fine Views may be feen.

XIII. That the Slopes of Mounts, &c. be laid with a moderate Reclination, and planted with all Sorts of Ever-Greens in a promifcuous Manner, fo as to grow all in a Thicket; which has a prodigious fine Effect.

In this very Manner are planted two beautiful Mounts in the Gardens of the Honourable Sir *Fifher Tench* at *Low-Layton* in *Effex.*

XIV. That the Walks leading up the Slope of a Mount, have their Breadth contracted at the Top, full one half Part; and if that contracted Part be enclofed on the Sides with a Hedge whofe Leaves are of a light Green, 'twill feemingly add a great Addition to the Length of the Walk, when view'd from the other End.

XV. That all Walks whofe Lengths are fhort, and lead away from any Point of View, be made narrower at their further Ends than at the hither Part; for by the Inclination of their Sides, they appear to be of a much greater Length than they really are; and the further End of every long Walk, Avenue, &c. appears to be much narrower than that End where you ftand.

And the Reafon is, that notwithftanding the Sides of fuch Walks are parallel to each other, yet as the Breadth of the further End is feen under a leffer Angle, than the Breadth of that Part where you ftand, it will therefore appear as if contracted, altho' the Sides are actually parallel; for equal Objects always appear under equal Angles, Q. E. D.

XVI. That the Walks of a Wildernefs be never narrower than ten Feet, or wider than twenty five Feet.

XVII. That the Walks of a Wildernefs be fo plac'd, as to refpect the beft Views of the Country.

XVIII. That

XVIII. That the Interfections of Walks be adorn'd with Statues, large open Plains, Groves, Cones of Fruit, of Ever-Greens, of Flowering Shrubs, of Foreft Trees, Bafons, Fountains, Sun-Dials, and Obelisks.

When in the Garden's Entrance you provide,
The Waters, there united, to divide :
Firft, in the Center a large Fountain make ;
Which from a narrow Pipe its Rife may take,
And to the Air thofe Waves, by which 'tis fed,
Remit agen : About it raife a Bed
Of Mofs, or Grafs ; but if you think this bafe,
With well-wrought Marble circle in the Place.
Statues of various Shapes may be difpos'd
About the Tube ; fometimes it is inclos'd
By dubious Scylla, *or with Sea-Calves grac'd,*
Or by a Brazen Triton 'tis embrac'd.
A Triton thus at Luxembourg *prefides,*
And from the Dolphin *which he proudly rides,*
Spouts out the Streams : This place, though beautify'd,
With Marble round, though with Arcueill *fupply'd,*
Yet to St. Cloud *muft yield, in this out-fhin'd,*
That there the Hoftel D' Orleans *we find ;*
The little Town, the Groves before fcarce known,
Enabled thus, will now give Place, to none.
So great an Owner any Seat improves ;
One whom the King, and all the People loves.
This Garden, as a Pattern, may be fhown
To thofe who would add Beauty to their own.
All other Fountains this fo far tranfcends,
That none in France *befides with it contends ;*
None fo much Plenty yields, none flows fo high ;
A Gulph, i'th' Middle of the Pond does lie,
In which a fwollen Tunnel opens wide ;
Through hiffing Chinks the Waters freely flide ;
And in their Paffage in a Whirlwind move,
With rapid Force into the Air above ;
As if a watry Dart were upward thrown.
But when thefe haughty Waves do once fall down,

Refounding

Refounding loud, they on each other beat,
And with a dewy Shower the Bafon wet.

XIX. That in thofe ferpentine Meanders, be placed at proper Diftances, large Openings, which you furprizingly come to;
and in the firft are entertain'd with a pretty Fruit-Garden, or
Paradice-Stocks, with a curious Fountain; from which you are
infenfibly led through the pleafant Meanders of a fhady delightful Plantation; firft, into an oven Plain environ'd with
lofty Pines, in whofe Center is a pleafant Fountain, adorn'd
with *Neptune* and his Tritons, &c. fecondly, into a Flower-
Garden, enrich'd with the moft fragrant Flowers and beautiful Statues; and from thence through fmall Inclofures of
Corn, open Plains, or fmall Meadows, Hop-Gardens, Orangeries, Melon-Grounds, Vineyards, Orchards, Nurferies, Phyfick-
Gardens, Warrens, Paddocks of Deer, Sheep, Cows, &c. with
the rural Enrichments of Hay-Stacks, Wood-Piles, &c.

Which endlefs are, with no fix'd Limits bound,
But fill in various Forms the fpacious Round.
And endlefs Walks the pleas'd Spectator views,
At ev'ry Turn the verdant Scene renews.

Thefe agreeable furprizing Entertainments in the pleafant
Paffage thro' a Wildernefs, muft, without doubt, create new
Pleafures at every Turn: And more efpecially when the Whole
is fo happily fituated, as to be blefs'd with fmall Rivulets and
purling Streams of clear Water, which generally admit of
fine Canals, Fountains, Cafcades, &c. which are the very Life
of a delightful rural Garden.

Of pleafant Floods, and Streams, my Mufe *now fings,*
Of chryftal Lakes, Grotts, and tranfparent Springs;
By thefe a Garden is more charming made,
They chiefly beautify the rural Shade.
You who employ your Time to cultivate
Your Gardens, and to make their Glory great;
Among your Groves and Flow'rs, let Water flow;
Water, the Soul of Groves and Flow'rs too.

Water,

Water, 'tis true, through Pipes may be convey'd
From hollow Pits; so Fountains oft are made,
By Art, when Nature aids not our Designs,
The pensile Machine to a Tunnel joins;
Which by the Motion of a Siphon straight,
The Element attracts, though by its Weight
It be depress'd; and thus, O Sein, thy Waves
Beneath Pontneuf, *the tall* Samarian *Laves,*
And pours them out above: But let all those
Who want these Helps, to him address their Vows,
Whose Arm, whose Voice alone can Water draw,
And make obdurate Rocks to Rivers thaw.

. And to add to the Pleasure of these delightful Meanders, I advise that the Hedge-Rows of the Walks be intermix'd with Cherries, Plumbs, Apples, Pears, Bruxel Apricots, Figs, Goose-berries, Currants, Rasberries, &c. and the Borders planted with Strawberries, Violets, &c.

The moft beautiful Foreft-Trees for Hedges, are the *English* Elm, the *Dutch* Elm, the Lime-Tree, and Hornbeam: And altho' I have advis'd the Mixing of thefe Hedges of Foreft-Trees with the aforefaid Fruits, yet you muft not forget a Place for thofe pleafant and delightful Flowering-Shrubs, the White Jeffemine, Honey-Suckle, and Sweet-Brier.

XX. Obferve, at proper Diftances, to place publick and private Cabinets, which fhould (always) be encompafs'd with a Hedge of Ever-Greens, and Flowering-Shrubs next behind them, before the Foreft-Trees that are Standards.

XXI. Such Walks as muft terminate within the Garden, are beft finifh'd with Mounts, Aviaries, Grotto's, Cafcades, Rocks, Ruins, Niches, or Amphitheatres of Ever-Greens, varioufly mix'd, with circular Hedges afcending behind one another, which renders a very graceful Appearance.

Befides the Fountains which to Art we owe,
That Falls of Water alfo can beftow,
Such, as on rugged Jura *we defcry,*
On Rocks; and on the Alps *which touch the Sky*
Where from the fteep Precipices it defcends,
And where America *itfelf extends*

To

To the rude North ; expos'd to Eurus' *Blaſt :*
On Canada's *bold Shore the Ocean paſt,*
There among Groves of Fir-Trees, ever-green,
Streams falling headlong from the Cliffs are ſeen ;
The Cataracts reſound along the Shore ;
Struck with the Noiſe, the Woods and Valleys roar.
Theſe Wonders which by Nature here are ſhown,
Ruellian *Naiads have by Art out-done.*
Into the Air a Rock with lofty Head
Aſpires, the haſty Waters thence proceed.
Daſh'd againſt rugged Places they deſcend,
And broken thus, themſelves in Foam they ſpend.
The Sound, as when ſome Torrent uncontroll'd,
With mighty Force is from a Mountain roll'd,
The Earth, with horrid Noiſe, affrighted groans,
Flints which lie underneath, and moiſten'd Stones,
Are beat with Waves ; th' untrodden Paths reſound,
And Groves and Woods do loudly ecch? round.
Nor ſhould it leſs deſerve of our Eſteem,
When from an even Bed diffus'd, the Stream
Runs down a poliſh'd Rock ; and as it flows,
Like Linen in the Air expanded ſhows.
The Textile Flood a ſlender Current holds,
And in a wavy Veil the Place infolds.

XXII. Obelisks of Trellip-Work cover'd with Paſſion-Flowers, Grapes, Honey-Suckles, and White Jeſſemine, are beautiful Ornaments in the Center of an open Plain, Flower-Garden, &c.

XXIII. In the Planting of a Wilderneſs, be careful of making an equal Diſpoſition of the ſeveral Kinds of Trees, and that you mix therewith the ſeveral Sorts of Ever-Greens ; for they not only add a very great Beauty thereunto, by their different Leaves and Colours, in the Summer ; but are a great Grace to a Garden in the Winter, when others have ſtood the Strip of their Leaves.

XXIV. Canals, Fiſh-Ponds, &c. are moſt beautiful when environ'd with a Walk of ſtately Pines, and terminate at each End with a fine Grove of Foreſt-Trees, or Ever-Greens.

Or,

Or, if an extenfive Canal terminate at one End in an elegant Piece of Architecture, with a Grove on each Side thereof,
and the other End in a Wood, Grove, &c. 'twill have a noble
and grand Afpect.

XXV. Groves of Standard Ever-Greens, as Yew, Holly,
Box, and Bay-Trees, are very pleafant, efpecially when a
delightful Fountain is plac'd in their Center.

XXVI. All Grafs-Walks fhould be laid with the fame Curvature as Gravel-Walks, and particularly in wet and cold
Lands; for, by their being made flat or level from Side to Side,
they foon fettle into Holes in the Middle, by often walking on,
and therein retain Wet, &c. which a circular furfaced Walk
refifts. The Proportion for the Heights of the Crown, or middle Part of any Grafs or Gravel-Walk, is as five is to one,
that is, if the Walk be five Foot in Breadth, the Height of
the Middle, above the Level of the Sides, muft be one Inch;
if ten Foot, two Inches; fifteen Foot, three Inches, &c.

XXVII. The Proportion that the Bafe of a Slope ought to
have to its Perpendicular, is as three to one, that is, if the
perpendicular Height be ten Feet, its Bafe muft be thirty Feet;
and the like of all others.

XXVIII. Diftant Hills in Parks, &c. are beautiful Objects,
when planted with little Woods; as alfo are Valleys, when
intermix'd with Water, and large Plains; and a rude Coppice
in the Middle of a fine Meadow, is a delightful Object.

XXIX. Little Walks by purling Streams in Meadows, and
through Corn-Fields, Thickets, &c. are delightful Entertainments.

XXX. Open Lawns fhould be always in Proportion to the
Grandeur of the Building; and the Breadth of Avenues to the
Fronts of Edifices, and their own Length alfo.

The entire Breadth of every Avenue fhould be divided into
five equal Parts: Of which, the Middle, or grand Walk, muft
be three Fifths; and the Side, or Counter-Walks on each Side
one Fifth each. But let the Length of Avenues fall as it will, you
muft always obferve, that the grand Walk be never narrower
than the Front of the Building.

The moft beautiful and grand Figures for fine large open
Lawns, are the Triangle Semicircle, Geometrical Square, Circle
or Elipfis, as the Figures A, B, C, D, E.

D d   XXXI.

XXXI. The Circle, Elipſis, Octagon, and mix'd Figures compoſed of Geometrical Squares, Paralellograms, and Arches of Circles, makes very beautiful Figures for Water, as may be ſeen in the ſeveral Parts of the Deſigns at the End hereof. But of them all, the Circle is the moſt grand and beautiful.

> *Nor will the plenteous Waters pleaſe you leſs,*
> *When in the Ground a Circle they poſſeſs :*
> *Which Figure with a Garden beſt agrees ;*
> *If on the graſſy Bank a Grove of Trees,*
> *With ſhining Scenes, and Branches hanging down,*
> *The Seats of Stone, and verdant Shores does crown.*
> *But whether they ſtand ſtill, or ſwiftly glide,*
> *With their broad Leaves let Woods the Rivers hide,.*
> *Beſtowing on each Place their cooling Shade ;*
> *For Springs by that alone are pleaſant made.*

XXXII. In the Planting of Groves, you muſt obſerve a re-gular Irregularity ; not planting them according to the common Method like an Orchard, with their Trees in ſtraight Lines ranging every Way, but in a rural Manner, as if they had receiv'd their Situation from Nature itſelf.

XXXIII. Plant in and about your ſeveral Groves, and other Parts of your Garden, good Store of Black-Cherry and other Trees that produce Food for Birds, which will not a little add to the Pleaſure thereof.

> *- - - - - We wandring thro' a Grove,*
> *Trees green beneath us, and all Shade above,*
> *Mild as our Friendſhip, ſpringing as our Love ;*
> *Hundred of chearful Birds fill ev'ry Tree,*
> *And ſing their joyful Songs of Liberty.*

XXXIV. Where Water is eaſy to be had, always introduce a Baſin or Fountain in every Flower and Fruit-Garden, Grove, and other pleaſing Ornaments, in the ſeveral private Parts of your rural Garden.

> *Ye Springs and Fountains in the Woods reſound,*
> *And with your Noiſe the ſilent Groves confound.*

XXXV.

XXXV. The feveral Kinds of Foreft-Trees make beautiful Groves, as alfo doth many Ever-Greens, or both mix'd together; but none more beautiful than that noble Tree the *Pine.*

'Twas in a Grove of pleafant Pines he ftray'd;
The Winds within the quiv'ring Branches play'd,
And dancing Trees, a mournful Mufick made.
The Place it felf was fuiting to his Care,
Uncouth and favage as the cruel Fair :
He wandred on, unknowing where he went,
Loft in the Wood, and all on Love intent.

XXXVI. In the Difpofition of the feveral Parts of Gardens in general, always obferve that a perfect Shade be continued throughout, in fuch a Manner as to pafs from one Quarter to another, &c. without being obliged at any Time to pafs thro' the fcorching Rays of the Sun.

O bleft Abodes ! O dear delicious Shade !
Had I for you, or you for me been made,
How gladly would I fix my wandring Courfe
With you? How willing bear the World's Divorce?
And only bleft in yours, her Charms forget,
Renounce her Pleafures, and to yours retreat.

XXXVII. There is nothing adds fo much to the Beauty and Grandeur of Gardens, as fine Statues; and nothing more difagreeable, than when wrongly plac'd : as *Neptune* on a Terrace-Walk, Mount, &c. or *Pan,* the God of Sheep, in a large Bafin, Canal, or Fountain. But to prevent fuch Abfurdities, take the following Directions.

For open Lawns and large Centers :

Mars, God of Battle, with the Goddefs *Fame*; *Jupiter,* God of Thunder, with *Venus,* the Goddefs of Love and Beauty; and the Graces *Aglaio, Thalia,* and *Euphrofyne* ; *Apollo,* God of Wifdom, with the nine Mufes, *Cleio, Melpomene, Thalia, Euterpe, Terpficoce, Erato, Calliope Urania,* and *Polymnia* ;

Minerva

Minerva and *Pallas*, Goddesses of Wisdom, with the seven Liberal Sciences; the three Destinies, *Clotho, Lachesis,* and *Atropos*; *Demegorgon* and *Tellus,* Gods of the Earth; *Priapus,* the Garden-God; *Bellona,* Goddess of War; *Pytho,* Goddess of Eloquence; *Vesta,* Goddess of Chastity; *Voluptia,* Goddess of Pleasure; *Atlas,* King of *Mauritania,* a famous Astronomer; *Tysias,* the Inventer of Rhetorick; and *Hercules,* God of Labour.

For *Woods and Groves:*

Ceres and *Flora; Sylvanus,* God, and *Ferona,* Goddess of the Woods; *Actæon,* a Hunter, whom *Diana* turn'd into a Hart, and was devoured by his own Dogs; *Eccho,* a Virgin rejected of her Lover, pined away in the Woods for Sorrow, where her Voice still remains, answering the Outcries of every Complaint, &c. *Philomela,* a young Maid ravish'd by *Tereus,* who afterwards imprison'd her, and cut out her Tongue; which cruel Action *Progne,* Sister to *Philomela* and Wife to *Tereus,* reveng'd, by killing her own Son *Itis,* whom she had by *Tereus,* and mincing his Flesh, dress'd up a Dish thereof, which she gave her Husband *Tereus* to eat, (unknown to him,) instead of Meat. *Philomela* was afterwards transformed into a Nightingale, and *Itis* into a Pheasant; and lastly, *Nuppæa* Fairies of the Woods.

For *Canals,* Basons, *and Fish-Ponds :*

Neptune, Palemon, Paniscus, and *Oceanus,* Gods, and *Dione, Melicerta, Thetis,* and *Marica,* Goddesses of the Sea; *Salacia* Goddess of Water; *Naiades* Fairies of the Water; and the Syrens *Parthenope, Lygia,* and *Leusia.*
Niches to be adorn'd with *Dii minores.*

For *Fruit-Gardens and Orchards :*

Pomona Goddess of Fruit, and the three *Hesperides, Eagle, Aretusa,* and *Hisperetusa,* who were three Sisters that had an Orchard of golden Apples kept by a Dragon, which *Hercules* slew when he took them away.

For

For Flower-Gardens :

Flora and *Chloris,* Goddeffes of Flowers; and alfo *Venus, Diana, Daphne,* and *Runcina* the Goddefs of Weeding.

For the Vineyard :

Bacchus God of Wine.

For Mounts, high Terrace-Walks, &c.

Æolus, God of the Winds and *Orcedes* Fairies of the Mountains.

For Valleys :

The Goddefs *Vallonta.*

For private Cabinets in a Wildernefs or Grove :

Harpocrates God, and *Agerona* Goddefs of Silence, *Mercury* God of Eloquence.

For fmall Paddocks of Sheep, &c. *in a Wildernefs :*

Morpheus and *Pan* Gods of Sheep ; *Pates* the Shepherds Goddefs; *Bubona* the Goddefs of Oxen; and *Nillo* a famous Glutton, who ufed himfelf to carry a Calf every Morning, until it became a large Bull, at which Time he flew it with his Fift, and eat him all in one Day.

For fmall Enclofures of Wheat, Barley, &c. *in a Wildernefs :*

Robigus a God who preferved Corn from being blafted ; *Segefta* a Goddefs of the Corn, and *Tutelina* a Goddefs, who had the Tuition of Corn in the Fields.

For

For Ambufcadoes near Rivers, Paddocks, or Meadows:

For thofe near a Canal or River, *Ulyffes,* who firft invented
the Shooting of Birds; and for thofe near a Paddock, wherein
Sheep, &c. are kept, *Cacus* flaying by *Hercules.* For *Cacus* being a Shepherd, and a notorious Theif of great Strength and
Policy, ftole feveral Sheep and Oxen from *Hercules,* who per-
ceiving his Lofs, lay in Ambufh, and took *Cacus* in the Fact,
for which, with his Club, he knock'd out his Brains.

Laftly, for Places of Banquetting:

The God *Comus.*

Where Bees are kept in Hives:

The God *Arifteus.*

Thefe general Directions, with the preceding deliver'd in
the Cultivation of the feveral Kinds of Fruit and Foreft-Trees,
Ever-Greens, and Flowering-Shrubs, join'd with the moft ufeful Obfervations on the feveral Defigns hereunto annex'd, is fully fufficient for any Perfon whatfoever, to defign, lay out, and
plant Gardens in general, in a more grand and beautiful Manner than has been done before. I therefore fhall now conclude
for the prefent, in the Words of *Rapin* on the Happinefs of a
rural Seat;

> *And bleft is he, who tir'd with his Affairs,*
> *Far from all Noife, all vain Applaufe, prepares*
> *To go, and underneath fome filent Shade,*
> *Which neither Cares nor anxious Thoughts invade,*
> *Does for a while, himfelf alone poffefs,*
> *Changing the Town for rural Happinefs.*
> *He, when the Sun's hot Steeds to th' Ocean bafte,*
> *E'er fable Night the World has overcaft,*
> *May from the Hills, the Fields below defcry,*
> *At once diverting both his Mind and Eye;*

Or,

Or if he please, into the Woods may stray,
Listen to the Birds, which sing at Break of Day:
Or, when the Cattle come from Pasture, hear
The bellowing Ox the hollow Valleys tear
With his hoarse Voice. Sometimes his Flowers invite:
The Fountains too are worthy of his Sight.
To ev'ry Part he may his Care extend,
And these Delights all others so transcend,
That we the City now no more respect,
Or the vain Honours of the Court affect;
But to cool Streams and aged Groves retire,
And th'unmix'd Pleasures of the Fields desire,
Making our Beds upon the grassy Bank,
For which no Art but Nature we must thank.
No Marble Pillars, no proud Pavements there,
No Gall'ries, or fretted Roofs appear.
The modest Rooms to India nothing owe;
Nor Gold, nor Ivory, nor Arras know:
Thus liv'd our Ancestors when Saturn reign'd,
While the first Oracles in Oaks remain'd.
A harmless Course of Life they did pursue,
And nought beyond their Hills, their Rivers knew.

F I N I S.

NEW
PRINCIPLES
OF
GARDENING.

PART VII.

Of the KITCHEN GARDEN.

INTRODUCDION.

MONGST the feveral parts of Gardening, which in general are delightful and advantageous, none is more neceffary to be well underftood, than that of the right Ordering and Cultivation of Sallets, throughout the feveral Seafons of the Year. And in Confideration, that a Work of this kind might be very ufeful to every one, if communicated to the Publick in a manner abfolutely practicable, and free from the feveral *Chimera's,* and Imaginations fo much ufed by our late theorical Writers on the feveral parts of Gardening,

which

which greatly deceives every one who follows their Directions; I shall therefore demonstrate the true and genuine Cultivations of those wholesome *Vegetables,* in a more concise, familiar and authentick manner, than has been done before.

CHAP. I.

Of the right Ordering and Cultivation of the several Sallet Herbs which are in Season, during the Months of January, February *and* March.

SECT. I.

Of Alexanders.

1. *Its Names.*

ALEXANDERS is called in Latin *Hippoſelinum*, in Greek ιπποσέλινον or great Parsley of *Gaza Equapium.* 'Tis also called *Oluſatrum*, or the black Pot-Herb, and by many *Sylveſtre* or wild Parsley. The *Germans* call it *Groſz Epffich*, The *French Alexandre*, and the *Engliſh Alexanders.*

2. *Its Deſcription.*

The Form of the Leaves of this Vegetable is like unto those of Smallage, but something larger, being smooth and of a very deep green. When it's suffered to grow up to Seed, it will rise about eighteen Inches high. Its Blossoms are white, and the Seed is black when ripe in *Auguſt,* and very bitter, but of an aromatic Smell. The Root is of a black Colour without, but white within, and may be eaten.

3. *Its Temperature.*

The Seed is hot in the second Degree, and almoſt dry in the third. Its Roots are of a moderate heat, as are also the Leaves, Stalks, *&c.*

4. *The*

4. *The Medicinal Virtues.*

A Decoction of the Root made with Wine, will expel Wind, provoke Urine, and is excellent against the Strangury, as also are the Seeds.

5. *The Parts for use in Sallets are,*

(1.) The fresh Sprouts, Tops and Stalk, while tender, being blanch'd. (2.) The Root being peeled, and eaten raw or boiled in Soup, is very good for the Stomach, and its tender Shoots make an excellent Pickle.

6. *Its Proportion or Quantity in a Sallet is discretionally, and is eaten with Oyl, Pepper, Salt,* &c.

7. *Its Cultivation.*

The Seed may be sown as soon as ripe in *August,* or in the *March* following. It delights in good mellow Land, being sown thin; its Seed is not produced under two Years growth, after being gathered and sown in *August,* in small Borders of three Foot in breadth, *&c.*

SECT. II.

Of Asparagus.

1. *Its Names and Kinds.*

ASPARAGUS is called in *Latin* (1.) *Asparagus Sativus,* Garden Asparagus. (2.) *Asparagus Palustris,* Marsh Sperage. (3.) *Asparagus Petræus,* Stone or Mountain Sperage. (4.) *Asparagus Silvestris,* wild Sperage. (5.) *Asparagus Silvestris Spinosus Clusii,* wild thorny Sperage; but of all these kinds we cultivate none but the first, which is called in *Greek* ἀσπάραγος, in *High Dutch Spargen,* in *Low Dutch Asperges* and *Coralcruut* or *Herba Coralli,* Coralwort in respect to its red Berries; in *Spanish Asparagos,* in *Italian Asparago,* in *French Asperges,* and vulgarly in *English* Sparrow-grass.

2. *Its*

2. Its *Description.*

The tender Shoots, which naturally begin to come forth about the End of *March,* are soft and brittle, and of divers Sizes, some being very small, as the Size of a Goose-quill, and others as large as a Man's Thumb, and oftentimes larger, being in Taste when raw like unto green Beans. The Top or Bud is of the form of a Sparrow's Bill, and from thence vulgarly called Sparrow-grass. When the young Shoots are about eight Inches in height (or thereabouts) they open their soft scalic Tops or Buds, and break out into divers Branches, adorned with small hairy-like Leaves, mixed with yellowish Blossoms, which afterwards produce Berries wherein the Seed is inclosed. These Berries are first of a green Colour, and afterwards become red, of the Size of a common Pea; and make a very beautiful Appearance, being mixt amongst their beautiful verdant Leaves. The Roots are of a very soft and spungy Nature, and when planted in rich Land, as I shall in its Place direct, prosper well, and continue for many Years.

3. Its *Temperature.*

Is temperately hot and moist.

4. The *Medicinal Virtues.*

The young Shoots being eaten, as hereafter directed, are very nourishing, and is a Cordial Diuretic, good for the Kidneys and Bladder, loosens the Belly, and very much helps Digestion.

5. The *Parts for use are,*

The tender Shoots when grown about three Inches in height, being carefully cut with a Knife, whose Edge must be ground very thin, and afterwards hacked with the Edge of another Knife, so as to be rough like the Teeth of a small Saw, or otherwise fil'd, as the Teeth of a fine Saw. The Knife being thus prepared, place the end of the side of the Blade close down by the side of the Asparagus, cutting it off about three Inches within the Ground. But before you put down your Knife, as aforesaid, open the Ground with the point of your Knife, to see if there are not other young Buds coming through the Surface, which care must be taken of to preserve; and

when

when you are cutting the Afparagus off, as aforefaid, be careful that you don't turn your Knife about, which oftentimes deftroys three or four other Buds as would have fucceeded the firft. Alfo be careful that you don't jaub, or haftily thruft down your Knife into the Head of the Roots from which the young Shoots arife; for by fuch doings I have known many fine Pieces of Afparagus killed. But to prevent fuch Misfortunes, care muft be taken to plant the Roots a fufficient Depth, as I fhall in its Cultivation direct.

6. *The* Proportion *or* Quantity *to be eaten,*

Is arbitrary, its white Parts being fcraped, and bound up in fmall Bundles and boiled, is eaten with melted Butter, Bread toafted, &c. alone, or with Chickens, Lamb, &c. well known to moft People.

7. *Its* Cultivation.

The proper Soil wherein Afparagus naturally delights, is a rich fandy Loam, and is thus cultivated.

(1.) Having made choice of fuch large and found Buds of the beft Kind (which firft appear in *April*) as may be thought neceffary; the *Michaelmas* following, when their Haulm is dead, their Seed will be fit to gather, at which Time obferve that you are not difappointed therein by Birds, which will deftroy the Seed, if Care is not taken to preferve it.

(2.) Your Seed, being arrived to its full Maturity of Ripenefs, gather all thofe large Stems elected, and ftrip off their Berries into a Tube, wherein put a little Water, and between the Palms of your Hands, rub the Berries to pieces, to feparate the Pulp of the Berries, which will fwim on the Surface of the Water, from the Seed that finks to the Bottom.

(3.) Having thus feparated the Seed from the Shell and Pulp of the Berry, pour off the Water, and lay the Seed to dry on a dry Floor, &c. obferving to lay it very thin, and to keep it ftirring about once a day, till perfectly dry.

(4.) The Seed being thus faved, keep it in a dry Place until the middle of the next *March*, at which time it muft be fown either in flat-bottom'd broad Drills, made with the full breadth of a Hough, or at random in Borders about three Feet wide, being
cover'd

cover'd with the natural Earth made fine, about two Iaches thick.

And as Afparagus Plants of one Year's Growth are the very beſt of all others, therefore be careful to fow the Seed of a moderate Thickneſs, that the Plants may receive their full Nouriſhment, and not ſtarve one another by their being too numerous.

(5.) The beſt Seaſon for planting *Afparagus* in light or hot Lands, is *April*, and in ſandy cold Lands, the beginning of *May*, and not in the beginning of *March*, as Mr. *Bradley* direꞓs in his new Improvements, Part the Third CORRECTED, page 141. For to my certain Knowledge, I have known many Labours loſt, by planting ſo very early, before that their Roots are diſpoſed to ſtrike, which they never fail of doing about the middle of *April*, and immediately grow away with good Succeſs. Whereas when they are planted at the beginning of *March*, before they are by the Heat of the Spring put into a State of Growth, and wet and cold Weather comes thereon; 'tis very rare that one Root in ten ever comes to one tenth the Perfeꞓion as thoſe planted in *April*.

(6.) The proper Seaſon for trenching and preparing the Land, wherein *Afparagus* is to be planted, is *November*, or the beginning of *December*, and not at the time of planting in *April*, &c. as has been always praꞓiſed.

The manner of performing this Work is as follows.

About the beginning of *November*, or ſooner, if the Ground will work, open a Trench the length or breadth of the Ground you intend to plant; of two Spit and two Crums in depth, which being done, throw into the Trench as much well rotted Horſe Dung, &c. as will fill it up about one Foot from the Bottom, and thereon caſt the firſt Spit of the ſecond Trench, which muſt be afterwards well mixed with the Dung underneath, by the help of a Dung-Fork, Sparrow-graſs-Fork, &c. before that the Crum and ſecond Spit come thereon. This bottom Spit being thus well worked in with the Dung, throw on the firſt Crum, and thereon a ſecond laying of Dung of the ſame Thickneſs of the former, and on that, the bottom Spit of the ſecond Trench; but herein obſerve that this bottom Spit of the ſecond Trench muſt be thrown into Ridges, and not levelled down as is uſual, and to cover ſuch parts of the Dung as is between the Ridges,

caſt

caft thereon the fecond Crum, and then begin again with a Foot thicknefs of Dung in the Bottom of the fecond Trench, which mix with the upper Spit of the third Trench, &c. till the whole is compleated.

The Quantity of Dung neceffary for one Rod of Ground, is about one good Cart Load and an half, or three quarters, if to be had. And altho' I have not hitherto mentioned any thing of the Care, as ought to be taken, in having the Land perfectly clean from Couch-grafs, Thiftles, Vervine, &c. yet that muft be carefully executed, or otherwife 'twill be of a very bad Confequence.

About the middle of *April,* when the Seafon of planting is arrived, and thofe Ridges fweetened and meliorated by the Winter's Frofts, &c. (for which I directed their being ridged) throw them down, and with a Dung-Fork, &c. mix the upper laying of Dung therein, and level it as you go on, ready for planting.

Having thus prepared the Ground fit for planting, fet out your Beds (which ought to be) four Feet in breadth, and the Alleys between them two Feet and half. This being done, divide the breadth of each Bed in four equal Parts, which being each one Foot, is the Diftance that the Rows muft be from one another.

The manner of planting *Afparagus* Roots with Dibbers is entirely wrong, for by crowding all their Fibres together the Earth cannot encompafs them, and therefore die in great Quantity. But to prevent fuch Loffes and Difappointments, obferve the following Direction, *viz.* Prepare a Line mark'd with Knots of Thread, at nine Inches apart, which fet on the firft Divifion of your Bed, and againft every Knot make a chop with a Spade, wide enough to receive one *Afparagus* Plant, which place againft the Knot of the Line about fix Inches below the Surface, fpreading their Root fingly againft the fide of the Chop, and clofing the Earth well between and over them, and in like manner proceed till the whole Plantation is completed.

The Cuftom of fowing Onions amongft the Plants in the Beds, and planting Colly-flowers or Artichokes in the Alleys, I cannot any wife commend, for they in general are Robbers of the Nourifhment as fhould be preferved with care for the *Afparagus* only, which will foon repay the Value of fuch Onions, Colly-flowers, &c. ten-fold. Therefore I recommend, that

Care

Care being taken to keep them perfectly clean from Weeds, and that no Plant of any kind be suffered to grow amongst them.

Towards *Michaelmas*, before that the young Haulm is decayed, examine the several Lines of all your Beds, to find what Number of Plants has miscarried; and in such places, when they have so missed, place down a small Stick, &c. which will inform you where to make good your Plantation the *April* following.

About the middle of *October*, divide the Alleys in the middle and on each side, set off the breadth of half a Spit, and then straining a Line on each side, chop out the Alleys, and throw them upon the Beds, which will raise the Beds about two Inches in height, whereby the Buds of the Roots will be about eight Inches deep, out of the Danger of the Knife in cutting, (as I observed before) Frosts, &c. and the Alleys exactly between the extream Lines of each Bed.

At the latter End of *February*, if the Spring be very forward, or beginning (but not later than the middle) of *March*, fork and rake the Beds, breaking the Earth very well, and picking out such Weeds as may have crept therein.

When *Asparagus* is planted very shallow, 'twill come much sooner in the Spring than that which is planted deeper; but then it is attended with these Misfortunes, 'tis always smaller, more exposed to the Winter's Frosts, subject to be killed by the Fork in forking, and by the Knife in cutting; so that altho' *Asparagus* be planted a moderate depth, and does not come in quite so soon, as that as is planted shallow; yet I cannot but recommend that manner of planting, because 'tis out of all the Dangers aforesaid, and is much larger and finer than the other.

About the middle of *October* cut down the Haulm, throw up the Alley, and at the End of *February*, or beginning of *March* following, fork and rake the Beds as before directed, and so in like manner every Year. When your Plantation has been thus managed three Years, 'twill then produce good *Asparagus*; but the less 'tis cut this third Year, the better it will be ever after; so that I would not advise you to cut longer than the End of *April* in the third Year, the middle of *May* the fourth Year, three Weeks in *May* the fifth Year, and the End of *May* every

Year

Year after. And in order to have this Plantation of a long Duration, you muſt every third Year lay on the Beds a good Coat of Horſe Dung, *&c.* well rotted, which Work ſhould be done at the end of *October*, or beginning of *November*, and at the ſame time the Alleys digg'd up, and ſpread over the Dung to preſerve the ſaline Particles from being exhauſted by the Sun, Wind, *&c.*

A Plantation cultivated according to theſe Directions, will produce the very beſt of *Aſparagus* in great Quantity, and continue thirty Years, and upwards. Having thus demonſtrated the true Practice of raiſing *Aſparagus* in the natural Ground without artificial Heats, I ſhall in the next place explain its Propagation by artificial Heats, as hot Beds of Horſe Dung, *&c.* The firſt Work to be done herein, is to provide or make choice of a piece of Land, that was very well dunged the laſt Year, and is very rich and mellow : Wherein plant the young Seedlings at the time, and in the ſame manner as before directed, excepting their diſtance and depth, which herein need not be ſo great; therefore if you plant them in Rows, about ſeven Inches apart, and four Inches aſunder in the Rows, with their Buds two or three Inches under Ground, 'tis fully ſufficient, becauſe that their Duration therein is but for two or three Years, or thereabouts.

Your Nurſery being thus planted of ſuch a Magnitude as is neceſſary, care muſt be taken to keep them clean from Weeds, for the ſpace of two Years after planting, at which time they are often uſed in the Hot Bed; but for my part, I cannot commend that Practice, having found by Experience that they produce much finer *Aſparagus* when let alone until the third or fourth Year after planting. And in order to have plenty of *Aſparagus* every Winter, *viz.* from the beginning of *November*, until the end of *March*, or a Week in *April*; you muſt every *April* make a new Plantation, that as you take up and force one Plantation this Winter, another may be coming in Readineſs to ſucceed that the next Winter, and after that another, and ſo on.

Being thus prepared with a good Stock of Plants, we will now proceed to the main Thing, that is, to receive a recompence for our Labour, which muſt thus be acquired.

C   At

At the latter end of *October* throw up in a heap six, eight, or ten Cart Loads of fresh Horse Dung, mixed with Sea-coal Ashes, and watered, if very dry; and in the Operation hereof observe, that you shake and separate the settled parts of the Dung, so that it may be all free and fit for working; also observe, that the Sea-coal Ashes be well mixed, for they add very much to the Duration of the Heat. After your Dung has laid in a heap, working for the Space of three or four Days, if the Quantity does not exceed three or four Loads, or six or seven Days, when as many Loads, &c. set out the Dimensions of your Bed, which in breadth should be about eighteen Inches more than the breadth of your Frame, so that the back and forepart of the Frame may stand about nine Inches within the upright of the Bed: The length of your Bed being always governed by the length of the Frames, I need not say any thing on that head more, than that the length of the Bed should be always as much longer than the Frame as it is in breadth, *viz.* eighteen Inches.

The Magnitude of your Bed being thus determined, place it direct East and West, that the reclining Glasses may be direct South. Then work up the same equally, shaking and mixing the Dung and Ashes in all parts alike, free from Clods, &c. But do not tread it down as you work it up, according to the common Way, for that Error is the cause of that violent Heat which always attends new Hot-Beds made that Way. Therefore to prevent such immoderate Heat, which oftentimes destroys good Plants, &c. and to cause a moderate moist Heat, of a long duration, most natural to all Vegetables, work up your Bed firm and tight with your Dung Fork, and, as I said before, equal in all its parts, of such a height as, when settled, to be about three Feet, or three Feet and half high: Making the back part some small matter higher than the foremost part, that it may lie a little sloping towards the Sun.

About three Days after your Bed is made 'twill have settled its self, at which time cover it about four or five Inches thick with any common sifted Earth, which encompass with Straw-bands pinned down, to preserve the Earth from falling from off the sides; and thereon place the *Asparagus* Roots as thick as possibly you can place their Buds together, without pruning any part of their Roots; covering them about three Inches thick with common Mould, sifted or skreen'd tolerably fine.

The

The Plantation being thus executed, let it remain in this State for fix or feven Days, if the Bed proves very hot, before you place the Glaffes on the Frames: Which may be very eafily difcover'd by thrufting three or four tolerable large Sticks into divers parts of the Bed at the time of making, which will be heated by the Bed in Proportion to the Heat, and by pulling thofe Sticks out and feeling them, may give a very good Judgment of the Heat of the Bed. At the aforefaid time of putting off the Lights of the Frames, add a Thicknefs of Earth more over the *Afparagus*, that will (with the former) bury the Buds about five Inches deep, and about three Days afterwards the Buds will appear above Ground, when you muft carefully obferve to give them as much Air as the Weather will permit, that they thereby may receive their natural green Colour, and a good Tafte withal. If the Nights are not very cold or frofty, one fingle Mat is a fufficient covering, and when very cold the Mats may be doubled. A Plantation of this Kind will produce very good *Afparagus*, plentifully every Day, for the fpace of a Month, and when the Bed begins to decline its Heat towards the end of the Month, cover the Glaffes every Night with frefh long Horfe Litter, which will draw the Bed very much, and caufe the Shoots to afcend with as much Vigour as if the Bed had been new lined.

It very often happens that good Plants will produce *Afparagus* longer than the Heat of the Bed continues, and at fuch times when the Heat of the Bed is in a manner over, take a cutting Knife as is ufed to cut Hay, Straw, &c. and cut down the fides and end of the Bed, and as much underneath the Frame, as will not caufe the Plants to fall, which fill up with frefh Horfe Dung, and Sea-coal Afhes, very firm and tight underneath, and about one Foot and half without at the Bottom, carried up diminifhing, fo as to be about eight Inches without the Frame at the Top.

This additional Dung is called the Lining of a Bed, and may be repeated as often as is neceffary, for it never fails of recovering the loft Heat, and continues the Growth of the Plants their whole Duration.

When the *Afparagus* Shoots begin to come fmaller than at firft, prepare more Dung, as before directed, and make another

Bed, to fucceed the firft, and after that a third, &c. during the whole Seafon.

If that your Earth grows dry 'tis requifite to give it a mode-rate watering, which thus prepare. In fome convenient part of your Bed place a large Pan or Pail of Water, at the time of your covering up at Night, and by the next Morning it will have received fuch a Heat, as is moft natural to the Heat of the Bed, and may then be fprinkled about, with a watering Pot and Rofe, without cooling or giving any check to the Heat of the Bed, or Growth of the Plants.

And as Heat and Moifture are the Principles of Vegetation, therefore never fuffer your Plants to be over dry and hot, which caufes their Shoots to be very fmall and infipid, which on the contrary, when moderately hot and moift, are very large and of a delicious Tafte.

N. B. That thofe Directions laid down for cutting *Aspara-gus* in the natural Ground, are to be obferved in the artificial Beds alfo : And the beft time for this Work is the Morning.

S E C T. III.

Of the white and red Beets.

1. *Their Names.*

A Beet is called in *Latin Beta,* by the *Grecians* Σεῦτλον, τεῦτλον, the *Germans Maugolt,* the *Spaniards Afelgas,* the *French de la Porée, des Jotes,* and *Betes.*

2. *Their Defcription.*

1. The white Beet is an Herb which produces very large, broad, fmooth and plain Leaves, from which afcends one, and fometimes two Stalks, of a tolerable thick Subftance channel'd on the outfides, from whence break out fmall Shoots, which produce much leffer Leaves than thofe at the Bottom, with their Clufters of Flowers or Bloffoms towards their extream parts, which is fuc-ceeded by its uneven prickly Seed; but neither Stalk, Bloffoms, or Seed are produced till the fecond Year after being fowed.

The

The Root is generally very large, and runs downward like unto a Parſnip, being attended with many fibrous Roots, which break out of its Sides.

2. The red Beet is of make and growth much like unto the white Beet, excepting its Colour of Leaves, Stalk, Bloſſoms, and Root, which laſt, when ſliced, produce wonderful fine delightful Colours. But beſides the common white and red Beets, there are many other Kinds, as the large *Turkey* red Beet, whoſe Leaves, Stalk, and Bloſſoms are of a very deep red, and its Root alſo, which in Form is very like unto our long rooted kind of Turnep. The variegated or ſtriped Beet, *&c.* whoſe difference is chiefly in Colour, more than Form.

3. *Their Temperature.*

The white Beets are temperately moiſt and cold, and the others in general are cold and dry.

4. *The Medicinal Virtues.*

Being boiled and eaten in Soop is a great looſener to the Belly, and its Juice ſnuffed up the Noſtrils gently draws forth Phlegm, and purgeth the Head.

5. *The Parts for uſe.*

The Leaves of the white Beet, boiled and eaten in Soop, are excellent good, as obſerved before : And the Leaves of the large red Beet, boiled and eaten with Oyl, Vinegar and Pepper, make a delicate Sallet. The Roots of the red Beet are chiefly uſed in the garniſhing of Diſhes, *&c.*

6. *The Quantity of either is at Pleaſure.*

7. *Their Cultivation.*

Altho' there be divers Kinds of Beets, as before deſcribed, yet their Difference makes no Alteration in their Culture. They in general love good ſandy moiſt Loam, are ſown in *March*, either in ſmall Borders, and afterwards tranſplanted out at about fifteen Inches apart, or in Quarters, ſingled out with a Hough, at the like Diſtances.

SECT.

S E C T. IV.

Of Broom Buds.

1. The Names.

THIS Shrub is called in *Latin Genista*, and by some *Genesta*, in *Italian Genestra*, in *Spanish Genestra*, or *Giestra*, in *High Dutch Pfrimmen*, in *Low Dutch Brem*, in *French Genest*, and in *English* Broom, and as 'tis supposed from its Usefulness in making good Brooms, for the sweeping of Houses, &c.

2. Its Description.

The Sort of Broom that I am now treating of, is the common Broom, which is found growing in most dry Pasture Lands well known to every good House-wife, and therefore needs no farther Description.

3. Its Temperature.

The Branches, Buds, Blossoms and Seed are hot and dry in the second Degree.

4. Its Medicinal Virtues.

The Decoction of the young Shoots, made with Water, is a great cleanser and opener of the Liver, Milt, and Kidneys; and with Wine, brings away by Stool all Kind of watery and dropsical Humours.

5. The Parts for use are,

The young Buds and small Flowers preserved in Pickle.

6. The Proportion or Quantity of them to be eaten in a Sallet is at Pleasure, they stir up, and create a very good Appetite, and are excellent against the Spleen and Scurvy.

7. The Culture of this Plant has not been as yet considered in the Garden, which I believe proceeds from its being naturally a plentiful Grower in most (if not all) Parts of this Kingdom without any Cultivation whatsoever.

4

most

SECT. V.

Of Brooklime.

1. Its Names.

BROOKLIME, or *Water Pimpernel*, is of four Kinds;
As first, That which is gathered and eaten in Sallets, called
Brooklime only, and in *Latin Anagallis seu Becabunga*. Secondly, That which is called *Water Pimpernel*, and in *Latin Anagallis Aquatica*. Thirdly, Small *Water Pimpernel*, in *Latin Anagallis Aquatica minor*. And lastly, Pale flowered *Water Pimpernel*, in *Latin Anagallis Aquatica minor flore pallido*.
But as my Business at this time is with the first only, therefore
I shall be very full in explaining its Virtues in Sallets, and pass
over the others in Silence.

2. Its Description.

The Stalks of this Herb are of a cylindrical Form, divided into divers Joints, from which spring their Leaves, that are of
a deep green, and placed opposite to each other. The Flowers
put forth from the Stalks of the Leaves, as 'twere from their
Bosoms, and are of a very beautiful blew Colour, not unlike
unto the Flowers of *Land Pimpernel*. Its Root is white, and
of a creeping Nature, like unto Spear-mint, breaking out Runners at every Joint, as also Its fibrous Roots.

3. Its Temperature.

Is temperately hot and dry.

4. Its Medicinal Virtues.

This Herb eaten in Sallets is good against the Scurvy, and
being stamp'd and its juice taken in Wine, helps the Strangury,
and Griefs of the Bladder, as Gravel, Stone, &c.

5. The Parts to be eaten in a Sallet are the tender Leaves.

6. The

6. The Proportion or Quantity that should be eaten in a Sallet, is an equal Quantity, *viz.* if the Sallet is composed of three Kinds of Herbs, there must be of Brooklime one third part; if of four Kinds, one fourth; if of five Kinds, one fifth, *&c.*

7. *Its Cultivation.*

This Herb delighting to grow by Rivers Sides, purling Streams, Brooks, *&c.* is there found in great Plenty, and therefore its Cultivation in Gardens is not regarded.

SECT. VI.

Of Cabbages, Savoys, &c.

ALtho' Cabbages, Savoys and Colly-flowers are now so called and distinguished from what is generally called Coleworts, yet they are all of the Colewort Race, as doth appear by their *Latin* Names. The Garden Colewort is called in *Latin Brassica vulgaris sativa*; the white Cabbage, *Brassica Capitata alba.* the red Cabbage *Brassica Capitata rubra*; the Savoy *Brassica Sabauda*; the Colly-flower, *Brassica Florida*, being no more than close growing (or headed) Coleworts, and the like of all others of the Cole Tribe.

2. *Their Description.*

To make an Attempt of informing Mankind what a Cabbage, Savoy or Colly-flower is, would be both a ridiculous and simple Thing, seeing that every Person living are perfectly acquainted therewith; and therefore I will, instead thereof, mention such Kinds as are worth our Notice.

The best Kinds of Cabbages are those which, tho' firm, close, and very large, yet are very light, as the true Sugar-loaf, the early white *Battersea*, and the *French* Cabbage; and of Savoys the same. But of all the several Kinds, the curdled Savoy, yellow in the middle, environed with deep green curdled Leaves, is, of all others, the most beautiful, sweetest, and despises the Severity of our Winters Frosts, which the other Kinds will not.

The

The red Cabbage is also worth our Notice, in Respect to its making a fine Sallet when pickled, or eaten raw with Oyl and Vinegar, being sliced very small.

N. B. That the best Cabbages, *&c.* are produced from such Stalks as are very short, and indeed, some are so very short, as for the Cabbage, when growing, to almost rest upon the Ground.

Colly-flowers are of the Cole Race, and their Leaves not much unlike the Colewort ; but as this Plant is not in Season, during these Months of *January, February* and *March,* I shall refer its Description to the proper Season.

3. *Their Temperature.*

All Coleworts, and others of the cole Race, are dry and binding.

4. *Their Medicinal Virtues.*

The Nature of Cabbages, *&c.* are such, that when they are boiled moderately, they are loosening, and when over much, astringent.

5. *The Parts for use are,*

The young Plants in the Spring, when well grown, their Leaves cabbaged ; and afterwards their tender Sprouts, which spring from the several Joints or Buds of the Stalks.

6. The Quantity to be eaten is at Pleasure.

7. *Their Cultivation.*

To be well furnished with Cabbages and Savoys, in the Months of *January, February* and *March,* sow the Seed at three different Seasons, *viz. March, April,* and *May,* which plant out in Rows at two Feet Distance from each other ; and the like in the Rows, in *July, August,* and beginning of *September.* That is, those sown in *March,* to be transplanted out in *July ;* those of *April,* in *August ;* and those of *May,* in *September ;* which will very orderly succeed one another, during the Months above-mentioned.

When the Heads of Cabbages are cut from the Stalks, ob-serve to cut them off sloping, with the Slope or Cut towards

D   the

the South; as also to cut away from the Stalk all the bottom
Leaves, to give Liberty for the free Growth of their Sprouts,
which are preferable to the Cabbages themselves, and will
plentifully furnish your Table till the middle of *April.*

N. B. My Reason for advising the aforesaid Care of
cutting off the Cabbages from the Stalks, is, that the Rains,
Snow, *&c.* may not rot them by falling on their upper-parts,
when cut off horizontally, and thereby be deprived of that useful second Crop of Sprouts.

SECT. VII.

Of Carrots.

1. *Their Names.*

OF CARROTS we have three Kinds, *viz.* The *yellow* or
orange Carrot, the *red Carrot,* and the *wild* or *white Carrot ;*
of which the yellow Carrot is the most valuable, called in *Greek*
ςαφυλῖνος, in *Latin Paſtinaca ſativa tenuifolia,* in *High Dutch
Geelruben,* in *Low Dutch Geel Peen, Geel Pooten* and *Geel
Wortelen,* in *French Carotte,* and *Racine jaulne,* in *Italian Paſtina-
ta,* in *Spanish Canahotta,* and in *English* yellow Carrot.

2. *Their Deſcriptions.*

1. The *yellow Carrot,* its Leaves are of a deep green, composed of many small Leaves like unto Fennel, from the midſt of
which rises its Stalk about four Feet in height, being pithy in
the middle, and somewhat hairy without, producing at its
extream parts round Tufts, which afterwards open into large
Tufts of Bloſſoms of a whitiſh Colour, which is ſucceeded by
their rough and hairy Seeds, of a very pleaſant ſweet ſmell when
rubbed.

The Root is of an Orange (rather than a Limon) Colour
both without and within, delighting in a deep ſandy Soil,
and very often grows to a large Size. I have had Carrots of
this Kind that have been twenty two Inches in Length, and of
twelve Inches and half Circumference at their greateſt End.
And altho' Carrots of a very large Size are much valued by
                                            many,

many, yet I cannot recommend them, fo much as thofe of a middling Size, which are always much fweeter, and nothing near fo watry and infipid as thofe very large ones are.

2. The *Red Carrot* is of the fame Form, both in Leaves, Stalk, Seed, and Root, but very rarely grows fo large. Its Leaves are of a dark reddifh green, and its Root of a blackifh red without, and yellowifh within; and is very feldom cultivated in our Gardens.

3. The *wild Carrot* is called in *Greek* ςαφυλῖνος ἄγριος, in *Latin Paftinaca Sylveftris tenuifolia,* by fome *Daucus,* in *High Dutch wild Paftenen, Vogol neft,* in *Low Dutch Vogels neft* and *wild Caroten, Crookens cruyt,* in *French Paftenade Saunage,* in *Englifh wild Carrot,* and after the *Dutch Birds neft.*

The Leaves of this Carrot are in Form very like unto the orange or yellow Carrot, but fomething whiter, and more hairy, as alfo are the Stalks, being a little rough withal. The Bloffoms are produced at the extream parts of the Stalks, as the others, but in much leffer Tufts, which when the Seed is ripening, are drawn together, fomething refembling the form of *Birds neft,* from which, by fome, it has been called *Birds neft.* The Roots are very fmall, of a mean length, and a whitifh Colour.

3. *Their Temperature.*

1. The Roots of the yellow or orange, and red Carrots are temperately hot, and fomething moift, and their Seeds hot and dry.

2. The wild Carrot, both Root and Seed, are hot in the fecond Degree.

4. *Their medicinal Virtues.*

1. The Virtues of the yellow or orange, and red Carrots, are very little more than that they are a pleafant Sallet, when boiled and eaten with Meats, &c. They are long digefting in the Stomach, and are fomething windy.

2. The wild Carrot, its Root being boiled in Wine, and the Decoction drunk, provokes Urine, and expells the Stone.

The Seed infufed in white Wine, and the Infufion being drunk, greatly helps the Dropfie, breaks and diffolves Wind,

cures

cures the Cholick, and is very good againſt the Stone and Gravel.

5. The Parts for the Kitchen uſe are the Roots only.

6. The Quantity or proportion is at pleaſure.

7. *Their Cultivation.*

The proper Soil (as I have before obſerved) for the yellow or orange Carrot, whoſe Cultivation I am now ſpeaking of, is a light ſandy Soil, rather than a ſtrong Loam, which generally infeſts them with numberleſs Quantities of Worms, and gives a very bitter inſipid Taſte. We muſt therefore furniſh our ſelves with ſound Seed of the beſt Kind; and make choice of a piece of ſuch light Land, as is moſt agreeable to their Nature.

This being done, cauſe the ſame to be well digg'd about the middle of *June*, and therein ſow your Seed, treading the Ground all over, that the Seed may be well ſettled therein; and being afterwards kept clean from Weeds, and ſingled out with a ſmall Hough, at about three Inches apart, will, by the *Michaelmas* following, be of a tolerable good Size, and fit for the Table.

But as my Buſineſs at the preſent is to provide a plenty of young Carrots, for the Months of *January*, *February* and *March*, I ſhall therefore give proper Directions for the ſame.

As ſoon after *Michaelmas* as the Carrots, before raiſed, are obſerved to have done growing, take them out of the Ground, cut off their Tops ſo cloſe to their Heads, as to leave none of the Leaves, *&c.* and dry them well in the Sun. Then having made choice of a dry piece of Ground, dig a Trench of two Feet deep, and about twenty Inches or two Feet in breadth, and of ſuch a length as is neceſſary.

This being done, place therein your Carrots, in regular courſes, one over the other, till the Trench is filled within ſix Inches of the Surface of the Earth, and then placing the Earth over them, well ſettled, in the Form of a Ridge, to caſt off the Water; you will have finiſhed your Magazine, from which you may be furniſhed with plenty of Carrots in a much better Manner, than when let growing all the Winter in the Ground;

which

which generally fills them full of the Worm and gives a very disagreeable earthy Taste. A Magazine or Pit of Carrots, well managed, will plentifully furnish the Table, not only the Months of *October*, *November* and *December* ; but *January*, *February*, *March* and *April* also. And if I may be allowed to give my Opinion, they are much preferable to those that are sown in *February* or *March*, which are fully grown when taken up in *September* or *October*.

N. B. That the manner of sowing Carrots in *February* or *March* for the Winter, is performed as before directed; but in the houghing or setting them out, care must be taken to leave them single, and not nearer to one another, than seven or eight Inches.

And as we are obliged to hough amongst them, twice at the least, 'tis generally practised in the first time of houghing, to leave them rather thicker than aforesaid, as at the Distance of five or six Inches; and at the second houghing, give them their proper Distance as before directed. If that your Carrots are very well grown when you come to the second houghing, be careful that the corner of the Hough don't cut or bruise their tender sides, which will cause them to grow deformed, and very disagreeable to the Eye.

When the Season for taking up these winter Carrots is arrived, as in *October*, and they have received their full Maturity of Growth, be careful in taking them out of the Ground, that they are not either broken or bruised with the Fork which in the Winter causes them to rot ; that they be well dried, and pitted as above directed, and entirely free from every part of their green Top, which never fails of making a very great rot amongst them, wherever it happens.

The manner of preserving Carrots in Sand where 'tis to be had, and sufficient Room within Doors also, is a very good Method ; but where large Quantities are required for large Families, *&c.* and very severe Frosts, 'twill not do; and therefore the aforesaid Method, which I have recommended, is much preferable thereunto.

And before that I conclude this Section, I shall speak a Word or two in Relation to the saving of Carrot Seed, and the manner of preserving a good Kind.

Amongst

Amongst the several Vegetables cultivated in Gardens, there are none so difficult to preserve from Degeneration as good Carrots; for if very great Care is not taken in the choice of those planted for Seed, they immediately degenerate, and soon after become wild, or very near thereunto.

The common received Notion amongst divers People, of good Carrot Seed once acquired, will always continue so, is absolutely false; and is the true reason of so many indifferent Kinds of Carrots now in *England.*

And to prove this, I made the following Experiment, *viz.* First, I made choice of a very beautiful orange Carrot, of a fine length and magnitude, which during the Winter, I preserved in Sand; and when *March* came, planted it in a very light sandy Loam, wherein it thrived with great Success, and produced several very large Heads of found Seed, which I gathered and saved very dry.

In *March* following I made choice of a fresh piece of Land, very light and agreeable to their Nature, wherein I sowed the Seed before saved, which soon after came up in great Plenty, and grew to a very large Size; but not above one in ten was truly as beautiful in Colour as their original; not but that the others were in general very good, some few excepted, which were perfectly white and wild.

Having received thus much Satisfaction from my Experiment, I was resolved to carry it on farther, and to that end I made choice of another Carrot, the second best, or degenerated one Degree of Colour from the original, which Carrot I preserved during the Winter, planted it in *March*, and it grew with good Success, and produced very near as much Seed as the former, which the Spring following I sowed, (as before) and the product was a very pale yellow, and a great many quite white, without so much as one of so good a Colour, as that from which I saved the Seed.

This last part of my Experiment gave me a plain Proof of the Cause of the several bad Kinds of Carrots in *England,* (as I before observed) as well as of the great Care that ought to be taken to preserve a good Kind. And 'tis my real Opinion that had I carried on the Experiment farther, they would at length become all white and wild, as the wild Carrots themselves are.

The

The firſt Motive that moved me to this Experiment, was from the prodigious great Care and Exactneſs obſerved by my Father Mr. *Daniel Langley*, Gardener at *Twickenham*, in his annual Choice of the beſt Carrots, from which he yearly raiſes great Quantities of Seed, and furniſhes many at very reaſonable Rates.

SECT. VIII.
Of Chervill.

1. *Its Names.*

COlumella calls Chervill *Chærephyllum*, in *Latin* 'tis called, *Cerefolium*, in *High Dutch Korffeskraut*, in *Low Dutch Kervell*, in *Italian Cerefoglio*, in *French Du Cerfueil*, and in *Engliſh Chervell* or *Chervil.*

2. *Its Deſcription.*

The Leaves of Chervil are ſlender, and very beautifully indented, being ſomething hairy and of a light green when young, but tending to a red when its Seeds are near ripe. The Stalk ſeldom riſes above one Foot, or thereabouts in height, and is very ſlender, at whoſe ends are ſmall Tufts, which produce white Flowers, that are ſucceeded by its Seed, of a long ſlender ſharp pointed Form.

And beſides this Kind of Chervil cultivated in Gardens for Sallets, there is another Kind, called the great *Chervil*, or *Myrrhe*, and in *Latin Cerefolium magnum*, whoſe Leaves are deeply indented like unto Hemlock, but of a very pleaſant Smell and Taſte, and by many called ſweet *Chervil.*

3. *Its Temperature.*

The Temperature of Chervil is temperately hot and moderately dry.

4. *Its Medicinal Virtues.*

The Nature of Chervil is ſuch, that if 'tis boiled in Wine,

and drank, it greatly provokes Urine; and its tender Leaves eaten in Sallets are very refreshing, and cherish the Spirits.

5. The Parts for use in Sallets, are the Seed-Leaves, and the next to them, being eaten with other Sallet Herbs in Compofition.

The green Tops or Seeds of Chervil, after the going off of the BlofToms, is an excellent Sallet, for cold and weak Stomachs, being eaten with Oyl, Vinegar, and a little Pepper.

6. The Quantity to be eaten in a Sallet, amongft other Sallet Herbs, is an equal part, as a third, a fourth part, *&c.* if the Sallet is compofed of three, four, *&c.* forts of Herbs.

7. *Its Cultivation.*

The ufual and beft Method of propagating this Sallet Herb, during the Months of *January, February* and *March,* is to make a gentle Hot-Bed, covered about feven Inches thick, with fine mellow Soil, and therein fow your Seed in little Drills, of an Inch deep, and about two Inches afunder, as alfo Creffes, Muftard, Radifh, Turnip, Spinage, and Lettuce : Wherein obferve that you make your Bed large enough to have two Crops, always fucceeding each other; and that whenever you gather a Sallet, be fure that you firft pull up the fame, and cut off the Roots when out of the Ground, and not leave them ftanding in the Bed, after their Leaves are cut away. Alfo obferve, that whenever you gather a Sallet, be it little or much, that you at the fame time fow as much as you gather, changing the Kinds of each Drill every time of fowing, that is, the Drill wherein you fowed Chervil the firft time, fow with Muftard the fecond; Turnips the third; Spinage the fourth, *&c.* ftill changing the Species; and thereby the Earth of one Bed will produce very good falleting as long as the Heat endures.

SECT. IX.

Of Chives.

1. Their Names.

CIVES are called in *Greek* Σχοινόπρασον, *Schænoprasum*, in *Dutch Bicfloack*, or *Junceum Porrum*, or *Ruſh Leeke*, in *French Brelles*, and in *Engliſh Cives, Chives, Civet* and *Sweth*.

2. Their Deſcription.

The Leaves of Chives feldom rife above four or five Inches high, of a long, flender, round form, like unto common Ruſhes, from which rife fmall and tender Stalks, at whofe extream parts are produced globular Bloſſoms. Their Roots are compofed of a great Number of very fmall Bulbs joined together, from which ſtrike great Quantites of fibrous Roots, in a perfect Matt down into the Earth. Their Taſte is between an Onion and a Leek, and are by many called the Leck-ruſh.

3. Their Temperature.

Hot and dry.

4. Their Medicinal Virtues.

Chives are great Provokers of Urine, but are hurtful to the Eyes, and do ingender hot and groſs Humours.

5. Their Parts for ufe are the tender Tops, eaten alone with Oyl, Pepper and Vinegar, or in Compofition with other Herbs.

6. The Quantity to be eaten, in Compofition with other Sallet Herbs, is an equal part.

7. Their Cultivation.

Chives are increaſed by their off-fets, or parting their Roots. They delight in the Shade, and love a light rich Land. The

E   beſt

beſt Seaſon to tranſplant them is in *March*, at which Time cut off Leaves or Graſs, and plant them in Borders, at about ſeven Inches apart in the Rows, as well as one Row from the other.

N. B. That a Border about three Feet and half in breadth (which will receive ſeven Rows) and twenty five or thirty Feet in length, is fully ſufficient to ſerve a very large Family. *Note alſo*, That the oftener Chives are cut, the finer their Leaves come, and conſequently more agreeable in Sallets, than thoſe Leaves that are coarſer and tough.

SECT. X.

Of Clary.

1. Its Names.

CLARY is called by the Apothecaries *Gallitricum*, as alſo *Oruala*, and by ſome *Tota bona*, but not properly; in *Italian Sciaria*, in *French Oruale*, in *High Dutch Scharlach*; in *Low Dutch Scharleye*, and in *Engliſh Clarie, Cleere*, or *Clary*.

2. Its Deſcription.

Altho' there be divers kinds of Clary, beſides the garden Clary, as the ſmall Clary called in *Latin Gallitricum alterum*, another ſort called *Jupiter's Diſtaff*, and in *Latin Colus Jovis:* The wild Clary, or *Oculus Chriſti*, called in *Latin Horminum Sylveſtre*, and the Clary with purple Leaves, *Horminum Sylveſtre foliis purpureis:* Yet that Clary of which I am now to treat on, is the garden Clary, without farther Regard to any other.

The Leaves of the garden Clary are of a broad oval Form, with their Edges a ſmall matter indented, of a whitiſh Colour, and ſomewhat rough and hairy, as alſo are the Stalks, which produce their Bloſſoms in *June, July* and *Auguſt*, that are not unlike thoſe of Sage, which are ſucceeded with long Husks, wherein is their Seed of a black Colour which ripens ſoon after. The Root is divided into many ſmall fibrous Roots, and the Herb in general is of a very ſtrong Smell. When its Seed is ripe, which is always the ſecond Year after ſowing, the Root,

2

Stalk

Stalk and Leaves immediately perish; so that to have this Herb always fit for use, 'tis best to sow a small Quantity every Year, to succeed each other, as they decay.

3. *The Temperature.*

Clary is hot and moderately dry in the third Degree.

4. *Its Virtues.*

The Leaves being stamped or fried whole with Eggs, in the manner of a Tansie, is a very great Strengthener to the Stomach, Eyes and Back.

5. The Quantity to be eaten is at Pleasure.

6. The parts for use are the young Leaves of the first Year's Growth, fried in fresh Butter, with Cream and Eggs, beaten with Sugar, and juice of Orange or Limon.

7. *Its Cultivation.*

The Seed being saved when ripe, and sow'd in *March*, in a small Border of about four Feet wide, and fifteen or twenty Feet long, will produce a very great Quantity, sufficient for any Nobleman's Family whatsoever, and delights in a rich sandy Loam.

SECT. XI.

Of Clivers or Goose-Grass.

1. *Its Names.*

CLIVERS is called in *Greek* ἀπαρίνη, *Aparine,* in *Latin Lappa minor,* but not properly. *Pliny* affirms it to be *Lappaginis Speciem,* of some *Philanthropos,* a Man's Friend, because that it takes hold of Garments, &c. when touched by them. In *Italian Speronella,* in *Spanish Presera,* or *Amordi Hortalano,* in *High Dutch Kleeb, Kraut,* in *French Reble ou Grateron,* in *Low Dutch Kleeferugt,* and in *English Goose-share, Goose-grass, Clever, Claver,* or *Cliver.*

E 2   2. *Its*

2. _Its Description._

Clivers or Goose-grafs, hath many fmall fquare Branches very rough and fharp, full of Joints, which are befet with fmall hairy Leaves, and are generally fix in Number at every Joint. The Flowers or Bloffoms are produced at the tops of the Sprigs of a white Colour, and very fmall, as alfo is the Seed which are of a fpherical Form, but indented or hollow on one Side.

The Roughnefs or Ruggednefs of this Plant being very great, 'tis reported by _Diofcorides_, that the Shepherds ufed this Herb, to ftrain or take the Hairs out of Milk, inftead of a Cullander, or other Strainer, now ufed.

3. _Its Temperature._

According to _Galen_, 'tis moderately hot and dry, and fome- what thin of parts.

4. _Its Medicinal Virtues._

Clivers being boiled and eaten in Soup, or fpring Pottage, prevents Fatnefs, and its Juice is good againft Poyfon, being drank in Wine.

5. _The Parts for ufe._

The tender Tops, gathered when young in the Spring.

6. The Quantity to be eaten, muft be proportional, to the other fpring Herbs eaten with it, as half if but two Kinds; three Parts if three Kinds; four Parts if four Kinds, &c.

7. _Its Cultivation._

This Herb being a great Delighter in Hedges, Ditches, &c. is very eafy to be had in great Plenty during the Spring and Summer, and therefore is never cultivated in our Gardens.

SECT. XII.

Of Cowslips.

1. *The Names.*

COwslips are commonly called *Primulæ veris,* and by some *Arthritica* and *Herba Paralysis,* good against the Pains of Joints, Sinews, &c. In *Italian Brache Cucult,* in *English Pettie Mulleins* or *Palsie-wort,* and vulgarly Cowslips.

There are also divers other Flowers of this Tribe that are very pleasant in Sallets; as first, the Field Oxelip, called *Primula pratensis inodora lutea;* secondly, double Paigles, *Primula hortensis Anglica;* thirdly, double Cowslips, *Primula veris flore geminato;* fourthly, the field Primrose, *Primula veris minor;* fifthly, the double white Primrose, *Primula veris flore pleno;* and lastly, *Primula flore viridi,* the green Primrose.

2. *Their Description.*

1. These kind of Flowers, are very nearly related to the Mulleins, and was by the Ancients called *Verbasculi,* small Mulleins. The *common Cowslips* being well known to every Boy, I need not trouble my Reader with any Description thereof.

2. The *Oxelip* differs but very little from the *Cowslip,* in the form of its Leaves, but are something lesser, as also are its Flowers, which fall very short of that delightful Smell, which the Cowslip greatly abounds in.

3. The *double Paigle,* called of *Pena Primula hortensis anglica omnium maxima & serotina Floribus plenis,* the greatest *English* garden Cowslip with double yellow Flowers, being also well known to every one, needs no Description.

4. The *double Cowslips,* or those that are two in a Hose, called Hose in Hose, is also well known, and therefore needs no Description. As also, the common white field Primrose, the garden double Primrose, and the green Primrose, whose Flowers are somewhat welted about the Edges, and therefore were called by *Pena, silvarum primula Floribus obscure virentibus fimbriatis.*

3. *Their*

3. *Their Temperature.*

Cowflips and Primrofes are of a dry Temperature, and little if at all hot.

4. *Their medicinal Virtues.*

The Flowers being eaten in Sallets, are very good againft the Gout and Palfie, and a Conferve made with their Flowers and Sugar prevaileth wonderfully againft the Palfie, Convulfions, Cramps, and other Difeafes of the Sinews.

5. *Their Parts for ufe.*

The Flowers being gathered and picked out of their Hofe are the parts to be eaten, being firft infufed in very good Vinegar, and eaten with other Sallet Herbs in Compofition.

6. The Quantity to be eaten in a Sallet is double the Quantity of any one of the other Herbs in the Compofition.

7. *Their Cultivation.*

Both Cowflips and Primrofes being very plenty, in moft moift meadow Lands, are therefore very feldom cultivated in our Garden. But if any one is defirous to encourage thefe Flowers in their Garden, which I cannot but acknowledge that they very well deferve, 'tis performed by parting their Roots, and tranfplanting their young Off-fets. And altho' thefe forts of Flowers are very common in Meadows and Fields, which make them of fo fmall a value among Florifts; yet when they are promifcuoufly planted amongft other Flowers, as Polyanthos's, Hyacinths, Daffodills, Wall-flowers, Flos Adonis, Virginia Stock, &c. they make as pleafant and delightful an Appearance, as thofe others which require much more Labour and Charge in their Cultivations. They begin their Bloom at the End of *February,* and continue to the End of *May,* the Cowflip excepted, which feldom comes into Bloom till *April.*

SECT.

SECT. XIII.

Of Corn Sallet.

1. *Its Names.*

COrn Sallet is called in *Greek* λευκολόχανον, in *Latin Lactuca Agnina latifolia*, in *Dutch Wytmoes*, in *English* the *white Pot-Herb*, or *Lambs Lettuce*, and *Corn Sallet.*

2. *Its Description.*

Corn Sallet is naturally an Inhabitant of the Field, but for its being a very refreshing pleasant Herb, is now received into our Gardens, and was introduced by the *French* and *Dutch*, who were the first that eat it in Sallets in *England.*

Its Leaves are in Form long and narrow, of a pale green (and was therefore called the white Pot-Herb) from which rises a slender Stem, about ten or twelve Inches high, wherein are several Joints, out of which proceed two Leaves, and between them small Stems, bearing at the Ends small Tufts of white Flowers, very close and compact together, which are afterwards succeeded by Seed.

3. *Its Temperature.*

This Sallet Herb is cold and something moist, like unto Cabbage Lettuce.

4. *The Medicinal Virtues.*

'Tis a very great loosener and refresher of the Spirits.

5. *The Parts for use.*

The tender *Tops* and Leaves.

6. The Quantity to be eaten in a Sallet, is double the Quantity of any one other Sallet Herb eaten in Composition.

7. *Its Cultivation.*

This Sallet Herb is raised from Seeds sown at any time of the Year, 'tis a very hardy Herb, will grow on most Lands, and

is

is an excellent good Sallet at all times, but particularly in the Winter and Spring.

SECT. XIV.

Of Garden and Water-cresses.

1. Their Names.

1. GArden Cresse is called in *Greek* κάρδαμον, in *Latin Nasturtium,* in *French Cresson,* in *Italian Nasturtio* and *Agretto,* and in *English Cresses,* borrowed from the *Germans,* who call it *Kersse.*

2. Water-cresses, in *Latin Nasturtium Aquaticum,* and *Laver Cratenæ,* and in *English* Brown, or Water-Cresses.

2. Their Description.

1. Garden-cresses, *Nasturtium Hortense,* or Town-cresses, has small narrow ragged Leaves, mordicant and hot in Taste. The Stalks are round, and generally rise near two Feet in height, producing many small white Flowers, which are succeeded by little flat Husks or Seed Vessels, like unto those of Shepherds Purse, wherein are contained Seeds of a brown reddish Colour, which when ripe (may be sown again, and) its Root then dies.

2. Water-cresses, the Stalks are weak and hollow, creeping upon the Ground, and strike Root at most of its Joints, which enables it to cover a large compass of Ground; the Leaves are compact, and their Edges something indented or jagged, growing exactly one against another, the end Leaf excepted, which stands alone. The Leaves are of a brown Colour above, and green underneath, which is the true sign to distinguish the physical Kind from the others. The Flowers are white, and appear in *July,* growing in spokie Rundles or Clusters, and the Root is a perfect Thrum or Bundle of Fibres.

3. Their Temperature.

1. Garden-cresses are hot and dry in the second Degree. And
2. Water-cresses are evidently the same.

2

4. *Their*

4. *Their Medicinal Virtues.*

Garden and Water Creffes being eaten raw in Sallets, are very good againft the Scurvy, and are very loofening and re-frefhing.

5. *The Parts for Ufe.*

Of Garden Creffes, the Seed Leaves; and the next to them —— Of Water Creffes, their tender Leaves and Shoots.

6. *Their Proportion in Sallets.*

The Quantity of each in a Sallet, where are many other Herbs that are cold and moift, as Cucumbers, Lettuce, &c. is of each three Times the Quantity of any other Kind of Sallet Herb ufed therein.

7. *Their Cultivation.*

Garden Creffes muft be fown on gentle Hot-Beds, during the Months of *January, February,* and the firft Fortnight in *March,* as directed for Chervil, after which they may be fown in the natural Ground under a South Wall, &c.

The Water Creffes are beft in *March,* when they firft appear, and as they delight in gravelly Springs, running Brooks, &c. are never cultivated in the Garden.

S E C T. XIV.

Of Cucumbers.

IN Confideration that many ingenious Gardiners raife early Cucumbers, and oftentimes cut Fruit for the Table in *March,* and fometimes in *February,* I have therefore plac'd them amongft the firft Salleting, notwithftanding that I cannot recommend their being eaten fo very foon as *February* or *March,* they being much too cold for the Weather of thofe Months.

1. *The*

1. *The Names.*

Cucumbers, are called in *Latin Cucumis sativus* or Garden Cucumber, in *Italian Concomero,* in *Spanish Cogombro,* in *High Dutch Cucumern,* in *Low Dutch Coucommeren,* and in *English Cucumber,* and vulgarly *Cowcumber.*

2. *Their Description.*

Altho' there be divers Kinds of Cucumbers, as the long and short prickly Cucumber, the long and short smooth Cucumber, the white Cucumber, the *Turky* Cucumber, the Adders Cucumber, Pear fashion Cucumber, *Spanish* Cucumber, wild Cucumber, &c. yet I cannot recommend any but the long and short prickly, the smooth and *Turky* Cucumbers, which in general are well known, and therefore need no Description.

3. *Their Temperature.*

All Sorts of Cucumbers are temperately cold and moist in the second Degree.

4. *Their medicinal Virtues.*

Cucumbers in general are soon putrified in the Stomach, but do not much nourish the Body, and what is, (as before) is cold and moist, and therefore not good. Being eaten raw with Oyl, Pepper, Salt and Vinegar provokes Urine, sharpens the Appetite, opens and cools the Liver, and helps the Chest and Lungs that are inflamed.

5. *The Parts for Use.*

When Cucumbers are very young and pickled, 'tis usual to eat the out-side Rind of the Fruit with them; but when they are largely grown, as fit for slicing, to be either fried, stew'd or eaten raw, they are generally pared, and then used. 'Tis a very great Custom amongst a great many People to make choice of the very largest Cucumbers, believing them to be the best, which are not, but instead thereof, are the very worst, except such as are quite yellow. Therefore in the Choice of Cucumbers, I recommend those that are about three Parts grown, or hardly so much, before those very large ones, whose Seed are
generally

generally large, and not fit to be eaten, excepting by such Perfons whose Stomachs are very hot.

6. The Quantity to be eaten is at Pleafure.

But herein obferve, that 'tis better to eat too few, than too many; and if your Stomach will bear, to eat a good many Onions fliced amongft them, 'tis much better than to eat them alone.

7. *Their Cultivation.*

The Cucumbers that are eaten in this Seafon, being raifed on Hot-Beds, I fhall now proceed to give proper Directions for the Performance of the fame as practifed by every good Gardiner, who raifes this Fruit.

The firft Work to be done, is to prepare a Parcel of frefh Horfe-Dung and Sea-Coal Afhes, as directed for the forcing of Afparagus, Sect. II. and about the End of *December*, or Beginning of *January*, make a very ftrong Bed, of fuch a breadth and length, as may exceed the Bignefs of your Frame about fix Inches all round, and three Feet and a Half or four Feet high, when fettled. And in the making of this Seed-Bed, obferve that the Dung be equally fettled with the Fork, but not trod down, as is ufual, for that caufes the Bed to fire and burn very much on a fudden, which when over lofes its Heat prefently, and chills the Plants: Whereas on the contrary, if a Bed be made, as directed for the forcing of Afparagus, its Heat will come gradually, and endure a very long Time.

About two Days after the Bed is made, place on the Frame and Lights, and fix or eight Days after that, earth the Bed with dry, rich, light Mould, preferv'd from the Winter's Rain in fome Out-Houfe, &c.

The Thicknefs of Mould need not exceed feven or eight Inches, which, the Day after earthing, will have received a fufficient Heat for the fowing of your Seed, which is beft done in little Drills about an Inch deep, at about two Inches afunder; and if the Weather is not very cold, I would advife that you cover the Lights every Night very thinly; for as the Bed is now coming into its Heat, if you fhould cover very thick, as many do, you would fet the Bed on fire by drawing its Heat up fo very haftily, which clofe covering never fails of doing.

The

The Heat of your Bed being moderately drawn, will caufe the Seed to appear above Ground about the fourth or fifth Day after fowing, at which Time give them all the Air and Sun that is poffible, fo as not too much, whereby you may lofe your Plants by too much Air, which is of as bad a Confequence as when they are ftifled for want of Air; which is difcover'd by their being of a very pale Colour, inftead of a lively Green, and very much drawn up and long ftem'd.

The only Care that is now to be taken, is more to defend them from cold Air, and to ftrengthen, than to draw and force them. And during all this Work, great Care muft be taken to wipe away the cold Steam, which by the Morning is condenfed into Water, hanging in Drops on the Glaffes, which is beft performed by a Woollen Rag, *&c*. This cold Steam is prefent Death to every Plant it falls on, and therefore great Care muft be taken to prevent its ill Effects. If your Lights are well made and firm, 'tis fufficient if you turn the Glaffes inftead of wiping them; and indeed is much the better way, becaufe 'tis fooner done, and the Bed lefs expofed to the Air. If you find that the Bed heats very much, and a great Quantity of Steam arifes, 'tis beft to abate the Covering, and to give a little Air in the Night; for in fhort, if they have not good Air, they are foon deftroy'd: And in the Day Time, when the Sun fhines very freely, be fure that they have fufficient Air, or otherwife the Steam that is then drawn up, will immediately kill them.

In the giving Air to Cucumbers, obferve that 'tis given in fuch Parts of the Frame, where the Wind cannot affect the Air of the Bed, which oftentimes kills the Plants.

Thefe Directions being duly obferved, your young Seedlings will thrive with good Succefs, and become very good Plants.

When they begin to fhew their third Leaves, they muft be tranfplanted into fmall Flower-Pots or Baskets, of feven or eight Inches Diameter, and four or five Deep, as directed by Mr. *Bradley*, in his *New Improvements*, Part III. Page 118. at about four Inches apart, placing four Plants in a Basket or Pot: And as Mr. *Bradley* obferves, that of the two, the Baskets are the beft, being made open on their Sides with Oziers: I do alfo recommend the fame, in regard to their great Conveniency in removing Plants from one Bed to another, as they decreafe in Heat, without any ways difturbing the Roots of the Plants,

4

which

which cannot be avoided when they are grown too large for the Pots; and besides, if a Bed happens by Winds suddenly to work and heat, and thereby scald or burn, the Baskets, tho' very hot, are instantly cool at raising up, which Pots are not, for they retain the burning Heat a long Time.

The Baskets are best when made with young Oziers, which must, before they are used, be cast into scalding or boiling Water, to prevent their growing when in the Hot-Bed.

Your Plants being thus managed, will be very close jointed, if you have allow'd them sufficient Air: And when they are arrived into their second or third Joint, make a good strong Ridge of about three Feet in Height when settled, which when its Fury of Heat is over, as will be in about ten Days or a Fortnight after making, then earth it in those Places where your Plants are to stand for good, and the next Day afterwards place or plant your Baskets of Plants therein, at the Height of seven Inches above the Dung; and at the same Time observe to cover the other Parts of the Ridge with Earth very thinly, to prevent the Steam of the Dung rising, which is present Death to these Plants at all Times. When you find that the Earth of your Bed grows dry, 'tis necessary to give the Plants Water, which prepare by its standing one Night within the Frame, before 'tis used, as directed for Asparagus forced, Sect. II.

Having thus transplanted your Plants for good, observe the Temperature of the Bed, and as its furious Heat declines, make good the remaining Earth within the Frames, always remembring to allow them sufficient Air, and that they are not any ways affected by the cold Steam within the Bed, or by any which may arise from the out Parts, which may be prevented, by covering the Dung from whence it arises, with any common Earth or Mould.

Your Plants being thus govern'd, will soon make great Progress; and that they may break out in many Runners, from which comes the Fruit, 'tis best to pinch or cut off with a Penknife the third or fourth Joint of every Plant, always observing to peg down every Runner, that they may not be burnt or destroy'd by the Glass (which too often happens) when their tender Shoots bear against it.

The

The Fruit springs forth from between the Stalks and Leaves, and appears very large before that the Blossom at its end opens ; and when these Blossoms blow strong and large, 'tis a very great proof of the Vine being in a good State of Health : So also 'tis to be observed in young Plants, when they hold their Seed Leaves with Strength and good Colour. And besides these Blossoms produced at the end of the Fruit, there are others, which grow at the Joints, called false Blossoms, which never produce any Thing; and are therefore by Gardiners picked off, as soon as ever they appear, to prevent their drawing any Nourishment from the Vines, which is supposed to prejudice the Fruit belonging thereunto.

As to Mr. *Bradley*'s Opinion of the male Dust contain'd in these male Blossoms, and convey'd by the Air or Wind, to the female Blossoms at the end of the Fruit ; I am not so good a Philosopher, as to confirm or speak one Word of the same. Perhaps it may be so, and that he may have seen, and been privy to such like Sports more than I have as yet thought on ; but I can affirm this for Truth, as also can many good Gardiners at *Twickenham* and other Places besides ; That I have raised many a good Crop of Cucumbers in very great Perfection, on whose Vines I never suffer'd one single false (or male) Blossom to open, or even attain one fourth part of its Growth ; for as soon as ever they appear'd, I instantly displaced them (as every good Gardiner always does) and never could observe, that for want of their familiar Conversation with the female Blossoms at the ends of the Fruit, did ever lose one single Cucumber thereby : However as I am not so proper a Judge of Procreation, as Mr. *Bradley* may be, I shall submit to his better Judgment.

When your Vines are tolerably grown, and several Fruit set, be careful that they are not check'd, or starved for want of Water, which will cause the Fruit to be both deform'd and of a bitter Taste : And as the Vines make their Progress, stir up the Surface of the Earth at the Ends of their Shoots very gently, that their tender Roots may the easier strike therein ; for the Nature of the Roots of a Cucumber is such, as to extend themselves as far from the main Stem within the Ground, as the Vines do without. The extension and size of the Roots, and Vines of every Kind of Cucumber, is always in proportion to the magnitude of its Fruit ; as for Example : The *Turky* Cucumber, whose Fruit is very large, produces a much larger Vine, and extends it self much farther than the long prickly Cucumber, and that also much larger, and of greater extent, than the short early prickly Cucumber.

Therefore seeing that every different Kind of Cucumber is of a different Growth ; great Care should be taken in their Planting that they are dispos'd of, at such Distances, as is proper and suitable to their respective Growth.

The different Growth of Cucumbers being thus considered, as to their Distance, each Hole from one another ; we should also consider the number of Plants necessary for each Hole according to their difference of Growth ; for was we to place but one or two at most of the short prickly Cucumber Plants in one Hole, which is fully sufficient for the *Turky* Kind, we should not receive a half Crop ; and on the contrary, if of the *Turky* Cucumber we plant three or four Plants, as is usually done with the prickly Kind, their Vines would rob one another of their Nourishment, and run into Confusion.

'Tis observable, that new Cucumber Seed draws a much greater Nourishment, and is less fruitful, than such Seed as is six or seven Years old; their Vines being more luxuriant, and less prolifick, with their Joints at a very great Distance ; which in old well saved Seed, are very close and nearly situated together. Now in order for the Discovery of the Cause, why old Seed should produce a much better Crop of Cucumbers, than new Seed, I have made the following Experiment, wherein I have discovered the Cause.

Having early in the Year made choice of the very best and earliest Cucumbers that came to perfection in the Spring (which must always be observed, and not delayed to the latter part of the Crop, when the Fruit has not half its Strength and Goodness) to save Seed from when rotten ripe ; I then washed it out and dried the same in the Sun, and put it into a Seed Bag, very secure from Mice, which are great Lovers of this kind of Seed, and therefore must be carefully guarded against.

This being done, I took part of the Seed, and caused it to be sewed up in a small Linen Bag, which about the beginning of *August* I put into the Watch Pocket of my Breeches, wherein it remain'd till the end of *December* following ; at which
Time

Time I took it out of the Linen Bag, and obferved that it had fhrinked very much, and was become very hard. And having prepared a Seed Bed, I fow'd the fame, as alfo fome of the fame Seed, as was kept in my Seed Drawers, and others of eight Years old, of the fame Kind: The Seed that was kept in the Seed Drawer, of one Year's Age, came up immediately: But the others, *viz.* That of eight Years old, and that of one Year preferved in my Pocket, as aforefaid, did not come up within two Days after the firft, and were much weaker: However, being very eager to fatisfy my Curiofity herein, I gave them an equal Attendance in every part of their Government, and at length found, that the Seed of one Year's Growth, kept in the Seed Drawer, produced very large Vines, and little or no Fruit; but the Seed of one Year, which I preferved in my Fob, produced rather a much better Crop, than that which was eight Years old: From which it appear'd, that the moderate dry Heat of my Body, communicated to it when in my Watch Pocket, had the very fame Effect as when gradually dried by time in the Term of feven or eight Years.

When hot Beds or Ridges decay very much in their Heat, let them be lin'd as before directed for Afparagus, Sect. II. and when many Ridges or Frames are placed before one another, cut away as much of the old Dung as is neceffary, and fill up the Alleys or Spaces between, even to the top of the Ridges, with frefh Horfe Dung, covering it with indifferent Earth, to prevent the Steam from rifing, which (as I faid before) is deftructive to your Plants.

The lefs that their Vines are difturbed on any Account, the better for the Veffels which convey the Juices to the Fruit, for being very tender, they are eafily bruifed and prejudiced by every Accident, &c. that caufes their removal.

The more Shade every Fruit poffeffes, the better it grows; for when Fruit of any Kind is fully expofed to the Sun, before they have done growing, the direct Beams of the Sun dry and pinch the Veffels of it, (as Mr. *Bradley* obferves) that the Sap cannot pafs with fuch Freedom, as in thofe Fruits growing in the Shade, whofe Veffels are open and free: Therefore always remember that the immediate Heat of the Sun is only neceffary for the ripening the Juices of Fruit, when fully grown, and giving its natural Colour, and not for the Growth of it, as many have thought.   **When**

When a Bed grows cool, if under the Vines you cover it with Mofs, fo as not to difturb or damage them, 'twill draw a frefh Heat, and endure a long time.

Whenever you water Cucumbers, be careful that the force of the Water do.not difplace their Roots, and that you wet their Leaves as little as poffible, which Work is beft done in an Evening, and thereby will be dry by the Morning: And if the Weather is warm in *March* or *April,* and inclinable to Rain, take off the Lights, and let them have a gentle Shower; 'twill add very much to their Increafe and Welfare; after which lay on the Glaffes, which will draw up a frefh Heat to the Moifture then received, and caufe them to flourifh and thrive greatly.

This firft Crop is generally preferved by the Frames to the very laft; and that your Table may not be deftitute of a fecond Crop, to fucceed the firft, 'tis highly neceffary and very commendable to fow a fecond Crop, at the back of your Frames, about the middle of *February,* and a third Crop about the middle of *March;* both of which, when in the fecond or third Joint, may be tranfplanted out for good on Ridges, and preferved with Bell, or fquare Glaffes, inftead of Frames, being fhaded with Mats for the fpace of a Day or two after Planting, till they have ftruck Root, and able to endure the Sun; as alfo every Night to preferve them from the Cold.

N. B. That thefe Ridges need not be made fo very ftrong, as directed for the firft Crop.

N. B. That the fowing and tranfplanting of Melons has no fort of difference from that of the Cucumber: Therefore whoever are Lovers of this noble Fruit, may fow their Seeds about the middle of *February,* and order them, in every Refpect, as the fecond Crop of Cucumbers, the pruning of their Vines, and manner of watering excepted, which is thus performed.

1. *The Manner of Pruning.*

When your Plants are in the fecond Joint, cut or nip that off, and 'twill caufe two other Runners to break out from the Stem, at the Seed Leaves, which ftop at the third Joint, and all others alfo, as they come forth.

This Method being duly obferved, will caufe the Vines to throw out great plenty of Fruit, which when fet, ftop the Vine whereon it grows, at two or three Buds or Joints beyond the

G   Fruit,

Fruit, which will caufe it to grow away with good Succefs. The nearer the Fruit is fet to its Root, the better; becaufe the Sap is not fo much fpent in a fhort Paffage from the Root, as when it has a long way to travel before it arrives at the Fruit, when the Fruit fets very remote from the Root, as at the very extreme part of the Vine.

It often happens in both Melons and Cucumbers, as well as in Fruit Trees, that there are many very weak Shoots or Vines, which are called water Shoots, never producing any Thing more than Leaves and falfe Bloffoms, which greatly rob the Fruit of its Nourifhment, and therefore ought to be pruned away.

Melons in general require a much lighter dryer Earth, and a greater Heat than Cucumbers do, which delight in frequent Refrefhings of Water, and will not thrive without it. In the watering of Melons, obferve that you place a Bell Glafs over their Roots, to prevent the Water coming to them, which inftantly caufes them to canker or rot, and foon die; and at all Times 'tis very neceffary to preferve their Roots as well from the cold of the Night, as the Rains alfo.

The Nature of a Melon is fuch, that when their Fruit is fet, they delight to be fhaded by their Leaves, to have moderate Waterings when the Earth is extreme dry, and not to be kept very moift, which caufes their Fruit to have a watery and infipid Tafte.

As foon as the Fruit is fully grown, it cannot be too much expofed to the Sun; and that it may receive the very greateft Advantage thereby, I advife that a Bell or fquare Glafs be placed over the Fruit, which fhould be laid on plain Tiles, and turned every Day till ripe, which is known by their agreeable Odour, as well as by the fmall Cracks about the end of the Stalk, as if it was feparated from the Fruit in order to be difcharged, having then perform'd its great Office. When Melons are to be fent ten, twenty, or thirty Miles, 'tis beft to cut them a Day or two fooner than when ripe, and to be eaten immediately; and in the cutting of a Melon obferve, that you cut its Stalk to the length of one Joint at leaft, with a Leaf or two alfo: It adds a great Beauty to the Fruit when at Table.

To enumerate the feveral Kinds of Melons would be too tedious a Task, and not any way ferviceable: Therefore I fhall only add, that the very beft are thofe of a middling Size, and

not

not thofe as large as Pumkins, which by many are moft valued, for want of better Judgment therein.

The *Melon* is called in *Greek* μῆλον, *viz.* An Apple, in *Latin Melo*, in *Italian Mellone*, in *Spanifh Melon*, in *High Dutch Melaun*, in *Low Dutch Meloenen*, in *French Melons*, and in *Englifh Melon*, or *Musk Melon*.

The Meat of the Musk Melon is very cold and moift, and much harder of Digeftion than the Cucumber; and when any Perfon eats too much of it, it lies very long in the Stomach, and very often caufes *Agues, Fevers,* &c.

The *Italians* and *Spaniards,* who have them in much greater Perfection than we can in *England,* are faid to eat them, more to reprefs the rage of Luft, than for any medicinal Virtue.

SECT. XVI.

Of Elder Buds and Flowers.

1. *Its Names.*

THIS Tree is called in *Greek* ἀκτή, in *Latin Sambucus,* in *High Dutch Holunderholder*, in *Low Dutch Vlier*, in *Italian Sambuco*, in *Spanifh Sauco, Sauch, Sambugueyro*, in *French Hus* and *Suin*, in *Englifh Elder* or *Elder Tree*, bearing large Bunches of black Berries which are ripe in *September*.

But befides this black Elder, there is another Kind, which produces white Berries, called by divers People *Sambucus Sylveftris*, wild Elder; but *Matthiolus* calls it *Montana* or Mountain Elder.

2. To give a Defcription of Elder would be needlefs, feeing that 'tis known by every Boy that ufes a Pop-gun.

3. *Its Temperature.*

The Temperature of Elder, according to *Galen*, is of a drying Quality, and moderately digefting.

4. *The Medicinal Virtues.*

The tender Buds and Leaves of Elder, boiled in Broth or Soup, open the Belly, purge all manner of flimy Phlegm, and cholerick Humours; as alfo doth the middle Bark, but in a more violent Manner.

The Leaves pounded with Deers Suet are good for hot Swellings and Tumours, and greatly help the Gout.

The inner and green Bark is a very ftrong Purge; being ftamp'd, and the Juice prefs'd out and drank in Wine, is very good againft Choler and watery Humours, and efpecially the Dropfy.

The Flowers gathered in *April* or *May* and dried, being fteep'd in Vinegar, are very wholefome for the Stomach, fweeten the Blood, create an Appetite, cut, and make thin all grofs and raw Humours.

5. *The Parts for Ufe.*

The young Buds and tender Leaves for Pottage.

The Flowers being dried for Vinegar, and

The Berries, which are ripe in *September*, for Syrup or Wine; of which Kinds, the white is the moft agreeable for Wine, it being free from that very ftrong Tafte which the black Elder much abounds in. About five Years ago I drank part of a Bottle of white Elder Wine, made by that *ingenious* Nurfery Man, Mr. *Peter Mafon* of *Ifleworth* in the County of *Middlefex,* which was fo very foft, and of fuch a delicious Tafte, that 'twas judged by many, who were competent Judges of good Wine, to be as good a White Wine as they had ever tafted before: And 'tis a very great pity that this, as well as many other *Englifh* Wines, are not propagated much more than have hitherto been done.

6. The Quantity of Buds or Leaves, to be ufed in Pottage, muft be a proportionable part with other Soup Herbs: And the Flowers for Vinegar are at pleafure; as alfo are the Quantity of Berries for Wine.

7. *Its Cultivation.*

Both Kinds of Elder are increafed by Slips or Cuttings, and will thrive in any fort of Land that is tolerably good, and are often found growing wild in Hedges, Woods, *&c.*

And altho' 'tis but very little regarded by Gardiners, yet I am well affured, that were they to plant it in Hedges, running *Eaft* and *Weft,* it would not only be a great Prefervative, by

breaking

breaking off the cold *Northern* Winds from their tender Plants; but by its Produce of Flowers and Berries, would turn to a very great Account alfo.

SECT. XVII.

Of Garden Endive.

1. *Its Names.*

ENDIVE is called in *Greek* Σέρις ἥμερος, in *Latin*, *Intybum fativum*, and of fome *Endivia*, in *Italian Scariola*, in *Spanifb Serraya Enuide*, and in *Englifb Endive.*

2. *The Defcription.*

Garden Endive is a Sallet Herb, whofe Leaves are very long and narrow with jagged Edges, and fomething curling, like unto the curled Endive, but the Leaves are much larger; from which in the Spring rifes a round and hollow Stalk, divided towards the upper part into many fmall Branches, which being broken, immediately iffues out a great Quantity of Sap, like unto Milk, but of a bitterifh Tafte.

On the extreme parts of the Stalk its Flowers are produced, which are of a blue (and fometimes a white) Colour: The Root is long and white, with fmall Fibres breaking out of its Sides, which in general die as foon as the Seed is ripe.

3. *Its Temperature.*

Endive is cold and dry, in the fecond Degree, and being fomething bitter, doth cleanfe and open.

4. *Its Medicinal Virtues.*

This Herb being eaten raw in Sallet with Oil and Vinegar, &c. comforts weak and feeble Stomachs, cools and refrefhes Stomachs over heated, cools the hot burning of the Liver and opens its Obftructions, caufes Sleep, and is very good in hot burning Fevers.

5. *The*

5. *The Parts for Use.*

The tender Leaves, when blanch'd as hereafter directed.

6. The Quantity or Proportion in a Sallet is generally two Roots in small Sallets, and more in larger, at Pleasure.

7. *Its Cultivation.*

Endive is an excellent Winter and Spring Sallet, and highly deserves our Care, in respect to its excellent Virtues before described.

It loves a very rich Soil, and must be sown about the beginning of *May* for the first Crop; the beginning of *June* for the second; the beginning of *July* for the third, *&c.* When it has grown in the Seed Bed to a tolerable good Size, transplant it in Beds, or in single Rows between your *Sellery* at about eight Inches apart; and when 'tis well grown, take some Bast-mat, and tye some of it up, *viz.* as much as may be required in a Week's Use, and the next Week after tye up the like Quantity, and so on during the whole Season: But whenever you tye any up, be sure that 'tis perfectly dry, or otherwise 'twill immediately be rotten and disappoint you of your Hopes.

The Ancient's Method for blanching of Endive was as follows. First, They sow'd their Seed in *July* and *August*, from which came very good Plants, which would endure the Winter; and were planted out at about the Distance of seven or eight Inches, as practised by the modern Gardiners: And when the Winter came on, that the Endive had done growing, they used to take it up in a very dry Day, and bind up the Leaves together, with small Withs or Bast-mat, and then bury it in the Ground with the Roots upward, to prevent the Earth's getting amongst the Leaves, which would instantly rot them; and as they had Occasion for them during the Winter, they used to take them, even at any Time, either in Frost, Snow, *&c.* when they were finely blanched, and in greatest Perfection.

This manner of preserving Endive is certainly the very best, for let the Winter have ever so much Snow, Rains and Frosts, which soon destroy this Sallet Herb, it cannot any ways affect, or damage their Leaves, being buried as aforesaid.

SECT. XVIII.

Of Fennel.

1. *Its Names.*

FENNEL is called in *Greek* μάραθρον, in *Latin Marathrum* and *Feniculum*, in *Italian Finocchio*, in *Spanish Hinoio*, in *High Dutch Fenckell*, in *Low Dutch Venckell*, and in *English Fennel.* Of Fennel there are two Kinds, *viz.* The common and the sweet Fennel, which last, in the Space of two Years, will degenerate and become common Fennel.

2. *The Description.*

Both these Kinds of Fennel being perfectly known to every one, need no Description.

3. *Their Temperature.*

Hot and dry in the third Degree.

4. *Their medicinal Virtues.*

The tender Suckers being eaten in the Spring as a Sallet, are very good for the Lungs, Liver and Kidneys, opening their Obstructions and comfort the inward parts. The Seed drunk in Wine, expels Wind, eases the pain of the Stomach, and prevents Retchings to vomit. The green Leaves, being eaten in Sauce with Mackerel, *&c.* cause great Quantities of Milk in the Breasts of Women who suckle young Children.

The Decoction of Fennel drunk, provokes Urine, easeth the Pain of the Kidneys, and is very good against the Stone; as also are the Roots, being boiled in Wine and drank, and are likewise very good against the Dropsie.

5. *Their Parts for Use in Sallets or Sauce.*

1. The Stalks and Suckers, whilst young, for Sallets, being peeled and eaten as Sellery, and

2. The green Leaves for Sauce, *&c.*

6. The

6. The Quantity of young Shoots in an indifferent large Sallet to be about ten, but the green Leaves are at Pleasure.

7. *Its Cultivation.*

Both kinds of Fennel delight in good mellow deep Land, and are increased by Seed sown in the Spring, which was ripened at the end of the preceding *August*; or it may be increased by dividing the Roots, which are lasting for many Years.

In the Spring, before the Root puts forth its tender Shoots, cover the Top about six Inches thick with Earth, which will blanch the young Shoots, as they make their Way through it, and will be fit for Use as soon as above Ground.

S E C T. XIX.

Of Garlick.

1. *Its Names.*

GARLICK is called in *Greek* σκόροδον, in *Latin Allium*, by the *Germans Knoblauch*, in *Low Dutch Look*, in *Spanish Aios, Alho*, in *Italian Aglio*, in *French Ail* or *Aux*; the *Bohemians* call it *Czesnek*, and the *English Garlick*, or *Poor Man's Treacle.*

2. *Its Description.*

Garlick is a bulbous rooted Herb, covered with very thin Skins, (finer than Gold-Beater's Skin) of a very light white Colour towards the Bottom, (from whence the fibrous Roots break forth) and of a very light purple towards the upper Part or Bud, from which ascends the Stalk; the Bulb, or Root consists of many small Cloves, which have a general Communication at the Bottom of the Bulb: The Leaves are green, and in form much like unto those of the Leek.

At the end of two Years its Stalk springs up, (as aforesaid) bearing at its end a little Pod, which when open'd produces a tuft of Flowers, covered with a white skinny Substance, wherein, when ripe, are round black Seeds, but are never saved for any use.

3

3. *Its*

3. Its Temperature.

Garlick is of a very sharp, hot and dry Nature, in the Fourth Degree, according to *Galen*.

4. Its Medicinal Virtues.

It being eaten, heats the Body very much, attenuates thick and grofs Humours, cuts fuch as are tough and clammy, and confumes them; opens Obftruftions, and is a very great Enemy to cold Poifons, and bitings of venomous Beafts, for which Virtues, *Galen* called it *Theriaca Rufticorum*, or the Husbandman's Treacle.

It greatly helps an old Cough, provokes Urine, breaks and confumes Wind, and is very good for a Dropfie proceeding from a cold Caufe. It kills Worms in both Men and Children, being eaten raw by Men, and boiled in Milk for Children.

'Tis a very great help to a cold Stomach, and is a very great Prefervative againft Contagions and Peftilence.

5. The Parts for Ufe at Table,

Are the Cloves, more to rub the Plates withal to give a Relifh to the Meat, than to eat the Cloves themfelves.

6. The Quantity is at Pleafure.

7. Its Cultivation.

Garlick is very eafily increafed from the Cloves of its Root, which is beft done in *March*, being then planted in light fandy Loam, (rather then ftiff cold Land, wherein it will not thrive) in a Border, about five or fix Inches fquare from one another; and in *July*, when the Leaves turn yellow, the Roots muft be taken up, and very well dried in the Sun, otherwife they will foon rot, as will all other Roots that are to be kept the Winter, if not well dried at firft taking up.

N. B. That *Rocambole*, by fome called *Spanifh Garlick*, is a very ufeful Vegetable, and is much efteemed for its high Relifh in Sauces. The Parts for Ufe are the fmall Cloves or little Bulbs, contained in the Head of the Stem. It delights in

H   a light

a light frefh Land, and is propagated by planting the Off-fets of the Roots in *March*, as directed for Garlick.

Efchalots, or Shallots, being of the fame Family with the Garlicks, are therefore annexed hereunto.

They are of great Ufe in Sauces, and therefore a Kitchen Garden ought not to be without them. They delight in the fame Land as the Rocambole, and are propagated in the fame Manner.

About the Beginning of *July* their Blades will turn yellow, and ought then to be taken up, well dryed, and laid up for Ufe.

N. B. That a Border of four Feet wide, and about thirty five or forty Feet long is fufficient for a very large Family.

SECT. XX.

Of Hop Tops, or young Hops.

1. The Names.

OF Hops there are two Kinds, the one called *Lupus Salictarius*, the manured Hop in Hop Gardens, and the other *Lupulus Sylveftris*, the wild Hop; in *High Dutch* they are called *Hopffen*, in *Low Dutch Hoppe*, in *Spanish Hombrezillos*, in *French Houblon*, and in *English Hops.*

2. Their Defcription.

The Garden Hop being fo univerfally known, needs no fort of Defcription; and the wild Hop, having little or no Difference from the Garden Hop, excepting that its Leaves and Bloffoms are much leffer, which I fuppofe to be caufed by its not being cultivated as the other, is alfo needlefs to defcribe; knowing that there are but few Boys in the Country, but are well acquainted with Hops and Hop Tops.

3. Their Temperature.

The tender Shoots or Tops, Leaves and Flowers of Hops, are hot and dry in the fecond Degree.

4. *Their*

4. *Their Medicinal Virtues.*

The tender Sprouts or Tops being boiled, and eaten as Asparagus, cleanse the Blood, provoke Urine, and comfort the Entrails.

5. *The Parts for Use,*

Are the young Shoots or Tops gathered in *March* and *April,* when they first come up, and about eight Inches in height above Ground.

6. The Quantity to be eaten is at Pleasure.

7. *Their Calculation.*

The Hops from which the young Shoots are gathered, are generally from those that grow wild in Hedges, and do naturally love a very rich fat Soil. To lay down proper Directions (in this Place) for the Propagation of Hops, for the sake of their Flowers only, would be a Subject very foreign to our purpose, therefore I shall omit that for the present, and pursue our other Sallet Herbs, as they come in order.

SECT. XXI.

Of Lettuce.

1. *Its Names.*

CABBAGE LETTUCE is commonly called *Lactuca capitata,* and *Lactuca sessilis.* PLINY calls it, *Lactuca Laconica:* Columella, *Lactuca Bœtica:* Petrus Crescentius, *Lactuca Romana,* and in *English Cabbage Lettuce.*

But besides this common Cabbage Lettuce, there are many others which cabbage very well, as the *Capaseen* Lettuce, the Brown *Dutch* Lettuce, the *Roman* Lettuce, the *Imperial* Lettuce, and the *Silesia* Lettuce: To which I may add divers *French,* and Goss Lettuces which are extreme good, and cabbage very well with a very small Assistance of the Gardiner in tying them close up.

H 2   To

To make a Description of the several Sorts of Lettuce is need-less, in regard to their being so well known to every Person.

2. Their Temperature.

All Kinds of Lettuce are moderately cold and moist.

3. Their Medicinal Virtues.

This Sallet being eaten raw, allays Heat, Choler, Thirst, ex-cites Appetite, and represses Vapours; and when boiled and eaten in Soup, or (as Spinach) with Meat, makes the Body loose and open.

4. The Parts for Use,

Are the young Lop Lettuces sown on gentle Hot Beds, as before directed for Chervil, Sect. viii. and Cresses, Sect. xiv. or such Lettuces as have endured the Winter, which were sown the August before.

5. The Quantity in a Sallet.

Of whatever Number and Kinds of Herbs the Sallet is com-posed of, the Quantity of Lettuce ought to be equal to one of those Parts, viz. If composed of three Kinds, to be one third part, if of four Kinds, one fourth, &c.

6. The Cultivation.

The best Sort of Lettuce, for the Service of these three Months, is the Brown Dutch Lettuce, which if sown in Au-gust, may be transplanted out in September for good, and is best when in a light rich Loam, under a South Wall. And for small Lettuce in Salleting, the Lop Lettuce sown on a Hot Bed, as be-fore directed, is as good as any other Kind.

To have Lettuces cabbaged very early in the Spring observe the following Directions, viz. About the middle or end of August sow Brown Dutch, Imperial and Silesia Lettuce in the Border of a South Wall, which will be fit to transplant out for good about a Month or five Weeks after sowing, provided that you keep them moist by Refreshings of Water given in a Morning, if the Season is very dry.

N. B. That the Reason why I advise their being water'd in a Morning is, in regard to the Coldness of the Nights which often

often happen at this Time, which if water'd then, would rather chill and check the Growth of the Plants, than forward
them; and the like of all others.

Your Plants being of a sufficient size for transplanting, dig
up a *South* Border, that is very rich and of a light Nature, wherein plant your Lettuce, the brown *Dutch* at six Inches, the
Silesia at nine Inches, and the *Imperial* at a foot Distance
from each other, and the nearer you plant them to the Wall,
the easier you may preserve them in Snow and frosty Weather, by covering, *&c.*

And altho' I did not before take Notice of the *Capaseen*
Lettuce, yet we must not forget to sow some of that at the
same Time; for 'tis a beautiful yellow, well tasted Lettuce, and
one of the first which cabbages in the Spring.

And as these several Kinds of Lettuces differ in their height,
we should therefore consider how to dispose of them, in such a
manner that they may all receive an equal Benefit of the Winter's Sun.

First then the *Imperial* being of the greatest Growth, ought
to possess the back or hindermost part of the Border, next the
Wall; and in the next Line before that, the *Silesia*; next before
that, the Brown *Dutch*, and lastly the *Capaseen* Lettuce without.

N. B. That about the middle of *September* you should sow
a second Crop to succeed the first, which, when planted out,
may be so planted, as to be help'd forward, and shelter'd from
bad Weather, by the Assistance of Bell and Square Glasses, which
at those Times are of no other Use.

N. B. Also, that the *Roman* Lettuce is more tender than
the preceding Kinds, and will seldom bear the Frosts, so that
we very rarely make use of it for this Season.

About the middle of *February*, when our hot Beds are grown
too cold for our Cucumbers, sow therein Brown *Dutch*, *Silesia* and *Imperial* Lettuce, which by the middle of *March* may
be transplanted out on some other decay'd Bed, or a new one
made very weak on purpose, under Square or Bell Glasses, and
they will be finely cabbaged and fit for the Table in *April.*

The Cabbage Lettuce which is sown in the Autumn, and cabbages in the Spring, is certainly very good; but nothing near
so fine as that raised early in the Spring, as before directed,
whose Leaves are in general tender, and much easier for the

Stomach,

Stomach, which the others are not, being harden'd by the Winter's cold.

In *March* all the Kinds of Lettuce are sown in the open Ground amongst Carrots, Parsnips, &c. which should be repeated in every Month, or rather oftner during all the Summer Season, that we may always have a constant and plentiful Supply of them.

It is observable, that if you leave Lettuce Plants in the Seed Bed, and suffer them to grow therein to their greatest Perfection, they never are near so well cabbaged, as the others which were drawn from thence and transplanted : Therefore 'tis evident, that transplanting of Lettuce contributes greatly to their cabbaging.

The Lettuces of any Kind whatsoever, which are design'd for Seed, are best when planted under a Wall or Pale, that when the Stalks are in Bloom, they may be tacked thereunto with a Nail and Thread, which will not only preserve them from being annoy'd by Wind, but greatly helps the Seed in ripening, when the Season is very wet and cold, as oftentimes happens.

N. B. That such Lettuces as produce large and fine Cabbages early in the Spring are those that must be chosen to let run for Seed; and altho' you make choice of the very best Plants for Seed, yet notwithstanding those Seeds will degenerate, if often sown in the Earth wherein the mother Plant grew : Therefore to prevent such Degeneration, the only Method is, to keep changing the Land wherein 'tis sown, which may be done, by being sown in different Parts of your Garden, or by exchanging the same Kind of Seed, raised in some other Garden, by an honest Brother Gardiner, whose Care and Word may be depended on.

N. B. That the *Imperial* Lettuces, designed for Seed, must have their Cabbages cut on the top, at right Angles, or thereabouts, to give leave for the Stem to rise : But make not the Incisions so large as to let in the Rains, which will instantly rot the Plant : Therefore a very small Incision is sufficient.

All Lettuces shew a Kind of a Down on their Seed Pods, when their Seed is ripe, at which Time they should be pull'd up, and set to dry, in a *Tool-house, Green-house, &c.* and then rub'd or thrash'd out, and kept for use.

4   S E C T.

SECT. XXII.

Of Leeks.

1. *Its Names.*

THE Leek is called by the *Grecians* πράσον, in *Latin Porrum*; but *Palladius* in the masculine Gender calls it *Porrus*; the *Germans Lauch*, the *Spaniards Puerro*, the *French Porreau*, and the *English Leek* or *Leeks*.

2. *Its Description.*

The Leaves of the Leek are of a very dark green, and in Form somewhat broad, and very long; having a Keil or Crest in the backside, and in Taste and Smell are something like unto the Onion.

The Stem rises from the midst of its Leaves, which also rise with it on the Sides, bearing on the top a globular Head of small Flowers which are succeeded by black Seed, very like unto that of the Onion.

The Bulb or Root is long and slender, and especially when 'tis not transplanted. Therefore to have Leeks with very large bulbous Roots, Care must be taken, that they may be transplanted into a rich and light Soil.

3. *Their Temperature.*

Hot and dry.

4. *Their Medicinal Virtues.*

The Root being boiled, brings up raw Humours that offend the Chest. A quarter of an Ounce of Leek Seed, with the like weight of Myrtle Berries, being beaten and drank in Wine, stop the spitting of Blood, which has continued a long time, and is an excellent Remedy against gross and tough Humours.

5. *Its ill Effects.*

Leeks being hot and dry, ingender bad Blood, offend the yes, is very bad for those that are by Nature hot and cholerick, and with some is very disagreeable to the Stomach.

6. *Their*

6. Their Parts for Use.

The bulbous Root, and hard part of the Stem, with some of the tender Leaves.

7. The Quantity is generally at Pleasure, being chiefly eaten in Spring Pottage, which may be made in less or greater Quantity as desired.

8. Its Cultivation.

The Leek (as I observed before) delights in a light rich Soil, and is sown in *March*, either in Borders to be afterwards transplanted out or thinly in Quarters, to remain there, and be houghed out as Onions, at about four or five Inches apart.

But the best Way is to transplant them in *July* at the aforesaid Distance, which will very much contribute to their largeness;

and if possible, make use of wet Weather at planting; for 'tis much more natural to every sort of Vegetable, than any Water that can be given to them: However if the Season proves dry, they must be plentifully watered at planting.

The Seed (as before said in its Description) is not produced till the second Year; and as soon as the Seed Vessels begin to open, cut off the globular Heads of Seed, and tye them up with Lines to the Cieling, so that their Heads may hang clear of one another, and be the sooner dry, at which time the Seed may be beaten out of its Husks, and kept for Use in a very dry Place, free from Wet, Damps, &c.

SECT. XXIII.

Of White Mustard.

1. Its Names.

MUSTARD, is called by the *Athenians* νᾶπυ, in *Latin Sinapi*, by the *Germans Senff*, by the *French Seneue* and *Moustarde*, in *Low Dutch Mostaert Saet*, in *Spanish Mostaza* and *Mostalla*, the *Bohemians Horcice*; *Pliny* calls it *Thlaspi*; and some others *Saurion*.

I   2. Its

2. *Its Description.*

The Leaves of the white Muſtard, when fully grown, are large and rough, like unto thoſe of the Turnep, but much rougher, and not near ſo large. The Stalk is round, rough and hairy, divided into many Branches, which produce yellow Flowers, that are ſucceeded by long, ſlender, rough Cods, wherein is contained round Seed, which, when ripe, is of a whitiſh Colour, ſomething inclining to yellow, being very ſharp and mordicant.

Beſides this Kind of Muſtard, there are two other, the one called *Sinapi Sativum alterum*, Field Muſtard, whoſe Stalks and Leaves are in Form like unto the preceding, only ſmaller, and are more white and rough. The Flowers are alſo yellow, but the Seed is brown like unto Rape, and not quite ſo biting as the former. The other Kind of Muſtard is called *Sinapi Sylveſtre*, wild Muſtard, whoſe Leaves are like thoſe of the Shepherd's Purſe, but rougher and more deeply indented, with a Stalk growing about two Feet in height, bearing at its Ends, or upper Parts, ſmall yellow Flowers, conſiſting of four Leaves only, which are ſucceeded by ſmall ſlender Cods, wherein is contained the Seed of a reddiſh Colour, but ſmaller than both the preceding, and not ſo biting.

3. *The Temperature.*

Hot and dry in the fourth Degree.

4. *The Medicinal Virtues.*

White Muſtard being eaten, when in its Seed Leaves, quickens, and revives the Spirits, ſtrengthens the Memory, expels Heavineſs, and prevents the vertiginous Palſie.

The Seed of Muſtard pounded or bruiſed with Vinegar, is an excellent Sauce, it helps Digeſtion, warms the Stomach, and excites Appetite.

5. *The Parts for Uſe,*

The Seed Leaves for Sallets, and its Seed when ripe in *July* or *Auguſt*, but of their ſeveral Seeds to make Muſtard with for Sauce, the Field Muſtard is the beſt.

I

6. *The Quantity in a Sallet.*

If the Sallet is compofed of four Kinds of Herbs, the Muftard muft be one fourth Part, if of five Kinds, one fifth, &c.

7. *The Cultivation.*

The manner of cultivating this Sallet Herb is directly the
fame as the Chervil and Crefles, in Sect. VIII and XIV.

SECT. XXIV.

Of Spear and Garden Mint.

1. *Its Names.*

MINT is called in *Greek* ηδύοσμος and μινθή, the *fweet Smell.*
(*vide Pliny*, Lib. XIX. Chap. VIII.) It hath changed the
Name amongft the *Grecians,* whereas otherwife it fhould be called *Mintha,* from whence our ancient Writers derived the Name;
for ηδύς fignifies Sweet, and οσμός Smell: The *Italian* and
French call it *Mentha,* as the *Latines;* the *Spaniards Terva
buena* and *Ortelana;* in *High Dutch Muntz;* in *Low Dutch
Munte,* and in *Englifh Mint.*

2. *Their Defcription.*

1. Garden Mint, called in Latin *Mentha Sativa rubra* comes
up in the Spring, with reddifh coulour'd Buds, fucceeded by
Stalks of a fquare Form, and fomething hairy, whofe Leaves
are of a deep green Colour, and indented on their Edges,
like unto the Teeth of a Saw. The Root grows very fhallow, divided into many Joints, from which iffues forth many
fibrous Roots, as well as its Stalks: It delights in moift rich
Land, and loves to extend its Roots to a very great Length.

2. The Leaves of *Salvia Romana,* or Spear Mint are very
long and narrow, and in Form not unlike the Willow, but
whiter, fofter and more hairy; and the Roots are of the fame
Form as the red Garden Mint, and love the fame Soil alfo.

3. *Their*

3. *Their Temperature.*

Mint is hot and dry in the third Degree, and according to *Galen,* fomething bitter and harſh.

4. *The Medicinal Virtues.*

The tender Tops of Mint being eaten raw, wonderfully help and ſtrengthen a weak Stomach, and dry up all ſuperfluous Humours, cauſe a very good Digeſtion, and are very powerful againſt nervous Crudities.

Mint being diſtilled, the Water is very good againſt Gripings and Pains in the Bowels, the Head-ach, and Vomiting.

And being boiled in Wine and drank, is good againſt the Gravel, Stone and Strangury.

5. *The Parts for Uſe in Sallets.*

The tender Tops when firſt ſpringing out of the Ground.

6. *The Quantity in a Sallet.*

When young Mint is eaten in Compoſition with other Herbs. The Quantity is $\frac{1}{7}$, $\frac{1}{4}$, $\frac{1}{5}$, &c. if the Sallet is compoſed of 3, 4, 5, &c. Kinds of Herbs: But when eaten alone with the Juice of Orange and Sugar, the Quantity is at Pleaſure; as alſo when uſed in Soups, Sauces, &c.

7. *The Cultivation.*

Mint is propagated by parting the Roots any time in *February* or *March,* being well water'd at planting, if a dry Spring.

To have young Mint very early in the Spring, you may take up ſome of the Roots and put them in the back part of your hot Beds, or ſtrewing a few Seacoal-Aſhes on the Border wherein it grows, and placing thereon ſome ſquare Melon or Bell Glaſſes, they will cauſe the Mint to ſpring very early.

When Mint is about ten Inches, or one Foot in height, 'tis then in its greateſt Perfection for drying: Therefore then cut it cloſe to the Ground, being perfectly dry, otherwiſe let it remain till it is, and drying it in the Shade, tye it up in Bunches for the next Winter's Uſe.

SECT. XXV.

Of Nettle Tops.

1. *Its Names.*

NETTLE is called in *Greek* Αχαλήφη, in *Latin Urtica urens* of its burning and ftinging Quality.

2. *The Defcription.*

This Herb being fo well known, and fo eafy to be found, even in the very darkeft of Nights, needs no kind of Defcription.

3. *The Temperature.*

Stinging Nettles are temperately dry, and a little hot, fcarce in the firft Degree, and of fubtile parts.

4. *Medicinal Virtues.*

Being boiled in fpring Pottage, makes the Body foluble, provokes Urine, expells the Stone out of the Kidneys, and purifies the Blood.

The young Tops being ftamped, and the juice fnuffed up the Noftrils, ftop the bleeding of the Nofe.

5. *The Parts for Ufe.*

The young Shoots or Tops, when firft out of Ground in the Spring.

3. *The Quantity.*

When fpring Pottage, or Soup is made with Nettle Tops, Clivers, Elder Buds, *&c.* there muft be of each an equal Quantity, in Proportion to the Quantity of Soup made.

7. *The Cultivation.*

Nettles growing fo very common almoft under every Hedge, are therefore never cultivated on purpofe in the Garden.

4   SECT.

SECT. XXVI.

Of Citron, Orange and Limon Seedlings.

1. *Their Names.*

1. THE CITRON *Tree* is called in *Greek* μηλέα μιδίκη, in *Latin Malus Medica,* and *Malus Citria*; the Fruit is called in *Greek* μῆλον μιδικὸν, in *Latin Malum Medicum,* or *Malum Citrium* and *Citromalum. Æmylianus* in *Athenæus* shews that *Juba* King of *Mauritania* has made mention of the *Citron,* and calls it *Malum Hespericum :* But *Galen* denies the Name of *Malum Medicum,* and justifies it to be *Malum Citrium,* adding that those who call it *Medicum,* call it so on purpose, that none should understand what they say; which is very common amongst Apothecaries, Attorneys, *&c.* however the Apothecaries call the Fruit, *Citrones ;* in *High Dutch Citrin Opffell, Citrinaten ;* in *Low Dutch Citroenen ;* in *Italian Citroni,* and *Cedri ;* in *Spanish Cidras ;* in *French Citrons ;* in *English Citron Apple,* or *Citron.*

2. The second kind of Citron, is that which we call Limon, 'tis called in *Latin Limonyum Malum,* in *Low Dutch Limonen,* in *French Limons,* and in *English Limon, Lemon,* or *Lemmon.*

3. Oranges called *Malum Aurantium* or *Aurengium,* of the yellow Colour of Gold. Some call them *Arantia* of *Arantium,* a Town in *Achaia,* or *Arania* in *Persia;* the *Italians* call it *Arancio,* in *High Dutch* 'tis called *Pomeranken,* in *Low Dutch Araengie Appelin,* in *French Pommes d'Orenges,* in *Spanish Naransas,* and in *English Orange.*

2. *Their Description.*

1. The *Citron* is a Tree which never was known to grow very large, but is generally very full of Wood. The Branches are of a tough and pliable Nature, and the bark of a deep Colour.

The Leaves are of a light green, long and broad, very smooth, and of a very delightful sweet Smell. The Branches

are

are adorned alfo with fmall Thorns, from whofe lower parts next the Branch the Bloffoms are produced, each compofed of five fmall Leaves of a whitifh Colour, fomething inclining to a purple. The Fruit is of a fpheroidical Form, and very often larger than a Limon; whofe Kind is of a light golden, or yellow Colour, fet with feveral Wart like Knobs, and of a very pleafant Smell.

The Limon Tree differs very little from the Citron, except in its Bloffoms, which are much whiter, and Fruit much lefs.

The Orange Tree does naturally grow much larger than either Citron or Limon, but the Form of its Leaves and Shoots differ very little from either of the preceding. The Flowers are very white, of a very pleafant fweet Smell, and the Fruit of a globular or fpherical Form.

N. B. That this Defcription is to be underftood as general, and not particular to any one kind of Citron, Limon or Orange, of which there are great variety of Sorts, which particularly to defcribe would be both needlefs as well as endlefs; and indeed I cannot but acknowledge, that as my Defign here is to fpeak of the Excellency of the young Seedlings when eaten in a Sallet only, I might have omitted even what is above delivered; but confidering that the various Names and general Defcription might be an Entertainment to fome, I therefore thought it neceffary that the fame fhould not be omitted.

3. *Their Temperature.*

Moderately hot and dry.

4. *Their Medicinal Virtues.*

The Flowers or young Seedlings being eaten raw, are exceeding grateful and comforting to the Stomach.

The Rind of Citrons being eaten, is very good againft all Poifons. There is now extant, in the third Book of *Athenæus*, a Story of a Malefactor, who being convicted of divers notorious Offences, was condemned to be devoured of Serpents; but the Convict by Accidence, having eaten divers Citrons on the Day that his Execution was defigned, and being caft amongft the Serpents, remained in Health and Safety; for inftead of their coming to devour him, as they had many others, they

4

ran

ran away into their Holes, without doing the leaſt hurt imagi-
nable. Hence 'tis very plain that there is nothing in this
Life but has its Oppoſite or Abhorrency.

Limons diſtilled with their Rinds, &c. and the Water being
drank, provokes Urine, diſſolves and expells the Storſe.

If to two Ounces of Limon Juice, you add the like Quantity of good Brandy, or the Spirit of Wine rectified, and drink
it at the coming of an Ague, it will take away the ſhaking Fit ;
and if taken three Times in like manner, never fails of a perfect
Cure, provided that the Perſon afflicted be covered very warm
in a Bed at the Time of taking, and kept ſome Time after in
a breathing Sweat.

The Kernels of either Citron, Limon, or Orange, being
eaten, kill and expel Worms, and mightily reſiſt Poiſon.

5. The Parts for Uſe.

The young Seedlings, when about an Inch or thereabouts in
height above Ground, and the Flowers, being firſt infuſed in
Vinegar.

6. The Quantity of each in a Sallet.

If the Sallet is compoſed of four other Herbs, the Quantity
of Seedlings muſt be equal to any one Quantity of the other
Herbs, and the like of the Flowers; ſo that each will be one
ſixth Part of the whole, and the like of others.

7. The Cultivation.

The Kernels being ſown on a moderate Hot-Bed, as directed
for Chervil, Creſſes and Muſtard, in Sections viii, xiv and
xxiii, and cut as other ſmall Salleting, give a very agreeable
and grateful Taſte, when eaten in Compoſition with other
Sorts of Salleting. The Flowers are to be gathered as required.

SECT.

SECT. XXVII.

Of Onions.

1. *Their Names.*

THE Onion is called in *Greek* κρόμμυον, in *Latin Cepa*, and many Times *Cepe*, in the neuter Gender.

The ancient Writers called it by the Name of the Place where it grew, fome being called *Cypria*, *Sardia*, *Cretica*, *Samothracia*, *Afcalonia*, of a Town in *Judea*, otherwife called *Pompeiana*.

Columella faith, that there is one fort called *Marifca*, which the Countrymen call *Unio*, and from thence the *Frenchmen* call it *Oignon*, if *Ruellius* is right, who is of that Opinion.

And 'tis fuppofed that the *Low Dutchmen* call it *Aueuim*, of the *French* Word corrupted. They are alfo called *Setaniæ*, when very little and fweet, and are thought to be thofe which *Palladius* calls *Cepullæ*, though he called them *Parvæ Cepæ*, or little Onions.

2. *Its Defcription.*

The Form of young Onions for Sallets, as well as the Bulbs for Sauce being well known to every one, needs no fort of Defcription; and for its Seed which is produced the fecond Year, 'tis alfo well known to every Gardiner.

3. *Their Temperature.*

Onions are hot and dry in the fourth Degree, but not fo extream hot as Garlick.

4. *Their Medicinal Virtues.*

Being eaten raw in Sallets or boiled in Sauce, raife the Appetite, deftroy Phlegm, and corroborate the Stomach.

5. *Their Ill Effects.*

Their Bulbs being eaten raw in too great a Quantity, dull the Senfes, hurt the Eyes, caufe over much Sleep, and over-heat the Body.

6. *The*

6. The Parts for Use.

The young Seedlings when as large as a Wheat Straw for *Sallets*, and the *Bulbs* or *Roots* for *Sauce*, when full grown.

N. B. That the kinds of *Onions* worth the *Gardiner's* Care is the *Spanish Onion*, which is generally very large, and sweet; and the *Strasbourg Onion*, which is more mordicant, and keeps much longer than the former.

7. The Quantity for Use.

The Quantity of young Onions in a Sallet, should be equal to two thirds of any one sort of Herb contained in the Sallet, and the Bulbs or Roots for Sauce at Pleasure.

8. Their Cultivation.

Onions are best cultivated in rich Soil, and are sown at the end of *February*, or beginning of *March*, and when they are almost large enough to draw for Salleting; they must be houghed out, at about two Inches and half, or three Inches apart, and when fit for Salleting may be drawn for Use, leaving those which you intend for a Crop, at five or six Inches Distance from one another, and by so doing, you will have a plentiful Crop, and very large, which they cannot be, when left nearer to each other, as is common amongst many.

In sowing of Onion Seed be careful in allowing Seed enough, for it is of such a Nature, that there is seldom more than one Seed in five that is found. Therefore when you sow sparingly, you are very often disappointed of a full Crop, which is easily prevented, by allowing a sufficient Quantity of Seed at first sowing.

When your Onions are about three Quarters grown, it is usual to press down their Tops quite flat to the Ground, to prevent them from robbing the Bulbs of their proper Nourishment, and hinder their being very large, and as often as they rise, they must be pressed down again till the Root has done growing, which is known by the Leaves changing their Colour, at which Time they must be pulled up, and laid in Parcels to dry in the Sun, being turned every Day, till very dry; and then taking them away, lay them thinly on the Floor of a Greenhouse, *&c.* to dry more thorowly, which when

K   done,

done, fort the large from the fmall ones, and tye them up in Ropes, &c. for ufe.

If this Work is performed with great Exactnefs in Refpect to their being thorow dry, and fo kept afterwards, many of them will remain found and good till the middle of *April*. About the beginning or middle of *February*, feveral of them will begin to *fpire* or fhoot out, it then being their Seafon to be planted for Seed; and at that Time prepare a piece of rich mellow Land, wherein they may be planted in Rows, about one Foot afunder (that there may be Liberty to come between them, to deftroy the Weeds, &c.) and in the Rows, four or five Inches apart.

When the Stalks begin to open their globular headed Flowers, which are fucceeded by their Seed, 'tis good to fecure them from the Affaults of the Wind, with fmall Stakes placed in their Rows at fix or eight Feet Diftance, to which tye Lines of Packthread or Bafs-Matt on each Side the Stalks towards their Top; which will preferve them from being broken down by the Winds.

When the Seed Veffels begin to open, gather, and dry them as directed for the Leek Seed, Sect. XXII. &c.

SCALIONS or Off-fets of Onions produced in the Spring, when the Onions are growing to Seed, fupply their Place till fucceeded by a frefh Crop; they are hot and dry, but not fo much as the Onion; they quicken the Appetite, correct Crudities, and promote Concoction. The Parts for Ufe are the bulbous Part, and tender Stalks; and the Quantity to be eaten in a Sallet or in Soup is at Pleafure.

S E C T. XXVIII.

Of Garden-Parfley.

1. *Its Names.*

PARSLEY is called in *Greek* σέλινον, but this kind is called σέλινον κηπαῖον, *viz. Apium hortenfe*; the *Apothecaries* and *Herbarifts* call it *Petrofelinum*; 'tis called in *High Dutch Peterfilgen*, in *Low Dutch Trimen Peterfelie*, in *French*

3

du

du Perfil, in *Spanish Perexil Julivert* and *Salfa,* in *Italian Petrofello,* in *English Perfele, Parfely, common Parfely,* and *Garden Parfley.*

2. *Its Defcription.*

Garden Parfley being fo very common and ufeful, is known to every one, and therefore needs no Defcription.

But that my Reader may not be deceived in the Parfley, whofe Leaves are crifped or curled, called *Apium crifpum five multifidum,* or *curled Parfley,* he is to underftand that, that is alfo a *Garden Parfley,* as the former, whofe Leaves are fmooth, and of the fame Ufe.

The other Parfleys are firft, the water Parfley or Smallage, called in *Greek* ηλιοσέλινον, of *Gaza paludapium;* in *Latin Paluftre Apium,* and *Apium rufticum,* in *High Dutch Epffich,* in *Low Dutch Eppe,* and by many *Jouffrouwmerk,* in *Spanish* and *Italian Apio,* in *French d' L'ache,* in *English March* marifh Parfley, and *Apium aquatile,* or water Parfley, but the true water Parfley is *Hydrofelinum,* or *Sium majus.*

Secondly, mountain Parfley, called by the *Grecians* ὀρεοσέλινον by the *Latins Apium Montanum* and *Montapium.*

Thirdly, Stone Parfley, of which there are two kinds, the one called *Petrofelinum Macedonicum Fuchfii,* or baftard Stone Parfley, and the other *Petrofelinum Macedonicum verum,* or the true Parfley of *Macedonia.*

Fourthly, Wild Parfley *Apium Sylveftre five Thyffelium :* And

Laftly, Baftard Parfley with white Flowers, called in *Greek* καυκαλίς, in *Latin Caucalis albis floribus,* and by fome *Daucus fylveftris,* or wild Carrot, but very improper. The *Ægyptians* call it *Sefelis,* and the *English Baftard Parfley,* and *Hensfoot.*

Thefe laft five kinds being of no ufe in our Sallets, I fhall not defcribe them, or fpeak of their Temperatures, Virtues or Cultivations.

3. *The Temperature of Garden Parfley.*

Garden Parfleys are hot and dry, the Seeds are more fo, as hot in the fecond Degree, and dry almoft in the third, and the Roots are moderately hot.

4. *Their*

4. *Their medicinal Virtues.*

Both of thefe Garden Parfleys being eaten in Sauce, provoke Urine, are very grateful to the Stomach, open Obftructions, and are good againft the Stone, as alfo are the Seeds, being taken inwardly.

5. *The Parts for Ufe.*

The young tender Leaves, proceeding from the Crown or Heads of the Roots.

6. *The Quantity.*

Parfley is very feldom eaten in Compofition with other Sallet Herbs, and therefore whenever it is, the Quantity is at Pleafure.

7. *The Cultivation.*

Parfley delights in mellow rich Land, and is propagated from Seed fown in *March*, in fmall Drills at the edge of a Border, &c. or all over the Border in general.

N. B. That when your Parfley begins to grow ftrong, or rather too rank for Ufe, 'tis beft to cut down part of it clofe to the Ground, which will caufe it to fhoot afrefh, and be very young and tender fit for Ufe.

The Seed lies a very long time in the Ground before it comes up, 'tis produced the fecond Year, and is ripe in *July* or *Auguft*.

SECT. XXIX.

Of the Parfnip.

1. *Its Names.*

THE ancient *Herbarifts* called the *Garden Parfnip* in Greek ϛαφυλῖνος, and *Paftinaca*; and therefore fome of the latter called or furnamed it *Latifolia*, or broad leaved, to diftinguifh it from the other Garden Parfnip with narrow Leaves, which is truly called *Staphylinus*, *viz.* the Garden Carrot.   Some

Some Phyſicians not knowing to what Herb the Parſnip could be compared, have feign'd the wild Kind to be *Panacis Species* or a kind of Allheal; others have named it *Bancia*, and ſome *Brancia Leonina*, but the Garden and wild Parſnip are now called, in *Latin*, the firſt *Paſtinaca Latifolia Sativa*; and the latter *Paſtinaca Latifolia Sylveſtris.*

2. *The Deſcription.*

The Leaves of the Garden Parſnip are very broad, conſiſting of many ſmall indented Leaves, placed on a large Stalk one oppoſite to the other. The Stalk riſes from the Head of the Root in the ſecond Spring, divided into many Joints, from which Leaves come forth of the ſame Form, as thoſe on the Head of the Root, but much leſs. The Seed is produced in ſpokie Tufts growing at the top of the Stalk; 'tis of a circular, flat, and very thin Form, and is ſeldom good after the firſt ſaving.

The wild Parſnip is like unto the Garden Parſnip, in Leaves, Stalk, Tufts, yellow Bloſſoms and Seed, but all together much leſs; the Root is ſmall and of a woody Subſtance, not fit to be eaten, which the Garden Parſnip is, its Root being very white, ſweet, and ſoft when boil'd, and an excellent Root for the Kitchen.

3. *The Temperature.*

The Root of the Garden Parſnip is moderately hot and dry.

4. *The Medicinal Virtues.*

Parſnips are a much greater Nouriſher than Turnips or Carrots, they provoke Urine, and are very good for the Stomach, Kidneys, Bladder and Lungs.

5. *The Parts for Uſe.*

The Roots when full grown, being preſerved for theſe Months, as directed for Carrots Sect. VII.

6. The Quantity is at Pleaſure.

7. *Their Cultivation.*

The natural Soil for Parſnips is a very deep rich ſandy Loam, wherein the Roots will become very large. The

The Land wherein they are sown should be digged very deep, or rather trenched, and being sown about the end of *February*, or beginning of *March*, will be fit to hough out about the middle of *April*, at which time leave them about eight or ten Inches asunder, which will give sufficient room for their being large; which they cannot be, when they are left at the Distance of five or six Inches, as directed by a late Writer, on the Theorical Parts of Gardening, Part 3. Page 126. And as Radishes, Lettuces, Spinage, *&c.* are of a very short Duration in the Spring, therefore amongst your Parsnip Seed, mix their Seeds to be sown thinly, and thereby you may receive their Benefit, without the least Prejudice to the young Parsnips. 'Tis the common Practice amongst many Gardiners, to give their Parsnips but two Houghings: But I am well assured by Experience that the oftener either Parsnips, Carrots, *&c.* are houghed, the better they thrive, for the oftener that the Crust of the Earth is broke, and the deeper they are houghed, the more Liberty they have to swell, which they cannot do, when the Ground is very hard, and baked with heat about them. For it is not their being kept clear from Weeds only, which causes their Growth, so much as often and deep houghing the Surface of the Ground, which not only gives Liberty for their swelling, but for the Rains, Heat, *&c.* to act with greater Freedom and Power.

To prove this, sow a piece of Parsnips, Carrots, *&c.* at the proper Season (as aforesaid) and when they are come up hough one part of them as before directed, and only weed the other by hand without houghing, keeping them both very clean from Weeds, during the whole Summer, and in *October*, which is the Season to take them up, you'll find those that were continually hough'd, *&c.* will be ten times larger and better tasted than the others, that were always kept clean from Weeds and never hough'd, and the like of other Vegetables in general.

SECT.

SECT. XXX.

Of Potatoes.

1. *Their Names.*

CLu*sius* calls Potatoes, *Battata, Camotes, Amotes,* and *Ig-nanes,* and in *Englisb* they are called *Potatoes, Potatus,* and *Potades.*

2. *Their Description.*

To defcribe Potatoes would be a needlefs Work, feeing that they are now very well known by moft (if not every) Perfon in *England.* But as there are divers Kinds of them that grow very well in *England* (which I fuppofe came originally from *Ireland,* they being very plentiful in that Country) it will not be amifs to fay fomething of their Kinds.

The firft is the white Kidney Potatoe, fo called, in regard to its Form, which is the true Form of a Sheep, or Hogs Kidney.

The fecond is the white round Potatoe of Colour and Tafte like unto the preceding, as alfo its Skin which is very thin ; both thefe Kinds are very pleafant in Tafte, and oftentimes very large, but don't increafe fo much as the following.

The third Kind is that, which is called the *Lancafbire* Potatoe, of a very pale reddifh Colour, and of a very large Growth, but very watery and infipid in Tafte to what fome of the others are, and efpecially when planted in a cold and wet Land.

The fourth Kind is the red Potatoe, with a rough Coat, the very beft of any, and the greateft Bearer: 'Tis a Potatoe that is generally very large, and of a much finer Tafte than the *Lancafbire,* and a much better Bearer, but does not come fo very early, for which that is moft valued.

3. *Their Temperature.*

The Roots of Potatoes are temperately dry.

4. *Their*

4. *Their Medicinal Virtues.*

They comfort, nourish and strengthen the Body.

5. *The Parts for Use.*

The Roots, *viz.* The Potatoes themselves being preserved from the Frosts in a warm Cellar, *&c.*

6. The Quantity is at Pleasure, being boiled and eaten with roasted Mutton, boiled Beef, *&c.* and require a great deal of Butter, Gravy, *&c.* They are oftentimes baked and eaten with baked Meats, or roasted in the Ashes, and eaten with Butter as an Egg, when boiled in the Shell. I have seen divers of the *Irish* People boil and eat 'em with Milk, Cheese, or Salt only, which for my part is not so agreeable, as when eaten with Mutton, Beef, *&c.* as before delivered.

7. *Their Cultivation.*

The best Land for Potatoes is a light sandy Loam, and rather a green Sward than any other, not but that they will do very well in Land which is cultivated every Year.

The proper time for planting them is *February*, at which time the Ground being digged, they are planted in Rows, at a Foot apart from one another in the Rows, and the Rows at fifteen Inches asunder, and about six Inches deep. But instead of planting these small Potatoes, 'tis best to take some of the very largest, and cut each of them into as many Pieces as there are Buds, planting one Bud or Piece in a Hole, instead of a whole small Potatoe as is usual.

When they are come up, (or sooner if the Ground is foul with Weeds) they must be houghed, and so continued during the whole Summer, till their Haulm shades the Ground and prevents the Growth of the Weeds.

When their Haulm produces Blossoms, their Roots are then knotting for Potatoes, which may be discovered at that time by taking up their Roots, wherein they then appear in great Plenty. And I have often experienced, that those Roots which I have taken up to observe the Progress of their Growth, have been always much larger than the others, which were not then disturbed: For 'tis always a certain Rule, that those Roots, whose Haulm is very short and thick, has the very best Potatoes. And

And thofe whofe Haulm is very rank and large, have feldom any that are worth taking up. The Nature of moft Potatoes is to run with their Roots in a kind of Mat, about fix Inches round the Stem, at whofe bottom are often found very good middling Potatoes ; but the very beft are generally about eight or nine Inches in depth, near to the Place of the Mother Plant.

In the digging up Potatoes, obferve that you place the Spade at a proper diftance from their Roots, that you don't cut them, and that you fearch the bottom of every Hole, left the beft Potatoes are left behind : When Potatoes are planted about fix or eight Inches apart, as directed by the aforefaid Theorical Writer page 132. they feldom are fit for any other Ufe than to feed Hogs, as alfo when planted under Trees ; therefore of thofe beware, left after a great Expence, you have a fruitlefs Harveft.

Soon after *Michaelmas* their Haulm decays, and 'tis then that you are to take them out of the Ground, and keep them in a warm Cellar (from the Frofts) for Ufe.

SECT. XXXI.

Of Penny Royal.

1. *Its Names.*

PENNY ROYAL is called in *Greek* γλἤχων, and oftentimes βλήχων, in *Latin Pulegium*, and *Pulegium regale*, to diftinguifh it from *Pulegium montanum*; in *Italian Pulegio*, in *Spanifh Poleo*, in *Dutch Poley*, in *French Pouliot*, and in *Englifh Penny Royal, Pudding Grafs, Pulial Royal*, and by fome *Organie*.

2. *Its Defcription.*

The common Penny Royal, called *Pulegium regium vulgatum*, is fo well known, needs no Defcription.

3. *Its Temperature.*

Penny Royal is hot and dry in the third Degree, and according to *Galen*, is of fubtile Parts.

L

4. *The*

4. *The Medicinal Virtues.*

Being boiled in Wine, and drank provokes Urine, and expels the Gravel in the Kidneys.

Being taken with Honey, it cleanses the Lungs and Breast from all gross and thick Humours: And with Water and Vinegar asswageth the inordinate desire to vomit, and Pains of the Stomach.

5. *The Parts for Use.*

The tender Shoots for the Kitchen Use, and the Stalks, Leaves, &c. when near full grown for Distilling.

6. The Quantity of either is at Pleasure.

7. *The Cultivation.*

Penny Royal delights in moist and shady Places, and is therefore planted in *North* Borders. It loves a good holding Loam, and is propagated by Slips, planted any time in *March.*

S E C T. XXXII.

Of Radish.

1. *Its Names.*

RADISH is called in *Greek*, of *Galen, Theophraftus, Dioscorides*, and other ancient Writers, ῥαφανίς. By Apothecaries, *Raphanus* and *Sativa Radicula*; and by others *Raphanus Sativus*, the Garden Radish, in *High Dutch Rettich*, in *Low Dutch Radiis*, in *French Raifort*, in *Spanish Ravano*, in *Italian Raphano*; by the *Bohemians* 'tis called *Rzedfew*; and in *English* Radish.

2. *Its Description.*

The Garden Radish produces very large Leaves, whose stalky part at bottom is of a dark reddish Colour, and the upper or leafy part very rough, and of a pale green, being indented on its Edges, not much unlike the Leaves of Turnips.

The

The Stalks are round, of a reddifh and pale green Colour, divided into many fmall Branches, at whofe Ends fpring forth fmall light purpled colour'd Flowers, each confifting of four Leaves only, which are fucceded by fharp pointed Pods, feemingly puft or blown up, and full of a fpungious or pithy Subftance wherein is contained the Seed, which when ripe is of a light brown Colour, of a round Form, and much larger than the Seed of Turnip. The Root is of a taper Form, running down about fix or eight Inches, with divers fmall Fibres breaking from its Sides: The top part of the Root is of a very dark or blackifh red, its middle part of a beautiful red, and the lower part quite white; as alfo are the inward Parts in general, and of a fharp or mordicant Tafte.

The beft Kinds of Garden Radifhes now in being, are the Dwarf or fhort top Radifh which comes very early, and the *London* Radifh, that fucceeds it, and continues a long while.

3. *Their Temperature.*

According to *Galen,* Radifhes are hot in the third Degree, and dry in the fecond.

4. *Their Medicinal Virtues.*

The tender Leaves, or Roots of Radifhes, being eaten raw in Sallets, procure a good Appetite, provoke Urine, diffolve cluftered Sand, and expel it.

The diftill'd Water of Radifh expels the Gravel and Stone in the Kidneys.

5. *Their Ill Effects.*

Being eaten before Dinner, are troublefome to the Stomach, and caufe much Belching.

6. *Their Parts for Ufe.*

The Seed Leaves, and Roots when as large as the thick part of a common Tobacco Pipe, and the Seed-Pods make a very fine Pickle.

7. *The Quantity for Ufe.*

The Quantity of Seed Leaves, in a Sallet of fmall Herbs, ought

ought to be three times the Quantity of any other; and for the Radish Roots, they may be eaten at Pleasure.

8. *Their Cultivation.*

All kind of Radishes love a sandy Loam, that they may freely strike down with their Roots. To have Radishes early in the Spring, at the end of *August*, or beginning of *September*, sow some Seed under a warm Wall; or rather on a decay'd Hot-Bed, that during the time of Frosts, Snow, *&c.* they may be preserved therefrom; and about the middle of *February*, or sooner, they will be fit for the Table. And that these may be succeeded by a second Crop, at the end of *September*, or rather a little sooner, sow some Seed in the Border of a *South* Wall, that they may get above Ground in their Seed Leaf, before their Growth is stopt by the Winter's Cold; and if they are preserved from very great Frosts and Snow in the Winter, they will be in Season about the middle of *March.*

To have the seedling Leaves for eating in Composition with other Sallet Herbs, you must sow it in little Drils, on a gentle Hot-Bed, during *January*, *February*, and the first Week in *March*, as directed for Chervil, Sect. VIII.

SECT. XXXIII.

Of Horse Radish.

1. *Its Names.*

HORSE RADISH is vulgarly called *Raphanus Rusticanus*, or *Magnus*, and by many *Raphanus Sylvestris*, in *High Dutch Merrettich*, *Krain* or *Kren*, by the *Low Germans Meradiis*, and in *English*, *Mountain Radish*, *Great Raifort*, and *Horse Radish*; and in the *North* part of *England* 'tis called *Red Cole.*

2. *Its Description.*

Horse Radish being now so well known to every one, 'tis needless to give its Description.

3. Its

3. *Its Temperature.*

Horfe Radifh is hot and dry in the third Degree, and has a drying, cleaning, digefting Quality.

4. *Its Medicinal Virtues.*

Being eaten with Vinegar, as Sauce, it heats the Stomach, and caufes a very good Digeftion.

5. *The Parts for Ufe.*

The Roots being very white, and about two Years Growth, are the Parts for Ufe, when fcraped, or grated very fine.

6. The Quantity is at Pleafure.

7. *Its Cultivation.*

The natural Soil for Horfe Radifh is a rich fandy Loam, and is thus propagated.

Firft open a Trench as is ufual for trenching of Land three Feet wide, and a full Spit and half deep, and therein place Cuttings of Horfe Radifh, each having two Buds at leaft, at about fix Inches apart; then moving your Line, fet out the next Trench, which muft be but half the breadth of the former, and caft its Earth to the further Side of the firft Trench, without laying any Roots in this fecond Trench. This being done, fet out the third Trench equal to the firft, *viz.* three Feet, and cafting its Earth into the others, will make them good; then in the bottom of this third Trench place the Horfe Radifh Cuttings all over at the Diftances aforefaid; and afterwards fetting out a half Trench, as the fecond, caft in the Earth, and in like manner proceed till the whole Piece is fo planted.

This Method being obferved, you will have your young Shoots come up in good Order, in Beds of three Feet wide, with Alleys of one Foot and half between them, which gives leave for their being kept clean from Weeds.

If this Work is performed in *October*, the young Shoots will be up in the Spring, and at *Michaelmas* fome will be fit for Ufe; by the *Michaelmas* following, they will in general be fit for Ufe.

3

When

When your Horse Radish is become large enough for the Table or Market, in taking it up, 'tis best to trench the Ground back again, observing to bury its Prunings in the bottom of Trenches, which will come up again, and produce a new Crop, whose Roots will be fine and smooth, free from Knots, Canker, &c.

SECT. XXXIV.

Of Rampion.

1. Its Names.

RAMPIONS are called by many, *Alopecuros*, because that the Ear or Spike of Flowers are very like unto *Alopecuron*, or Fox Tail, which is another Herb; and by others it has been called *Rapunculum Alopecuron*, that it may differ from the true and right *Alopecuros*, or Fox Tail. In *Latin* 'tis called *Rapuntium majus*, and in *English* **Great Rampion**, or **Garden Rampion**.

2. Their Description.

The Leaves of the Garden, or great Rampion, are tolerably large, smooth and plain, very like unto those of the Beet.

From the Head of the Root spring up divers Stalks, set with the like Leaves, but decreasing in their Magnitude, as they approach the top. The Flowers are produced at the top of the Stalks in a thick Cluster, like unto an Ear of Wheat in Form; and before they are open'd they appear like small crooked Horns, after which, when full blown, they are like small Bells (which makes me believe them to be of the Bell Flower Tribe) being sometimes purple, and at other times white.

3. Their Temperature.

The Roots are of a cold Temperature and something binding.

4. Their Medicinal Virtues.

'Tis reported by many, that the Decoction of the Roots are good for all Inflammations of the Mouth, and Almonds of the Throat, &c. and is a very great Nourisher. 5. *The*

5. *The Parts for Use.*

The Roots boiled, and eaten with Oyl, Vinegar and Pepper; the Seed Leaves, or young Tops in Composition.

6. *The Quantity.*

When a Sallet is composed of five, six, &c. sorts of Herbs, and of each a Pugil, *viz.* as much as is generally taken up with the Thumb and two Fingers; to such a Sallet we generally add twelve Roots; and of the Seed Leaves or tender Tops an equal Quantity with any other Herb, Radish excepted.

7. *Their Cultivation.*

Rampions delight in a shady, rich and strong Soil.

The Seed is sown early in the Spring, and the Plants are afterwards transplanted out in a shady Border, at the Distance of four or five Inches, wherein they remain (being kept clean from Weeds) till fit for Use.

S E C T. XXXV.

Of Garden, or Spanish Rocket.

1. *Its Names.*

ROCKET is called in *Greek* ευζωμον, in *Latin Eruca sativa*, in *Italian Ruchetta*, in *Spanish Oruga*, in *High Dutch Rauckenkraut*, in *French Roquette*, in *Low Dutch Rakette*, and in *English Rocket*, or *Racket*.

2. *Its Description.*

The Leaves of Garden Rocket are very like unto those of Turnips, but not altogether so large, or rough.

When it runs up to Seed, the Roots break out into two or three Branches, or Stems which produce Flowers of a whitish, and sometimes yellowish Colour, and are succeeded by small long Pods, wherein are contained the Seeds, which in Form are very like unto Rape Seed, but much less.

2   3. *Its*

3. Its Temperature.

Rocket is hot and dry in the third Degree, therefore *Galen* advifes it not to be eaten alone, being rather too hot for the Stomach.

4. The Medicinal Virtues.

Being eaten in Compofition with other Sallet Herbs that are cold, as Lettuce, Purflane, *&c.* is very wholefome for the Stomach, and provokes Urine, but when eaten alone, caufeth the Head-ach.

5. The Parts for Ufe,

Are the young and tender Leaves.

6. The Quantity.

If the Sallet is compofed of cooling Herbs, as before obferved, there may be one Pugil, or equal Quantity of Rocket.

7. Its Cultivation.

The Seed is ripe in *September*, and fhould then be fown; it delights in a warm rich Soil, and is very hardy, efpecially the *Roman* Rocket, which is an Annual, and dying every Year, as foon as its Seed is ripe, rifes again from its own Seed, if fuffer'd to fall.

SECT. XXXVI.

Of Red Sage.

1. Its Names.

SAGE is called in *Greek* ἐλιλίσφακος , in *Latin, Italian* and *Spanifh Salvia,* in *High Dutch Salben ,* in *French Sauge ,* in *Low Dutch Sauie* ; and in *Englifh Sage.*

2. Its Defcription.

To defcribe red Sage, which is fo well known, would be needlefs, and therefore I fhall only add, that the Flowers are in bloom in the Months of *June* and *July.*　　　3. *Its*

3. *Its Temperature.*

Sage is hot and dry almoſt in the third Degree.

4. *The Medicinal Virtues.*

Sage is ſingularly good for the Head and Brain, quickens the Memory, and ſtrengthens the Sinews.

5. *The Parts for Uſe.*

The young and tender Leaves, and Flowers eaten in compoſition with other Herbs.

6. The Quantity is at Pleaſure.

7. *Its Cultivation.*

Red Sage is propagated from Layers, or Slips twiſted at the lower end, and planted in *September* or *October*, or if planted in *March* or *April* they will grow, but not near ſo well as when planted in the end of Autumn.

. The other Kinds of Sage, *viz.* The Tea Sage (called by many Sage of Virtue) the Mountain Sage, and the Wormwood Sage, are propagated in like Manner ; and as they are in general well known, they need no Deſcription.

S E C T. XXXVII.

Of Sampier.

1. *Its Names.*

THERE are three different Kinds of Sampier, the firſt called *Rock Sampier*, the ſecond *Thorny Sampier*, and the third *Golden Sampier* ; but the *Sampier* eaten in Sallets is the *Rock Sampier*, which is called in *Greek* κρίθμον, in *Latin Crithmum marinum*, and by many *Bati* ; in *High Dutch Meerfenchell*, which is in *Latin Fæniculus Marinus*, Sea Fennel ; in *Italian Fenocchio marino, Herba di San Pietro*, and hereupon divers call it *Sampetra* ; in *Spaniſh Perexil de la mer, Hinoiomarino, Fenolmarin*, and in *Engliſh* Sampier, or Rock Sampier,

becauſe

becaufe it delights to grow on Rocks, Clefts, &c. as at *Dover,*
Winchelfea, &c. and by fome 'tis called *Creftmarine.*

2. *Its Defcription.*

Rock Sampier is very like, in its Leaf, unto that of Purflain,
but fomewhat lefs, and of an aromatick Tafte.

From the Head of the Root rifes the Stalk, which, as it
rifes, fends forth many collateral Branches, on whofe ends grow
fpokie Tufts of white Flowers, like unto thofe of Fennel or
Dill, which are afterwards fuccceded by Seed in Form very
like unto Fennel Seed, but much larger. The Root is generally very thick, and of a very agrecable pleafant Smell.

3. *Its Temperature.*

Sampier, according to *Galen,* is dry and warm.

4. *The medicinal Virtues.*

The Leaves being pickled, and eaten in Sallets with Oil
and Vinegar, are very good for the ftopping of the Liver, Milt,
Kidneys and Bladder; it gently provokes Urine, and excites
an Appetite.

5. *The Parts for Ufe.*

The tender Leaves and Shoots.

6. *The Quantity to be eaten in a Sallet.*

When a Sallet is compofed of four Kinds of Herbs, there
muft be of Sampier one fourth part, when of five Kinds, one
fifth, &c.

N. B. Sampier being an Inhabitant of Rocks, Clefts, &c. is
therefore gather'd from thence in great Plenty, and feldom or
ever cultivated in the Garden.

SECT. XXXVIII.

Of Scorzonera.

1. Its Names.

SCORZONERA, or *Viper Grass*, called by the *Spaniards* Scorzonera, in *Latin Viperaria five Scorzonera*, and sometimes *viperina*, or *serpentaria*, because 'tis of force against the Poisons of Vipers; for *Vipera*, or a Viper is called in *Spanish Scurzo*, and in *English* 'twas first called *Scorzoner*, and now *Scorzonera*, from the *Spanish* Name, or Vipers Grass.

2. Its Description.

Scorzonera or Vipers Grass, hath long and plump Leaves, with a large Rib or Stem down the middle of a light green Colour.

The Stalk rises from the Crown of the Root, bearing Leaves of the same Form, but smaller, and yellow double Flowers on its top part.

The Root is almost like a Carrot, its Colour without is black, and white within, yielding a milky Juice, as do the Leaves also.

And besides this kind of Vipers Grass called *Scorzonera*, there are five other Kinds; as first, *Viperaria humilis*, Dwarf Vipers Grass; secondly, *Viperaria Hispanica*, *Spanish* Vipers Grass; thirdly, *Viperaria Hispanica humilis*, Dwarf *Spanish* Vipers Grass; fourthly, *Viperaria Pannonica*, *Hungary* Vipers Grass; and Lastly, *Viperaria Pannonica angustifolia*, narrow leafed Vipers Grass.

These last Kinds being of no Use in our Gardens, I shall not trouble you with their Description.

3. Their Temperature.

Temperately hot and moist.

4. Their Medicinal Virtues.

The Root being eaten, causes chearfulness.

5. Their Parts for Use.

The Roots.　　　　　　M 2　　　　　　6. The

6. The Quantity is at Pleasure.

7. Their Cultivation.

Scorzonera delights in a sandy Loam, 'tis propagated by Seed sown in *March*, which ripen'd the *July* or *August* before.

SECT. XXXIX.

Of Scurvy Grass.

1. Its Names.

SCURVY Grass or Spoonwort, so called in regard to the Leaves being of the form of a Spoon, called in *Latin Cochlearia rotundifolia,* or round leafed Scurvy Grass. And besides this Kind there is another Sort which is more common called *Cochlearia Britannica,* the common *English* Scurvy Grass.

2. Its Description.

The round leaf Scurvy Grass is of a very low Growth, producing many Leaves from the Head of the Root, which are of a round hollow Form, and a very deep shining green Colour. The Flowers or Blossom rise from the Head of the Root, of a white Colour, and are generally in Bloom about the middle of *May,* and the Seed ripe in *June.*

The common Scurvy Grass being well known, needs no Description.

3. Its Temperature.

Hot and dry.

4. Its Medicinal Virtues.

Being steeped in Ale and drank, is very good against the Scurvy, and is a great Sweetner of the Blood.

5. The Parts for Use.

In Sallets, the very young and tender Seed Leaves; and in Drink, Distilling, &c. the larger Leaves more grown.

6. The

6. The Quantity in Sallets.

The Quantity eaten with other Herbs is at Pleasure, as also in Drink, &c.

7. The Cultivation.

The Seed gather'd when ripe in *June* or *July*, may be sown on a fresh Border any time in the Spring; it delights in a moist Soil wihch is not fully exposed to the Sun.

SECT. XL.

Of Sellery.

THERE is no Herb adds so rich a Flavour to our Spring Sallets, as blanch'd Sellery. It is a Herb generously hot, and very easily propagated. To describe this Herb would be a needless work, seeing that its great Use has made it universally known to every one; and therefore I shall pass over that, and proceed to the Propagation thereof.

To have Sellery very early, 'tis best to sow the Seed upon an old decay'd Hot-Bed at the end of *February* or beginning of *March*, and when the Seed is come up, and about three Inches high, or thereabouts, prepare a Border of a light and rich Nature, or rather a decay'd Hot-Bed, and therein prick out the young Plants at four Inches apart, giving them good Waterings when required.

Having thus transplanted them out, when they are about seven or eight Inches high, and become good strong Plants, you must then plant them out for good, which perform as follows, *viz.* Having made choice of a good piece of Land proper for the purpose, strain a Line the whole length thereof, which chop out with your Spade, and then remove it parallel to the first, at about eight or ten Inches distance, *viz.* equal to the breadth of one Spit.

That being done, dig out the first Spit, about eight or nine Inches deep, throwing the Earth on each side of the Trench, and about three Feet from the first Trench, dig a second, and

after

after that a third, &c. The Trenches being thus open'd, 'twill
not be amiss if in the bottom of every Trench, you prick in
a tolerable good Coat of well rotted Horse-dung, and especially if your Land is poor, 'twill greatly add to the Growth of
your Sellery.

The Trenches being thus prepared ready for planting, take
an old Knife or piece of a Sythe, and cut out the Plants, putting them into a shallow Basket with Care, that you do not
knock off the Earth from their Roots, and plant them in the
bottom of the Trenches, at about six or seven Inches apart.
Having first pruned their Heads to about five or six Inches in
length.

Some are so curious as to tye up their Leaves together with
a small piece of Bast, that they may not, when a little flag'd
at first removing, lie down upon the Ground.

After your Plantation is ended, be sure to give them a very
good Watering, and indeed at all other Times, when the Earth
is dry.

When your Plantation is about nine or ten Inches in height,
you must earth them up within four or five Inches of the top,
and so continue during all the time of their Growth.

About six or seven Weeks after earthing up, they will be
whiten'd, that is, what we call blanch'd, and are then fit for the
Table.

To have a plentiful Supply of Sellery, 'tis best to sow and
raise Plantations at different Times, about one Month after
the other, by which Means we may be well furnish'd throughout the whole Year.

The most gross or rank strong Roots are more fit for
Soup, than for Sallets; therefore I advise that the midling
sized Sellery be chosen for Sallets with their small Suckers,
which break out from the sides of their Roots.

I have seen some Gardiners, who have been very curious in
the splitting of the blanched Leaves of Sellery with a Pin, which
being afterwards thrown into clean cold Water curl themselves
up, and make a very agreeable Figure, when well disposed
of amongst the other Sorts of Sallet Herbs.

The number of Roots eaten in a Sallet is generally about
five or six, when of other Kinds there is but a Pugil of each,
viz. as much as one commonly takes up between his two Fingers and Thumb.

Sellery

Sellery may be eaten in Composition with other Sallet Herbs, or alone, with Oil, Vinegar, Salt and Pepper.

SECT. XLI.

Of Skirrets.

1. Its Names,

THE *Skirret* is called in *Greek* σισαρον, in *Latin Sisarum*, by the *Germans Sierlin, Tragus Zamgarten Rapunkelen*, in the low Countries *Suycker Wortelen*, viz. Sugar Roots, and oftentimes *Scrillen*, in *Spanish Cherinia*, in *Italian Sisara*, in *French Cheruy*, and in *English Skirret* or *Skirwort*.

2. Its Description.

The Leaves of the *Skirret* consist of many small Leaves fastned to one Rib, very like unto those of a Parsnip, but lesser, smoother and of a deeper Green. The Stalk rises from the Head of the Root, bearing at its ends little spokie Tufts of white Flowers; the Roots are of a white Colour, and of a very sweet and pleasant Taste.

3. Their Temperature.

The Roots, which are their Parts for Use, are moderately hot and moist.

4. Their medicinal Virtues.

They create an Appetite and provoke Urine: And according to *Hieronymus Heroldus*, the Women of *Swevia* prepare the Roots hereof for their Husbands, and know full well wherefore and why, &c. I suppose they find a secret Pleasure therein, for they are very great Provokatives.

5. The Parts for Use.

The Roots eaten either raw, in Composition, or boiled and eaten with Vinegar, Oyl, Salt, &c.

6. The Quantity is at Pleasure.

4   *7. Their*

7. Their Cultivation.

The *Skirret* delights in a light, rich and moist Soil, and may be propagated by sowing the Seeds in *March*; but are more generally raised from Slips or Sets planted in the same Month.

The manner of increasing them is as follows. In *March*, when they begin to shoot forth their Leaves, take up the Roots, and part or divide them into as many Slips as possible, taking away all the old Roots, and preserving none but the fresh growing Fibres. This being done, take a large Hough, and draw deep Drills, about six Inches in depth, wherein place or plant the young Slips at about five or six Inches distance from each other, and during all the time of their Growth keep them well water'd, which will add very much to their Growth.

SECT. XLII.

Of Sorrel.

1. Its Names.

THE Garden Sorrel is called in *Greek* ὀξαλὶς, and ἀναξυρὶς, and by *Galen* ὀξυλάπαθον, *viz.* *Acidum lapathum*, or *Acidus Rumex*, sower Dock, the *Germans* call it *Sawrampher*, in *Low Dutch Surckele* and *Surinck*, the *Spaniards Azederas*, *Agrelles*, and *Azedas*, in *French Ozeille*, and *Surelle Aigrette*, and in *English* Garden Sorrel.

The several Kinds of Sorrel are seven, *viz.* the first called in *Latin Oxalis sive Acetosa*, Sorrel. The second, *Oxalis tuberosa*, knobbed Sorrel; the third, *Oxalis tenuifolia*, Sheeps Sorrel; the fourth, *Oxalis Franca seu Romana*, round Sorrel, called also *French* Sorrel; and fifthly, *Oxalis Crispa*, curled Sorrel; sixthly, *Oxalis minor*, small Sorrel; and lastly, *Oxalis minima*, the smallest Sorrel: But *French* Sorrel is the best for Sauce, Sallets, &c.

2. Their Description.

The several Kinds of Sorrels being well known to every one, need no Description.

4

3. Their

3. *Their Temperature.*

Moderately cold, moist and acid.

4. *The Medicinal Virtues.*

Cools a hot Stomach, creates an Appetite, opens the Obstructions of the Liver, and asswages the Heat thereof. It cuts tough Humours, and strengthens the Heart.

5. *The Parts for Use.*

The tender young Leaves.

6. *The Quantity in a Sallet.*

The Quantity of Sorrel in a Sallet is generally at Pleasure, some loving a greater Quantity of acid than others : But the usual Quantity is an equal part, proportionable to the other Sorts of Herbs, as a fourth part, when the Sallet is composed of four Kinds of Herbs; a fifth, when of five, &c.

7. *Its Cultivation.*

The Garden and *French* Sorrels are propagated from Seeds sown in *March* in Drills on the edge of a Border, and make a very handsome and profitable Edging.

S E C T. XLIII.

Of Spinach, or Spinage.

1. *Its Names.*

SPINAGE was anciently called *Spinachia,* and *Spinachium olus,* and by some *Hispanicum olus. Fuchsius* calls it Επιναχία ; the *Arabians* and *Serapio* call it *Hispane,* the *Germans Spinet,* the *French Espinas,* and the *English Spinach,* or *Spinage.*

2. *Its Description.*

It is supposed by many *Herbalists* that *Spinach* is a Sort of *Orach* ; the Leaves being soft and tender, of a dark green

N   Colour,

Colour, full of Juice, sharp pointed, and deeply indented towards the Stalk end. The Stalk rises about a foot and half high, and is hollow within; bearing on its top divers Clusters of Flowers, which are succeeded by a prickly Seed, and is therefore called prickly Spinage. But besides this Kind of Spinage, whose Leaves are deeply indented, there is another Kind called round Spinage, on Account of its Leaves being of a round Form, without being indented, as in the other.

3. *Their Temperature.*

Spinage is cold and moist, almost in the second Degree.

4. *The Medicinal Virtues:*

Laxative and emollient.

5. *The Parts for Use.*

The tender Seed Leaves when eaten in a Sallet, and the well grown Leaves when used in Soup, &c.

6. *The Quantity.*

When the young Seed Leaves are eaten in Composition, there must be the same Quantity of them as of other small Sallet Herbs, Radish excepted.

7. *The Cultivation.*

Spinage is propagated by Seed, and to have a plentiful Store thereof during the Winter and Spring, we must sow the Seed about the beginning, middle, and end of *August*, on good rich Land, which when come up, and large enough to hough out, must then be run over with a hough, and left at about five or six Inches apart; and as I before directed its being sown at three different Seasons, so you must observe in the Spring also, to keep sowing sufficient Quantities every Fortnight; for in the Spring 'tis very rare to find that one Crop will last longer than a Fortnight.

The prickly Spinage is of the same Taste when boil'd as the round Leaf, but is not so much esteem'd by Gardiners.

SECT.

SECT. XLIV.

Of Succory.

1. *Its Names.*

SUCCORY is called in *Greek* κιχώριον, in *Latin Cichorium sativum*, the *Germans* calls it *Wegwarten*, the *Italians Cichorea*, the *Spaniards Almerones*, the *Bohemians Czakanka*, and the *English Cichory* and Succory. *Pliny* named the broad Leaf Succory *Hedypnois*, and the bitterer *Dioscorides* calleth πικὺς, in *Latin, Intybum sylvestre, Intybum agreste, Intybum erraticum,* and *Cichorium*.

2. *The Description.*

Garden Succory is of two Sorts, the one with broad Leaves, and the other with narrow deeply indented : The Leaves of the first Kind are something hairy, and very like unto those of Endive. The Stalk rises from amongst them dividing its self towards the top, into many Branches, whereon grow little blew Flowers consisting of many Leaves, which are afterwards succeeded by white Seed. The Root is of a long duration, producing a white milky bitter Juice, as also doth the Leaves and Branches when broken.

3. *The Temperature.*

Cold and dry in the second Degree.

4. *The Medicinal Virtues.*

Being eaten raw in a Sallet, comforts the weak and feeble Stomach, cools the Liver, and opens the Obstructions of Urine.

5. *The Parts for Use.*

The Leaves being blanch'd, or whiten'd as the Endive, Sect. XVII.

6. The Quantity to be eaten in a Sallet is at Pleasure, it

being

being more pleasing to the Stomach than the Taste; 'tis also very good being boiled in Soup.

7. *The Cultivation.*

Succory is encreased by sowing the Seed in *July*, and ordered in every Respect as the Endive, Sect. XVII.

S E C T. XLV.

Of Tansie.

1. **T**ANSIE, called in *Latin Tanacetum*, being universally known, needs no Description.

2. *Its Temperature.*

The Garden Tansie is hot in the second Degree, and dry in the third.

3. *The Medicinal Virtues.*

Tansie being eaten with eggs fried, or in a Tansie, *&c.* is very good for the Stomach : For if any bad Humours cleave thereunto, it doth perfectly concoct them, and scowre them downwards.

The Seed of Tansie is a singular and approved Medicine against Worms, for in what sort soever it be taken, it kills and expells them; and being drunk with Wine, is very good against the pain of the Bladder, and stoppage of the Urine.

4. *The Parts for Use.*

The young and tender Leaves.

5. The Quantity is at Pleasure.

5. *The Cultivation.*

Tansie is increased by parting the Roots, and planting them any time in the Spring : 'Tis a valuable Plant, and ought not to be wanting in our Kitchen Garden.

The

The ingenious Mr. *Bradley* tells us, in his new Improvements, Part III. page 172. that he has experienced the great Virtue of this Herb, and found that one handful being boil'd in a half pint of ftrong White Wine, and the Decoction drank as hot as is poffible to be drank, immediately removes the pain of the Gout in the Stomach.

When Tanfie is qualified with the Juice of Spinage and fried, 'tis very pleafant and grateful to the Stomach, and efpecially being eaten hot with the Juice of Orange and Sugar.

SECT. XLVI.

Of Tarragon.

1. *Its Names.*

TARRAGON is called in *Greek* πολυείδος, in *Latin Draco,* in *Italian Dragoncellum,* in *French Dragon,* and in *Englifh* Tarragon.

2. *Its Defcription.*

Tarragon hath long and narrow Leaves, of a deep green Colour, broader and longer than thofe of *Hyffop,* with flender brittle round Stalks, about which hang fmall round Flowers of a yellow Colour mixed with black like unto thofe of common Wormwood.

The Root is long, with many Fibres breaking out of the Sides and extending themfelves like unto Couch Grafs.

3. *The Temperature.*

Tarragon is hot and dry in the third Degree.

4. *The Medicinal Virtues.*

Very good for a cold Stomach, being eaten raw in a Sallet.

5. *The Parts for ufe.*

Their tender Tops, or young Leaves.

6. *The*

6. The Quantity.

This Herb being well mixt in a Sallet, gives it a very agreeable Relish, altho' some cannot endure any part of it in a Sallet. When a Sallet is composed of six or seven Sorts of Herbs, and of each a Pugil, to them may be added about twenty five large Leaves of Tarragon , and the like of a Sallet of any other Size.

7. The Cultivation.

This Herb delights in a warm Exposure, and is increased by Slips taken from the Roots, and planted any time in the Spring.

S E C T. XLVII.

Of Turnips.

1. Its Names.

THE Turnip is called in *Greek* γογγύλη, in *Latin Rapum*, and by some *Rapa*. The *Lacedemonians* call it γαστηρ, in *High Dutch Ruben*, in *Low Dutch Rapen*, in *French Naueaurond*, in *Spanish Nabo*, and in *English Turnip* and *Rape*.

2. Their Description.

To describe the several parts of a Turnip, which is already well known, would be a needless work, and therefore I shall pass over the same in Silence, and only add, that the very best Kinds are the yellow and flat white Turnip, red on the upper part, and of these the best are those of a midling Growth ; the very large ones being, for the most part, either sticky and hard, or woolly and soft like unto the Pith of an Elder Tree.

3. Their Temperature.

Windy and moist.

4. The

4. The Medicinal Virtues.

The young tender Shoots or Tops, boiled and eaten provoke Urine. The Decoction of Turnips is good against a Cough and Hoarfness of the Voice, being drank in an Evening with a little Sugar, or Quantity of clarified Honey.

5. The Parts for Use.

The Seed Leaves when eaten in Salleting, the Roots when boil'd, and the tender Tops in the Spring for Soup.

6. The Quantity for Use.

The Quantity of the Seed Leaves to be eaten in a Sallet is an equal part with others; but the Roots and tops are at Pleasure.

7. Their Cultivation.

The fweeteft Turnips are produced on a light fandy Loam. The time of fowing Turnips to come in, for the Months of *January*, *February* and *March*, is *Auguft*: But to have them fooner for the Months of *October*, *November* and *December*, they may be fown in *June* or *July*; and indeed I can't fee any Reafon why we may not fow them earlier, as in *March*, *April* or *May*, that thereby our Table may be plentifully fupplied throughout the Summer. However let them be fown at any time, the manner of fowing and ordering after is the fame. To explain the Method of fowing Turnip Seed for a Crop, is as needlefs as to defcribe what fort of a Root a Turnip is: The only Care therein is, that you do not fow them too thick, which will caufe a very great Trouble and Expence in their houghing, or too thin, whereby you will be deprived of a Crop. Their proper diftance ought to be about feven or eight Inches, and twice houghing them over is generally fufficient.

If in the Winter the Frofts are very fevere, 'tis beft to pull them up and pit them, as directed for the Carrots, Sect. VII. or keep them in Sand in a warm Cellar.

The manner of fowing Turnips for young Salleting is the very fame with that of Creffes, Muftard, Chervil and Radifh.

Having

Having thus given a general Account of the feveral Sorts of raw and boil'd Salleting for the Months of *January,* *February* and *March,* I fhall now proceed to the Conftruction of two Tables, of which the firft will exemplify all the feveral Herbs in their refpective Degrees of Heat, Cold, Moifture, *&c.* by the help of which we may be capable of compofing a Sallet to any Degree required : And the fecond Table, the feveral Kinds of Herbs good againft every one particular Difeafe, the whole being digefted in an alphabetical Manner, for the more ready finding any part required.

A Table of the Degrees of Heat, Cold, &c. *contain'd in the feveral Sallets, for the Months of* JANUARY, FEBRUARY and MARCH.

Sallet Herbs hot and dry.

BROOM Buds 2^d Degree.
Chives.
Clary 3^d Degree.
Garden Creffes 2^d Degree.
Water Creffes.
Elder Buds and Flowers.
Fennel 3^d Degree.
Garlick 4th Degree.
Hop Tops 2^d Degree.
Leek.
Muftard 4th Degree.
Mint 3^d Degree.

Onions almoft in the 4th Degree.
Penny Royal 3^d Degree.
Radifh hot in the third Degree, and dry in the fecond.
Horfe Radifh 3^d Degree.
Garden Rocket 3^d Degree.
Red Sage almoft in the 3^d Degree.
Scurvy Grafs.
Tanfie, hot in the fecond, and dry in the third.
Tarragon 3^d Degree.

Sallet Herbs temperately, &c.

Brooklime.
Chervil.
Clivers.

Orange and Limon Seedlings.
Parfnip.

Sallet Herbs temperately hot and moist.
Carrot, Scorzonera, and Skirret.

Sallet Herbs generously hot.
Sellery.

Sallet Herbs cold and moist.

White Beet.　　　　　　Lettice.
Cucumber 2ᵈ Degree.　　Spinage.

Sallet Herbs cold and dry.
Red Beet, Endive and Succory.

Sallet Herbs cold and something binding.
Rampions.

Sallet Herbs moderately cold and acid.
The several Sorts of Sorrel.

Sallet Herbs dry and binding.
The several Kinds of Cabbages, &c.

Sallet Herbs temperately dry, and little or nothing binding.
The several Sorts of Cowslips, and Nettle Tops.

Sallet Herbs windy and moist.
The several Sorts of Turnips.

Sallet Herbs warm and dry.
Sampiers.

Sallet Herbs nourishing.
Asparagus, Parsnips, Potatoes, and Rampion.

TABLE II.

Of the several Effects, which the Sallets for JANUARY, FEBRUARY *and* MARCH *have on human Bodies.*

1. BLOOD *to cleanse and sweeten.*

ELDER Buds, Hop Tops, Nettle Tops, and Scurvy-Grass.

2. DIGESTION *to help.*

Asparagus, Mustard, and Horse Radish.

3. DROPSIE *acquired by Cold.*

Broom Buds, and Garlick.

4. FATNESS *to prevent.*

Clivers boil'd in Soup, *&c.*

5. HEAD *and* BRAIN.

Red Sage.

6. HUMOURS (*gross*) *to make thin.*

Garlick, Nettle Tops, and Sorrel.

7. LUNGS *to strengthen.*

Leek, Parsnip, and Penny-royal.

8. MEMORY *to strengthen.*

Red Sage.

9. LIVER *to cool.*

Broom Buds, Endive and Sellery.

10. LOOSENING.

White Beet, Cabbage, Corn Sallet, Elder Buds, Hop Tops, Nettle Tops, and Spinage. 11. RE-

11. Refreshing.

Corn Sallet, Creſſes, and Scorzonera.

12. Obstructions *to open.*

Garlick, Hop Tops, Onions, Sampier, and Sorrel.

13. Scurvy.

Brooklime, Scurvy-Graſs.

14. Stomach, *cold and feeble.*

Chervil, Clary, Elder Buds, Garlick, Leek, Muſtard, Mint, Orange Seedlings, Onions, Parſnip Penny-royal, Horſe Radiſh, Garden Rocket, Tanſie, Tarragon, and Alexanders.

15. Stomach *hot.*

All the Sorts of Lettice and Sorrels.

16. Stone *and* Gravel.

Wild Carrot, Water Creſſes, Fennel, Mint, Nettle Tops, Parſnip, Penny-royal, and Radiſh.

17. Urine *to provoke.*

Aſparagus, wild Carrot Seed, Chervil, Chives, Water Creſſes, Endive, Fennel, Garlick, Hop Tops, Nettle-Tops, Onions, Parſnip, Penny-royal, Radiſh, Sampier, Skirret, Scurvy-Graſs, Tanſie and Turnips.

18. Wind *in the Stomach.*

Garlick.

19. Worms.

Garlick.

20. *To excite an* Appetite.

Cucumbers, Muſtard, Radiſh, Sampier, Skirret, and Sorrel.

TABLE

TABLE III.

1. *The raw Sallets for* JANUARY, FEBRUARY *and* MARCH, *are, The*

YOUNG Tops of Alexanders.
Brooklime.
Chervil.
Chives.
Cowflips.
Corn Sallet.
Garden Creffes.
Water Creffes.
Cucumber.
Endive.
The young Shoots of Fennel.
Lettice.
White Muftard.
Tarragon.
Mint.
Orange and Limon Seedlings.
Young Onions.
Radifh.
Horfe Radifh.
Rampion Seed Leaves and Tops.
Red Sage.
Sampier.
Scorzonera.
Sellery.
Sorrel.
Spinage.
Succory.
Turnip.

2. *The boiled Sallets for* JANUARY, FEBRUARY, *and* MARCH *are, The*

Afparagus.
Beets.
Cabbages and Coleworts.
Savoys.
Carrot.
Clivers.
Elder-Bubs.
Hop-Tops.
Turnip.
Lettice.
Leeks.
Nettle-Tops.
Onions.
Parfnips.
Potatoes.
Rampion.
Skirrets.
Spinage.

3. *The pickled Sallets for* JANUARY, FEBRUARY, *and* MARCH *are,*

The Broom-Buds, red Cabbage, Cucumbers, fmall Onions, Radifh Pods, French Beans, Walnuts, Nafturtium Seeds, Berberries, Mufhrooms, &c.

Before that I proceed to the Sallets for the Months of *April,*

April, May and *June*, 'twill not be amifs, if I firſt lay down proper Directions for the gathering and ordering of a Sallet after the beſt Manner : And altho' I place theſe Directions now immediately after the Sallets for *January, February* and *March ;* yet the ſame is to be obſerved at all Times throughout the whole Year.

DIRECTIONS *for the gathering, ordering, and dreſſing of a Sallet.*

In the Choice of Sallets obſerve,

Firſt, That the Kinds are young and delicate.

Secondly, That they are picked very clean from imperfect, ſlimy, *&c.* Leaves.

Thirdly, That each Kind be waſh'd ſeparately in two clean Waters.

Fourthly, That they are well drain'd in a Cullender, and afterwards ſwing'd dry in a clean Napkin.

Fifthly and Laſtly, That every ſort be proportion'd as directed in the preceding Sections, and laid ſingly in the Diſh, in ſuch a Manner, as to form a pyramidical, or other agreeable Figure.

N. B. That during the Months of *January, February* and *March*, Sallets may be cut at any time of the Day ; but when the Weather increaſes in heat, the beſt time to gather or cut a Sallet, is about eight or nine of the Clock in the Morning, to be afterwards kept in a cool place, till within one Hour before 'tis eaten, at which time, it ſhould be waſh'd as before directed, and not immediately before 'tis eaten, as practiſed by many.

And when you are obliged to cut a Sallet in very hot Weather, put it into Spring Water for the ſpace of half an Hour or more, and then take it out, and order it as before directed.

And having thus gather'd and waſh'd your Sallet, the next Work is the dreſſing, wherein obſerve,

Firſt, That the Oil be very clean, ſmooth, light, and perfectly ſweet, without any ſort of rancid Smell.

Secondly, That the Vinegar, or other acid, be perfectly clear and freſh.

Thirdly, That the Salt be of the brighteſt and beſt refined Kind, and moderately dry.

Fourthly, When Sugar is uſed, that it be the very beſt refined.

Fifthly, That the Vinegar, Salt and Sugar, be proportioned to the heat or cold of the Stomach, as near as can be.

Sixthly,

Sixthly, That the Sallet be compofed of fuch Herbs as are agreeable to both Weather and Conftitution; which laft may be performed by the Directions of the firft Table, and the former by Difcretion.

N. B. That Sallets fhould be fo chofen, as to be agreeable to both Weather and Conftitution, as is faid before, *viz.* thofe which are hot, for cold Weather and cold Stomachs; the temperate ones, for temperate Weather, and the very cool ones, for very hot Weather, as well as hot Stomachs.

N. B. That Sallets may be fo mix'd, as to be hot and moift, hot and dry, temperate, *&c.* as for Example, Onions and Cucumbers being mix'd together, *viz.* double the Quantity of Cucumbers as of Onions, the one being cold and moift in the fecond Degree, and the other hot and dry in the fourth Degree.

This Mixture moderates the oppofite Natures of both, and caufes them together to be of a temperate Quality, and the like of all others.

The beft Difhes to drefs Sallets in, are *China* Difhes, on Account that the Oil and Vinegar are difagreeable to both Silver and Pewter.

The Oxoleon.

Take of clear and perfect good Oyl Olive three parts; of fharp Vinegar, Limon, or Juice of Orange one part; and therein let fteep fome Slices of Horfe Radifh, with a little Salt, and fome in Vinegar alone; gently bruife a pod of *Guinea-*Pepper ftraining both the Vinegars apart, to make ufe of either, or alone, or of both as they beft like. Then add as much good dry Muftard grated as will lie upon an half Crown piece, beat and mingle all thefe very well together; but pour not on the Oyl and Vinegar, till immediately before the Sallet is ready to be eaten; and then with the yolk of two new laid Eggs boil'd, fquafh and bruife them all into mafh with a Spoon: And Laftly, pour it all upon the Herbs, ftirring and mingling them till they are well and throughly imbib'd, not forgetting the fprinkling of Aromatick Flowers that are in Seafon, as well as thin flices of red Beet, Horfe Radifh, Berberries, *&c.*

N. B. That the Liquids may be made more or lefs acid, as is moft agreeable to the Tafte.

C H A P.

CHAP. II.

Of the several Sallet Herbs, Roots, &c. for the Months of April, May *and* June.

SECT. I.

Of Asparagus.

THE several Names, Description, Temperature, medicinal Virtues, Parts and Quantity for Use, being already declared at large in the first Part hereof, needs no Repetition: And therefore, as this Herb is now in its greatest Perfection, I therefore advise that great Care be taken in the cutting, as I have before advised, and that the latest time of cutting be never longer than the first Week in *June.*

SECT. II.

Of Artichoke.

1. *Its Names.*

THE Artichoke is called in *Greek* καινάρα, in *Latin Cinara* of *Cinis*, Ashes, a Manure wherewith it delights to be dress'd, in *Italian Carcioffi Archiocchi*, in *Spanish Alcarrhofa*, in *High Dutch Strobildern*, in *Low Dutch Artichoken*, whereupon divers call it in *Latin Articocalus*, and *Articoca*, in *French Artichaux*, and in *English Artichoke.*

2. *Its*

2. Its *Description.*

ARTICHOKES being univerfally known, I need not give any Defcription thereof; but as they by Degeneration are now become of many Kinds, fome good, and other very bad, I fhall by the way advife, that when Plantations of this Herb is made, that the Slips are taken from a very good Kind, as from thofe planted in the Neat-Houfe Gardens near *London*, or other Places, where the Kind is known to be very good.

3. Their Temperature is windy, and medicinal Virtues little or any at all.

4. The *Parts for Ufe.*

The young Leaves blanch'd, and the Chokes when fully grown, before they offer to bloffom.

5. The Quantity of either is at Pleafure.

6. Their *Cultivation.*

Artichokes delight in a warm, rich and deep Soil, and are propagated from Suckers or Slips, taken off and planted in *March* or *April*, in Holes or Cups as pickling Cucumbers, about two Feet and half apart in Lines, and about four Feet diftant from each other. In every Hole or Cup you muft plant three Plants in the Form of an equilateral Triangle, at about eight or nine Inches apart, having firft prun'd their Heads to about the fame Number of Inches.

This young Plantation being kept very well water'd will thrive very ftrongly, and many of them produce good *Chokes* about *September*, but I cannot recommend that they fhould ; for it very often happens that they die after, or are greatly weaken'd thereby. Therefore to prevent the Lofs of your Plantation, as foon as the young *Chokes* appear, break them off, and the Plants will be greatly ftrengthen'd thereby.

When you flip Artichokes, be careful of leaving a fufficient number of Slips behind for a Crop, which ought always to be confidered, with refpect to the ftrength of the Plant.

Therefore when your Plants are very ftrong, you may allow to each Root, three Heads, or four at the moft, and to thofe that are weaker, two or three at the moft.

When

When the old Stems have done blowing, which is about *July*, break them off clofe to the Ground, and their Roots will afterwards break out and furnifh themfelves with frefh Shoots for the Winter.

About the middle of *November* they require to be dig'd, and at the fame time their large fpreading Leaves muft be pruned away; and inftead of flat digging them, they muft be ridged in fuch a Manner, as the Roots may ftand in the middle of every Ridge, to preferve them from the Frofts of the Winter, which if they prove to be very hard, you muft not fail to defend them with frefh Horfe Dung, or other long Litter, that will keep the Frofts from their Roots.

When Artichokes are planted in ftrong wet and cold Lands, they feldom laft longer than the firft Year.

N. B. That altho' I advifed the breaking of the young Chokes or Flowers of the young Plantation, which is intended for future Times; yet 'tis very neceffary that a fmall piece be planted every Year, and fuffer'd to grow up to large *Chokes* fit for the Table, to fucceed thofe produced from the old or mother Plants in *June*.

S E C T. III.

Of (Lisbon *and* Windfor) *Beans.*

1. *Its Name.*

THE Bean is called in *Latin Faba,* and that which we call the great *Windfor,* or Garden Bean, *Faba major hortenfis,* the great Garden Bean, and the Hog or Horfe Bean, originally growing wild, was called *Faba Sylveftris,* the wild Bean.

2. *Their Defcription.*

To defcribe what a Garden Bean is, would be a needlefs Undertaking, feeing that every Boy is well acquainted therewith: And therefore I fhall proceed to the Defcription of fuch Sorts as are moft advantageous and worth our Notice.

P   The

The Bean having very great Varieties, it would be endlefs, as well as ufelefs, to defcribe all its feveral Kinds, and as there are but two Kinds that are very good, and valuable among Gardiners, therefore I fhall take notice of thofe two, and o-mit all the other. The firft is the *Spanifh* or *Lisbon* Bean, which in Nature is hardy enough to endure moft of our Winters Frofts, *&c.* and produces an early Crop about the end of *April* or beginning of *May.*

This Kind of Bean is commonly planted under *Eaft*, *South* or *Weft* Walls, in *October*, or *November*, at about fix or eight Inches diftant from the Wall, and the like diftance in the Row: And altho' by this Means they come in very early in the Spring, and at firft gathering receive a kind Welcome, or if fold, a tolerable good Price; yet I cannot by any Means advife their being planted fo very near to the Fruit Trees, which, if great care is not taken, are very much damaged thereby. I have too often feen, that for the fake of three or four Beans, not worth one Penny, a good Peach or other Fruit Tree, worth half a Crown, has been deftroyed, by fuffering thofe Beans to grow fo very near, as totally to deprive the Tree of its pro-per Nourifhment, and thereby became (if not quite dead) good for nothing and irrecoverable.

And befides, it is not the Lofs of the prime Coft and Ex-pence of planting it only, but the great Difappointment and Lofs of one Year, which is a very great part of a Man's Life.

Now that this Practice may be laid afide, the Fruit Trees no ways injured, and the Table be well and early furnifh'd with a good Supply; I advife that about the end of *Auguft*, or mid-dle of *September*, you plant or fet as many of thefe early Kinds of Beans, in an open Border, at about three Inches every way diftant from one another, as you may have Occafion for, for your firft Crop, which when grown about three Inches or there-abouts in height, muft be taken up and tranfplanted againft fuch parts of your Walls as are naked, but never nearer to the Root or Stem of any Fruit Tree, than three Feet on each fide thereof at the leaft: And others may be tranfplanted in Lines about fix Inches apart, at two Feet and half afunder. But the neareft Line of thofe planted from the Wall, muft not be nearer to the firft than fix Feet at the neareft. A Plantation of this Kind will produce a much greater Crop, and earlier,

than

than thofe fet with the Dibber, and not tranfplanted afterwards.

In *March* when your Beans are in full Bloffom pinch off
their Tops, and carefully cut away all Suckers that may break
out, and grow from the bottom of their Roots; which if
carefully perform'd, as they firft appear will caufe the mother
Stem or Stalk to fet its Bloom and produce its Beans a fortnight or three Weeks fooner than if let run, without being
top'd and fucker'd.

And as foon as the Stalks are cleared of their Beans, pull
them up, and clear the Ground; or if you cut them down
clofe to the Ground, they will break out again, and produce
a fecond Crop.

By the time thofe planted under your Walls are gone, the
others planted from the Walls will fucceed, and produce fuch a
plentiful Crop, as will afford a very confiderable fupply to
a Family. And that our Table may be always furnifh'd;
'tis beft to plant fome others in open Quarters, at different
Times, *viz*. Some about the middle of *December*, other about
the middle of *January*, and again about the middle of *February*, at which time we may begin to plant our noble large Bean,
called the *Windfor* Garden Bean, and continue Plantations
thereof during the Months of *March, April, May* and *June*:
And if the Weather happens to be very dry at any of thofe
Times of Planting, 'tis beft to foak the Beans in Water before
they are planted, as alfo to water the Drills wherein they are
fown; for in thefe hot Months, 'tis better to drop them in
Drills at five or fix Inches apart, than to plant them with Dibbers, as in the Spring.

If the Seafons continue very hot, be fure to let them have
Water enough, and particularly when in Bloffom and Fruit,
'twill very well anfwer your Labour.

SECT.

SECT. IV.

Of Balm.

1. Its Names.

BALM is called in *Greek* μελισσόφυλλον, of *Pliny Melittis*; in *Latin Melissa Apiastrum* and *Citrago*, of some *Melissophyllon* and *Meliphyllon*, in *Dutch Consille de greyn*, in *Italian Cedronella* and *Arantiata*, in *Spanish Forongil*, in *French Poucyrade ou Melisse*; and in *English Bawme* or *Balm*.

2. The Description.

The common Balm, called in *Latin Melissa*, is very well known to most People, being valued by many for its fragrant Smell, which is not much unlike that of the Citron: But besides the common Balm, there is another Kind much more valuable called *Melessa Turcica*, the *Turky* Balm, whose Leaves are of a more acute Form and more indented, producing small Clusters of purple Flowers: The Root is small, and dies at the very first approach of Winter, 'tis propagated by Seed sown in *April* or *May*, and loves a rich Soil.

3. Their Temperature.

Balm is hot and dry in the second Degree, according to *Avicen.*

4. The Medicinal Virtues.

Balm being infused in Wine, and that drank, comforts the Heart, drives away Melancholy, and is good against the Bitings of venomous Beasts.

Serapio affirms it to be comfortable to a moist and cold Stomach, to stir up Concoction, to open the Brain and drive Sorrow and Care away.

Avicen, on the Infirmities of the Heart, affirms that Balm makes the Heart merry and joyful, and strengthens the vital Spirits, which I suppose good Wine will do alone also.

5. *The*

5. *The Parts for Use.*

The young Shoots, or tender Leaves.

6. The Quantity is at Pleasure.

7. *Its Cultivation.*

Balm is a very useful Herb for Distilling, as well as for using in Wine, and therefore should never be wanting in our Kitchen Garden. 'Tis propagated by parting the Roots any time in the Spring, and will thrive very well in most Kinds of Garden Soils.

SECT. V.

Of the Beet.

THE two Kinds of Beets being already described in Section III. Part 1. with their Culture, &c. I need not say any more thereon, but that they are now in their greatest Perfection, and are of very great Service in Soups, &c.

SECT. VI.

Of Borage.

1. *Its Names.*

BORAGE is called by many *Borago,* of the ancient Writers βούγλωσσον, which is in *Latin Lingua Bubula: Pliny* calls it *Euphrosinum,* because it makes a Man merry and joyful, as testified by the old *Latin* Verse,

> *Ego Borago gaudia semper ago.*
> Thus English'd
> I Borage bring always Courage.

'Tis called in *High Dutch Burretsch,* in *Low Dutch Bernagie,*
in

in *Italian Boragine*, in *Spanish Boraces*; and in *English Borage*.

2. *The Description.*

Of *Borage* there are four different Kinds, *viz.* The Garden *Borage*, call'd in *Latin Borago hortensis*; the white flower'd *Borage*, *Borago flore albo*; the never dying *Borage*, *Borago semper virens*; and a fourth Kind whose Leaves are like unto the last, but much thinner, lesser, rough and hairy, dividing its self into many Branches at the Head of the Root, which produce very beautiful fair red Flowers. And altho' there is this variety of *Borage*, yet the three last are to be rejected; the first being for our use only. The Leaves of Garden *Borage* are broad, rough and of a very deep green Colour, and generally lying flat upon the Ground: From the Head of the Root, amongst the Leaves, rises a Stalk, sometimes about eighteen or twenty Inches high, divided at the upper part into many Branches, producing beautiful blew Flowers, each composed of five Leaves, which are succeeded by Seed, ripe in the Autumn.

3. *Its Temperature.*

Borage is evidently moist, and temperately hot and cold, or rather a mean between both.

4. *Its Medicinal Virtues.*

The Flowers being eaten in Sallets, exhilarate and make the Mind glad.

The Leaves being boiled in Soup make the Body soluble.

Dioscorides and *Pliny* affirm, that the Leaves and Flowers being put into Wine and drank, drive away all Sadness, Dulness, and Melancholy, and make Men and Women glad and merry.

A Syrup made of the Flowers comforts the Heart, purges Melancholy, and quiets the phrantick or lunatick Person.

The Flower of *Borage* made up with Sugar performs all the aforesaid, with greater force and effect.

The tender Leaves being eaten raw in a Sallet, with other Sallet Herbs, create good Blood, and especially in those that have been lately Sick.

     5. The

5. The Parts for Use.

The Flowers and tender Leaves, when eaten in a Sallet, the Leaves, or young Tops with their Blossoms, when used for a cool Tankard, in Wine, &c.

6. The Quantity of either is at Pleasure.

7. Its Cultivation.

Borage delights in good rich mellow Loam, and is raised from Seed sown in the Spring.

SECT. VII.

Of Buglofs.

1. Its Names.

BUGLOSS is thought to be a kind of *Borage*, degenerated therefrom; but as *Dioscorides*, *Pliny*, and other ancient Fathers have divided them, I shall therefore follow their Rule of *Buglofs*: There are two Kinds, the one called *Buglossa*, and *Buglossa Domestica*, or Garden *Buglofs*; and the other *Lange de beefe*, in *Latin Lingua bovis*, and *Buglossum luteum*, and of some *Hieracio cognatum*, and *Buglossa Sylvestris* or wild *Buglofs*.

2. Their Description.

The Leaves of the common or Garden *Buglofs*, are longer than those of the *Borage*, sharp pointed, rough and hairy, and longer than the common size of Beet Leaves.

The Stalk rises to the same height as the *Borage*, and is divided into many Branches also, which produce Flowers of a bluish Colour, something inclinable to a purple before they are open'd, and when quite open'd, more inclinable to a blue.

The Root is long, thick, grofs, and of a long Duration. The other wild Kind, called *Lange de beefe*, is much less, but the Leaves more rough, like unto the Tongue of an Oxe, from which it took its Name.

3. The

3. *The Temperature and Virtues.*

The Leaves and Flowers are of the fame Temperature as the *Borage*, and their Virtues alfo.

4. *The Parts for Ufe.*

The fame as of the *Borage*.

5. The Quantity is at Pleafure alfo.

6. *The Cultivation.*

'Tis encreafed as the Borage from Seed, but its Root doth not die in the Winter as the *Borage*, wherein is the only difference between them.

SECT. VIII.

Of Burnet.

1. *Its Names.*

OF Burnet there are two Kinds, the one called Garden Burnet, and in *Latin Pimponella Hortenfis*, and the other *Pimpinella Sylveftris* or wild Burnet.

The later Herbarifts call Burnet *Pimpinella Sanguiforba*, that it may differ from the other, and yet 'tis called by many *Sanguiforba*, and *Sanguinaria*.

Gefner chufes to call it *Peponella* of the fmell of Melons to which it is like, and by others 'tis called *Pimpinella*, or *Bipennula*, and *Solbaftrella*; in *High Dutch* 'tis called *Kolbleskraut*, her *Gots Bartlin*, *Blutkraut*, *Megelkraut*, in *French Pimpennelle*, *Sanguiforbe*, and in *Englifh* Burnet.

2. *The Defcription.*

The Leaves of Garden Burnet are very fmall, indented, and thick fet upon fingle Stems or Ribs, each Leaf oppofite to another, and withal fomewhat hairy.

The Stalk rifes from the Head of the Root, bearing divers of thofe compofed Leaves on its Sides, dividing themfelves

into

into several Branches towards their Tops, whereon they produce little round Heads of small brown purpled colour'd Flowers which are succeeded by Seed, closely placed together. The Root is, in make, not much unlike that of a small Parsnip, and smells something like a Melon.

The wild Burnet is much larger in all its Parts, but has not that pleasant smell as the other.

3. *The Temperature.*

Garden Burnet is temperately cold.

4. *The Medicinal Virtues.*

The tender Leaves being eaten in a Sallet, with other Herbs, make the Heart merry and glad, as also being put into Wine, to which it yieldeth a pleasant Taste in Drinking.

5. *The Parts for Use.*

The young Sprigs or Shoots in Wine, the tender Leaves in Sallets.

6. The Quantity is at Pleasure, as of Balm, Borage, and Buglofs.

7. *The Cultivation.*

Burnet produces its Blossoms from *June* to the end of *August*, at which time, or very soon after, the Seed is ripe, which may be sown in the Spring, and the young Plants, when large enough, transplanted out in Borders at six or eight Inches distant from one another.

S E C T. IX.

Of Chervil, Cresses, Corn-Sallet, white Mustard, Radish, Spinage and Turnip.

CHERVIL being an excellent Sallet Herb, is still to be cultivated, but need not be sown upon old decayed hot Beds under Glasses, &c. as before. The Season being now

Q   warm

warm enough for its Growth in the natural Borders, as the heat of the Spring advances, make choice of such Borders to sow your Seed in, as are not so fully exposed to the heat, as a *South* Border.

When you find your young Salleting begins to start, or run away as soon as out of Ground, then remove your place of raising to some *East* Border, which the Sun will depart from about eleven in the Morning, and your Salleting will be much finer: And whenever you find that in very hot Weather your Salleting begins to run, as before in the *South* Border, then remove to a *North* Border, wherein you may raise it with Pleasure.

N. B. That what is here delivered in relation to the sowing of Chervil, the same must be understood in the sowing of Cresses, Corn-Sallet, white Mustard, Radish, Spinage, Turnip, Lettuce, &c. and all other small Salleting in general.

S E C T. X.

Of Indian Cresses.

INDIAN Cresses, called in *Latin Nasturtium Indicum*, is raised from Seed sown early on a hot Bed, at the back of Cucumbers, Melons, &c. which produce great plenty of Flowers very early, that are very beautiful and agreable in our Sallets.

There are two Kinds of *Nasturtiums*, the one of a small Growth, which is that commonly raised in a Hot-Bed, and the other of a larger Kind, which would run beyond the Bounds of a Frame if planted therein.

And altho' the small Kind is raised in a Frame for the sake of having them early, yet it will grow very well in the natural Earth, as also will the larger Kind.

The Seeds which succeed the Flowers, being gathered before they are fully ripe, and pickled, make a fine Sallet in the Winter.

When

When this Plant is planted at the foot of Standard Trees, or clofe under Hedges of Elm, Hornbeam, &c. they make a very agreeable and pleafant Figure, being tyed up in and about the fame. Their Branches are many, and incapable of fupporting their own Weight, and therefore require help.

Their Nature is, to extend themfelves a very great way from their Roots, and delight in a rich moift Soil.

Their Leaves are of a round Form and light green Colour, and in Tafte and Smell like unto the Garden Crefles.

The Flowers are difperfed throughout the whole Plant, of a yellow Colour, intermixed with Purple ; having a Spur or Tail, exactly as the Larkfpur or Larkheel, but much larger. The Seed is rough, of a brown Colour, and in Form very like unto the Beet, but fmaller.

SECT. XI.

Of Cucumbers.

THE Cucumbers raifed on hot Beds, having hitherto plentifully furnifh'd our Tables, we may now make fmall Holes in the natural Ground, and be plentifully ferved therefrom.

The only care to be obferved herein is, that the Ground be tolerably rich, and if not, to be made fo.

The Manner of performing the fame is as follows, Firft, fet out the diftance of your Holes, which ought to be about four Feet (fquare) from one another ; then if the Ground was dug before, open fmall Holes about eighteen Inches over, and one Spit deep, and therein throw a Spit or two of good rotten Horfe-dung, which work in and mix very well with the Earth, and having work'd it very fine, form it with a Concavity like unto a Bafon, as termed by Gardiners, *viz.* hollow like unto a Difh to receive the Water: And therein fow at leaft ten or a dozen Seeds, at about two Inches apart from each other, and the like Depth ; for 'tis much better to have too many Plants than too few ; and if the Seafon be very dry at the time of fowing, 'twill not be improper to give the

Seed

Seed a gentle refreshing of Water, as also at all times when above Ground, if the Weather proves hot and dry.

About the middle of *May* is a very good time to sow, in the very same manner, such Quantities as you may have occasion to pickle, which will also furnish your Table, during the Months of *July* and *August*, plentifully: For be as careful as possibly you can, some will escape your Eye, which will appear the next time of gathering and be fit for the Table.

'Tis a Practice amongst many to put the Seed, at the time of sowing, all in a heap, which causes the Plants to grow in a Cluster, but in my Opinion cannot thrive so well, as when each Plant is about two Inches apart. There is another Practice amongst many Gardiners, to sow their Seed for Pickling on a gentle Hot-Bed, and afterwards transplant them into their Holes at the distances aforesaid. Now I confess that this Method is a very good one, when the Land design'd for them is not clear of its first Crop, at the Time when 'tis the Season for the Seed to be sow'd; for whilst the Crop is clearing away, the Seed is coming up, and when quite clear'd, the Plants may be taken up with Earth, and transplanted therein, and the Land fully crop'd again.

But where Land has not a Spring Crop in like manner 'tis much better, and less extensive, first, to sow the Seeds in the Holes where they are to remain as before directed, and thereby the Trouble and Danger of transplanting is saved.

When young Cucumbers are thus transplanted, they should be shaded with Flower-Pots, &c. for the space of three or four Days, in which time they will have struck Root, and be able to withstand the heat of the Sun.

And as I directed in Sect. XV. Part I. continually to keep the Earth about their Roots from binding, by often removing it gently; so you must observe the very same herein, and when they are arrived into their third Joint, to peg them down, and raise the fresh Earth amongst their Stems, which will cause them to strike fresh Roots therein, and grow away strongly.

As soon as ever you observe them to turn out Fruit, you must not fail of giving them plentiful Refreshings of Water, otherwise the Fruit will dwindle and die away, and you'll be disappointed of your Hopes.

The

The beſt Kind for pickling is the long prickly Cucumber, the choiceſt of which leave for Seed, as before directed in Sect. XV. Part I.

SECT. XII.

Of the Collyflower.

THE Collyflower is called in *Latin Braſſica florida,* and *Cauliflora,* and in *Italian Cauliſiore,* is one of the moſt delicious boil'd Sallets that we have in *England,* and the moſt difficult to have of a good Kind.

The greateſt Care herein, is to be well furniſh'd with good Seed; otherwiſe all the Labour will prove unſucceſsful: But that being taken for granted, about the beginning, or tenth Day of *Auguſt* at lateſt, prick or dig up a ſmall Border that is in tolerable good Heart, and therein ſow your Seed; or if you have any decay'd Hot-Bed, 'tis better to make uſe of that, in which ſow your Seed, giving it when dry gentle refreſhings of Water, and when the Plants are come up, and in their firſt Leaf, excluſive of their Seed Leaves, then tranſplant them upon ſome other well prepared Bed, at about three or four Inches diſtance from each other; and therein let them remain till near *Michaelmas,* at which time 'tis beſt to tranſplant them out for good in the Places where they are to bloſſom: And for fear of loſing any by Froſts, *&c.* plant in every place where you intend one to continue, five Plants, and in ſuch a Compaſs, as all to be cover'd with a ſquare or Bell-Glaſs during the Severity of the Winter: And if they all endure the Winter's cold, 'tis a very eaſy thing for the Gardiner, with his Trowel, to take up and tranſplant ſuch as are unneceſſary in that place, in ſome other prepared part of the Garden.

But that we may not be diſappointed of a Crop, in Caſe we ſhould loſe all thoſe planted out at *Michaelmas* under the Glaſſes, we muſt, at the ſame time, tranſplant other Plants, either on a very warm *South* Border, to be hooped and covered over in time of Froſts and Snow, (which laſt is the moſt

preju-

prejudicial to them) or on an old decay'd Hot-Bed, where
we can place over them a Frame and Glaffes to preferve them;
or in large Flower-pots, to be lifted into the Greenhoufe, &c.
during all fuch hard Weather; and in the Spring, when all
the cold Blafts are blown over, tranfplant them out for good
in Rows about two Foot and half apart, and the Rows three
Feet afunder.

The Soil wherein you plant Collyflowers ought to be very
rich and naturally moift, and for want of the laft, great Care
muft be taken to give them plenty of Water, and always clean
from Weeds.

When Collyflowers are planted out for good at *Michaelmas*,
and withftand the Winter's Frofts and Snow, they never fail
of producing better Flowers, and much fooner than thofe
planted out in the Spring; for whilft they are recovering their
Removal, the other is going forward, getting very ftrong Roots,
which enable them to produce thefe Flowers about three Weeks
fooner than the other.

However, altho' they don't come in fo very foon as the other,
yet they come in a very good time to fucceed them, and therefore I advife their being planted at both Seafons.

And that your Table may not be deftitute of this matchlefs
Sallet, I advife, that at the beginning of *March* you fow more
Seed upon a gentle Hot-Bed, which when in their firft Leaf
tranfplant out at about three Inches apart, and as the heat of
the Spring comes on, make them more acquainted with the
Air; fo that when they are large enough to tranfplant out, they
may be perfectly hardy, and not any ways unacquainted with
their Removal.

About the middle of *April* we may fow another fmall Quantity of Seed in the natural Ground, which being ordered as
the others before directed, will produce Flowers that will fucceed the former, as well as produce large Flowers in the
Autumn.

When their Flowers begin to appear, break down over them
two or three of their Leaves, to preferve them from the Rains,
and heat of the Sun, which caufe them to be either green
or yellow, inftead of a beautiful white; and during all this
Work, great Care muft be taken to keep them well water'd,
for 'tis what they are great lovers of; and efpecially at firft

4   planting

planting in *May, &c.* If the conveniency and quantity of your Water is such, that you can flow their Alleys between them, 'twill add a much greater Nourishment to them than the common way of watering the Holes only.

It often happens, that many of the last Plantation, if planted in a shady Place, will not produce their Flowers 'till after *Michaelmas,* at which time such Plants should be taken up with the Earth to their Roots, and planted upright in Sand, within a Greenhouse, *&c.* giving them plenty of Water at planting, which will produce very good Flowers fit for use in the Winter, even until *Christmas,* as I have often experienced.

To continue a good Kind of Seed, make choice of some of the very best and earliest Flowers, which let run to Seed, securing them from the Injuries of Winds, by Stakes, *&c.* And as soon as the Seed Vessels and Seed are fully perfected, cut away the whole Stem, and carry it into your Greenhouse, and there let it be throughly dry'd before you rub or thrash it out: For as Mr. *Bradley* ingeniously observes, 'tis not necessary to leave the Seed upon the Plants till the Pods are dry, lest they shed the Seed, or be damaged by Rains, Mill-dews, *&c.*

SECT. XIII.

Of Dill.

1. *Its Names.*

DILL is called in *Greek ἄνηθον,* in *Latin Anethum* and *Anetum,* in *High Dutch Dyllen,* in *Low Dutch Dille,* in *Italian Anetho,* in *Spanish Eneldo,* in *French Avet,* and in *English Dill* and *Anet.*

2. *Its Description.*

Dill for the generality produces a little Stalk, about sixteen or eighteen Inches high, round in form, and jointed like unto Fennel, as also are the Leaves which are finely cut, but much smaller. The Flowers are very small and of a yellow Colour, growing in spokie Tufts like unto those of Parsnips, but nothing near so large.   The

The Seed is round, flat and thin, in form very like Parf-nip Seed, and has a fmell very like unto Caraway Seed.

3. *Their Temperature.*

According to *Galen*, Dill is dry in the end of the firft, and hot in the end of the fecond Degree.

4. *The medicinal Virtues.*

The Decoction of the Tops of Dill dried, and likewife of the Seed, being drank, allays Gripings and Windynefs, and provokes Urine.

5. *The Parts for Ufe.*

The green Tops and Bloffoms in *July*, being then ufed in the pickling of Cucumbers.

6 The Quantity is at Pleafure, in proportion to the Quantity of Cucumbers pickled.

7. *Its Cultivation.*

The Seed being ripe about the end of *Auguft*, may be fown any time in *February* or *March*, and a very fmall Quantity is fufficient for a large Family.

SECT. XIV.

Of French or Kidney Beans.

1. *Their Names.*

THIS Herb is called by *Hippocrates*, *Diocles*, *Theophraftus*, and moft of the other ancient Writers δόλιχον, and fome others call it λόβον, and λόβιον, in *Latin Siliqua*.

Diofcorides calls it *Smilax*, becaufe it climbs up Branches, Sticks, &c. as *Smilax* doth. Others call it φασέολον, a Diminutive derived from φάσηλος; for φάσηλος and φασέολος, are not one and the fame Pulfe called by different Names, as fome fuppofe; but are different from one another, as *Galen* has very plainly proved, in his firft Book of the Faculties of Nourifh-

3 ments.

ments. The *Dutch* call it *Turcksboomen*, the *French Feues de Romme*, and the *English* call it *Kidney Bean*, in regard to the *Bean* being of the form of a *Kidney*. It is alſo called *Sperage Bean*, *Faſelles* or long Peaſon, Garden *Smilax*, which I ſuppoſe to be taken from *Dioſcorides*, who, as I ſaid before, named it σμίλαξ κηπαία, viz. *Smilax hortenſis*, *Garden Smilax*; the *English* alſo call it *Roman* Bean, and many *French* Bean.

2. *The Deſcription.*

The white *Kidney Bean*, called in *Latin Phaſeolus albus*, hath long and ſmall Branches growing very high, taking hold with its claſping tendrels upon Poles, Sticks, Branches of Trees, &c. as Hops do, for without ſuch Supporters, they are not able to bear their own Weight, and therefore run rambling upon the Ground, which cauſes them to be almoſt fruitleſs or barren, to what they are when ſtick'd with Branches of Trees to climb upon. Their Leaves are very round on that part whereunto the Stalk is fix'd, and the oppoſite part very acute. Their exterior form is very like unto the *Ivy* (but are not ſmooth) each Stem or grand Rib having three Leaves, the one at the end thereof, and the others near thereunto, oppoſite to one another. The Flowers are produced from the upper part of thoſe grand leaf Stalks, at their communication with the grand Stem or leading Branch, and are of divers Colours, as white, red, pale, mixt, &c. which are ſucceeded by long Cods, whereof ſome are ſtraight and others crooked, wherein their Seed or Beans are contained, and when ripe are of a ſhining white Colour.

But beſides this white *Kidney Bean*, there are many other Sorts cultivated in our Gardens, and I believe more for Variety's ſake, than that they are better, or even as good, as the white *Kidney Bean*: However, as moſt ingenious Gardiners think it worth their while to give them place in their Gardens, I ſhall not diſpute them a place herein, of which the firſt is the *black Kidney Bean*, called in *Latin Phaſeolus niger*; the ſecond, the *red Kidney Bean*, called in *Latin Smilax hortenſis rubra*; the third, *Smilax hortenſis flava*, or the *pale yellow Kidney Bean*; the fourth, the *Kidney Bean* of *Braſil*, called in *Latin Phaſeolus Braſilianus*, and the Party-colour'd *Kidney Bean* of *Ægypt*, called *Phaſeolus Ægyptiacus*.

R   3, Their

3. *Their Temperature.*

The *Arabian Herbarists* allow them to be of a hot and moist Nature, but I don't find that our *English Herbarists* have taken any Notice of their Temperature.

4. *Their medicinal Virtues.*

The Cods being boiled when young make an excellent Sallet, they gently loosen the Belly, provoke Urine, create good Blood, and are very great Nourishers.

The Beans themselves, when ripe and dry, are eaten by many, being boiled and butter'd, but are very unwholesome.

5. *The Parts for Use.*

The Cods when about half grown, so as, when broken, not to have Strings on their Sides, holding the parts together: And when used for pickling, they must be very young, and fresh gathered.

6. The Quantity is at Pleasure.

7. *Their Cultivation.*

Altho' I did not mention the different Kinds of white *Kidney Beans* in the Description, yet I cannot proceed to their Culture, before I explain the same.

Of the white Kidney Beans there are divers Kinds, which to mention in general, would be both a needless and endless Work, and therefore shall describe but one Kind; for in fact, I cannot recommend any other, and that is the true *Battersea Bean*, which is of the same form as the others, but very small, 'tis a very great Bearer, comes early, and of an excellent delicious Taste; all which Qualifications are not to be found in any other Bean of the *Kidney Tribe.*

This Kind of *Kidney Bean* delights in a light, warm, fresh Soil, (and not in wet, for that is present Death to them) if it takes them before they are above Ground; therefore to sow them very early in wet Weather, is needless, for 'tis very seldom or ever that they escape being rotted by the wet: But if the Spring is not over dry, we may begin to sow some for our first Crop, about the latter end of *March*, or a Week sooner,

pro-

provided you give your felf the trouble to fow them in the following manner, *viz.*

About the middle of *March* (your Ground being dig'd) draw Drills (under, or near unto a *South* Wall) at about two Feet and half or three Feet apart, or rather double Drills, within a Foot of one another, and then leaving a fpace between them of four Feet, wherein may (at the Seafon) be planted a Crop of Savoys to fucceed them when done bearing. Your Drills being thus drawn drop in your Beans about an Inch diftant from one another, and cover up the Drills with the Earth, leaving a fmall Ridge over the Beans to throw off the Rains.

This being done, ftrain a Line within three Inches of the Beans in the Drills, and with your Spade chop out, and open a fmall Trench, about three or four Inches deeper than the bottoms of the Drills, which leave open till your Beans are above Ground, and got out of their Seed Leaves, for then they are paft all the Dangers that can happen from wet; and then fill them in again and earth up the young Plantation as is ufual.

The Reafon of my advifing thofe Trenches, is to draw off the great Rains, *&c.* (if any fhould happen) from the Beans, which, if invaded by it, would deftroy them. This Method of opening Trenches, I have practifed with very great Succefs in divers Springs, and often in very wet ones; for let the Spring be ever fo wet, thefe Trenches never fail of preferving the Beans from it. When you make ufe of fingle Drills, 'tis beft to draw them *Eaft* and *Weft*, that the Trench may be made on the *South* fide, the better to receive the advantage of the Sun, to keep dry that part of the Drill next thereunto. But when you make ufe of double Drills, they muft be drawn *North* and *South*, that the Morning Sun may dry that Drill next to the *Eaft*, and the Afternoon Sun that next to the *Weft*: For was you to draw double Drills *Eaft* and *Weft*, the hindermoft Drill towards the *North* could have very little or no help from the Sun in keeping it dry.

As foon as you find your Beans are in a thriving State, then they muft be thin'd, and left at about five or fix Inches apart, and thofe which you draw from them may be tranfplanted at the fame Diftances, in fome other warm part of your Garden.

The Reafon why I advife their being fown fo very thick is, that in cafe fome fhould fail by badnefs of Seed, wet, *&c.*

there

there should, notwithstanding those Accidents, be a full and sufficient Crop, which otherwise could not be, if sown at their proper Distance, as they ought to grow in, when such Miscarriages happen.

As soon as they begin to run out with their Tendrels, they should be stick'd with Sticks, Branches, *&c.* about four or five Feet in height, whereon they will soon take hold, and run up without any Assistance.

When their Cods are arrived to a sufficient magnitude fit for the Table, they must be gather'd, and not suffer'd to hang on till very old, which stops the Growth of the Vines, and hinders a further Product; for the nature of these Kinds of Beans are such, that the oftner you gather and keep them down, the more they prosper and bear. This Sort of *Battersea Bean* never runs up so high as another Sort of white *French* Bean, (which is also a very good Kind) whose Form is the same as the other, but much larger, and its Nature is such, that if it is not sticked, it will not produce any Quantity of Cods, to what it never fails of performing, when sticked. I have had plentiful Crops of this Kind, which have ran up Sticks upwards of eight Feet high, producing great Quantities of Cods at their several Joints as they go up. It delights in a very rich Soil, and to be kept very moist during the time of its blooming and bearing.

The duration of one Crop of *French* Beans being but for the space of three Weeks, or thereabouts, we must therefore every three Weeks, after our first time of sowing, sow other Pieces that will be sufficient for our Use, until the middle or end of *July*, to succeed one another throughout the Summer: And if the Seasons prove very dry at the times of sowing, and the Weather very hot, then 'tis best to water the Drills very well, before you sow or drop the Beans therein, which will contribute very much to their immediate Growth, but you must not water them after being sown, before they are out of Ground, lest it rot them.

To have Kidney Beans sooner than these Methods here laid down are capable of producing, you must make gentle Hot-Beds, and thereon raise them at any time, from *August* until *March*, wherein the greatest Care is, to give them all the Air that can possibly be allow'd them, or otherwise they will decay and be worth nothing.   S E C T.

SECT. XV.

Of the several Kinds of Lettice.

THE Season being sufficiently warm in *March*, we may then sow all sorts of Lettice, and repeat the same every three Weeks or a Month throughout the Summer, that we may have a constant Supply, by their succeeding one another.

And as I advised in the sowing of Chervil and other small Salletting (Sect. IX.) to remove to shady Borders as the heat increased; so I must also advise herein.

The best Kinds of Lettice for our Table, are the Gofs-Lettice, the *Silesia* Lettice, divers Kinds of *French* Lettices, the *Imperial* Lettice, the *Roman* Lettice, and the *Brown Dutch* Lettice, which in general (the first excepted) cabbage very well, and are extremely fine tasted.

The Gofs-Lettice is not inferior to any, and of an excellent Flavour; but generally requires the Gardiner's Assistance to tye up the Leaves with Bast-mat, or otherwise it seldom is cabbaged or fit for the Table.

In the transplanting of all the several Kinds of Lettice (which contributes very much to their cabbaging, as has been before observed in Sect. XXI. Part. I.) great Care must be taken to allow them proper room for their Growth: As for Example, an *Imperial Lettice* requires more Liberty for its Growth, than the *Brown Dutch*, and the *Silesia*, more than the *Capaseen*, &c. Therefore that we may not croud our Plantation, and damage it thereby, or plant too thin, whereby we lose much Ground, which can't well be spared in many Gardens, observe the following Directions, *viz.* Plant the *Capaseen* Lettice about four Inches apart from one another, the *Brown Dutch* at six Inches, the *Roman* and *French* Lettices at eight Inches, the *Silesia* at nine or ten, as also the Gofs-Lettice, and the *Imperial* at one Foot, and if the Land is very rich at fifteen Inches every way. And if this Method of planting be truly executed, and the Lettices supply'd in dry Seasons with plenty of Water, you will be sufficiently furnish'd with the best Kinds of Lettices in their greatest Perfection. SECT.

S E C T. XVI.

Of Onions.

THE Onions neceffary for our Sallets are thofe that are
very young, and that we may be well furnifh'd with
them, they muft be fown every Fortnight or three Weeks at
moft, by which Means they will be always very young, tender,
and fit for our Purpofe.

S E C T. XVII.

Of Orange and Limon Seedlings.

THE feedlings of Oranges and Limons being raifed, and
eaten in Sallets, (as before directed in Sect. XXVI. Part
the 1ft.) are very grateful to the Stomach; and altho' I mention
them here again, being proper amongft our Sallets for thefe
Months, yet their Culture is the very fame as before, the difference of the Weather's heat only excepted.

S E C T. XVIII.

Of Purflane.

1. *Its Names.*

PURSLANE is called in *Greek* ἀνδράχνη, in *Latin Por-*
tulaca, in *High Dutch Burkelkraut,* in *Italian Procac-*
chia, in *Spanifh Veraolagus,* in *French Poupier,* and in *Englifh*
Purflane and *Porcelaine.*

2. *Their Defcription.*
We have two Kinds of Purflane cultivated in our Gardens,
4   the

the one called the green, and the other the golden Purflane, but are both vulgarly called *Garden Purflane*.

The Stalks of both Kinds are in their Form like unto one another, as alfo their Leaves, the difference being in their Colour only; and to defcribe their Forms of Leaves, Stalks, &c. would be but a needlefs Work, they being well known to every one that delights in Sallets, and therefore I fhall proceed to their Temperature.

3. *Their Temperature.*

Purflane is moift in the fecond Degree, and cold in the third.

4. *Its Medicinal Virtues.*

Purflane being eaten in Sallets, cools a hot Stomach, rectifies inflamed Blood, provokes Urine, and is very good for the Bladder and Kidneys.

The Juice of Purflane being drank, ftops the bloody Flux, fpitting of Blood, and all other Fluxes whatfoever.

5. *The Parts for Ufe.*

The young and tender Shoots or Tops.

6. *The Quantity in a Sallet.*

This Sallet Herb not being in Seafon until the Weather begins to be very warm, and of fuch admirable Virtues, is therefore eaten in much greater Quantity, than any other fort of Sallet Herb. The common Quantity is fix times as much as of any other, young Radifh excepted.

7. *Its Cultivation.*

Purflane of both Kinds are raifed from Seeds fown in *March* under Glaffes upon a decay'd Hot-Bed, or in *April,* in fome very warm place in the natural Ground: It delights in a rich Soil, and to be plentifully water'd in hot Weather.

SECT.

SECT. XIX.

Of Peafe.

1. *Their Names.*

THERE being divers Kinds of Peafe, are therefore called by many Names, and are diftinguifhed by their feveral Degrees of Magnitude, as well as by the Perfons or Places by whom they were firft cultivated.

The great Peafe are called by *Theophraftus* and other old Writers, in *Greek* πίσον, in *Latin Pifum Romanum*, or *Pifum majus*, in *French des Pois*, in *Low Dutch, Roomfcheerwiten*, and in *Englifh Roman Peafe*, or *Peafe of the Garden :* We have many other Sorts much fmaller, that are cultivated in the Gardens alfo, which the Ancients call'd *Pifum minus*, and in *Englifh little Peafe*, or the *common Peafe*.

But fince that Peafe were firft cultivated in Gardens they have been greatly improved, and now confift of a great many new Kinds, which our ancient *Herbarifts* and Gardiners never knew, or heard of.

The feveral Sorts of Peafe now cultivated in Gardens are as follow.

Firft, of fmall Peafe, *viz.* fuch as the Ancients called *Pifum minus, viz.*

The feveral Sorts of *Hotfpurs*, of which thofe are the beft that were firft raifed and improved by Mr. *Cox*, late of *Kew Green* near *Richmond* in *Surrey*, Nurfery Man, deceafed : And another Kind, called and known by the name of *Mafter's Hots*, firft raifed and improved by an ingenious Gardiner and Nurfery Man of that Name, now living at *Strand in the Green*, near old *Brentford* in *Middlefex*. The other Sorts of fhort and long Hotfpur Peafe, are the *Reading* Peafe, Rofe Peafe, and Dwarf Peafe.

Secondly, of large Peafe, fuch as the Ancients called *Pifum majus, viz.*

(1.) The

(1.) The *marrow Peafe,* vulgarly called *marrow fat Peafe.*
(2.) The fugar Peafe, vulgarly called fugar Polands.
(3.) The grey or blew Roncivals, or *Dutch* Admiral, and
(4.) The *Spanifh Marratta.*

And befides all thefe, there are many other Kinds, which are very difficult to diftinguifh from the abovenam'd, fome few excepted, whofe Names I fhall forbear to mention, knowing that thefe Sorts are not only the very beft Kinds, but will fuffice for any Garden, and plentifully furnifh the grandeft Table required.

2. *Their Defcription.*

To defcribe the Forms of the Leaves, Shoots, Cods, and Seed would be very unneceffary, they being fo well known; therefore I fhall only take notice of the difference of their Growth.

Firft then, all Sorts of Hotfpurs and *Readings* are of a midling Growth, rifing (when fticked) about two Feet and half in height, producing their Bloffoms at their feveral Joints, from the bottom to their Tops, which are of a white Colour, with a purple fpot in their middle. The firft Bloffoms are from the firft or fecond Joints, which at firft appearing before they are in Bloffom, are then faid to be in *Bell* (*a term ufed by Gardiners only.*) The Bloffoms of all other Peafe that are white, are of the fame Colour, but the Bloffoms of thofe Peafe as are grey, or any other Colour, are of a tranfparent blew on the outer Parts, and a very fine purple mix'd with crimfon within.

The Rofe Peafe, fo called in regard to their Bloffoms, which are produced at the extreme part of the Haulm (growing about the fame height as the Hotfpur) in a round Tuft or Clufter.

The Dwarf Peafe, fo named from the fmallnefs of their Growth, their Haulm being feldom above one Foot in height; 'tis a great Bearer, and a very fweet kind of *Pea.* There are a very fhort kind of Dwarf Peafe, that I have raifed very early on gentle Hot-Beds, which have produced great Quantities during the Months of *February, March* and *April,* that feldom rife higher than fix or eight Inches, and altho' fo very fmall,

yet

yet they will yield very near as many Peafe for the Quantity of Ground, as any of the largeft Kinds.

The other Kind of Peafe are in general of a much ftronger Growth, and will, when ftick'd, climb up five or fix Feet high, producing great Quantities of Cods as they afcend.

3. *Their Temperature and Virtues.*

As to their Temperature of Heat or Cold, neither the ancient or modern *Herbarifts* have difcovered in publick ; and 'tis my humble Opinion that they are neither hot or cold, but of a Temperature between both.

Galen, in his Book of the Faculties of Nourifhments, fays, that their whole Subftance are very near like unto that of *Lisbon* and Garden Beans, but are not fo windy, and withal, have not that cleanfing Quality as the Bean hath.

4. *The Parts for Ufe.*

The young Peafe or Seed, when near full grown, whilft green and tender, before they begin to turn, of a very pale white Colour, and mealy when boiled.

The tender Leaves, when about three Inches high, are an excellent boil'd Sallet.

5. The Quantity of either is at Pleafure.

6. *Their Cultivation.*

All the feveral Kinds of Peafe delight in good frefh Land, rather than that which is very rich with Dung, which caufes them to grow very rank.

The Seafon for fowing the firft Crop is about the middle of *October,* or beginning of *November,* and fometimes not till *December,* which I think is rather too late to have them early, and efpecially when the Winter proves very mild : But however, for fear it fhould not, 'tis beft to fow at both Seafons, and then, if the firft ftands the Winter's Froft, that Crop will come very early in *April,* and be fucceeded by the other in *May.* The Hotfpur Peafe are the Kinds we fow for our firft and fecond Crops, the *Readings* for the third, the marrow Peafe, fugar'd Peafe, *&c.* for the fourth, and the

dwarf

dwarf and marrow Peafe, &c. for the remaining part of the Summer.

The Hotfpur Peafe for the firft and fecond Crops may be fown at the times aforefaid in Drills, about two Feet and half diftant from each other, of a tolerable thicknefs in the Drills; for you muft always remember that you are not in danger of the Frofts only, but of Mice, Crows, and Slugs, againft which you muft carefully guard, otherwife few will come to your fhare; and for thefe Reafons 'tis beft to allow Seed enough at firft fowing.

When your Peafe begin to appear above Ground, be diligent in furveying them every Morning, and to deftroy all the Slugs you can find near them.

Slack'd Lime, and Sea Coal Afhes ftrewed upon the Drills, before the Peafe are come up, will prevent their being deftroy'd; be careful to do the fame after Rains; and when they are grown about four Inches high, draw up fome Earth on each fide clofe to their Roots to prefervo them from cutting Winds, &c.

It has been the common Practice for many Years amongft Gardiners, to fow one Drill of Peafe clofe under a *South, Eaft,* or *Weft* Wall, and very often under every one, when they have them; but I cannot recommend that Method, for it feldom fails of doing the Fruit Trees very great Damage: But however, I am not for entirely banifhing of Peafe from warm Walls, which caufe them to come much earlier; and therefore I advife that they be fown under fuch Walls, but not nearer than three Feet at the leaft.

When you fow Peafe in open Quarters, 'tis beft to draw their Drills *North* and *South,* that when the very cold and blafting *Eaftern* Winds do blow, they may be defended therefrom by fmall Ridges or Banks drawn up with a Hough on the *Eaftern* Sides thereof.

The ufual diftance that Hotfpur Peafe are fown, is about two Feet and half each Drill from the other: And when they are about eight or nine Inches high they fhould be well earth'd up, and ftuck with Sticks about three Feet high, and to prevent their being damaged by Winds, 'tis beft to place a double Row of Sticks, that the Peafe may be between them, and as they run up be fecured from the Winds, and much better expofed to the Sun, than when lying on the Ground.

To have Peaſe come in very early, obſerve to ſtop them as ſoon as they appear in Bell, that is, pinch off their leading Shoots, and 'twill cauſe them to ripen a full Fortnight before the others which are not ſo ſtopt ; and indeed 'tis very prudent to leave ſome untop'd to come in and ſucceed the firſt.

About the middle of *January* we ſow a third Crop, which may be of *Readings*, if you have not *Hotſpurs*, in the ſame manner as before directed ; as alſo again in the middle of *February* and *March*, for the pleaſure of Gardening conſiſts in having great plenty throughout the whole Summer, and not for a very ſmall Seaſon, and then no more, as is too often ſeen.

This laſt ſowing of Hotſpur or *Reading* Peaſe is very ſufficient for thoſe Kinds, and therefore we muſt about the beginning of *April* think of ſowing the other Kinds, *viz.* the Dwarf Pea, the Marrow Pea, the Sugar Pea, *&c.* which Sorts alſo ought to be ſown in *May* and *June*, and thereby we ſhall have a conſtant Supply throughout the Summer.

The manner of ſowing theſe laſt Kinds of Peaſe, differs very much from thoſe of the Hotſpurs, or *Readings*, as will appear by the following.

1. Dwarf Peaſe are ſown in Drills as the Hotſpur Peaſe, but with theſe Differences : Whereas Hotſpur Peaſe are ſown very thick in the Drills, to allow for Accidents, *&c.* or even free from them ; theſe muſt not be ſown, or drop'd nearer to one another than four or five Inches, excepting in a very wet Year, when the Slugs are very numerous, when they may be drop'd at about two Inches apart, to allow for ſuch a loſs : And inſtead of drawing the Drills at two Feet, or two Feet and half apart, they muſt not be more than eighteen or twenty Inches. And when Dwarf Peaſe are ſow'd for Seed, the diſtance between the Drills need not exceed one Foot ; becauſe there will be no occaſion to go between them, except to hough the Weeds, *&c.* till they are ripe and fit to pull up.

N. B. It is obſervable, that altho' a Perſon is as careful and nice as poſſible a Man can be, in the ſaving of Peaſe for Seed ; yet there are always, amongſt all Sorts of Peaſe, ſome few that will degenerate the very firſt Year of ſowing, and will not either be in bloom, or ripe ſo ſoon as the others, by a full Fortnight, and oftentimes three Weeks.

3

Theſe

Thefe degenerate Peafe are by the Gardiners called *Rogues,* and are difcovered by the Over-ranknefs of their *Haulm,* as well as by their late and untimely Produce.

The Reafon why I mention thefe degenerate Peafe is, that you may take a careful Survey of them amongft all your Peafe intended for Seed : For if they are not carefully pricked out from the others, but are fuffer'd to mix therewith, your Kind will immediately be worth nothing, and very much deceive every one that fows the fame.

The other Kinds of Peafe, as the *Marrow Pea,* the *fugar'd Poland,* the *Roncival, &c.* are alfo fubject to the like Degeneracy, which with a very little Care may be eafily prevented.

The large Kinds of Peafe are fown in Drills, as I directed for the large Kind of white *French* Beans, *viz.* in double Drills about fixteen or eighteen Inches apart, with Alleys between them of two Feet and half, or three Feet wide, and are ftuck with high Branches of Trees, *&c.* for them to run up ; which they in general delight to do, and will bear plentifully, which they never will do if not ftaked up, or if planted nearer, and have not fufficient Air.

The large Kinds of Peafe muft not be fown or drop'd nearer to each other in the Drills than three Inches, for they break out into many Shoots when above Ground, and become very thick and fruitful.

S E C T. XX.

Of the remaining Sallets for the Months of April, May *and* June.

THE remaining Sallet Herbs for thefe Months, are Cabbages, Parfley, Spinage, Succory, the *French* and *Greenland* Sorrels, Sampier, red Sage, Turnip and Mint, whofe Culture being delivered at large in the firft Part, need not be repeated here again ; and having thus gone through the two firft parts of the Year, I fhall now prefent you with Tables of the Temperatures, and medicinal Virtues of fuch Sallets as have been in Seafon for the laft Quarter. *A Ta-*

A Table of the Degrees of Heat, Cold, &c. contain'd in the several Sallet Herbs, for the Months of APRIL, MAY, *and* JUNE.

Sallet Herbs hot and dry.

BALM second Degree.
Garden Cresses, D°.
Dill, D°.
White Mustard 4th Degree.
Onions almost in the 4th Degree.

Radish hot in the third Degree, and dry in the second.
Horse Radish 3d Degree.
Red Sage, almost in the third Degree.

Sallet Herbs temperately hot and dry.
Chervil, and Seedlings of Oranges and Limons.

Sallet Herb hot and moist.
Young Carrots sown at *Michaelmas* last.

Sallet generously hot.
Sellery.

Sallet Herb cold and moist.

White Beet.
Cucumber.
Lettice.

Spinage,
and
Purslane.

Sallet Herb cold and dry.
Succory.

Sallet Herbs moderately cold and acid.
The several Kinds of Sorrel.

Sallet Herbs dry and binding.
The several Kinds of Cabbages, Coleworts and Colly-flowers.

Sallet

Sallet Herb nourishing.
Asparagus.

Sallet Herbs windy.
Artichokes and Garden Beans.

T A B L E II.

Of the several Effects, which the Sallets for APRIL, MAY *and* JUNE *have on human Bodies.*

1. *To excite Appetite.*
CUCUMBERS, Mustard, Radish, Onions and Sorrel.

2. *To help Digestion.*
Asparagus, Mustard and Horse Radish.

3. *Good for the Head and Brain.*
Red Sage.

4. *To attenuate gross Humours.*
Garlick, Onions, and Sorrel.

5. *Loosening.*
White Beet, Cabbage, Corn Sallet, and Spinage.

6. *Refreshing.*
Corn Sallet, Cresses and Chervil.

7. *To comfort the Heart.*
Balm, Borage, Buglofs and Burnet.

8. *To open Obstructions.*
Garlick, Onions and Sorrel.

9. *To*

9. *To help a cold and weak Stomach.*

Balm, Chervil, Garlick, Muftard, Mint, Orange and Limon Seedlings, Onions, and Horfe Radifh.

10. *To help a hot Stomach.*

All Sorts of Lettice, Purflane, and Sorrel.

11. *To provoke Urine.*

Afparagus, Chervil, Garlick, Onions, Purflane and Radifh.

12. *To ftop the fpitting of Blood or bloody Flux.*
Purflane.

TABLE III.

1. *The raw Sallets for* APRIL, MAY, *and* JUNE *are,*

BORAGE Flowers.
Chervil.
Cowflip Flowers.
Corn Sallet.
Garden Creffes.
Cucumber.
Lettices.
White Muftard.
Mint.
Nafturtium Indicum Flowers.

Orange and Limon Seedlings.
Young Onions.
Purflane.
Radifh.
Horfe Radifh.
Red Sage.
Sorrel.
Spinage.
Turnip in Seed Leaves.

2. *The boiled Sallets for* APRIL, MAY, *and* JUNE *are,*

Afparagus,
Artichokes.
Garden Beans.
White Beet.
Early Cabbages.
Coleworts.

Colly-flowers.
Carrot.
Lettice.
Kidney or French Beans.
Peafe.
Spinage.

3. *The*

3. *The pickled Sallets for* APRIL, MAY, *and* JUNE *are,*

Broom Buds.
Cucumbers.
Radifh Pods.
Walnuts.
Mufhrooms.

Red Cabbage.
Small Onions.
French Beans.
Nafturtium Seeds.
Berberries, &c.

As in the laft Quarter.

C H A P. III.

Of the feveral Sallet Herbs for the Months of July, Auguft, *and* September.

S E C T. I.

THE Sallet Herbs for this Quarter are Balm, Garden Beans, Beet, Borage, Burnet, Buglofs, Chervil, Garden Creffes, Corn Sallet, Cucumbers, Collyflowers, Cabbages, French Beans, the feveral Kinds of Lettice, Nafturtium Flowers, Onions, Purflane, Peafe, Sorrel, Tarragon and Melons: And as their Culture is already laid down in the preceding Parts, I refer you thereunto.

I   T A B L E

TABLE I.

Of the Degrees of Heat and Cold, &c. *contain'd in the several Sallet Herbs for the Months of* JULY, AUGUST, *and* SEPTEMBER.

Sallet Herbs hot and dry.

BALM second Degree.   Onions.
   Garden Cresses, Dº.   Horse Radish.
Tarragon.

Sallet Herb temperately hot and dry.
Chervil.

Sallet Herb hot and moist.
Carrots.

Sallet Herbs cold and moist.

White Beet.   Melons.
Cucumber.   Spinage.
Lettice.   Purslane.

Sallet Herbs moderately cold and acid.
The several Sorts of Sorrel.

Sallet Herbs dry and binding.
The several Sorts of Cabbages and Collyflowers.

Sallet Herbs windy.
Artichokes and Windsor Beans.

TABLE

TABLE II.

Of the several Effects, which the Sallets for JULY, AUGUST, *and* SEPTEMBER *have on human Bodies.*

1. *To create an Appetite.*
CUCUMBERS, Muſtard, Onions, and Sorrel.

2. *To help Digeſtion.*
Muſtard, and Horſe Radiſh.

3. *To make thin groſs Humours.*
Garlick, Onions, and Sorrel.

4. *Looſening.*
White Beet, Cabbage, Corn Sallet, and Spinage.

5. *Refreſhing.*
Corn Sallet, Creſſes, and Chervil.

6. *To comfort the Heart.*
Balm, Borage, Bugloſs and Burnet.

7. *To open Obſtructions.*
Garlick, Onions, and Sorrel.

8. *To help a cold and weak Stomach.*

Balm.	Mint.
Chervil.	Onions,
Garlick.	and
Muſtard.	Horſe Radiſh.

9. *To help a hot Stomach.*
All the Sorts of Lettice, Purſlane, and Sorrel.

10. *To provoke Urine.*
Chervil, Garlick, Onions, and Purſlane.

11. *To stop the spitting of Blood, or Bloody-flux.*
Purslane.

TABLE III.

1. *The raw Sallets for* JULY, AUGUST, *and* SEPTEMBER.

BORAGE Flowers.
Chervil.
Corn Sallet.
Garden Cresses.
Cucumber.
Lettice.
Mustard.

Melons.
Nasturtium Flowers.
Young Onions.
Purslane.
Horse Radish.
Sorrel.
Tarragon.

2. *The boiled Sallets for* JULY, AUGUST, *and* SEPTEMBER *are,*

Artichokes.
Garden Beans.
White Beet.
Savoys.
Collyflowers.

Carrot.
Lettice.
Kidney, or French Beans.
Pease.
Spinage.

3. *The pickled Sallets for* JULY, AUGUST, *and* SEPTEMBER *are as before,* viz.

Broom Buds.
Cucumbers.
Radish Pods.
Walnuts.
Mushrooms.

Melons.
Small Onion.
French Beans.
Nasturtium Seeds.
Berberries.

N. B. That the above Pickles are seldom eaten in these two last Quarters, except by some particular People, who delight more therein than raw Salleting, for whose Use they are herein inserted.

CHAP.

C H A P. IV.

Of the several Sallets, Roots, &c. for the Months of October, November, *and* December.

S E C T. I.

THE several Sallet Herbs for this Quarter are Beets, Cabbages, Savoys, Carrots, Cresses, Chervil, Clary, Corn Sallet, Endive, Garlick, Horse Radish, Lettice, Mustard, Onions, Parsnips, Potatoes, Parsley, Radish, Sellery, Spinage, red Sage, Sorrel, and Turnips both in Seed Leaves and Roots. And as the Culture of all these several Herbs are already declared, I shall proceed to the Tables of their Temperatures, *&c.*

T A B L E I.

Of the Degrees of Heat, Cold, &c. *contained in the several Sallet Herbs for the Months of* OCTOBER, NOVEMBER, *and* DECEMBÆR.

Sallet Herbs hot and dry.

CRESSES 2d Degree.
Clory 3d Degree.
Mustard 4th Degree.
Horse Radish 3d Degree.
Garlick 4th Degree.

Onions almost in the 4th Degree.
Radish 3d Degree.
Red Sage, almost in the 3d Degree.

Sallet Herbs temperately hot and dry.
Chervil, and Parsnips.

2

Sallet

Sallet Herbs temperately hot and moist.
Carrots, and Skirrets.

Sallet Herb generously hot.
Sellery.

Sallet Herbs cold and moist.
White Beet, Lettice, and Spinage.

Sallet Herbs cold and dry.
Red Beet, Endive and Succory.

Sallet Herbs dry and binding.
The several Sorts of Cabbages and Savoys.

Sallet Herbs windy and moist.
The several Sorts of Turnips.

Sallets nourishing.
Parsnips, Potatoes, and Rampions.

TABLE II.

Of the several Effects which the Sallets for OCTO-
BER, NOVEMBER, *and* DECEMBER, *have on*
human Bodies.

1. *To create an Appetite.*
MUSTARD and Onions.

2. *To help Digestion.*
Mustard, and Horse Radish.

3. *To make thin gross Humours.*
Garlick, and Onions.

2   4. *Loosening.*

4. *Loosening.*
White Beet, Cabbage, Corn Sallet, and Spinage.

5. *To cool the Liver.*
Endive, and Sellery.

6. *Refreshing.*
Corn Sallet, Cresses, and Chervil.

7. *To open Obstructions.*
Garlick, and Onions.

8. *To help a cold and weak Stomach.*

Chervil.	Mint.
Clary.	Onions.
Garlick.	Parsnip, and
Mustard.	Horse Radish.

9. *To help a hot Stomach.*
All Sorts of Winter Lettice.

10. *To provoke Urine.*

Chervil.	Parsnip.
Endive,	Radish,
Garlick.	and
Onions.	Turnips.

11. *Stone and Gravel.*
Wild Carrot Seed, Mint, Parsnip, and Radish.

12. *Wind in the Stomach.*
Garlick.

13. *Worms.*
Garlick.

TABLE

TABLE III.

1. *The raw Sallets for the Months of* OCTO-
BER, NOVEMBER, *and* DECEMBER.

CRESSES.   Chervil.
     Corn Sallet.   Endive.
Horfe Radifh.   Lettice.
Muftard.   Onions.
Parfley.   Radifh.
Sellery.   Spinage.
Red Sage.   Turnip.

2. *The boiled Sallets for the Months of* OCTOBER, No-
VEMBER, *and* DECEMBER.

Beets.   Cabbages.
Savoys.   Carrots.
Onions.   Parfnip.
Potatoes.   Parfley.
Spinage.   Turnips.

3. The pickled Sallets are the fame as in the preceding
Months.

CHAP.

CHAP. V.

Of the Names, Descriptions, Temperatures, Virtues and Cultivations of such Distilling, and other physical Herbs, as are absolutely necessary for the Service of all Gentlemen, (and other) Families in general.

SECT. I.

Of the several Distilling Herbs, necessary for the Use of every Family.

THE several Physick Herbs necessary to be cultivated for the Use and Service of a Family are, Angelica, Anniseed, Balm or Baum, Camomile, Carduus, Clary, Comfrey, Clove-gilli-flowers, Dragons, Dill, Dwarf Elder, Elicampane, Fennel, Featherfew, Hyssop, Lavender, white Lilies, Lavender Cotton, Lavender Spike, Liquorish, Mint, Marjoram, Marsh-mallows, Marygolds, Penny-royal, Parsley, Peonie, white Poppy, Rosemary, Rhue, red and damask Roses, red Sage, Tea Sage, Wormwood Sage, Savory, Solomon Seal, Saffron, Thyme, Tansie, Tobacco, Scurvy-grass, Violets and Wormwood. And as I have already explain'd the Culture of Balm, Dill, Fennel, Mint, Penny-royal, Parsley, red Sage, Tansie, and Scurvy-grass in the preceding Parts, I shall now proceed to the Descriptions, Culture, &c. of the others.

U

SECT. II.

Of Angelica.

1. *Its Names.*

GARDEN ANGELICA, is called in *Latin Angelica Sativa,* in *High Dutch, Angelick, Bruftwurtz,* or *Desheilighen Geyft Wurtzel,* that is *Spiritus Sanĉti Radix,* or the Root of the Holy Ghoft, as witneffed by *Leonhartus Fuchfius,* in *Low Dutch,* 'tis called *Angelijka,* in *French Angelic,* and in *Englifh Angelica.*

2. *Its Defcription.*

The Leaves of *Angelica* are very large and broad divided into many Parts or leffer Leaves, which are indented like unto the Leaves of *Spondilium* or Cow Parfnip, but grow much nearer to the Eye, are much thicker, of a deeper green, and of a ftrong Savour. The Stalk rifes up from the head of the Root, and very often rifes fix or feven Feet in height, and efpecially when 'tis planted in good Land. 'Tis very large and hollow, divided into many Joints, from which grow out other fmall Branches, at whofe ends grow Tufts of whitifh Flowers, very like unto thofe of Fennel, which are afterwards fucceeded by Seed.

It flowereth in *July* and *Auguft,* and the Seed is ripe in *September.*

The Root is generally very large, producing an oily Liquor when broken, and the whole Plant is of a very pleafant Smell.

And befides the aforefaid Kind of *Angelica,* there is another Kind, which in Form is exactly the fame, but the Leaves next the Ground are of a purple red Colour, the Roots of a more aromatick Savour, and the whole Plant of a leffer Growth.

The wild *Angelica,* called *Angelica Sylveftris,* delights in cold and moift Meadows, and is very like unto the Garden *Angelica,* excepting its Leaves, which are not fo much indented,

I   and

and are of a blackifh green and narrower, the Stalks are alfo much flenderer and fhorter, the Flower much whiter, the Root much lefs, and of not fo ftrong a Savour.

3. *The Temperature.*

The Garden *Angelica* is hot and dry in the third Degree.

4. *The Medicinal Virtues.*

The Roots of Garden *Angelica* is a fingular Remedy againft Poifon, the Plague, and other Infeƈtions taken by bad Air: For if the Heart is infeƈted by Peftilence, 'tis faid by many famous Men, that the Root being chewed in the Mouth, will inftantly drive it out again by Urine and Sweat.

'Tis a very great Opener of the Liver and Spleen, and extenuateth grofs and tough Phlegm.

The Leaves put into Wine and drank make the Heart merry. 'Tis a fingular Medicine againft Surfeits, and bad Stomachs, and cures the Bitings of mad Dogs, and all other venomous Beafts.

5. *Its Cultivation.*

The Seed is ripe generally in *September*, and may then be fown, or in the Spring following, and afterwards tranfplanted out at two Feet and half, or three Feet apart.

When the Plants are fuffer'd to run up to Seed, their Roots die foon after their Seed is ripe, but if you prevent its growing to Seed, by cutting off the Stem as it appears, 'twill endure a great many Years.

N. B. That the tender Stalks are of a very pleafant Tafte, when candied.

SECT. III.

Of Annifeed.

1. *Its Names.*

ANISE or ANNISEED, is called in *Greek* ἄνισον, in *Latin Anifum,* in *High Dutch Anifz,* in *Low Dutch Aniffaet,* in *Italian Anifo,* in *Spanifh Matahalua,* in *French Anis,* and in *Englifh Annifeed.* U 2   2. *Its*

2. *Its Description.*

The Stalk is round and hollow, divided into many Branches which are set with indented Leaves, and those that grow towards the top of the Branches are very like those of young Parsley, but the others nearer the Ground are much larger. On the ends of the Stalks, about the end of *June* or beginning of *July*, the Blossoms appear in spokie Heads or Tufts, like unto those of Parsnip, Parsley, *&c.* which are succeeded by Seed that ripens in *August*, which is of a very delightful Smell.

3. *The Temperature.*

According to *Galen*, the Seed of *Anise* is hot and dry in the third Degree, but by others 'tis said to be only hot in the second Degree, and not very dry; and indeed 'tis my Opinion, that it is so, for was it dry in the third Degree, it could not breed Milk in Women, as it is known to do. However, altho' *Galen* and others of his Time could not agree about the Temperature of this Herb; yet others of latter Days have found it by Experience to be dry in the first Degree, and hot in the second.

4. *The Medicinal Virtues.*

The Seed is very good for those who are troubled with Wind, Belchings, Upbraidings of the Stomach, Gripes, provokes Urine gently, and breeds plenty of Milk in the Breasts of Women who suckle young Children.

5. *Its Cultivation.*

This Herb is a Native of *Candie, Syria, Ægypt,* and other of the *Eastern* Countries; but if 'tis sown with us in a rich warm Soil in *May*, 'twill thrive very well, and ripen its Seed in *August* as aforesaid.

SECT.

S E C T. IV.

Of Camomile.

1. *The Names.*

CAMOMILE, is called *Chamæmelum,* and by some *Leu-canthemis,* and also *Leucanthemon,* especially the double Flower Camomile; and altho' there are four Kinds of this Herb, yet they are all call'd Camomile, as the single Camomile, the sweet naked Camomile, the double flower'd Camomile, and the *Romish* Camomile.

2. *Their Description.*

(1.) The single Camomile growing in great plenty on Commons, Meadows, &c. is well known to every one.

(2.) The sweet naked Camomile has no difference from the preceding, excepting in the Flowers, which are quite naked of those small white Leaves, which are placed round the lower part of their Flowers.

(3.) The double Camomile is of the same make as the two others, its difference consisting in the Flowers only, which are as close set with small white Leaves, as the last was wanting, being very like unto a double white Daisy.

(4.) The *Roman,* or Romish Camomile has many slender Stalks, but much stronger than any of the others, nor doth it creep upon the Ground, as the others do.

The Leaves are of a pale Colour, and their Flowers very like unto the single Kind.

N. B. The double Camomile is the best Sort for our Use, and therefore the others may not be regarded.

3. *Its Temperature.*

Camomile, according to *Galen,* is hot and dry in the first Degree, and is of thin Parts.

4. *Its Medicinal Virtues.*

Camomile is very good against the Cholick and Stone,

I   provokes

provokes Urine, and is moſt ſingular in Gliſters, againſt the aforeſaid Diſeaſes.

The Oil of Camomile is exceeding good againſt all manner of Aches, Pains, Bruiſes, Cold, Swellings, and ſhrinking of the Sinews.

The Decoction of Camomile made in Wine and drank is very good for a cold Stomach, ſower Belchings and Wind.

Galen reporteth, that the *Ægyptians* uſed it againſt Agues, wherein it had ſuch Succeſs, that for its great Virtue, they did therefore conſecrate it.

The Herb boiled in Poſſet-Drink, and drank, eaſeth the Pains of the Cheſt, expells tough and clammy Phlegm.

The Herb uſed in Baths cauſes Sweat, opens the Pores, eaſeth the Gripings and Gnawings of the Belly, ſoftens hard Swellings, and waſtes raw and undigeſted Humours.

5. *Its Cultivation.*

Camomile is encreaſed by parting the Roots, and is beſt when new planted every Year.

It delights in good mellow holding Land, and may be planted any time in *March,* in Beds or Borders, each Root a Foot apart.

SECT. V.

Of Carduus Benedictus.

1. *Its Names.*

CARDUUS BENEDICTUS or the *Holy Thiſtle,* is called by many Apothecaries *Cardo Benedictus,* and by ſome 'tis called *Atractylis* wild baſtard Saffron, and often *Atractylis hirſutior,* hairy wild baſtard Saffron.

Valerius Cordus names it *Cnecus ſupinus,* and in *High Dutch* 'tis called *Beſeegnete Diſtell, Kardo Benedict,* which laſt Name is known by the *Low Dutch,* in *Spaniſh* 'tis called *Cardo Sancto,* in *French Charaon Benoiſt,* or *Beneiſt,* and in *Engliſh Bleſſed Thiſtle,* but more commonly by the *Latin* Name *Carduus Benedictus.*

2. Its

2. *Its Description.*

The Stalks òf the *Blessed Thistle* are round, rough and pliable, divided into many Branches, most of which rest upon the Ground. The Leaves are jagged, and full of tender Prickles on their Edges, and on the Tops of their Stalks they produce Heads of Blossoms set with Prickles, and environ'd with sharp prickly Leaves. The Flowers are yellow, which are succeeded by long Seed, set with a sort of a hairy down on their Tops. The Root is white, and the whole Plant above Ground, *viz.* its Stalks, Leaves, and Heads of Blossom or Seed, are cover'd with a soft and thin downy Substance.

3. *Its Temperature.*

Hot and dry in the second Degree, and withal cleansing and opening.

4. *Its Medicinal Virtues.*

Carduus Benedictus, being boiled in Wine and drank hot, healeth the griping Pains of the Belly, kills and expells Worms, causes Sweat, provokes Urine, expels Gravel, cleanseth the Stomach, and is very good against a quartane Fever.

Hierome Bock witnesseth, that the Juice of *Carduus* taken in Wine or any other way, is singular good against all Poison, and according to *Joachimus Camerarius* of *Noremberg*, it helps the Inflammation of the Liver.

The Powder of the Leaves given in the quantity of half a Dram, is very good against Pestilence, provided that 'tis taken within twenty four Hours from the time of the Infection and the Party sweat upon the same.

N. B. That the Wine wherein the Leaves have been infused has the same Effect.

5. *Its Cultivation.*

The Seed of *Carduus Benedictus* is ripe in *September*, and should at that time be sown: It delights in good Land, and when large enough to transplant out, should be planted in Beds at one Foot distant each Plant from the other.

N. B. That the time of its greatest Perfection for physical Uses is *July* and *August*, when 'tis in its full Blossom.

S E C T.

SECT. VI.

Of Comfrey.

1. *Its Names.*

COMFREY otherwife called *Bugle*, is reckon'd amongft the Confoundes or wound Herbs, and is called by fome *Confolida media*, *Bugula*, and *Buglum*, in *High Dutch* 'tis called *Guntzel*, in *Low Dutch Senegroen*, and in *Englifh Brown Bugle*, *Sicklewort*, and *middle Comfrey.*

2. *Its Defcription.*

The Nature of this Herb is to fpread its felf and creep along the Ground like *Moneywort*. The Leaves are long and of a brownifh Colour. The Flowers grow in Parcels, encompaffing the Stalk towards the Top with fmall Intervals between each Parcel , and are of a fair blew Colour, and fometimes very white ; but I take the *Bugle* which produces white Flowers to be that called the white *Bugle*, and in *Latin Bugula flore albo.*

3. *The Temperature.*

This Herb is of a mean Temperature, being neither hot nor dry in any Degree whatfoever.

4. *The Medicinal Virtues.*

This Herb is very good for inward Burftings, Member torn, rent or bruifed, and therefore 'tis put into Potions that ferve for Nodes, in which 'tis of fuch wonderful Virtue, as to diffolve and wafte away congealed and clotted Blood.

Ruellius writes, that 'tis a common faying in *France*, that he who hath *Bugle* and *Sanickle*, needs no *Phyfician* or *Surgeon:* For its Virtues are fo great, that it does not only cure Wounds being inwardly taken, but outwardly alfo, being applied thereunto.

'Tis alfo very good for the Infirmities of the Liver, it takes away the Obftructions, and gives great Strength thereunto.

The Decoction of *Bugle* being drank, diffolveth clotted or congeal'd Blood within the Body, and heals all manner of Wounds either inward or outward.   The

The Deco&ion doth alfo open the ftoppings of the Liver and Gall, is very good againft the Jaundice, Fevers of long continuance, and cureth the rotten Ulcers of the Mouth and Gums.

In fhort, this Herb, called vulgarly *Comfrey*, and that called *Self-Heale*, are two of as good wound Herbs as any the Earth produces, and for which Reafon I recommend their Cultivations in the Phyfick Garden, to be ready at Hand upon every Occafion that may happen.

5. *The Cultivation.*

Bugla, or *Comfrey* delights in moift and fhady Lands, and is propagated by Seed fown in *March.*

SECT. VII.

Of Clovegilliflower.

1. *Its Names.*

THE Clovegilliflower is called by the modern *Herbarifts Caryophylleus flos*, of the fmell of Cloves, wherewith 'tis poffeffed: In *Latin*, of moft *Ocellus Damafcenus, Ocellus Barbaricus*, and *Barbarica*, in *Italian Garofoli*, in *Spanifh Clavel*, in *Low Dutch Ginoffelbloemen*, in *French Ocilletz*, and in *Englifh* Carnation and Clovegilliflower, and of fome 'tis called *Vetonica*, and *herba Tunica.*

2. *The Defcription.*

The Stalks and Leaves of the Clovegilliflower, have little or no Difference from thofe of the Carnation, which are well known to every one, and the Flowers are not unlike thofe of the clofe blowing Kinds, excepting in their Colour, which is all red, without any Streaks or Variegations of any other Colour whatfoever, and are as double as any of the Carnation Tribe, but are not near fo large as fome of them are.

There is another Kind of Clovegilliflower, which no way differs from the other in its Leaves and Stalks, that produces a fingle Flower, like unto a very large fingle Pink, which a

mongft Gardiners is called a *Stamel*, and is of no Ufe in Phyfick; therefore not to be entertain'd in a Garden.

3. *The Temperature.*

The Gilliflower is temperately hot and dry.

4. *The Medicinal Virtues.*

The Conferve made of the Flowers and Sugar is an exceeding good Cordial, and being eaten now and then comforts
the Heart beyond Expreffion, as alfo doth the Syrup being
drank in Brandy, and is very opening.

The Conferve is very good againft peftilential Fevers, ex-
pelling the Poifon and Fury thereof, and greatly comforts the
Stomach.

5. *Its Cultivation.*

The Clovegilliflower is propagated by Layers, as the Carnations (well known to every Gardiner and Florift) in *June*, or
the firft Fortnight in *July*; they love a light rich Soil, and are
very great Bearers, and I believe are therefore called in *Latin
Caryophyllus Multiplex.*

N. B. If the Flowers are gather'd when wet, and lay'd clofe
together, they will immediately heat and turn black.

S E C T. VIII.

Of Dragons.

1. *Their Names.*

THE Herb called *Dragon*, is called in *Greek* δρακόντιον,
in *Latin Dracunculus*, or *Dracontium*, and as there are
two Kinds cultivated in our Gardens, *viz.* the major, and the
minor, they are therefore called *Dracontium majus*, and *Dracontium minus*, and very often *Serpentaria major*, and of fome
Bifaria, and *Colubrina.*

Cordus calls it *Dracunculus, Polyphyllos*, and *Luph, Crifpum*,
and in *Italian* 'tis called *Dragontea*, in *High Dutch Schlan-
genkraut*,

genkraut, in *Low Dutch Speerwortele*, in *Spanish Taragontia*, in *French Serpentaire*, and in *English Dragon*, or *Dragon-wort*.

Apuleius calleth *Dragon Dracontia*, and to that adds many strange Names, but whether they agree with the greater or the lesser, or both, he has not demonstrated : As *Pythonion, Anchomanes, Sauchrowaton, Therion, Schænos, Dorcadion, Typhonion, Theriophonon*, and *Eminion*. *Athenæus* sheweth that *Dragon* is also called *Aronia*, because 'tis like unto *Aron*.

2. The Description.

The great *Dragon* riseth up with a straight Stalk about two Feet and half, and sometimes three Feet high, being generally very thick, smooth, and spotted with Spots of divers Colours, very like unto the Belly of a Toad, or back of a Snake, the Leaves are very large, consisting of seven or eight Parts, or rather so many lesser Leaves, which in Form are very like those of the Dock, being very smooth and slippery. And out of the top of the Stalk grows a long large Husk very like that of the *Cuckow Pintle*, but much larger, of a greenish Colour without, and Crimson within.

The *Pestal* which grows in the midst of the Husk is of a blackish Colour, very long, thick and blunt pointed, and when the Seed is grown pretty large, the Skin or Film that covers them being stretch'd and broken thereby, they appear like unto a Bunch of Grapes, which at first appears of a green, and afterwards of a red Colour and full of Juice, wherein are contain'd the Seed, which are somewhat hard.

The Root is bulbous, cover'd with a white thin peel, with many small fibrous Roots appendent thereto.

The lesser *Dragon* is like unto *Aron* or *Wake-Robin*, in Leaf, Husk, Pestal and Berry, but instead of their Leaves being sprinkled with black Spots, they are sprinkled with white Spots, and the Berries are not of a deep red as the other, but of a Colour inclining to Saffron. The *Bulb* is very like that of *Cuckow Pintle*, full of small stringy Roots and young Off-sets whereby 'tis propagated.

3. The Temperature.

Dragon is hot, and of thin Parts.

X 2

4. The

4. *The medicinal Virtues.*

The Root of *Dragon* cleanfes the Entrails, and attenuates thick and tough Humours.

The Leaves are good for Ulcers and green Wounds, being apply'd green, for when they are dry, they have very little Virtue to heal, and are of a more fharp or biting Quality than is neceffary for green Wounds.

Pliny affirms, that Serpents will not come near any one that hath *Dragons* about him. The diftill'd Water of *Dragons* is very good againft the Peftilence, or any peftilential Fever or Poifon, being drank warm with the beft Treacle or Mithridate.

S E C T. IX.

Of Dwarf Elder.

1. *Its Names.*

DWARF ELDER is commonly called *Danewort*, and in *Greek* χαμαιάκτη, that is, *Humilis Sambucus*, or low *Elder*, in *Latin Ebulus* and *Ebulum*, in *High Dutch Attich*, in *Low Dutch Hadich*, in *Italian Ebulo*, in *Spanifh Tezgos*, in *French Hiebles*, and in *Englifh Wallwort*, *Danewort* and *Dwarf Elder*.

2. *The Defcription.*

Wallwort or *Dwarf Elder* is very like the common Elder in its Leaves, fpokie Tufts of Bloom, and Fruit; but hath not woody Stalks, as the common *Elder* hath.

It produces green Stalks which die in the Winter, and are jointed as the young Shoots of *Elder*. The Leaves grow in Couples, and confift of many fmall Parts or leffer indented Leaves, which are placed upon a thick rib'd Stalk, and their Flowers are produced at the top of the Stalks in white Tufts, which are fucceeded by *Blackberries*, very like unto thofe of the common black *Elder*, wherein are contain'd fmall long Seeds.

The Root is very tough, of a reasonable size and length, and of greater Virtue than the Roots of the black *Elder.*

3. *Its Temperature.*

Hot and dry in the third Degree.

4. *Its Medicinal Virtues.*

The Roots of *Dwarf Elder* boil'd in Wine and drank is very good against the Dropsie, by purging away the watery Humours.

The Leaves waste and consume hard Swellings, being applyed as a Pultise, or in a Fomentation; one Dram of the Seed being drank in Ale, &c. is the most excellent Purger of watery Humours of any in the World, and therefore very good against the Dropsie.

5. *Its Cultivation.*

Dwarf Elder or *Danewort* is increased by parting the Roots in the Spring, and delights in mellow Land.

SECT. X.

Of Elicampane.

1. *Its Names.*

ELICAMPANE is called by the *Grecians* ἰλένιον, in *Latin Inula,* and *Enula,* and by some *Enula campana,* in *Italian Enoa,* and *Enola,* in *High Dutch Alantwurtz,* in *Low Dutch Alandt-wortele,* in *French Enula campane,* and in *English Elicampane, Scabwort,* and *Horse-heal:* And 'tis reported by some, that this Herb took its Name *Helenium,* of *Helena,* Wife to *Menelaus,* who had her Hands full of it, when *Paris* stole her away into *Phrygia.*

2. *The Description.*

The Leaves of *Elicampane* are very like those of the large *Comfrey,* but soft, and covered with a hairy Down, of a whi-

4   tish

tifh green, Colour on their upper Parts, and very white underneath, being flightly indented about the Edges.

The Stalk very often rifes four or five Feet high, and fomething more than a Finger's thicknefs, cover'd with a fort of downy Subftance, very like the upper part of the Leaves, and divided towards the upper part into many Branches, upon whofe extreme Parts are produced large round yellow Flowers, which are fucceeded by long and flender Seed.

The Root is very large, of a darkifh Colour without, and white within, whofe Subftance is fweet of Smell, but very bitter in Tafte.

3. *Its Temperature.*

The Root of *Elicampane* is hot and dry in the third Degree.

4. *Its Medicinal Virtues.*

'Tis good for fhortnefs of Breath, and an old ftanding Cough, the Root preferved is very good for the Stomach, and being eaten after Supper helps Digeftion, and keeps the Belly foluble. The Root taken with Honey or Sugar, made into an Electuary, cleanfes the Breaft, ripens tough Phlegm, and caufes it to be eafy fpit forth.

5. *Its Cultivation.*

This Herb is in bloffom in *June* and *July*, after which their Seed ripens, which fhould be fown as foon as gather'd; it delights in deep mellow frefh Land, and the Roots are in greateft Perfection in *April* or the Autumn.

SECT. XI.

Of Feverfew.

1. *Its Names.*

FEVERFEW is called by *Diofcorides* in *Greek* παρθένιον, of *Galen* and *Paulus*, Αμάραος; in *Latin* *Parthenium*, *Matricaria*, and *Febrifuga*, of *Fuchfius* Artemifia Tenuifolia,

I   in in *Italian Amarella,* in *Dutch Moedercruyt,* in *French Espar-goute,* in *English Fedderfew* and *Feverfew.*

2. Its *Description.*

Feverfew produces many small round Stalks divided into many Branches. The Leaves are tender, and as it were torn and jagged, and something indented on their Edges.

The Flowers are produced at the tops of their Branches, whose yellow Balls are environ'd with small white Leaves.

The Root is of a hard and tough Substance, and of a strong Smell and bitter Taste.

There is another Kind of *Feverfew,* called in *Latin Matricaria duplici flore,* or *Parthenium,* whose Smell, Stalk and Leaves are the same as the preceding; but the Flowers are double, and is therefore called in *English* double *Feverfew.*

3. *Their Temperature.*

Feverfew is dry in the second Degree, and hot in the third.

4. *The Medicinal Virtues.*

This Herb is of a cleansing Nature, and purges, opens, and fully performs all that bitter Herbs can do.

SECT. XII.

Of Hyssop.

1. Its *Names.*

HYSSOP is called in *Latin Hyssopus,* as also in *Italian, Spanish, French,* and *German.*

2. Its *Description.*

Hyssop being a very common Herb in the Garden, needs no Description, and altho' there be four Kinds of this Herb, yet their difference is so very little, as not worth the trouble of describing the same: but however it may not be amiss to declare their several Names.

The

The firft Kind is called in *Latin Hyffopus Arabum, Hyffop* with blue Flowers; the fecond *Hyffopus Arabum flore rubro, Hyffop* with reddifh Flowers; the third *Hyffopus albis floribus,* and laftly, *Hyffopus tenuifolia,* thin leafed *Hyffop.*

3. *The Temperature and Medicinal Virtues.*

A Decoction of *Hyffop* made with Figs, and the Mouth and Throat gargled therewith, ripens and breaks the Tumors and Impofthumes of the Mouth and Throat, and heals the Parts, fo as to fwallow with eafe.

A Decoction of *Hyffop* made with Figs, Water, Honey, and Rhue, being drank helps the Inflammation of the Lungs, an old Cough, fhortnefs of Breath, and the Obftructions of the Breaft.

The Syrup or Juice of *Hyffop,* taken with the Syrup of Vinegar, purgeth by Stool tough and clammy Phlegm, and expels Worms being eaten with Figs.

The diftill'd Water is alfo very good for the aforefaid Difeafes, but not with that Speed and Strength.

4. *Its Cultivation.*

The blew flower'd *Hyffop,* being the beft for our Purpofe, may be raifed from Seed fown in *March* or *April,* or propagated from Slips, planted any time in the Spring, and delights in a frefh mellow Soil.

S E C T. XIII.

Of Lavender Spike, fweet or Clothes Lavender, and Lavender Cotton.

1. *Their Names.*

1. LAVENDER SPIKE is called in *Latin Lavandula* and *Spica,* in *Spanifh Spigo* and *Languda,* of which there are two Kinds, the one called in *Latin Lavandula flore caruleo,* common *Lavender Spike,* and the other *Lavandula flore albo,* white flower'd *Lavender Spike;* the firft being the Male, and the fecond the Female.

2. The

(2.) The other Kind of *Lavender* common in our Gardens, and chiefly ufed by the common People, who put the Flowers amongft their Linen, is called in *Latin, Lavendula hortenfis minima,* the fmalleft *Lavender.*

(3.) *Lavender Cotton* is called in *Latin Chamæcypariffus,* and by the *Italians Santolina,* and there are many that would have it to be *Abrotanum fœmineum,* or the female Southernwood, but they are abfolutely as wrong, as thofe who take it to be *Scriphium,* Sea Wormwood; for 'tis impoffible to refer it to one particularly, becaufe 'tis a Plant participating of both Wormwood and Southernwood.

2. *Their Defcription.*

All the *Lavenders* being already well known, need no Defcription.

3. *Their Temperature.*

Lavender is hot and dry in the third Degree, and is of a thin Subftance, confifting of many airy and fpirituous Particles.

The Seed of *Lavender Cotton* is of a bitter Tafte, and is hot and dry in the third Degree.

4. *Their Medicinal Virtues.*

The blew Flowers of *Lavender,* exclufive of their Husks, being mixed with Cinnamon, Nutmegs and Cloves, made into a Powder and drank in the diftill'd Water, help the panting and paffion of the Heart, Giddinefs, and the Members fubject to the Palfie: As alfo doth the Conferve made of the Flowers with Sugar, taking the Quantity of a Bean in a Morning fafting.

The *Lavender Cotton* being given green or dry kills Worms in human Bodies, and if the Seed be taken, it hath the fame Effect, but expels them with greater Force.

Pliny fays, that *Lavender Cotton* drank in Wine is an excellent Medicine again the Poifons of Serpents and venomous Beafts.

5. *Their Cultivation.*

All the Kinds of *Lavender* are encreafed by Slips of the laft Year's Growth, planted in *March* or *April,* and delight in a light frefh Soil.　　　　Y　　　　　　S E C T.

SECT. XIV.

Of Liquorish.

1. *The Name.*

THERE are two Kinds of *Liquorish*, the one called *Glycyrrhiza Echinata Dioscoridis*, Hedge-hog *Liquorish*, and the other *Glycyrriza vulgaris*, common *Liquorish*.

The first is called in *Greek* γλυκύρριζα, in *Latin Dulcis radix* or sweet *Root*, and in *English Dioscorides*'s *Liquorish*.

And 'tis evident, that the other is *Glycyrrhiza* or *Liquorish*, altho' the Apothecaries call it by the corrupt Name of *Liquiritia*; the *Italians* call it *Regolitia*; and the *Spaniards Regaliza* and *Regalitia*; in *High Dutch Sufzhotz*, *Sufzwurtzel*; in *Low Dutch Callissiebout*, *Suethout*; in *French Rigolisse*, *Raigalisse* and *Reglisse*; and in *English* common *Liquorish*.

Pliny calls it *Scythica herba*, and I suppose, because 'tis a Native of *Scythia*, where it grows in great plenty.

2. *Their Description.*

The Hedge-hog *Liquorish*, is composed of several Branches of a woody Substance, rising about three or four Feet high, and adorn'd with Leaves of a light green Colour, consisting of many small Leaves set upon a large Rib, and somewhat glutinous in handling. The Flowers are produced out of small Knobs which grow upon short Stems, betwixt the foot of the Leaves and main Stem, clustering together, and making a round Form, which in Colour are very like the blew *English Hyacinth*, and are succeeded by round, rough, and prickly Heads, each consisting of divers rough or scaly compact Husks, wherein are contain'd flat Seeds; the Root is very straight, of a brownish Colour without, yellow within, and of a sweet and pleasant Taste.

The common *Liquorish* in its Stalks and Leaves are very like the former, except in their Colour and Magnitude, which are of a deeper green, and much larger. The Flowers are of a shining blew Colour, but are not produced in such thick Clusters as the former.   The

The Cods are of a fmall Magnitude, and in form like unto the *Tare.* The Roots are of a ftraight Make, much fweeter in Tafte than the other, of a brown or earthy Colour without, and of a beautiful yellow within.

3. *The Temperature.*

The common *Liquorifh* is temperately warm and moift.

4. *The Medicinal Virtues.*

The common fort of *Liquorifh* is good againft Hoarfenefs, Inflammation of the Lungs, Pleurifie, fpitting of Blood and Matter, Confumption, all Infirmities of the Cheft, and greatly helps fhortnefs of Breath, and decay'd Lungs.

It takes away Inflammations, mitigates the fharp and falt Humours, concocts raw Humours, and caufes eafy fpitting.

The Decoction being drank very much helps the Kidneys and Bladder that are ulcerated.

It cures the Strangury, and generally all Infirmities that proceed from fharp, falt, and mordicant Humours.

5. *Its Cultivation.*

The common *Liquorifh* thrives beft when planted in very deep mellow frefh Land, for its Nature is to run down very deep : Before that *Liquorifh* is planted, the Land muft be very well trench'd, full two Spit and both Crumbs in Depth ; and if 'tis trench'd in the Autumn, as directed for *Afparagus* in Sect. II. Part I. having the bottom Spit ridged, to be meliorated by Frofts, &c. during the Winter, 'twill very much add to the fuccefs of your Plantation.

Liquorifh is propagated from Runners, or fmall Roots, as thofe of Horfe Radifh, each being prun'd to about fix or feven Inches in length, and planted about eight or nine Inches apart, in Beds about three Feet wide, with Alleys of two Feet wide between them, for the conveniency of cleaning them, during the time of its Growth, which is generally three, and very oftentimes four Years.

And that you may (after three Years time) have a full Crop coming in every Year ; you muft therefore plant as much every Spring, as you have taken up the Autumn and Winter before, and thereby you will be plentifully and conftantly fur-nifh'd at all Times. Y 2 To

To preferve *Liquorifh* from drying after being taken up, you muft prepare a Bed of Sand within your Greenhoufe, *&c.* and therein place all the Roots in Beds or Rows, about half an Inch afunder, which will preferve them very moift throughout the whole Winter.

SECT. XV.

Of Marjorams.

1. *Their Names.*

MARJORAM is called in *Latin Majorana*, and *Amaracus*, and alfo *Sampfychum*, in *High Dutch Mayoran*, in *Spanifh Mayorana, Moradux*, and *Almoradux*, in *French Mariolaine*, and in *Englifh* fweet *Marjoram* or Summer *Marjoram*, and Pot *Marjoram* or Winter *Marjoram*.

2. *Their Defcription.*

Summer fweet *Marjoram*, or the great fweet *Marjoram* called in *Latin Majorana major*, is a low and fhrubby Plant, of a very light green Colour, and pleafant aromatick Smell. The Stalks are flender, rifing about one Foot in Height, divided into many fmall Branches, about which are placed divers fmall foft and hoary Leaves. The Flowers are produced near to the upper parts of the Stalks, in chaffy or fpiked white Ears. The Root is compact of many fmall Fibres, and the whole Plant is of a moft delightful aromatick Smell.

Pot or Winter *Marjoram*, called in *Latin Majorana major Anglica*, confifts of feveral fmall Branches, whereon are placed fuch Leaves as the former, but not fo hoary, nor of fo pleafant an aromatick Smell.

The Flowers are produc'd at the tops of the Branches in fmall Tufts, of a whitifh Colour, and withal fomething tending to a purple. The whole Plant is of a long Duration, which the other is not, for that being not able to endure the violence of the Winter, is then perifh'd. Whereas the Pot *Marjoram* keeps green all the Winter, and is therefore called Winter *Marjoram*.

And

And befide thefe two Kinds of *Marjoram*, there are two other Kinds, the one called *Marjoram gentle,* and in *Latin Majorana tenuifolia,* and the other *laced Marjoram,* in *Latin Epimajorana.*

The *Marjoram* gentle confifts of feveral Branches, which are adorn'd with foft and ruffet colour'd Leaves, of a very pleafant fweet Smell. The Flowers are produced at the very extreme parts of the Stalks, compofed of divers fmall Leaves of a white Colour, fomething ting'd with a blufhing red. The whole Plant is in form very like unto the great fweet *Marjoram,* but fomething leffer of Growth, and of a much finer Smell.

The laced *Marjoram,* or *Epimajorana*, is alfo a very fine Kind of *Marjoram,* and differs very little from the preceding. 'Tis a Native of *Candia,* where its Branches are adorn'd with Laces, or fmall Threads, which are not produced in this Climate.

The other Kinds of wild *Marjorams,* as the baftard *Marjoram* called in *Latin Origanum Heracleoticum,* the white baftard *Marjoram, Origanum Album,* the *Origanum Creticum* or wild *Marjoram* of *Candia,* the *Origanum Anglicum* or *Englifh* wild *Marjoram,* the *Tragoriganum* or Goats *Marjoram,* the *Tragoriganum Clufi,* or *Candia* Goats *Marjoram,* being very rarely cultivated in our Gardens, the firft two Kinds being fully fufficient ; I fhall therefore filently pafs over their Defcription, and proceed to the Temperature of the Summer and Winter *Marjorams.*

3. *Their Temperatures.*

Both the Summer and Winter *Marjorams* are hot and dry in the fecond Degree, and by fome faid to be the fame in the third Degree.

4. *Their Medicinal Virtues.*

Sweet *Marjoram* is a very good Remedy againft cold Difeafes of the Brain and Head, being dry'd and fnuff'd up the Noftrils.

Dryed fweet *Marjoram* mix'd with Tobacco and fmoaked, is very good for a cold Stomach, and being fteep'd in Ale or Wine and drank provokes Urine.

The Leaves boiled, and the Decoction drank, is very good for thofe that are entering into a Dropfie, provokes Urine and eafeth the Pains of the Belly.   The

The Leaves dried and mingled with Honey, and taken inwardly, diffolveth congeal'd and clotted Blood.

The Oil of *Marjorams* is very good againft the fhrinking of Sinews, Cramps, Convulfions, and all kind of Aches, proceeding from a cold Caufe.

5. *Their Cultivation.*

The Summer fweet *Marjoram* is raifed from Seed fown in *March* upon a very gentle Hot-Bed, and afterwards is tranfplanted out at about four Inches apart, or in fmall Flower-pots, as the Gardiner pleafes.

The Winter or Pot *Marjoram* is increafed by planting the Slips in *March* or *April,* at five or fix Inches apart, and delights in a moift frefh Land.

And becaufe, that the Summer fweet *Marjoram* will not endure the Sharpnefs of our Winters, we muft therefore gather and dry a fufficient Quantity for our Ufe, when 'tis well grown and fit for our Purpofe.

SECT. XVI.

Of *Marfhmallow.*

1. *The Names.*

THE common *Marfhmallow* is called in *Greek* Αλθαία, and Ιβίσκος; the *Latins* retain the Names *Althæa,* and *Ibifcus*, and fome others *Bifmalva* and *Malvavifcus,* as though they fhould fay *Malva Ibifcus* ; in *High Dutch* 'tis called *Ibifch,* in *Low Dutch Witte Maluwe,* and *Hemft,* in *Italian* and *Spanifh Maluavifco,* in *French Guimaulve,* and in *Englifh Moorifh Mallow, white Mallow,* and *Marfhmallow.*

The Tree *Mallow,* called in *Latin Althæa Arborefcens,* being but of little Ufe, I fhall not trouble my Reader with its Defcription, Temperature, *&c.* but fhall proceed to the Defcription of the Marfhmallow.

2. *Its Defcription.*

Marfhmallow is a kind of Mallow, whofe Leaves are very
2　　　　　　　　　　　　　　　　　　　　broad

broad towards the bottom of the Plant, and leſſer towards the
top, being very ſoft, of a whitiſh Colour, and ſlightly indented about the Edges.

The Stalks are ſtreight and round, of a grey Colour, and
often riſe about three or four Feet high.

The Flowers are produced at the ſeveral Joints of the Stalks
from the upper part of the Stem of each Leaf, where they joyn
to the ſeveral Stems, and are in Form like unto the wild Mallow, but not red as they are, being commonly white, and
ting'd with a purple. The Knob or Button, which ſucceeds
the Bloſſoms wherein their Seed is contain'd, is very like that
of the wild Mallow.

The Root is generally very large, tough, white within, containing a clammy and ſlimy Juice.

3. *Its Temperature.*

Marſhmallow is moderately hot, and drier than the wild
Mallow. The Root and Seed are more dry, and of thinner
Parts, and likewiſe of a digeſting, ſoftning, and mollifying
Nature.

4. *The Medicinal Virtues.*

The Leaves of *Marſhmallows*, digeſt, ſlacken, and mitigate
Pain, and are very good, being mixed in Fomentations and
Pultiſes, againſt the Stone, pain of the Sides, and of the Bladder.

The Decoction of the Leaves drank does the ſame, and not
only aſſwages the Pain, but eaſily expells it.

The Decoction of the Roots is very good againſt the Bloody
Flux, and that not by a binding Quality, but by mitigating the
Gripings and Frettings thereof ; for they are not of a binding
Nature.

The Roots boiled in Wine, and the Decoction drank expels
the Stone and Gravel, is very good againſt the Bloody Flux,
Sciatica, Cramps, and Convulſions ; and the Seed beaten to
Powder, and drank in good old Port Wine, ſtops the Bloody
Flux, and all other likes Iſſues of Blood.

5. *The Cultivation.*

Marſhmallow is encreaſed from Seed ſown any time in *September* or *March*, the Leaves and Stalks being incapable to
reſiſt

refift our Winter's cold, are thereby perifh'd, but the Root remains good, which in the *March* following fends forth a new quantity of Stalks, Leaves, and Flowers, which blow in *July* and *Auguft*; and the whole Plant fhould be gather'd for Ufe in *September*. The Roots are generally planted about one Foot apart, and delight in a moift frefh Soil.

<hr>

S E C T. XVII.

Of Marigolds.

1. *Their Names.*

THE MARIGOLD is call'd *Calendula*, in regard to its being in bloffom moft Months of the Year. It is alfo called *Chryfanthemum*, of its golden Colour, in *High Dutch Kingleblumen*, in *Low Dutch Goudt Bloemen*, in *French Soufii* and *Goude*, in *Italian Fior d'ognimefe*, and *Englifh Marigolds*, and *Ruddes*.

2. *Their Defcription.*

Of *Marigolds* there are a very great Variety, as firft, the greateft double *Marigold* called in *Latin Calendula multiflora, maxima*. Secondly, The next greater double *Marigold*, called *Calendula major polyanthos*. Thirdly, The fmaller double *Marigold*, called *Calendula minor polyanthos*. Fourthly, The double Globe *Marigold*, called *Calendula multiflora orbiculata*. Fifthly, The Straw coloured double *Marigold*, called *Calendula polyanthos melina*. Sixthly, The fingle *Marigold*, called *Calendula fimplici flore*. And Seventhly, The *French* or *African* Marigolds, called in *Latin Caryophyllus Indicus*, whereupon the *French* call it *Ocilletz d'Inde*. In *Low Dutch* 'tis called *Thunis Bloemen*, and in *High Dutch Indianifchnegelin*, that is the Gilliflower of *India*. *Cordus* calls it *Tanacetum Peruvianum*, becaufe its Leaves are like unto thofe of Tanfie, and of its being a Native of *Peru*, a Province of *America*, from whence 'tis thought 'twas brought into *Europe*.

To defcribe the Stalks, Leaves, &c. of thefe feveral Kinds, would be a very tedious and ufelefs Work, feeing that they are in general pretty well known.

2

3. *Their*

3. *Their Temperature.*

The Flowers of the firſt ſix Kinds of Marigolds are temperately hot, almoſt in the ſecond Degree.

The two laſt, *viz.* the *French* and *African* Marigolds, are
of a cold and poiſonous Quality, and altho' they produce very
beautiful Flowers, yet they are not to be uſed in either Meat
or Medicine; and therefore are only uſeful to mix amongſt
other Flowers for Variety's Sake.

4. *The Medicinal Virtues.*

The Flowers of the firſt Kind of Marigolds ſtrengthen and
comfort the Heart, and withſtand Poiſon, being boiled and
eaten in Soup, Broths, &c.

5. *Their Cultivation.*

The ſeveral Kinds of Marigolds begin their Bloſſoms in
April, and continue 'till the Winter's cold deſtroys them; and
as they are continually blowing and decaying, ſo they are continually ſucceeded by crooked Seeds, which may be ſown as
ſoon as ripe, or any time in the Spring.

It is obſervable, that thoſe Seeds which grow on the outermoſt
part of the Pods, or Heads, generally produce ſingle Flowers,
and thoſe of the middle part double: Therefore to preſerve a
good kind from degenerating, 'tis beſt to make uſe of thoſe Seeds
which grow in the middle, and to rejeƈt the other.

SECT. XVIII.

Of Garden Poppy.

1. *The Names.*

POPPY is called in *Greek* μήκων, in *Latin* Papaver, in
High Dutch Magſamen, in *Low Dutch Huel* and *Mancop,*
in *French* Pauot and *Oliette Gallobelgis* , and in *Engliſh* Poppy
and *Cheſs-boul.* The white Garden Poppy is called in *Latin* Papaver ſativum album, and that which hath black Seeds,

is furnamed of *Diofcorides* ἄγριον, or wild, and is, as he faith, called ῥοιάς, becaufe *Opium* is gather'd from it. But the black Garden Poppy is called *Papaver fativum nigrum.*

2. *Their Defcription.*

The Leaves of the white Poppy are of a very irregular Form, being long, broad, fmooth, and cut or jagged on their Edges very much, and of a very light green Colour.

The Stem or Stalk is very ftreight and brittle, and is very often towards the middle divided into two, three, four, or five fmaller Stalks, each bearing a white Bloffom, which before open'd, is enclofed with a foft green Husk, compofed of two light-colour'd green Leaf-like Skins, or Coats, between which the Bloffoms break forth, in which at the very firft appears a fmall Head, fet round or adorn'd with a great Number of fmall Petals or Threads, like to a Fringe; which Head, when fully perfected, is of a round Form, but fomething flat on the upper part, (excepting thofe who are degenerated from the true Garden Poppy, which are of a fpheroidical rather than a globular Form) whereon is placed a very beautiful Cover or Coronet.

The inward part of the Shell is wonderfully divided into many curious Cells, between which its white Seeds are gene-rated, and are many in Number. Out of one Poppy Head, which was produced from one Seed only, I have taken up-wards of twelve hundred Seeds, and all very found and good.

The Root runs down in the Ground, like a very fmall Parf-nip, with fome few *horizontal* Roots, breaking from the Sides of that which grows downright. When the Heads are be-ginning to turn hard, and become almoft dry, 'tis then that they are to be gather'd, which, when ftring'd, are hung up in Lines for Ufe.

The black Garden Poppy very little differs from the preced-ing in its Leaves and Stalks; but the Flowers or Bloffoms are not altogether white, they having a mixture of purple there-with, nor are their Heads near fo large as the white Poppy; and whereas the Coronet of the white Poppy is very clofe in all its Parts, fo, on the contrary, the Coronet of the black Poppy is open on the lower Parts thereof, through which it fheds its Seed, which when ripe is of a black Colour, and is therefore called the black Poppy.   And

And altho' by Garden Poppies, the white and black Kinds are underſtood only; yet there are many other Kinds cultivated in the Garden, but more for the ſake of their beautiful Bloſſoms, than for any medicinal Uſe; and ſuch are, firſt, the double black Poppy called in *Latin Papaver nigrum Polyanthon.* Secondly, The double white Poppy, or *Papaver album multiflorum.* Thirdly, The double purple Poppy, or *Papaver purpureum Polyanthon.* Fourthly, The ſcarlet double Poppy, or *Papaver multiflorum coccineum.* Fifthly, *Papaver album Polyanthon minus,* the ſmall double Poppy; and Laſtly, the wild double Poppy, called *Papaver multiflorum ſylveſtre.*

3. *Their Temperatures.*

All the ſeveral Kinds of Poppies are cold, as teſtified by *Galen.*

4. *Their Medicinal Virtues.*

The Heads of white Poppies being boil'd in Milk, cauſe Sleep, repreſs Diſtillations or Rheums, and come very near in force to *Opium,* but are more gentle.

Opium, or the hard Juice of Poppy Heads, is the ſtrongeſt of all.

Meconium (which is the Juice of the Heads and Leaves) is weaker, but either of them taken, either outwardly or inwardly, cauſes much Sleep, and if taken inwardly in too great a Quantity cauſes DEATH.

A piece of the white Poppy Shell, as large as a half Crown piece, being boiled in Milk or Wine, is a very good Quantity to be uſed, where Sleep is required; and if that has not the deſired Effect, you may double the Quantity, but never more, leſt the Conſequence proves fatal to thoſe that take the Decoction.

5. *Its Cultivation.*

The Seed of the Garden Poppies is ripe about the beginning of *Auguſt;* and if 'tis then ſown, 'twill come up before the Winter comes on, whoſe Froſts it reſiſts, and will come much earlier to Perfection than when ſown in *February* or *March,* as is uſual.

The

The white Poppy delights in a fandy frefh Loam, and is the chief that is cultivated for phyfical Ufes, which when the young Plants are about the fize of a half Crown, or fomething fooner, are to be thin'd with the Hough, as Turnips are, but muft be left at greater Diftances, *viz.* about ten or twelve Inches each Plant from the other; and when they are got about four or five Inches high, they muft be houghed over again with a great deal of Care; for wherever the corner of the Hough either cuts or bruifes any of the Plants, they immediately decay and become ufelefs.

And as I told you, in their Defcription, that they threw out *horizontal* Roots; therefore this laft time of Houghing, you muft take Time and Care to remove the Earth very deep, that thofe Roots may eafily ftrike therein, and receive their proper Nourifhment, otherwife, tho' clear from Weeds, they will become very fmall, and not worth your Labour.

SECT. XIX.

Of Rofemary.

1. *Its Names.*

ROSEMARY is called in *Greek* λιβανωτὶς ςεφανωματικὴ, in *Latin Rofmarinus Coronaria*, which Surname is given it, to diftinguifh it from the other *Libanotides*, which by fome *Herbarifts* are reckon'd to be Kinds of Rofemary; the *Italians* call it *Rofmarino coronario*, the *Spaniards Romero*, the *French* and *Dutch Rofmarin*, and the *Englifh Rofemary.*

2. *The Defcription.*

Rofemary is a fmall Evergreen Shrub, which when planted againft a Wall, will rife to feven or eight Feet high, but not near fo much when planted alone.

It confifts of many fmall Branches, which are very thick fet with fmall, long, and narrow green Leaves, fomewhat hard, and of an aromatick Tafte, and pleafant Smell, amongft which their Flowers are produced in very great plenty; firft in the Spring, and again in *Auguft*, being of a very light blue Colour, and pleafant Smell.　　3. *The*

3. *The Temperature.*

Rofemary is hot and dry in the fecond Degree, and of an aftringent or binding Quality.

4. *The Medicinal Virtues.*

Rofemary is given againft all Fluxes of Blood. The Flowers are very good againft all Infirmities of the Head and Brain, proceeding from a cold and moift Caufe. They dry the Brain, quicken the Senfes and Memory, and ftrengthen the mufcular Parts.

The diftill'd Water of the Flowers being drank every Morning and Evening, the firft and laft thing after rifing and going to Bed, takes away the Stench of the Mouth and Breath, efpecially when there are a few Cloves, Mace, Cinnamon and Annifeed fteep'd or infufed therein.

5. *Its Cultivation.*

Rofemary is increafed by Slips of the laft Year's Shoot, being twifted at the lower end, and planted in *March* or *April* in any kind of Soil.

N B. That Slips of two Years Growth will not ftrike Root, the Wood being too hard; the like of Lavender.

SECT. XX.

Of Garden Rue.

1. *Its Names.*

GARDEN RUE is called in *Latin Ruta hortenfis*, as alfo in *Italian*, in *High Dutch* 'tis called *Rauten*, in *Low Dutch Ruijte*, in *Spanifh Aruda*, in *French Rue de Jardin*, and in *Englifh Herb-Grace* and *Rue*.

There is another kind of Rue that is wild, called in *Greek* πήγανον, in *Latin Ruta fylveftris*, in *Galatia* and *Cappadocia* μῶλυ, and of feveral *Harmala*; the *Arabians* call it *Harmel*, and the *Syrians Befara.*

To give a Defcription of Garden Rue is needlefs, it being fo well known.

The wild Rue is very like the Garden Rue in Stalks, Leaves, Flowers, Colour, Tafte and Savour, but much lefs; it being an Annual, dies every Winter.

2. *The Temperature.*

Garden Rue is hot and dry in the latter end of the third Degree, and is of thin and fubtile Parts; wild Rue is hot and dry in the fourth Degree.

3. *The Medicinal Virtues.*

Garden Rue being taken, breaks and confumes Wind, digefts all grofs and tough Humours, and provokes Urine. Being boiled in Vinegar and drank, is very good againft Gripes, Stitches of the Side and Cheft, Shortnefs of Breath upon a cold Caufe, and Pains in the Joints.

The young Shoots being boiled, or rather fcalded and kept in a Pickle, and eaten, are a very great help to the Sight, whereof is written

> *Nobilis eft ruta, quia lumina reddit acuta;*
> *Auxilio rutæ, vir lippe videbis acute.*

The Juice of Rue made hot in a Pomgranate Rind, and dropp'd into the Ear, takes away the Pain inftantly. The Leaves of Rue, beaten and drank with Wine, are an Antidote againft Poifons.

The Leaves of Rue eaten with the Kernels of Walnuts or Figs ftamped together and made into a Pafte, are very good againft all infectious Airs, Peftilence, Plague, Poifon, &c.

Rue boil'd with *Dill*, Fennel Seed, and fome Sugar in Wine, and drank, affwages the Torments of the Belly, as Gripings, &c. the Pains in the Sides and Breaft, helps thofe that are fhort winded, or breathe with great Difficulty, is very good againft a Cough, and ftopping of the Lungs, and very much helps thofe that are inclining to the Dropfie.

N. B. That Rue ufed very often in Meat or Drink drieth up the natural Seed of Generation, as alfo the Milk of thofe that give fuck.

I   *N. B. Ruta*

N. B. Ruta Sylvestris, or the wild Rue, is much more vehement, both in Smell and Operation; and therefore the more virulent and pernicious, and not to be used in either Meat or Medicine.

4. *Its Cultivation.*

Garden Rue delights in a light, fresh, shady Soil, wherein is no Dung, that being its mortal Enemy; 'tis encreased by Slips planted any time in *March* or *April,* being twisted at the bottom at the time of planting.

S E C T. XXI.

Of Red and Damask Roses.

1. *Their Names.*

THE Rose is called in *Greek* ρόδον, and the Plant it self ροδώνια, and in *Latin Rosa,* and according to *Plutarch,* 'tis called *Rodon,* because it sends forth great plenty of Smell, or pleasant Odour.

The Red Rose is called in *Latin Rosa rubra,* in *French Rose Franche,* *Rose de Provins,* a Town in *Campaigne,* and by *Pliny Trachinia,* or *Prænestina.*

The Damask Rose is called in *High Dutch Leibfarbige Roosen,* in *Low Dutch Provencie,* and of some *Provincialis* or Rose of *Province,* in *Italian Rosa Incarnata,* in *French Melesia,* the Rose of *Melaxo,* a City in *Asia,* from whence 'tis thought 'twas first brought into these parts of *Europe.*

And as both of these Kinds of *Roses* are very well known, there needs no Description.

3. *Their Temperatures.*

Red Roses being dried, do bind and dry, and also cool, but Damask Roses are of a moist, airy and spirituous Nature.

4. *Their Medicinal Virtues.*

The distill'd Water of Roses is a great Strengthener of the Heart, and a very great Refresher of the Spirits.

The

The Juice of the Damask Rose makes the Belly soluble, as also will the Juice of the Musk Rose.

The Syrrup doth moisten and cool, allays the extreme Heat of hot burning Fevers, and quenches Thirst.

The Oil of Roses mitigates all kind of Heat, and will not suffer Inflammations or hot Swellings to rise, or being risen, it instantly asswages them.

The Conserve of Roses being taken fasting in the Morning, and the last thing at Night, comforts the Heart, and a weak Stomach that is moist and raw, strengthens the Liver, Kidneys, and other weak interior Parts.

5. *Their Cultivation.*

Both Red and Damask Roses are increased by Layers, or Suckers, and delight in a fresh sandy Loam.

The best time to transplant them is *October* or *November*, in Rows about three Feet apart; but in the Gardens about *London*, they generally plant them in the midst of their Straw-berry-Beds at the aforesaid Distance, or some small Matter more or less.

N. B. That the Red Roses are gather'd for Use when in Bud before they are near blown open, and the Damask Rose not till they are full blown.

SECT. XXII.

Of Saffron.

1. *Its Names.*

SAFFRON is called in *Greek* κροκός, in *Latin Crocus*, in *Arabick Tahafaran*, in *Spanish Acafron*, and in *English* Saffron.

2. *Its Description.*

Saffron is a bulbous rooted Flower, as the several Kinds of Spring and Autumn *Crocus's* are, but much larger. The Flower appears in the Autumn, and is of a purple Colour, something inclining to a blue, and not much unlike the blue

I

Crocus

Crocus that blows in the Spring. The Flower appears before the Leaves, wherein is contain'd a *Still* or *Piſtillum,* which is the pure Saffron its ſelf, and not the Flower wherein it grows.

This *Still* or *Piſtillum* of the *Saffron* Flower muſt be gather'd very early in a Morning before the Sun riſes, otherwiſe when the Sun begins to influence them, they ſhrink very much, and withdraw themſelves almoſt into the Earth.

The Soil wherein it has been known to thrive very well, as at *Saffron Walden,* is a ſhallow chalky Loam, not but I have ſeen very good Saffron produced in the Kitchen Garden of the Honourable *James Johnſtone* of *Twickenham,* whoſe Soil is inclinable to a brick Earth. And I my ſelf have had it in very great Perfection on a freſh ſandy Loam. So that 'tis my humble Opinion, it will thrive in moſt Sorts of Land, a hot Sand or Gravel, and cold Clay excepted.

3. *Its Temperature.*

Saffron is dry in the firſt Degree, and hot in the ſecond.

4. *The medicinal Virtues.*

Too much *Saffron* being taken prevents Sleep, but when taken with Moderation, 'tis good for the Head, revives the Spirits, expells Drowſineſs and makes the Heart merry.

It alſo ſtrengthens the Heart, concocts crude or raw Humours of the Cheſt, opens the Lungs, and removes Obſtructions.

'Tis an excellent Remedy for thoſe that have a Conſumption of the Lungs, when ten or fifteen Grains are given in good Stomach Wine, and is alſo a very great Reſtorer of Breath, where People breathe with great Difficulty ; 'tis alſo very good againſt a Surfeit, and *Yellow Jaundice.*

5. *Its Cultivation.*

The proper Seaſon for planting of *Saffron* is about *Midſummer,* at which time having digg'd and prepared your Ground, and divided the ſame into Beds about three Feet wide, with Alleys between of one Foot or fifteen Inches , plant therein your young *Bulbs* three or four Inches diſtant from one another, and about three Inches deep ; but that you may be ſure of their Growth, obſerve the following Method.

A a

Your

Your Beds being prepared and set out as before mention'd, strain a Line on the Edge or beginning of a Bed, by which draw a Drill with the corner of a small Hough about three Inches in Depth, and therein place your young *Bulbs* at about three Inches apart, with their bottom close to the Earth; then remove your Line three Inches farther into the Bed, and draw a second Drill, wherein place the *Bulbs* as before, and so on till the whole Bed is planted; then taking a Rake, level down the small Ridges of the Drills, and rake the Border or Bed level, and in like Manner proceed till your whole Plantation is ended.

This manner of planting being duly observed, you will have your new Plantation come up every Year in a very regular Manner, and if the *Bulbs* are all sound, there's none can miscarry, except such as are destroyed by Vermin.

The common Method of planting *bulbous* Roots with a Dibber, occasions many great Miscarriages; for the Hole made by the Shoe of the Dibber being much smaller at bottom than it is in the thickest part of the Dibber, prevents the Fibres of the *Bulb* from striking Root, and therefore must inevitably perish; for when the *Bulb* is put into the Hole and cannot get to the bottom, but sticks by the way at such a Depth as the Planter thinks is necessary, it then has but one only Chance for its Life, and that is, being carelesly put in the Hole, sideways, with the bottom of the Root to the side of the Hole, instead of being placed downward, as they ought to be planted.

This Chance I say is the only one, for then the Earth being contiguous to the fibrous part of the *Bulb*, it has Power to strike therein and preserve its Life; as also when the fibrous or lower part of the Root is placed upwards instead of downwards, and then at such times the leading Bud is obliged to extend its self in a *horizontal* Position (which is against their Nature) beyond the outside of its *Bulb* before it can proceed to its natural perpendicular Position. However, as 'tis a very difficult matter to beat some stubborn Humours out of their old Road who will sooner submit to a great Loss, than hearken to good Instructions; I have only this to say, that my particular Pleasure is to oblige the Wise and Curious, without any regard to the stubborn Coxcomb.

To give Directions for the keeping of your Plantation is needless, since that is natural to every good Gardiner.

The

You will reap the first Fruits of your Labour the second *September* after planting, at which time you'll gather about one fourth part of the Quantity that is gather'd in the third and fourth Years, when 'tis in its greatest Perfection ; and when your *Saffron* has thus remain'd in the Ground for the space of four Years, it must then be taken up, and replanted, as at the first time of planting four Years before : But to have always a full Crop, you should plant an equal Quantity every Year to come in and succeed the other that is taken up.

The manner of drying *Saffron* after 'tis gather'd, is perform'd by putting it between two Sheets of clean writing Paper, and dry it over a very gentle Heat.

At *Littlebury* near *Walden* in *Essex*, where *Saffron* grows in great plenty, every one that propagates it is furnish'd with a small Kiln, whereon they dry their *Saffron* with Charcoal Fires.

SECT. XXIII.

Of Savory.

1. *Its Names.*

SAVORY is called in *Greek* Θύμβρα, nor has it any truer Name in *Latin* than *Thymbra*, notwithstanding 'tis called *Satureia*, which is repugnant to *Columella*, an old *Latin* Author, who demonstrates a manifest Difference between *Thymbra* and *Satureia*, in his tenth Book ; wherein he says, that *Savory* has the Taste of *Time*, and of *Thymbra*, or Winter *Savory*.

Et Satureia Thymi referens Thymbræque Saporem.

Savory is called in *High Dutch Kunel Saturey* and *Sadaney*, in *Low Dutch Ceulen*, in *Italian Savoreggia*, in *Spanish Axedrea* and *Sagorida*, in *French Sarriette*, and in *English Savory*.

Of *Savory* we have two Kinds, the one called *Satureia hortensis*, or the Garden Winter *Savory*, and the other *Satureia hortensis æstiva*, or Summer *Savory*.

A a 2

2. *Their*

2. *Their Descriptions.*

(1.) Winter *Savory* is an Herb very like unto *Hyſſop*, but leſs, more tender and brittle. It conſiſts of many ſmall Branches, beautifully beſet with narrow ſharp pointed Leaves, which are ſomething longer than thoſe of *Thyme,* among which out of Husks grow white Flowers, ſomething inclinable to a light purple. The Root is very ſmall, as alſo are the ſeveral Branches (as is ſaid before) but are in general very hard.

(2.) Summer *Savory* has very little Difference from the Winter *Savory,* excepting that its Leaves are not ſo cloſe ſet together, and when its Seed is ripe in the Autumn, it immediately periſhes.

3. *Their Temperatures.*

Winter *Savory* is hot and dry in the third Degree, but Summer *Savory* is not quite ſo hot.

4. *Their Medicinal Virtues.*

Both Kinds of *Savories* doth naturally make thin, and cleanſe the Paſſages, and are very good againſt Wind, being boiled and eaten with *Beans, Peaſe, &c.* which are of a windy Nature.

5. *Their Cultivation.*

They are both propagated from Seed ſown in *March,* and delight in a freſh mellow Soil.

S E C T.   XXIV.

Of Self-Heal.

1. *Its Names.*

SELF-HEAL is called in *Latin Prunella,* and by ſome *Herbariſts Brunella,* and in *Engliſh Purnell,* Carpenters Herb, of their often uſing it to heal Cuts, Wounds, &c. alſo *Hooke-Heal, Sicklewort* and *Self-Heal:* And altho' 'tis a very common Herb in the Fields, and well known to every one; yet I cannot but recommend its being cultivated in the

Phyſick

Phyſick Garden, for of all Herbs that are growing, there are none more uſeful than this, and as 'tis no Stranger amongſt us, I ſhall omit the Deſcription.

2. *Its Temperature.*

Self-Heal is hot and dry, and ſomething binding.

3. *The Medicinal Virtue.*

The Decoction of *Self-Heal* made with Wine or Water, doth join and make whole and ſound all kind of inward and outward Wounds ; and the Herb being bruiſed with Oil of Roſes and Vinegar, and apply'd to the fore part of the Head, aſſwages the Pain thereof, and in ſhort, 'tis good againſt all the ſame Diſeaſes as the *Bugle*.

4. *Its Cultivation.*

Self-Heal doth naturally grow wild in moſt Fields in *England*, and keeps in Bloſſom for the greateſt part of the Summer, encreaſing its ſelf by Seed, which ripens at different times of the Summer, which then is ſhed, and from thence it riſes again. But when the Seed is carefully ſaved, and ſown about *Bartholomew-tide*, it will, by the next Summer, be greatly improved, which I have experienc'd to be true.

S E C T. XXV.

Of Solomon Seal.

1. *Its Names.*

SOLOMON's SEAL is called in *Greek* πολυγόνατον, in *Latin* likewiſe *Polygonatum*, of many Knees, which the *Greek* Word alſo imports ; by ſome 'tis called *Sigillum Salomonis*, and *Scala cœli*, in *High Dutch Weiſwurtz*, in *French Seau de Salomon*, of the *Hetrurians Fraſinella* or *Fraxinella*, and in *Engliſh Scala cœli*, Whitewort, Whiteroot, and *Solomon's Seal*.

Of *Solomon Seal* there are ſix Kinds, whereof there are but two worth our Notice, the one called in *Latin Polygonatum*,

natum, or *Solomon's Seal,* and the other called *Polygonatum Minus,* the fmall *Solomon's Seal.*

2. *Their Defcription.*

The firft kind of *Solomon Seal* hath long round Stalks, which for the moft part, are adorn'd with long furrow'd and rib'd Leaves, very like in form unto thofe of *Plantane,* which are generally placed all on one fide of the Stalk, with very fmall white Flowers, refembling the Flowers of *Lily Conval.* On the other fide when the Flowers are faded, there appear round Berries of a green Colour, which afterwards turn to a very dark or blackifh blue, which when ripe, are as large as Hotfpur Peafe, and of an exceeding fweet and pleafant Tafte. The Root is of a white Colour, and very full of Knobs or Joints clofe fet together, which in fome Places have very odd Marks, that the Ancients fuppofed to be the refemblance of an Impreffion or Mark of a Seal, from which it took the Name of *Sigillum Solomonis*; its Tafte is fweet at firft, and of a fharp Bitter at laft.

The fecond kind of *Solomon Seal,* differs but very little from the preceding, excepting in the Leaves which are narrower, and are placed round about the Stalk, and not on one fide only as the other. The form of the Flowers are the fame, but are of a light green Colour, and are fucceeded by Berries, as the former, but of a reddifh Colour. The Root is like unto the former, having fome few Fibres breaking out of its Joints.

3. *Their Temperature and Virtues.*

Diofcorides makes mention, that the Roots of *Solomon Seal* are excellent good to feal or clofe up green Wounds, being ftamp'd and laid thereon; whereupon he faith it was called *Sigillum Solomonis,* of the fingular Virtue that it hath in healing of Wounds, broken Bones, *&c.*

The frefh *Roots* of *Solomon Seal* being ftamp'd and applied to any Bruife, black or blue Spots acquired by Falls, *&c.* take them away in one night or two at moft.

Galen was of the Opinion, that neither the Herb or Root fhould be given inwardly; but People of lefs Capacity fince his time have experienc'd the contrary; for in *Hampfhire* and many other Places, 'tis adminifter'd inwardly with great Safety: For when any unhappy Accident happen'd, fuch as Bruifes, broken

2   Bones,

Bones, *&c.* in any part of the Body, their Remedy is to stamp the Roots, and give it the Patient in Ale to drink, which very speedily sodders or knits the Bones together, and that in a very strange manner; for altho' the Bones are but very indifferently placed and wrapp'd up, yet it never fails of Success. And when the like Accidents happen to Horses, or other Cattle, they stamp the Roots, and applying them as a Pultise, have the same Effect.

The Roots stamp'd, and applied in manner of a Pultise, and apply'd to Members that have been out of Joint, and newly restored to their Place, drive away the Pain, and knit the Joint very firm, and take away the Inflammation, if any.

The Roots stamp'd, and the Juice given to drink with Ale, or white Wine as before, or the Decoction thereof made in Wine, helps any inward Bruise, and disperseth congealed and clotted Blood: and in one Word, there is not such another Herb growing in the Earth that is known to be so good for Bruises, broken Bones, *&c.* as this of *Solomon Seal.*

4. *Its Cultivation.*

Both these Kinds delight in fresh mellow Land, and are increased by dividing their Roots, which may be planted any time in *March* or *April.*

SECT. XXVI.

Of Southernwood.

1. *Its Names.*

SOUTHERNWOOD is called in *Greek* 'Αβρότονον, in *Latin Abrotonum,* in *Italian Abrotano,* in *Spanish Yerva Combriguera,* and *Abrotano;* also in *High Dutch Stabwurtz,* in *Low Dutch Averoone,* and *Avercruut,* in *French Aurone* and *Auroesne,* and in *English Southernwood* and *Sothernwood;* and as this Shrub is very common and well known in *England,* it needs no Description.

2. *Its*

2. *Its Temperature*.

Southernwood is hot and dry in the end of the third Degree.

3. *The Medicinal Virtues*.

The Tops, Seed, or Flowers being boiled or ſtamped raw with Water and drank, are a very good Remedy for thoſe that are troubled with the Cramp, the *Sciatica*, and greatly help thoſe whoſe Sinews are ſhrunk.

Being taken in Wine, it kills Worms and expells them, and is very good againſt deadly Poiſon.

The Leaves of *Southernwood* boiled in Water until they be ſoft, and being ſtamp'd with Barley Meal and Hogs Lard, and apply'd as a Plaiſter, diſſolveth all cold Humours and Swellings.

4. *Its Cultivation*.

Southernwood or *Sothernwood* is increaſed by Slips planted in *March* or *April*, and delights in freſh mellow Land.

N. B. That when you plant the Slips, you muſt twiſt their lower Parts, as directed for *Lavender*, *&c.*

S E C T. XXVII.

Of Thyme.

1. *The Kinds and Names*.

THE ſeveral Kinds of *Thyme* cultivated in our Gardens are Pot *Thyme*, Limon *Time*, *Maſtick Thyme*, and *marum Syriacum* or *Cat Thyme*, which in general are well known to every one, and therefore need no Deſcription.

2. *Their Temperature*.

Theſe Kinds of *Thyme* are hot and dry in the third Degree.

2

3. *Their*

3. *Their Medicinal Virtues.*

Pot *Thyme* or Mother *Thyme* which grows wild in Meadows, being boiled in Water with Honey and drank, is very good againſt a Cough, and Shortneſs of Breath; it provokes Urine, and diſſolves congealed or clotted Blood.

4. *Their Cultivation.*

All the ſeveral Kinds of *Thyme* are raiſed either from Seeds ſown in *March* or *April,* or increaſed from Slips planted at the ſame time; but of theſe two Ways, I recommend the former. The Pot *Thyme* and Limon *Thyme* will thrive in any kind of Soil that is not over hot or cold; ſo likewiſe the Maſtick and Cat *Thyme,* provided they are planted in the warmeſt part of the Garden.

S E C T. XXVIII.

Of Engliſh *Tobacco, or yellow Henbane.*

1. *Its Names.*

ENGLISH Tobacco, or yellow *Henbane,* is called in *Latin Hyoſcyamus luteus,* and of ſome *Petum,* and *Petun,* and by others *Nicoſiana* of *Nicot* a *Frenchman,* who is ſaid to be the firſt that brought the Seed from the *Indies;* as alſo the Seed of the true or *Indian* Tobacco, for which this kind has been often taken.

2. *The Deſcription.*

This Herb when fully grown is about three Feet or more in Height, conſiſting of a very large green Stalk full of a ſpungious Pith, and is divided into many Branches, which are ſet with large Leaves that are very ſmooth, even, thick, and full of Sap or Juice.

The Flowers are produced at the top of the Branches, and are very orderly placed, being of a pale yellow Colour, and ſomething leſs than thoſe of the black *Henbane.*

The

The Cups wherein their Flowers are situated, are very like those of the *Henbane*, but much less, and without acute Points, wherein is placed the Husk or Pod, of a round Form full of very small Seeds, not much unlike those of *Marjoram*.

3. *The Temperature.*

This Herb is thought by some to be cold and moist, but according to *L'Obelius*, it rather heats than cools.

4. *The Medicinal Virtues.*

This Herb is very good against all Apostemes, Tumours, inveterate Ulcers, Blotches, &c. being made into an Unguent or Salve as following. Take of the green Leaves three Pound and a half, stamp them very small in a Stone Mortar, and put to them one Quart of *Olive* Oil : Having put them in a Brass Sauce-pan, &c. over a gentle Fire, let them boil until the Herb appears of a blackish Colour, keeping it continually stirring all the while ; and when it will not boil or bubble any more, take it off and strain it, and put the clear Oil (which will then be of a green Colour) over the Fire again, with an Addition of half a Pound of Bees-wax, four Ounces of Rosin, and two Ounces of good Turpentine, and when they are all melted together, pour it out into a large Gallypot, &c. for Use.

This green Salve thus made, is of very great Use to all Families, and is what they ought to be never without.

'Tis also of great Service, being apply'd to Burnings, green Wounds, Cuts, &c.

This most useful Herb is raised from Seed, which is ripe in the Autumn, and may at that time be sown, or in the *March* following : The Seed is very hardy and will resist our Winter's cold, and wherever 'tis planted, and suffer'd to grow up to Seed, 'tis very difficult to get clear of it again. It delights in fresh rich mellow Land, and when the Plants are of the bigness of a half Crown or more, are transplanted into Rows at a Foot asunder each Plant from the other.

S E C T.

SECT. XXIX.

Of Violets.

1. *Their Names.*

THE Violet is called in *Greek* ἴον, of *Theophrastus* both ἴον, and μελάνιον, in *Latin Nigra Viola*, or black Violet of the blackish purple Colour of the Flowers. The Apothecaries retain the *Latin* Name (which is something wonderful, for they seldom care to call any thing by the true Name as other People do) *viz. viola*, or *Herba violaria & mater violarum*; in *High Dutch* 'tis called *Blanviel*; in *Low Dutch*, *violeten*; in *Italian viola mammola*; in *Spanish violata*; in *French violette de mars*; and in *English* Violet.

Nicander in his *Geoponicks* believes (as *Hermolaus* sheweth) that the *Græcians* did call it ἴον, because that some certain *Nymphs of Ionia*, gave that Flower first to *Jupiter*; and others say, that it was called ἴον, because that when *Jupiter* had turn'd the young Damsel *Io*, whom he tenderly loved, into a *Cow*, the Earth brought forth this Flower for her Food, and as it was made for her Sake, received that Name from her. And thereupon 'tis thought that the *Latins* also called it *viola*, as though they should say *vitula*, by leaving or blotting out the Letter *t*.

Servius also reporteth, that for the same Cause, the *Latines* do likewise Name it *vaccinium*, alledging the place of *Virgil* in his *Bucolicks*.

Alba ligustra cadunt, vaccinia nigra leguntur.

Notwithstanding *Virgil* in his 10th *Eclog.* shews that *Vaccinium* and *Viola* do differ.

——*Et nigræ violæ & vaccinia nigra.*

Of Violets we have a very great Variety, as first, The purple Garden Violet, called in *Latin Viola nigra sive purpurea.* Secondly, The white Garden Violet called *Viola flore albo.* Thirdly, The double purple Garden Violet called *Viola martia purpurea multiplex.* Fourthly, The double white Violet called

Viola

Viola martia alba multiplex. Fifthly, The yellow Violet, called *Viola martia lutea.* And Laftly, Dog's Violets, or wild Violets, called *Viola canina fylveftris.* Thefe feveral Kinds of Violets are in general very common, and therefore need no Defcription.

2. *Their Temperature.*

The Flowers and Leaves of Violets are cool and moift.

3. *Their Medicinal Virtues.*

The Flowers are good for all Inflammations, efpecially of the Sides or Lungs. They take away the Hoarfnefs of the Cheft, allay the extreme Heat of the Liver, Kidneys and Bladder, mitigate the fiery Heat of burning Agues, temper the Sharpnefs of Choler, and take away Thirft.

The Leaves of Violets being taken inwardly, do cool, moiften, and make the Body foluble; and being outwardly apply'd, mitigate all Kind of hot Inflammations.

The Syrup of Violets foftens the Belly, and purges Choler.

The Decoction of Violets is good in hot Fevers, and the Inflammation of the Liver, and other interiour Parts; as alfo is the Juice, Syrup, or Conferve of the fame.

The Syrup is alfo very good againft the Inflammation of the Lungs and Breaft, againft the Pleurifie and Cough, againft Fevers and Agues in young Children; and efpecially if you put to one Ounce of Syrup eight or nine Drops of Oil of Vitriol mix'd together, giving the Child a Spoonful at a time.

The fame being given as aforefaid is very good againft burning Fevers, and peftilential Difeafes, greatly cooling the inward Parts, and comforting the Heart.

4. *Their Cultivation.*

Violets are increafed by parting their Roots, they love a good mellow Soil, and delight very much, when partly fhaded. The beft time to make new Plantations of Violets, is the latter end of *March* when they have done blowing, and are planted in Beds of three Feet wide, about nine Inches apart.

S E C T.

SECT. XXX.

Of Wormwood.

1. Its Names.

WORMWOOD is called in *Greek* ἀψίνθιον, and is named of *Apuleius Abfinthium rufticum*, Country Wormwood, or *Peafants* Wormwood, in *Latin* 'tis called *Abfinthium latifolium five ponticum*, and *Abfinthium latifolium*, broad leaf'd Wormwood, to diftinguifh it from the *Abfinthium tenuifolium feu Romanum*, or fmall leaf'd *Roman* Wormwood, commonly called *Abfinthium Romanum*, and in *Low Dutch Roomfche alfene*. The *Italians* call Wormwood *Affenfo*; the *Spaniards Axenxios, Affenfios*, and many of them *Donzell*; the *Portuguefe Alofna*; in *High Dutch Weronmut, wermut*; in *French Aluyne*; and in *Englifh Wormwood*.

And as both the common and *Roman* Wormwood are very plentiful throughout moft, or all Parts of *England*, therefore I need not trouble you with their Defcriptions.

2. Their Temperatures.

The common or broad leaf'd Wormwood is hot in the fecond Degree, and dry in the third.

The fmall leaf'd or *Roman* Wormwood is alfo hot and dry, and bitter alfo, but nothing near fo much as the other, its greateft Force being in binding.

3. The Medicinal Virtues.

Wormwood is very good for a weak Stomach, that is troubled with Choler, for it cleanfes through its Bitternefs, and by its binding Quality, it ftrengthens and comforts the Stomach.

'Tis oftentimes a good Remedy againft a long and lingering Ague, efpecially *Tertians*, it greatly ftrengthens the Stomach, creates an Appetite, and clears away Obftructions, bad Humours, &c. by Urine.

The Herb being boiled in Milk, or the Seed given in Treacle to young Children or older grown People, kills and expels Worms out of the Guts. The

The Herb withſtands all Putrifactions, and is good againſt a ſtinking Breath, and prevents Moths from deſtroying Clothes.

4. *Their Cultivation.*

Both the Kinds of Wormwood are either raiſed from Seeds ſown, or Slips planted in *March*, and will thrive in any Sort of Garden Soil.

And as I have now paſs'd through the ſeveral Kinds of Phyſick Herbs neceſſary for the Uſe of every Family, as appears by their ſeveral Virtues; I ſhall now conclude with *an excellent Receipt for a Conſumption, or Shortneſs of Breath,* which I have known by Experience to have made ſound and perfect Cures of ſome Hundreds of poor afflicted People, who after a long and expenſive Time have been given over by ſome of our learned D--o--c--t--o--r--s as incurable.

The Receipt is as follows.

Take of *Solomon Seal, Comfrey* Leaves and Roots, *Marſhmallows, Hyſſop,* Pot *Thyme,* Mother *Thyme, Succory, Agrimony, Plantane* Leaves and Roots, *Clivers, Nettle Tops, Scabious* both Kinds, *Dandelion, Roſemary, Violets* (or their Leaves if the Flowers are gone,) ſcarlet *Strawberry* Leaves, *Ground-Ivy, Borage* Leaves, *Balm, Mint, Pimpernel,* and of *Colts Foot,* each one Handful.

- Of *Couch-graſs* Roots, and five leafed Graſs, each one Handful and half, with a ſmall Quantity of *Rue*, and one Head of *Garlick*.

Of *Figs* one pound ſliced, of *Raiſins* in the *Sun*, one pound ſtoned, and one quarter of a pound of *Liquoriſh* ſliced.

Put all theſe Ingredients into a large Saucepan with one Gallon of Water, and boil them till one half of the Water is conſumed: Then ſtrain off the Liquor and let it ſtand and ſettle, which being done, pour it off clear, and boil it up with one pound of brown *Sugar-candy,* and four pound of the beſt double refined *Sugar;* and when all the Scum is boil'd and taken off, and the Syrup appears clear and ſparkling, 'tis then completed, and is fit for Uſe. The manner of keeping it is in Glaſs Bottles, being well dry'd when put in, and bound over with a piece of Leather pierced full of Holes inſtead of a Cork.

N. B. That

This Border to, Sown and Planted with Thyme Parsley majoram Savory and other Sweet Herbs

W E S T.

Parsnips
Mixed with Lettice
Radish & Spinage
20 rod

6   6

Savoys
Planted Betwixt
Kidny Beans

15

...hokes &c.
3 rod

6

Early Peale
succeeded by Pickling
Cucumbers
30 rod

9

Potatoes
14 rod

**English
Saxifrage**
10 rod

3

...nd for
...eans
...ceeded by Winter
Spinage

6

Dwarf &c.
Peale
32 rod

3

Beets 6 rod
Skerrets 4 rod
Alexander Rocket
Sampieer Scurvie:
ra each 2 rod

6   6

Ridishes
6 rod

Chives
6 rod

9

15

N. B. That the afflicted must take three Spoonfuls every four Hours, or oftner if their Stomach will bear it, and 'tis best taken when suck'd from off a *Liquorish Stick,* cut jagged at the end.

To say any more in the Praise of this excellent Syrup is superfluous, for whoever makes Use of it will receive such Benefit as will be sufficient to establish its Praise, so that I need not give my self any farther Trouble than what I have already done, in communicating it for a publick Good, which will always be my only Study, *durante vita.*

F I N I S.

This Border to Sown and Planted with Thyme Parsley majoram Savory and other Sweet Herbs

Parſnips
Mixed with Lettice
Radiſh & Spinage
20 rod

Savoys
Planted Betwt
Kidny Beans
15

Early Peaſe
Succeeded by Pickling
Cucumbers
20 rod
9

hokes 90
3 rod

W
E
S
T.

Potatoes
14 rod

Engliſh
Saxifrage
10 rd
3

ndſor
eans
ceded by Winter
Spinage

Dwarf &c
Peaſe
32 rod
3

Beets 6 rod
Skerrets 4 rod
Alexander Rocket
Sampier & Scarzinel:
ra each 2 rod

Kichalots
6 rod
9

Chives
4 rod
15

N. B. That the afflicted must take three Spoonfuls every four Hours, or oftner if their Stomach will bear it, and 'tis beft taken when fuck'd from off a *Liquorifh Stick,* cut jagged at the end.

To fay any more in the Praife of this excellent Syrup is fuperfluous, for whoever makes Ufe of it will receive fuch Benefit as will be fufficient to eftablifh its Praife, fo that I need not give my felf any farther Trouble than what I have already done, in communicating it for a publick Good, which will always be my only Study, *durante vita.*

F I N I S.

THE General Hiftory of the vaft Continent and Iflands of *America*, commonly call'd the *Weft-Indies:* From the firft Difcovery thereof to this prefent Time. With the beft Accounts thofe People could give of their Antiquities. Collected from the Original Relations fent to the Kings of *Spain.* By *Antonio de Herrera*, Hiftoriographer to his Catholick Majefty. Tranflated into *Englifh* by Capt. *John Stevens.* In 6 Vol. Illuftrated with Cuts and Maps.

A new Journey through *Greece, Ægypt, Paleftine, Italy, Swifferland, Alfatia* and the *Netherlands.* Written by a *French* Officer who travell'd thofe Countries in the Years 1721, 22, 23. Now firft done into *Englifh.*

Surveying improv'd, or the whole Art, both in Theory and Practice, fully demonftrated. In four Parts. I. Arithmetick, Vulgar and Decimal. II. All Definitions, Theorems and Problems; with plain Trigonometry, and whatever elfe is neceffary to the Theory of Surveying. III. The Defcription and Ufe of Inftruments proper to be ufed in practical Surveying. IV. How to Meafure, caft up, plot or divide any parcel of Land; to take inacceffible Heights and Diftances; with Surveying Counties, Roads, Rivers, *&c.* Alfo to reduce a Plan to a Profpect; and to correct any Survey by Aftronomical Calculation; with Directions for making tranfparent Colours for Maps. To which is added, an Appendix concerning Levelling, and conveying Water to any poffible Place affign'd; with 96 Figures engrav'd on Copper. By *Henry Wilfon.*

A New Verfion of all the Books of the New Teftament, with a Literal Commentary on all the difficult Paffages. To which are added, I. An Introduction to the reading of the Holy Scriptures, intended chiefly for young Students in Divinity. II. An Abftract or Harmony of the Gofpel-Hiftory. III. A critical Preface to each of the Books of the New Teftament, with a general Preface to all St. *Paul's* Epiftles. Written originally in *French* by *Meffieurs De Beaufobre* and *Lenfant*, by the Order of the King of *Pruffia.* Done into *Englifh* with additional Notes.

A New Dictionary of Heraldry, explaining the Terms us'd in that Science, with their Etymology, and different Verfions into *Latin.* Containing all the Rules of Blazon, with Reafons for the fame. The original Signification of Bearings. And a concife Account of the moft noted Orders of Knighthood, that are, or have been; and of Honours and Dignities, Ecclefiaftical, Civil, or Military. Illuftrated with 196 Devices in Copper. The whole defign'd to make that Science familiar. Revifed and corrected, with a Letter to the Publifher, by Mr. *James Coats.*

M. Murray